CW00970934

Reconsidering Southern Labor History

UNIVERSITY PRESS OF FLORIDA

Florida A&M University, Tallahassee
Florida Atlantic University, Boca Raton
Florida Gulf Coast University, Ft. Myers
Florida International University, Miami
Florida State University, Tallahassee
New College of Florida, Sarasota
University of Central Florida, Orlando
University of Florida, Gainesville
University of North Florida, Jacksonville
University of South Florida, Tampa
University of West Florida, Pensacola

RECONSIDERING SOUTHERN LABOR HISTORY

Race, Class, and Power

EDITED BY

MATTHEW HILD AND

KERI LEIGH MERRITT

University Press of Florida

Gainesville · Tallahassee · Tampa · Boca Raton

Pensacola · Orlando · Miami · Jacksonville · Ft. Myers · Sarasota

Published in the United States of America

First cloth printing, 2018
First paperback printing, 2020

25 24 23 22 21 20 6 5 4 3 2 1

Library of Congress Cataloging-in-Publication Data
Names: Hild, Matthew, editor. | Merritt, Keri Leigh, 1980– editor.
Title: Reconsidering southern labor history : race, class, and power / Edited by Matthew Hild and Keri Leigh Merritt.
Description: Gainesville : University Press of Florida, 2018. | Includes index.
Identifiers: LCCN 2017055300 | ISBN 9780813056975 (cloth : alk. paper)
ISBN 9780813068312 (pbk.)
Subjects: LCSH: Working class—Southern States—History. | African Americans—Employment—Southern States—History. | Southern States—Social conditions.
Classification: LCC HD8083.S9 R43 2018 | DDC 331.0975—dc23
LC record available at https://lccn.loc.gov/2017055300

The University Press of Florida is the scholarly publishing agency for the State University System of Florida, comprising Florida A&M University, Florida Atlantic University, Florida Gulf Coast University, Florida International University, Florida State University, New College of Florida, University of Central Florida, University of Florida, University of North Florida, University of South Florida, and University of West Florida.

University Press of Florida
2046 NE Waldo Road
Suite 2100
Gainesville, FL 32609
http://upress.ufl.edu

Contents

Acknowledgments

We would like to thank Susanna Delfino, who suggested at a meeting of the Southern Industrialization Project that we put this book together. We would also like to thank the contributors, whose time and effort made this book possible.

Introduction

MATTHEW HILD AND KERI LEIGH MERRITT

"You are kept apart that you may be separately fleeced of your earnings," the famous Populist leader Tom Watson once told a crowd of white and black laborers. "You are made to hate each other because upon that hatred is rested the keystone of the arch of financial despotism which enslaves you both. You are deceived and blinded that you may not see how this race antagonism perpetuates a monetary system which beggars both." Thus, with three short sentences Watson laid bare the indomitable labor problem that had plagued the South since the times of slavery, continuing—frustratingly—even today. Yet while problems concerning labor history have seemingly increased in recent years, as union membership wanes, labor laws become more punitive, and real wages decline, labor history itself has experienced somewhat of an existential crisis.[1]

The decline of labor history over the past twenty years or so may have been slow and steady, but the decline has nevertheless happened. As Alan Draper wrote in 1996, "southern labor history is in ferment."[2] Edited collections of essays have served a vital role in helping to keep the field alive since then. In 2001, Glenn T. Eskew published *Labor in the Modern South*, which featured essays by noted historians focusing primarily upon the mid- to late twentieth century.[3] One of the most influential U.S. labor historians of the past forty years, the late Robert H. Zieger, edited three collections of essays on southern labor between 1991 and 2012, all of which focused upon the twentieth century.[4] *Reconsidering Southern Labor History: Race, Class, and Power* is the first collection of essays on southern labor history in six years, and its broad chronological sweep distinguishes it from most of its recent predecessors.[5] By showcasing a new generation of scholars, it demonstrates new methodologies and perspectives and seeks to link the past history of southern labor with the present-day issues of the

American working class. Studying both the contentions and connections among the races, the essays included in this volume highlight the deep inequities resulting from slavery. Labor history is particularly relevant for the South, a region consistently ranked the poorest in the nation. The Deep South—an area that had the highest rates of slavery—is rated poorer still, indicating that the legacies of slavery are still salient.

In many ways, the problems that have beset southern labor for the past century and a half—unfree labor, low wages, lack of collective bargaining rights, and virulent and sometimes violent repression of those who have tried to organize unions—have become the problems of workers across the United States, as the regional convergence of labor markets has pulled wages and conditions for workers across the nation closer to those of southern workers rather than the reverse. By addressing the troubled state of labor and the deep inequalities inherent today, we will use this volume to demonstrate how the South's long history of worker exploitation and labor practices have become standard fare throughout America.

The reason for this change in history's focus is multifaceted but primarily emerges from several different issues.[6] First, the scholars themselves—in general—seem to come from higher classes than did the scholars of the mid-twentieth century. In reality, even at its "cheapest," it takes an incredible amount of money to get through years of both undergraduate and graduate school, and coming through debt free is very rare, even while holding assistantships. It certainly helps to be independently wealthy or have family money. Very few people from working-class backgrounds are able to make it through Ph.D. programs, especially ones at elite institutions, an essential part of getting a tenure-track job. When many scholars are monetarily privileged, labor history has very little appeal. People tend to study what they know—they study themselves to a degree—and perhaps the pronounced shift to business and economic history best demonstrates this hypothesis. As Chad Pearson wrote, "departmental-based scholarly trend-setters have, with greater subtlety than their cost-cutting administrative colleagues, challenged the subject academically, insisting that labor and working-class history is no longer fashionable." Indeed, most professors are not leftists—they are liberals or, perhaps increasingly, neoliberals. Still, turning the focus from labor—and laborers—onto business history, the history of capitalism, and the histories of technology melds history with economics, which is certainly a welcome prospect, but at the same time it minimizes the focus on actual human beings—the workers, the laborers, the people. In doing so, much of the history of the last generation has centered on things and processes rather than on people, ultimately making history less humanistic.[7]

Second, both university administrations and students have added to labor history's recent struggle to stay relevant. Although there were certainly innovations in labor history in departments in the 1960s and 1970s, Pearson held, during the conservative backlash of the 1980s and 1990s, "business-aligned conservative administrators . . . attacked, and in some cases dismantled, labor studies departments, including those that have educated trade unionists." This institutional hostility of administrators clearly helped reduce the number of positions available. Another possible reason may be that students themselves have shunned the subject, as the decline of unions has likely lessened curiosity about labor—and the labor movement—greatly. Many modern-day students view labor as individual; the self-made mantra is strong, and very few recognize any collective economic interests with others. They often see work as a path to self-fulfillment, and not as a subject to be studied.[8]

Finally, the funding situation in higher education—the humanities especially—has drastically changed over the last few decades. With grant and research money specifically earmarked for certain topics, and with money increasingly coming from private sources, traditional labor history rarely receives funding. Instead of universities funding research, companies and even private citizens now compose a sizable percentage of research grantors, and they are often very specific about what types of research deserve funds. Sometimes, universities receive so much money that donors get to control curriculum. This model is certainly the case for the Koch Brothers, who donated $23.4 million to universities in 2014, up from more than $19.3 million in 2013. Of course, nearly all of the funding promotes the Kochs' conservativism and devotion to laissez-faire capitalism.[9]

These developments came to light in a rather visible way at the University of Alabama at Birmingham (UAB) between 2008 and 2011. Alabama has long had one of the strongest labor movements of any southern state, and during the early 1970s representatives of the United Steelworkers district office, the AFL-CIO's Alabama Labor Council, and the UAB prepared a proposal to create a labor education program at the university. With the encouragement of Governor George Wallace, the state legislature provided funding in 1971–72 for the creation of the Center for Labor

Education and Research (CLEAR) at UAB. CLEAR proved to be a great success, eventually teaching more than three thousand students in labor education classes each year while serving another twenty-five hundred students per year in workplace safety training programs.[10] But after more than three and a half decades of providing a home and significant support for CLEAR, in May 2008 UAB suddenly took the odd step of requesting that the state legislature remove a $650,000 line-item appropriation for CLEAR from the university's budget. CLEAR's director, the labor historian Glenn Feldman, attributed this unexpected development to the new dean whom UAB's business school had hired in March 2008. The dean had previously served as chief executive of CompBenefits Corporation, a major health benefits provider, and a former colleague of Feldman described the dean as "very business-oriented" and "certainly not a friend of labor." The former colleague added that the dean "was pretty clear that he did not feel that the labor movement had any business in academe or that academe had any business spending time on the labor movement." CLEAR moved to Jefferson State Community College in Birmingham before closing in 2011. Feldman remained on the faculty at UAB after filing two lawsuits and a complaint with the U.S. Equal Employment Opportunity Commission.[11]

Perhaps due partly to these facts, labor history does still get written, but it is usually considered African American history, gender history, or the "new political" history. Instead of focusing on unions and movements, it is generally written under the catch-all "working-class history" moniker. Indeed, by the 1970s the category of gender often subsumed the stories of working-class women, just as the title of African American history replaced scholarly pursuits concerning black laborers. Cultural history, along with charting the "rise of the right," helped marginalize the term "labor history" as well. Still, no matter the terminology, the fact is that fewer people are writing about the poor and working classes in general.[12]

One of the few labor historians left with that title, Eric Arnesen called for changes to labor history nearly twenty years ago, and they remain relevant today. He claimed that historians needed to reexamine the role of the state, as well as "federal agencies, the law, and the judiciary in establishing racial rules in the workplace, policing working-class racial conflict, and legitimizing employment or union discrimination." He also called into question employers' racial policies, noting that the current rage is to blame white workers for their own racism, while letting "capital largely off the hook, with workers dividing themselves and capital merely walking away with the proverbial shop."[13] In yet another essay, Arnesen took scholars of "whiteness" studies—particularly David Roediger—to task for failing to address basic labor history questions. Focusing on the "arbitrary and inconsistent definitions" of whiteness, he challenged DuBois's notion of a "psychological wage" for white workers. While leftist labor historians have adopted a "sharply critical stance toward the American labor movement and white male workers for their failure to live up to historians' hopes and expectations," Arnesen suggested that the concept of failure of worker solidarity across racial lines rested on a faulty premise. Not all white laborers acted with similar interests, class-based or not. Indeed, the entire idea of "false consciousness" needed to be reexamined.[14]

Yet Arnesen's comments are not only pertinent to today but also ring painfully true throughout the South's entire past, all the way back to the days of slavery. Indeed, the one antebellum topic that produced racial tension between slaves and poor whites was labor. While most of the time poor whites seemed to direct their anger at slave owners or hirers instead of at the slaves themselves, there were occasional instances of racial violence between the two groups of workers. Yet instead of recognizing labor relations as a complicating issue between black and white workers, historians have generally presented both an incomplete and inaccurate version of the region's social relations.

Essays by Thomas Brown, Kristin O'Brassill-Kulfan, Brett Derbes, and Angela Diaz all expound upon this fact, showing the variations in labor issues over time and in different regions of the South. Brown studies Charleston in the early national period, finding that when the white working class began to organize, it was often due to labor competition from slaves and free people of color. O'Brassill-Kulfan ponders similar themes in an examination of vagrancy laws in the Upper South. Researching mobile free blacks, she suggests that labor regulation was intimately intertwined with poor laws. Derbes demonstrates that penitentiary workshops emerged in the antebellum years in the Deep South, thrived during the Civil War, and developed into the modern prison-industrial complex. And Diaz uses the Cart War between white workers and Mexican teamsters to show what happened when race and labor intersected in 1850s Texas. Indeed, all of these articles seem to confirm Karl Marx and Friedrich Engels's maxim that "labor cannot emancipate itself in the white skin, where in the black it is branded."[15]

In the aftermath of the Civil War, the labor situation in the South was thrown into near total disarray. With emancipation, an entirely new class of laborers was free to compete for jobs and wages, greatly complicating an already tense state of affairs. Yet things were not slated to end as they did. As W.E.B. DuBois wrote, "the South, after the war, presented the greatest opportunity for a real national labor movement which the nation ever saw or is likely to see for many decades." Unfortunately, the demographic catastrophes that free people faced, along with the failure of land redistribution and the early withdrawal of U.S. troops, gave former slaveholders a chance to quickly reassert power. Using terroristic violence to buttress the entire system, the former southern elite expanded the region's criminal justice system as a way to re-enslave (or threaten to re-enslave) African Americans who refused to labor on their terms. Furthermore, by inflaming the racial prejudices of working-class whites, upper- and upper-middling-class whites helped ensure segregation, thus prohibiting the emergence of biracial unions. With an overwhelmingly rural population and without the emergence of a unified working class, laborers wielded very little power. With the rise of sharecropping and debt peonage, the southern working class had little chance to extricate themselves from often dire poverty.[16]

Two essays on Reconstruction further examine the links among politics, law, and labor. Stuart MacKay studies the writings of Carl Schurz, which provide insight into how Republicans first saw the ideology of free labor, how these ideologies were challenged in the postwar South, and how free labor was transformed from being considered as a "natural" process to one where political action would be necessary to implement it. Then, Linda Tvrdy uses *Haskins v. Royster*, a 1874 North Carolina Supreme Court case, to show how difficult it was to overcome long-standing practices embedded in local legal culture to secure lasting change in labor law. Indeed, she writes, most of the work of implementing new constitutional values fell to state legislators, lawyers, and judges applying them at the state and local level. The law governing the conditions of labor was no exception.

During the late nineteenth century, organizations such as the Knights of Labor and the People's (or Populist) Party seemed to hold significant promise for helping southern workers find some solidarity across the color line. The Knights made considerable inroads in the organization of black farmers and industrial workers in the South during the 1880s.[17] The

Knights and the Populists alike espoused a view of the political economy in which citizens were either "producers" or (as labeled in the Knights' constitution) "social parasites."[18] Both organizations supported greenback monetary policies and equal protection for the rights of labor and capital, while opposing the convict lease system and the use of prison contract labor.[19] James F. Foster, a Knights leader in Paulding County, Georgia, spoke to the appeal that the Populist Party held for a variety of working-class southerners when he wrote in 1892 that "when the signal is given for a [Populist] political rally the laboring men of farms and factory join hands and march in unbroken columns to the [site] of action."[20] While Foster's words may seem hyperbolic, the Populists swept Paulding County in the national, state, and county elections in 1892–93 and maintained that success for three years.[21]

The Populists also built upon the Knights' groundwork in trying to assemble an interracial coalition. In Georgia, not only did Tom Watson make direct appeals to poor whites and blacks, but African American leaders, most notably the Reverend Henry S. Doyle, also tried to build a movement of the poor of both races.[22] In Texas the Populists received very little support from black voters in 1892, but black support for the party increased in 1894 due in large part to the efforts of the teacher and preacher John B. Rayner and a corps of additional black organizers.[23] Some forty years after the Populist movement's demise, C. Vann Woodward wrote that "never before or since have the two races in the South come so close together as they did during the Populist struggles."[24]

Several essays in this volume deal with the promise and the failures of Populism and unions during that era. Deborah Beckel examines the role of the Knights of Labor, very much a biracial group in North Carolina, and the white and "colored" branches of the Farmers' Alliance, in helping the Populists and Republicans combine to wrest control of the state government from Democrats from 1894 until 1898. Dana M. Caldemeyer's essay on non-unionism demonstrates, however, that unions did not always unite workers, due to racial divisions and a host of other reasons, even when workers desired reforms and a chance to make their voices heard. T.R.C. Hutton's piece starkly illustrates yet another significant obstacle to unionism in the South during the Gilded Age: the willingness and ability of hired "gunmen of capitalism" to use armed force to snuff out efforts at unionization and labor activism in the southern Appalachian mountain region. Yet even after the promise of Populism had faded, and in spite of the particular obstacles faced by African Americans who demonstrated the courage and resolve to unionize, unions could still provide black workers with a vehicle for engaging in grassroots protest that played a role in the larger civil rights movement, as Theresa A. Case shows in her essay on the participation of black Texas railway shopmen in a national strike in 1922.

The problems of the late nineteenth and early twentieth centuries compounded and culminated in the disastrous Great Depression. "It is my conviction," said President Franklin D. Roosevelt, "that the South presents right now, in 1938, the Nation's No. 1 economic problem." Southern politicians responded to this pronouncement from the part-time Georgian with indignation, and the *Manufacturers' Record*, the mouthpiece of southern manufacturers and industrialists, declared, "Quite the opposite is true. The South represents the nation's greatest opportunity for industrial development."[25] To the extent that this hyperbolic, defensive statement contained any kernel of truth, much of its accuracy was predicated on the low wage scale and lack of unionization in the region compared to those of other sections of the nation. Indeed, the man often heralded as the original "New South" prophet, Henry W. Grady, extolled Georgia's potential for manufacturing in 1874, claiming that "labor is thirty percent cheaper than in New England."[26] President Roosevelt expressed astonishment in 1934 when he learned that farmers in Georgia paid seasonal black farm laborers a mere fifty cents per day. "Somehow," he wrote, "I cannot get it into my head that wages on such a scale make possible a reasonable American standard of living."[27]

As many of these essays show, closely related to the South's low wages was the region's relative lack of union membership. Two of the cornerstones of Roosevelt's New Deal, the National Industrial Recovery Act of 1933 (which was invalidated by the Supreme Court in 1935) and the National Labor Relations Act (or Wagner Act) of 1935, provided protection for the right of workers to organize, and some southern workers viewed them as tantamount to encouragement from the president himself to form unions. The general textile strike of 1934 that swept across much of the South ended, however, "in disaster," as the labor historians Melvyn Dubofsky and Foster Rhea Dulles put it, and five years later, the rate of union density (the percentage of nonagricultural employees who belonged to unions) was only 10.7 percent across thirteen southern states, just under half the rate of 21.5 percent in the rest of the nation.[28] And while World War II greatly aided the South's efforts at industrialization, it also sparked interest in labor unions again. In 1946 the Congress of Industrial Organizations launched "Operation Dixie," a major southern organizing drive. This effort ended largely in failure in 1953, although it did contribute to the region's burgeoning civil rights movement.[29]

Yet the changes wrought from the lessons of the Great Depression and World War II had only a small impact upon labor history itself. Prior to the advent of "new labor history" in the 1960s, relatively little had been written about southern labor history. Most of the few works that had been published examined labor in the New South's leading industry, the cotton textile industry. Some of these works were essentially "first drafts" of this history that examined recent and contemporary developments during the 1920s and 1930s.[30] Not until 1967 did a monograph appear that provided a fairly comprehensive (albeit institutional) examination of southern labor history: *Labor in the South* by F. Ray Marshall. Marshall, who later served as the secretary of labor under President Jimmy Carter, surveyed the southern labor movement from the end of the Civil War through the mid-1960s.[31]

But it was not until the 1980s that the "new labor history" would have a significant impact upon the field of southern labor history. The development of oral history programs greatly aided this development, as most vividly shown in the publication in 1987 of *Like a Family: The Making of a Southern Cotton Mill World*. This book drew upon hundreds of interviews with mill workers to present a thorough examination of the evolution of the southern textile industry from the late nineteenth century to the 1930s, focusing in particular on the lives of workers in the mills and in their communities.[32] Over the next decade or so, many other books followed that utilized the framework of new labor history and, in many cases, oral history to examine not only southern textile workers but also workers in other southern industries, such as coal mining, iron and steel, and dockworking. Scholars also published works focusing on labor and civil rights, showing these fields to be more intertwined than had previously been understood or acknowledged.[33]

Carrying on this tradition, Erin Conlin overlaps the experiences of African American and Latino farmworkers in postwar Florida, showing their shared encounters with coercive labor structures, state hostility, economic marginality, racial discrimination, and bleak working conditions, including extensive pesticide and chemical exposure. The workers' personal testimonies, combined with a rich trove of archival and secondary sources, create a strong case study that grounds the broader narrative of southern labor in a local community, poignantly illustrating how major trends play out in the everyday lives of workers. Michael Sistrom examines the Mississippi Freedom Labor Union's attempts to establish communal housing for displaced workers, demonstrating a shift in goals from requesting civil rights from the country's lawmakers to demanding a share of political and economic power. He shows that after a series of plantation strikes in the summer of 1965, many black Mississippians left behind the borrowed tactics of organized labor, experimenting instead with new types of direct action and separatist self-rule that were part of the maturing and varied philosophy of Black Power.

Similarly, Joseph Hower focuses on Memphis's public workers and their struggle for union recognition, arguing that the labor movement took on a distinctive form because of its integral ties to the Black Freedom Struggle. Though these relationships were strained by the onset of the fiscal crisis in the mid-1970s, they survived into the late twentieth century, bolstering black political power in southern cities and providing a model and foundation for the revival of civil rights unionism in the early twenty-first century. And Joseph Thompson focuses on two factories in metropolitan Atlanta, showing how African American laborers combatted southern white supremacy with the best means at their disposal. His comparative study reveals the federal government's sometimes-unintended role in the maintenance of Sunbelt white supremacy and exposes the ways organized labor, the Black Freedom Struggle, and the military-industrial complex shaped the political economy of the postwar South.

Despite the progress of the Civil Rights Era, however, certain forms of labor injustice remained unchanged, even when they were repeatedly challenged. Even as the twenty-first century got under way, the southern economy continued to be reliant upon forms of unfree labor. Just how reliant became all too clear in 2006 in the small eastern Georgia town of Stillmore. In May of that year, federal immigration agents inspected the records of the Crider, Inc., poultry plant and found that about 700 employees, approximately 70 percent of the workforce, were suspected illegal immigrants.[34] The company fired many of the immigrants, and hundreds of them left town over the summer. Then, on Labor Day weekend, agents raided the Crider plant as well as some homes in the area, arresting and cuffing more than 120 illegal immigrants, mostly men. Stillmore mayor

Marilyn Slater protested, telling reporters, "This is like the Gestapo was back in Germany in World War II, coming to snatch people out of their homes and all. That's not America. That's not the way it should be." Many of the arrested immigrants immediately found themselves being taken in vans to processing centers in Savannah, Atlanta, and Dalton.[35]

After this purge of most of the company's Hispanic employees, Crider suddenly found itself struggling to meet its labor needs. The company raised its starting pay to the range of seven to nine dollars per hour, which was more than one dollar an hour more than what most immigrant workers had been paid. African Americans soon filled some (though far from all) of the vacant positions. "For the first time since significant numbers of Latinos began arriving in Stillmore in the late 1990s," according to the *Wall Street Journal*, "the plant's processing lines were made up predominantly of African Americans." But many of these African American workers soon began complaining about long workdays, harsh supervisors, and allegedly dangerous working conditions, and company officials in turn complained of higher turnover rates and lower productivity with these workers. Of course, pay disputes arose as well.[36] By the end of the year, Crider resorted to employing felons who were being bussed to Stillmore daily from a diversion center in Macon, nearly one hundred miles away.[37] Still about 300 workers short of the size of the workforce before the intervention of the Immigration and Customs Enforcement agents, Crider officials decided once again that their labor problems could be solved by turning to immigrants: they began bringing Laotian Hmong refugees (entire families) to Stillmore from Minnesota and Wisconsin, apparently still unable or unwilling to satisfy their labor needs with local citizens.[38]

Two essays in this collection echo these concerns, explaining the modern-day struggles of business and labor. First, Adam Carson uses Fort Smith, Arkansas, to show that the power wielded by the business community over the media and civic institutions not only was used to ward off attempts at labor organization but also sought to unite the community in a mutual effort to create local prosperity. Then, David Anderson and Andrew McKevitt explore the arrival of the foreign-owned automobile factories in the South, finding that almost all of the region's automobile branch plants were unionized, thanks to company-wide contracts with the United Auto Workers (UAW). When it came to so-called basic industry, therefore, union density rates in the South matched those in the North. So, when southern politicians and boosters promised foreign-owned manufacturers a union-free industrial environment, they were, in essence, promising to remake the region's industrial sector into a bastion of the open-shop.

In the penultimate essay, Alan Draper demonstrates the importance of labor history by comparing the labor and civil rights movements, arguing that both shifted their earlier goals based on social rights and recognition to more concrete concerns about economic equality. With the two movements progressing along parallel lines, Draper writes, it is little wonder that the trajectories of their historiographies also resemble each other. Yet he also cautions readers not to measure the success of these movements against the high standards that activists applied but to instead use the more sober benchmarks that workers and African Americans used to assess their own lives. Both scholars and citizens need to view these movements through the practical lens of ordinary people that bottom-up historians are supposed to offer.

With the final chapter, Bethany Moreton shows how many problems of the South's past, from slavery to the region's long period of one-party rule by conservative Democrats, have contributed to the current crisis in the American job market where jobs are being devalued and destroyed. She further explains how past problems of the South, such as hyperincarceration and disfranchisement, have reemerged to once again undermine the principles of equal opportunity and democracy. Moreton raises questions that policymakers will need to consider carefully if the nation's recent trend of falling income and rising poverty is to be arrested.

Reconsidering Southern Labor History, therefore, seeks to bring all of these disparate topics together in a concerted examination of labor strife and activism in the South over the past two centuries. Although the essays are varied, they all concern similar themes, and all speak to issues that are still relevant to both the southern and American working classes today. In an increasingly "southernized" America, solving the problems associated with the exploitation of the working classes is not only desirable but imperative. As President Barack Obama said in 2010, "it was the labor movement that helped secure so much of what we take for granted today. The 40-hour work week, the minimum wage, family leave, health insurance, Social Security, Medicare, retirement plans. The cornerstones of the middle-class security all bear the union label." These cornerstones have never been secure for many working-class southerners, and now are becoming less secure for all working-class Americans. It is our hope that these essays, taken together, will spark meaningful discussion of these problems, and will also help contribute to their solutions.[39]

Notes

1. Thomas E. Watson, "The Negro Question in the South," *Arena* (Boston) 6 (1892): 540–50.

2. Alan Draper, "The New Southern Labor History Revisited: The Success of the Mine, Mill and Smelter Workers Union in Birmingham, 1934–1938," *Journal of Southern History* 62, no. 1 (1996): 87–108 (quote on 87).

3. Glenn T. Eskew, ed., *Labor in the Modern South* (Athens: University of Georgia Press, 2001).

4. Robert H. Zieger, ed., *Organized Labor in the Twentieth-Century South* (Knoxville: University of Tennessee Press, 1991); Robert H. Zieger, ed., *Southern Labor in Transition, 1940–1995* (Knoxville: University of Tennessee Press, 1997); Robert H. Zieger, ed., *Life and Labor in the New South* (Gainesville: University Press of Florida, 2012).

5. An exception, albeit one that examines only one state, is Robert Cassanello and Melanie Shell-Weiss, eds., *Florida's Working-Class Past: Current Perspectives on Labor, Race, and Gender from Spanish Florida to the New Immigration* (Gainesville: University Press of Florida, 2009).

6. Thanks to Bob Hutton, Joseph E. Hower, Michael Miles, Emily Senefeld, Rob Townsend, Daniel Vivian, and Gabriel Winant for input on this question via Twitter.

7. Chad Pearson, "From the Labour Question to the Labour History Question," *Labour/Le Travail* 66 (Fall 2010): 196, 198.

8. Pearson, "From the Labour Question to the Labour History Question," 196.

9. Dave Levinthal, "Koch Brothers Supersize Higher-Ed Spending," Center for Public Integrity, December 15, 2015, https://www.publicintegrity.org/2015/12/15/19007/koch-brothers-supersize-higher-ed-spending.

10. "Alabama Labor Archives and History, Center for Labor Education and Research Collection Finding Aid," Alabama Center for Labor Education and Research, http://www.alabama-lah.org/findingaids/CLEAR_Finding_Aid.pdf, 1. On the strength of labor unions in Alabama relative to those in other southern states over the last eighty years, see F. Ray Marshall, *Labor in the South* (Cambridge, MA: Harvard University Press, 1967), 299 (table 5); and Bureau of Labor Statistics, "Economic News Release," table 5 ("Union affiliation of employed wage and salary workers by state, 2014–2015 annual averages"), http://www.bls.gov/news.release/union2.t05.htm.

11. Peter Schmidt, "An Angry Professor Mounts His Own Labor Protest in Alabama," *Chronicle of Higher Education*, July 12, 2010 (quotes); "Alabama Labor Archives and History, Center for Labor Education and Research Collection Finding Aid," 1; Greg Garrison, "UAB Professor, Historian of the South, Studied Race, Politics, Faith," AL.com, October 23, 2015, http://www.al.com/living/index.ssf/2015/10/southern_historian_left_a_lega.html. Glenn Feldman passed away on October 19, 2015.

12. Pearson, "From the Labour Question to the Labour History Question," 199, 207, 222, 226.

13. Eric Arnesen, "Up from Exclusion: Black and White Workers, Race, and the State of Labor History," *Reviews in American History* 26, no. 1 (1998): 156.

14. Eric Arnesen, "Whiteness and the Historians' Imagination," *International Labor and Working-Class History* 60 (Fall 2001): 3, 4; David R. Roediger, *The Wages of Whiteness: Race and the Making of the American Working Class* (New York: Verso, 1999); also see Brian Kelly, *Race, Class, and Power in the Alabama Coalfields, 1908–21* (Urbana: University of Illinois Press, 2001), and Michelle Brattain, *The Politics of Whiteness: Race, Workers, and Culture in the Modern South* (Princeton: Princeton University Press, 2001).

15. Elizabeth Fox-Genovese and Eugene D. Genovese, *Slavery in White and Black: Class and Race in the Southern Slaveholders' New World Order* (New York: Cambridge University Press, 2008) (quote on 10).

16. W.E.B. DuBois, *Black Reconstruction in America: An Essay toward a History of the Part Which Black Folk Played in the Attempt to Reconstruct Democracy in America, 1860–1880* (New York: Free Press, 1992; first published 1935), 353.

17. Melton A. McLaurin, *The Knights of Labor in the South* (Westport, CT: Greenwood, 1978), ch. 7; Matthew Hild, *Greenbackers, Knights of Labor, and Populists: Farmer-Labor Insurgency in the Late-Nineteenth-Century South* (Athens: University of Georgia Press, 2007), esp. chs. 2 and 3.

18. *Constitution of the General Assembly, District Assemblies, and Local Assemblies of the Order of the Knights of Labor of America* (1885), in Terence Vincent Powderly Papers (Glen Rock, NJ: Microfilming Corporation of America, 1974), microfilm, p. 59, reel 64.

19. Robert C. McMath Jr., *American Populism: A Social History, 1877–1898* (New York: Hill and Wang, 1993), 79; Hild, *Greenbackers*, 160, 166, 187; Ernest W. Winkler, ed., *Platforms of Political Parties in Texas* (Austin: University of Texas, 1916), bulletin of the University of Texas no. 53, 297, 299. The Populists' opposition to convict leasing varied from state to state.

20. James F. Foster to John W. Hayes, August 14, 1892, in John William Hayes Papers (Glen Rock, NJ: Microfilming Corporation of America, 1974), microfilm, reel 8.

21. W. A. Foster Jr. with Thomas A. Scott, *Paulding County: Its People and Places* (Roswell, GA: W.H. Wolfe Associates, 1983), 238; Steven Hahn, *The Roots of Southern Populism: Yeomen Farmers and the Transformation of the Georgia Upcountry, 1850–1890* (New York: Oxford University Press, 1983), 280–81.

22. Omar H. Ali, *In the Lion's Mouth: Black Populism in the New South, 1886–1900* (Jackson: University Press of Mississippi, 2010), 105–6.

23. Hild, *Greenbackers*, 165–66, 186–87.

24. C. Vann Woodward, *Tom Watson, Agrarian Rebel* (New York: Oxford University Press, 1963; first published 1938), 222.

25. George Brown Tindall, *The Emergence of the New South, 1913–1945* (Baton Rouge: Louisiana State University Press, 1967), 599.

26. *Atlanta Daily Herald*, March 14, 1874.

27. Arthur M. Schlesinger Jr., *The Age of Roosevelt: The Coming of the New Deal* (Boston: Houghton Mifflin, 1958), 274. The quotation is from a letter that Roosevelt wrote

to Georgia governor Eugene Talmadge but which the president decided to send under the signature of the director of the Federal Emergency Relief Administration, Harry L. Hopkins.

28. Douglas Flamming, *Creating the Modern South: Millhands and Managers in Dalton, Georgia, 1884–1984* (Chapel Hill: University of North Carolina Press, 1992), 196; Melvyn Dubofsky and Foster Rhea Dulles, *Labor in America: A History*, 8th ed. (Wheeling, IL: Harlan Davidson, 2010), 250; Marshall, *Labor in the South*, 299 (table 5). The thirteen southern states referred to here include all eleven ex-Confederate states plus Kentucky and Oklahoma.

29. Barbara S. Griffith, *The Crisis of American Labor: Operation Dixie and the Defeat of the CIO* (Philadelphia: Temple University Press, 1988).

30. See, for example, Paul Blanshard, *Labor in Southern Cotton Mills* (New York: New Republic, 1927); Tom Tippett, *When Southern Labor Stirs* (New York: Jonathan Cape and Harrison Smith, 1931); and George Sinclair Mitchell, *Textile Unionism and the South* (Chapel Hill: University of North Carolina Press, 1931).

31. On Marshall's tenure as secretary of labor, see Gary M. Fink, "F. Ray Marshall: Secretary of Labor and Jimmy Carter's Ambassador to Organized Labor," *Labor History* 37 (1996): 463–79.

32. Jacquelyn Dowd Hall, James Leloudis, Robert Korstad, Mary Murphy, Lu Ann Jones, and Christopher B. Daly, *Like a Family: The Making of a Southern Cotton Mill World* (Chapel Hill: University of North Carolina Press, 1987).

33. See, for example, Flamming, *Creating the Modern South*; Daniel Letwin, *The Challenge of Interracial Unionism: Alabama Coal Miners, 1878–1921* (Chapel Hill: University of North Carolina Press, 1998); Henry M. McKiven Jr., *Iron and Steel: Class, Race, and Community in Birmingham, Alabama, 1875–1920* (Chapel Hill: University of North Carolina Press, 1995); Eric Arnesen, *Waterfront Workers of New Orleans: Race, Class, and Politics, 1863–1923* (New York: Oxford University Press, 1991); Michael K. Honey, *Southern Labor and Black Civil Rights: Organizing Memphis Workers* (Urbana: University of Illinois Press, 1993).

34. Jim Wooten, "Thinking Right: Immigration: What's the Story Here?" *Atlanta Journal-Constitution*, September 21, 2006.

35. Mary Lou Pickel, "Immigration Issue Ripples Both Ways: Raid of Illegals Hits Home in Georgia Town," *Atlanta Journal-Constitution*, September 25, 2006.

36. Evan Perez and Corey Dade, "An Immigration Raid Aids Blacks—For a Time," *Wall Street Journal*, January 17, 2007.

37. Jim Wooten, "Liberals Go Nowhere with Same Old Deal," *Atlanta Journal-Constitution*, December 3, 2006.

38. Perez and Dade, "Immigration Raid Aids Blacks"; Jerry Gonzalez, "Legislator's Divisive Tactics Won't Succeed," *Atlanta Journal-Constitution*, June 29, 2007.

39. "Fighting for the Middle-Class, One Grievance at a Time," American Postal Workers Union, AFL-CIO, http://www.apwu.org/news/deptdiv-news-article/fighting-middle-class-one-grievance-time, accessed January 4, 2017.

1

The Early Republic and the Old South

1

Origins of the Charleston Mechanic Society

White Labor Activism and Slave Competition in Charleston, South Carolina, in the Early National Era

THOMAS BROWN

Over the course of the eighteenth century, the North American colonies experienced increasing class stratification in the major urban areas, setting the ground for labor activism.[1] When the working class did begin to organize, it was around the interest of specific trades, and led by the elite members of those trades. Furthermore, competition from slaves and free people of color—not class stratification—was often the motivating factor for labor organization in the early national period. This process manifested with particular clarity in Charleston in the 1790s. This chapter examines the interaction between race and class in early labor activism.

Scholars of white labor in eighteenth-century Charleston, South Carolina, have portrayed Charleston's mechanics as part of a broader middle class, downplaying and even ignoring class divisions among non-elite whites. A number of misleading assertions appear in the literature, including that Charleston's mechanics in the early national era did not develop class consciousness, ceased participation in outdoor politics after the revolution, and never formed an organization that unified mechanics as a class for political purposes. Previous scholars have deemphasized or even ignored the role of slave competition in motivating white labor organization, and paid even less attention to the political ramifications of class divisions among the Charleston mechanics.[2]

In 1794, Charleston artisans from various trades came together to engage in collective action against competition from slaves. This essay will analyze the emergence of the Charleston Mechanic Society, demonstrating that Charleston mechanics engaged in political action not unlike that of their counterparts in other cities of the South during the early national era.[3] It will demonstrate that, contrary to claims by previous scholars, Charleston mechanics did develop class consciousness and did organize as a class, did engage in outdoor politics, and did develop their own organic leaders. Slave competition was the primary proximate issue motivating Charleston's mechanics to organize and engage in politics.

The Revolutionary War's end was a boon for tradesmen, who were needed to reconstruct Charleston's ruined buildings. Rising wages were to the disadvantage of the planter elite, who called for wage regulation, and for bringing in mechanics from the northern states or Europe. Charleston's mechanics reacted with anger to plans to increase competition or otherwise hold down their pay. They also complained of slave competition and of planters refusing to pay old labor debts.[4]

For the white laboring class as a whole, slave workers were competition, driving down wages. Slaves were competition for skilled as well as unskilled white laborers, although some journeymen could find work supervising a slave crew of mechanics. However, a class cleavage among mechanics created different perspectives on slave labor within the mechanic class. Wealthier mechanics faced a different set of incentives. Slave-owning mechanics could train and sell skilled slave artisans to planters. They could keep their trained slaves and use them to increase their own business's productivity. They could hire out their skilled slaves, or even allow the slaves to conduct business on their own account. The manufacturing tradesmen—saddlers, cabinetmakers, coachmakers, and silversmiths among them—were the most likely to profit directly from slave labor, and members of these trades were least likely to be involved in political action against slave competition.[5]

Those who suffered most from slave competition were coopers and members of the building trades. A Carpenters Society formed in 1783, amidst concerns over slave competition. Thirty-six carpenters and bricklayers petitioned the state legislature, complaining of "having Scarce had employ Sufficient to Support their families, owing to the number of Jobbing Negro Tradesmen, who undertook work for little more than the Stuff would Cost." They asked for a law prohibiting black tradesmen from hiring themselves out. The city council responded by requiring slaves on hire to obtain a badge from the city, and by preventing slaves from hiring out on their own account.[6]

Both the South Carolina house and senate formed committees to address the petition, including several wealthy master mechanics in the legislature who owned slaves themselves. The committee report endorsed the mechanics' petition. It recommended an ordinance prohibiting any slave from working "at any Mechanical Occupation except under the direction of some white Mechanic" and instituting fines for violators. However, reflecting the interests of the wealthy mechanics on the committee, the report also permitted any mechanic to employ his own slaves "in doing any Necessary private work or business of [his] own" without penalty. The legislature rejected the recommended ordinances and instead revived a colonial act from 1740 that permitted an owner to hire out his slaves by giving written permission.[7] Legal restrictions on slave mechanics were rarely enforced, as evidenced by petitions to the South Carolina legislature from white mechanics concerned about slave competition. The South Carolina state archive preserved at least thirteen such appeals.

In 1793, amid concerns over a rumored slave rebellion, a group of white shoemakers in Charleston published a notification that they would report neighbors who were illegally renting space to slaves for the purposes of commerce. The white shoemakers believed that some slaves had an unfair economic advantage in obtaining raw goods below market value, and that in any case the right to engage in these professions belonged "to freemen only." The shoemakers offered a reward of two pounds for any offender they could convict of illegally renting to slaves.[8]

The white shoemakers' concerns were a response to slaves such as Friday. When Friday escaped from his owner, the runaway ad described Friday as "a shoemaker by trade. He has carried on that business in a small house near the New-Market."[9] Friday's enterprise was illegal, but his owner showed no qualms about describing it in the newspaper ad—even though the owner should have been subjected to a fine for allowing Friday to run his own business in a house on his own account. Such public candor suggests that slave businesses were not uncommon and rarely regulated.

The white tailors responded in agreement with the shoemakers. The tailors argued that slave competition was "prejudicial to the true interest of South Carolina in general, and of the tradesmen in particular; and that they operate very much and very unfairly to the disadvantage of the handicraft citizens of this state." The tailors complained that "the honest, industrious and fair tradesman, who is bound to pay the state tax, city tax, poor tax, road tax, and all other legal assessments . . . is in justice entitled to privileges which the slave, who is liable to no such duties, can have no claim to." The tailors offered their own two-pound reward for the conviction of white offenders who rented to slave entrepreneurs or who otherwise violated the restrictions on slave participation in the trades.[10]

Hairdressers published their own similar grievance, as did a group of painters, glaziers, and paper hangers. In late 1793, meetings were organized to bring a number of these trade groups together, and to "invite those that are not incorporated" to organize and attend.[11] This emergent labor activism resulted in white coopers taking their grievances to the state legislature. In December 1793, "in behalf of the Whole," eight members of "The Society of Master Coopers of Charleston" petitioned the legislature, complaining about the "inattention" given by local authorities to the laws regulating slave commerce. "At present as well as for considerable Time past," the coopers observed, "the Slaves of Charleston have been privileged (although illegally) to sell traffick and barter, as well as to carry on different Trades and Occupations free from the Direction or Superintendence of any white Person whatever." The coopers complained that the slave mechanics worked "to their own Emolument and the great and manifest Injury of the mechanical part of the Community, selling their Commodities and working at their Trades much lower and at much cheaper Rates, than those persons who are privileged by their Citizenship." The coopers argued that such "Privileges encourage Negroes in Stealing as well as destroy that Subordination which the Situation of this State requires from the Slave towards his master and all other Citizens." The coopers asked the legislature for an act of incorporation, with "Privileges and Rights as are usually granted in such Cases."[12]

In January 1794, scarcely a month after the coopers' petition, the Charleston City Council repealed its law forbidding slave owners and overseers from permitting slaves to "carry on any mechanic or handicraft trade of themselves, in any shop or otherwise in this city." The city council justified this move by resolving that "the operation . . . of the above ordinance has been found highly injurious to the citizens of Charleston."[13] The Charleston elites had responded to the white coopers' petition with a resounding rebuke. Not only had the coopers failed to gain any ground—but the city government had taken away the entire legal basis for their grievance. As a result, labor activism would come to a boil in 1794.

Two months later, in March 1794, the "committees of the different branches of mechanics" began organizing a "Mechanical Society" to represent their broader interests as a class.[14] A month after that, in April, the new society submitted a petition to the city council, which rejected it. The mechanics called another meeting to discuss the setback.[15] The society appointed a committee to draft a petition "for redress of their grievances" to the state legislature, and then met again a few days later to discuss the draft petition.[16] On April 19, the entire society held a meeting at Harris's hotel to sign the petition.[17] The society's petition to the legislature has not been preserved in the state archive, but it would appear to have failed. Nonetheless, the society continued to meet monthly at Harris's hotel, establishing rules, requiring dues to be paid three times a year, holding elections, and otherwise giving all appearances of an established organization.[18] The following year, it held half-year and anniversary dinners, drawing a hundred attendees.[19]

In 1794, as Charleston's mechanics were organizing, the city's elites might have had good reason to pay closer attention to the white working class's grievances. During the summer of 1793, refugees from Sainte-Domingue arrived in Charleston with eyewitness horror stories of the slave rebellion under way. The island's fall had been hastened, in part, by the French elite's refusal to consider the needs of their own white working class.[20] The whites of Charleston were also outnumbered by slaves and free people of color and had comparable reasons to be concerned about potential slave revolts. White Charlestonians needed a united front that would discourage slave rebellions before they started. Still another security threat stemmed from the recent international hostilities between the French and British, which the locals feared would affect Charleston.

These security concerns created an opening for the new Mechanic Society to engage in symbolic politics. The mechanics exploited the opportunity by constructing a new wooden fortification in the city, donating the labor. While Congress provided some federal funding, the new fortification expanded beyond the original plans due to "mechanical labor being done gratis by the carpenters of the city."[21] The white mechanics' donation was successful in winning them notice and acclaim from the elite class. In November 1794, the Mechanic Society formally presented its donation to Governor Moultrie in a public ceremony. The governor named the new structure "Fort Mechanic" to honor its builders.[22]

Charleston mechanics also formed a militia, the "Mechanical Blues."[23] By building the fort and marching in formation as a militia, the mechanics publicly asserted their significance to the city's security. Amidst news of slave rebellion on Saint-Domingue and the ensuing flood of French refugees, the city's elites could not escape the fact that working-class whites were necessary to ensuring the physical security of the broader white population in the face of potential slave revolts. Fort Mechanic was the symbolic expression of that reality. The new Mechanic Society found another opportunity to participate in outdoor politics in the fall of 1794. In October, the city formed a committee to organize a parade celebrating the new Orphan House. Brickwork for the new building had been contracted by Anthony Toomer, president of the Mechanic Society and a local representative to the legislature. The parade would proceed to the Orphan House from the Charleston Exchange, a large building that served as the symbolic center of the city's economy.[24]

The *City Gazette* published the processional order, which starkly revealed the city's prevailing class hierarchy. At the head of the parade were the Masons, followed by the planters and the agricultural society. Next in line were the officers of the branch bank, followed by the federal civil servants and the tax collectors. Then came the leaders of the merchant class: the officers of the local banks and the chamber of commerce, followed by the merchants, the port pilots, the harbor masters, and the masters of various ships.[25]

Only after the planters, government luminaries, merchants, and sea captains had marched were the mechanics lined up. The city's parade committee called for representatives from the mechanics' societies to help organize their own participation in the procession.[26] While it is not clear whether the order in which the mechanics decided to march indicates a status hierarchy within their own class, the *City Gazette's* list of forty-two mechanical trades—from the pump-makers at the front to the coach painters in the rear—does indicate how Charleston society of the time defined the boundaries of the mechanical class.[27]

The symbolism of the Orphan House parade functioned on many levels for Charleston society. The movement on behalf of widows and orphans was begun in the 1737 by the South Carolina Society, founded by artisans, but by 1763 that society had long since been taken over by the upper classes. Still, the Orphan House functioned as an insurance policy for the white working class, ensuring that their children would be taken care of in case of their incapacity or demise. It was still an institution for the white workers—even if they had lost control of its governance.[28]

A large-scale public orphanage for the benefit of the white working class functioned as the city's symbolic inclusion of white workers into the fold. The parade of all of Charleston's whites, from all classes, was a physical display of white unity. It reflected the common cause among the whites against a potential black common enemy, thus preserving an economy based on slave labor primarily owned by the elites. While poor whites had access to a charity hospital and orphan house, destitute blacks faced incarceration in the city's public work house.[29] Thus the Orphan House was symbolic of the elites' need to build racial solidarity among whites of all classes, while papering over class differences. Nonetheless, the parade's processional order simultaneously functioned to symbolically reinforce those class differences.[30]

By parading to the Orphan House, and by marching as the Mechanical Blues, the mechanics engaged in outdoor symbolic politics as a unified class. By organizing their own militia, and by organizing their own marching procession to the Orphan House, the mechanics affirmed control of their own social order. They publicly affirmed their existence, their role in city life, and their solidarity as a class.

But, outdoor political displays aside, how much solidarity was there among the mechanics? Previous scholars of Charleston labor have largely ignored class divisions among workers—not only the class divide between free labor and slave labor but also the cleavages among the white mechanic class itself. The mechanic societies that emerged in Charleston in the late eighteenth century were not labor unions in the modern sense. They were led and populated solely by master mechanics who were often more employer than employee. Could they truly represent the broader class of mechanics?

The individual trade societies restricted membership to master mechanics by setting rules that effectively excluded apprentices and journeymen.[31] The societies' elected leaders were relatively wealthy men who owned successful manufacturing firms or contracting businesses and held political office. The Charleston Mechanic Society followed this pattern, limiting membership to free white mechanics and setting a lower age limit for membership of twenty-one.[32] Slaves and free people of color were excluded by the race requirement. The age limit effectively excluded apprentices. While journeymen were not specifically prohibited from joining, none are found in the society rolls.[33] Applicants had to be sponsored by two current members and pay twelve dollars upon acceptance. This must have been too high a bar for journeymen to cross.

The economic status of many of the Mechanic Society's founding members in 1794 can be established by examining surviving documents. The society's leaders routinely won public works and state building contracts. A number of the founding members would move out of the petit bourgeois master mechanics class and eventually become prominent capitalists and politicians.[34]

There are indications of internal divisions among the mechanics. Even after the Charleston Mechanic Society was founded in 1794, the individual mechanical trade societies persisted, with the carpenters and tailors being especially active.[35] Carpenters were particularly riven by class differences between masters and journeymen. It was common in Charleston for house- and road-building jobs to be carried out by slave carpenters working under white supervision. Carpenters who were in a position to obtain those supervisory jobs could claim good wages, while other carpenters found their opportunities limited by slave competition.[36] A similar dynamic appeared among the tailors, some of whom also regularly hired out their own slaves to make or mend clothes and shoes.[37] Evidence of some division among the mechanics appeared in February 1796, when the "journeyman house carpenters," excluded from membership in the existing Carpenters Society, held their own meeting at a local tavern.[38]

The Mechanic Society's early activism against slave competition began to pay off. In January 1796, two years after the city council had struck down the city statute regulating slave competition with white mechanics, the Grand Jury of the District of Charleston presented a grievance indicating growing support for the white mechanics among the electorate. The grievance noted "that slaves, who are mechanics, are suffered to carry on various handicraft trades on their own account to the great prejudice of the poor white mechanics in this city."[39]

More than two and a half years after the mechanics lost their legal battle when the Charleston City Council rescinded the statute restricting slave competition, the mechanics won a major victory. In August 1796, the city council passed an ordinance that once again banned slave mechanics from working independently, prohibited slaves from teaching each other the mechanical trades, and restricted slaves from occupying buildings or working without a ticket.[40] The statutory language was a virtual verbatim copy of the laws that had been rescinded in January 1794. It had taken two and a half years of activism on the mechanics' part just to get back to where they had started.

Previous scholars have read the mechanics' constitution, observed that mutual aid for widows and funerals was the rationale given to the legislature for incorporating in 1798, and assumed that the question was closed—ignoring the political tumult over slave competition that surrounded the society's initial formation in 1794.[41] But a careful analysis of the Charleston Mechanic Society's emergence conclusively demonstrates that slave competition was the primary issue motivating the society's formation.

Mechanics would continue to petition the legislature requesting relief from slave competition throughout the antebellum era. It is clear that slave competition motivated activism and organizing among the mechanical class, but questions remain. The leaders of the Mechanic Society were economically successful employers and entrepreneurs—and slave-owners. Why did the relatively wealthy, slave-owning entrepreneurs of the mechanical class lead their societies in activism against slave competition on behalf of the less-advantaged white mechanics who did not own slaves? More regulation of skilled slave labor would have been to the slave-owning master mechanics' disadvantage.[42]

The society members may have had some degree of class consciousness and solidarity with their apprentice and journeyman brethren. Even the wealthiest mechanics still owned far fewer slaves and real property than the planter elite, and were not accepted into the upper crust of Charleston society. All of them had once been manual laborers as apprentices and journeymen, and likely still thought of themselves as mechanics, even as their fortunes improved.[43]

There is also a more instrumental explanation for their activism. Many of the Mechanic Society's members were active in electoral politics. Of the two hundred members from the Society's inception in 1794 through 1820, more than half held a political office.[44] Other mechanics were their natural constituency. South Carolina's voting laws allowed any white man to vote who owned a town lot or who had paid three shillings in tax. However, there were more extensive property-owning qualifications that would have barred all but the wealthiest mechanics from political office.

This meant that journeymen were unlikely to be able to run for office, but they could vote for one of the elite master mechanics to represent their interests.[45]

The minor concessions against slave labor won by the Mechanic Society may have been a small price to pay for the elite slave-owning master mechanics, in exchange for an advantageous political position and access to lucrative public works contracts. The Mechanic Society, by situating itself as representing the entire class of mechanics, was able to curb the more radical urges of the journeymen, while retaining their political support. The resulting legal environment still permitted the elite mechanics to own and use slave mechanics' labor to their own profit. In fact, the legislative wins by the Charleston Mechanic Society further consolidated skilled labor under the control of master mechanics, by requiring skilled white oversight of slave mechanics. The Charleston Mechanic Society was much more than a mutual aid society, but it was not a precursor to a labor union. It was a means for elite mechanics to secure and advance their advantages.[46]

The racial politics of labor in the early national period, as manifested in the emergence of the Charleston Mechanic Society, influenced the subsequent trajectory of labor unionism. In postbellum Charleston, black workers began to organize unions. Although radical editors encouraged black labor to collaborate with white unions, this occurred only rarely. More often than not, a strike by workers of one race would be quashed by bringing in workers of the other race. For example, in 1866, black mill employees were fired for striking, and replaced by white laborers who were willing to work at the old wage.[47]

Thus the capitalist class learned to exploit a labor market split by racial competition.[48] The strategy was to pit black workers against white workers in order to drive down labor costs. Prior to 1893, the American Federation of Labor (AFL) prohibited racial restrictions in union membership. However, in the years after the Panic of 1893, the AFL moved from inclusive industrial unionism toward craft unionism segregated by race.[49] Indeed, Jim Crow segregation advanced contemporaneously with segregated unions. When unionism was at its peak in the mid-twentieth century, industries in many locales still had separate unions segregated by race. Other twentieth-century labor organizations, such as the Industrial Workers of the World (IWW) and the Congress of Industrial

Organizations (CIO), attempted to fight against labor segregation, but with little success until too late.

The formation of the Charleston Mechanic Society in the 1790s thus presages the historical trajectory of labor unionism throughout the nineteenth and well into the twentieth century. The threat of competition from workers of color was a primary motivation behind labor organization not only in Charleston but also across the nation. The inability of labor to organize across color lines would repeatedly undercut the effectiveness of unionization.

The story of labor activism in Charleston suggests that the question of whether racism in the United States originates from the elites or the masses may be framed too broadly to enlighten and may even obscure understanding of the process as it played out on the ground. An analysis of labor activism in Charleston makes clear that there was political and financial advantage to be gained by encouraging and exploiting racial competition, and that the leaders of the Charleston Mechanic Society came to exploit that advantage.[50]

Notes

1. Gary Nash, *Class and Society in Early America* (Englewood Cliffs, NJ: Prentice Hall, 1970).

2. Analyses of Charleston mechanics include Emma Hart, *Building Charleston: Town and Society in the Eighteenth-Century British Atlantic World* (Charlottesville: University of Virginia Press, 2009); Bradford L. Rauschenberg, "Evidence for the Apprenticeship System in Charleston, South Carolina," *Journal of Early Southern Decorative Arts* 29, no. 1 (2003): 1–67; Mary Catherine Ferrari, "Artisans of the South: A Comparative Study of Norfolk, Charleston and Alexandria, 1763–1800" (Ph.D. diss., College of William and Mary, 1992); and Nicole Marlene Summers, "A Prosopography of the Charleston Mechanic Society, 1794–1820" (master's thesis, University of South Carolina, 1999).

3. Analyses of white labor activism in other southern cities include Diane Barnes, *Artisan Workers in the Upper South: Petersburg, Virginia, 1820–1865* (Baton Rouge: Louisiana State University Press, 2008); Michele Gillespie, *Free Labor in an Unfree World: White Artisans in Slaveholding Georgia, 1789–1860* (Athens: University of Georgia Press, 2004); and Charles G. Steffen, *The Mechanics of Baltimore: Workers and Politics in the Age of Revolution, 1763–1812* (Champaign: University of Illinois Press, 1984).

4. Richard Walsh, *Charleston's Sons of Liberty: A Study of the Artisans, 1763–1789* (Columbia: University of South Carolina Press, 1959), 108.

5. Walsh, *Charleston's Sons of Liberty*, 124.

6. "Carpenters and Bricklayers Petition," 1783, series S165015, items 159 and 258, South Carolina Department of Archives and History, Columbia (hereafter SCDAH).

7. Walsh, *Charleston's Sons of Liberty*, 124–25.

8. *The City Gazette* (Charleston, SC) (hereafter just *Gazette*), November 6, 1793. (Note that the *Gazette* used several slight variations on its title during the time period under study.)

9. *Gazette*, March 19, 1793.

10. *Gazette*, December 7, 1793.

11. *Gazette*, November 30, 1793, December 6, 1793. The shipwrights also began to organize a few weeks later, although their motivation is not stated (*Gazette*, December 17, 1793); *Gazette*, November 20, 26, 1793.

12. "Cooper's Petition," December 11, 1793, Records of the General Assembly, document 64, SCDAH.

13. *Gazette*, December 16, 1794.

14. *Gazette*, March 4, 1794. The "committees of the different branches of mechanics" met in March. The *Gazette* refers to subsequent meetings variously as the mechanic, mechanics, or mechanical society. Because the group eventually incorporated as the "Charleston Mechanic Society" that is the term used in this article, unless the *Gazette* is being quoted directly.

15. *Gazette*, March 7, 1794.

16. *Gazette*, March 11, 1794.

17. *Gazette*, March 19, 1794.

18. *Gazette*, May 23, 1794; June 6, 1794; June 20, 1794; July 18, 1794; November 10, 1794.

19. On April 6, 1795, the Mechanic Society held an anniversary dinner and elected officers. About one hundred people attended (*Gazette*, March 28, 1795). Names of officers in the April 10, 1795, issue.

20. Thomas O. Ott, *The Haitian Revolution, 1789–1804* (Knoxville: University of Tennessee Press, 1987).

21. "Halsey Map," Preservation Society of Charleston, http://www.halseymap.com/flash/window-print.asp?HMID=63.

22. *Gazette*, November 18, 1794, December 9, 1794.

23. *Gazette*, October 8, 1796.

24. *Gazette*, October 18, 1794.

25. *Gazette*, October 18, 1794.

26. *Gazette*, October 16, 1794.

27. *Gazette*, October 18, 1794.

28. John Murray, *The Charleston Orphan House: Children's Lives in the First Public Orphanage in America* (Chicago: University of Chicago Press, 2012).

29. Murray, *The Charleston Orphan House*.

30. Timothy Lockley, *Welfare and Charity in the Antebellum South* (Gainesville: University Press of Florida, 2007).

31. Walsh, *Charleston's Sons of Liberty*, 132–33. The Barbers Society rules specifically excluded apprentices. The coopers and tailors societies also only admitted master mechanics. The carpenters' society admitted few members, indicating a similar class bias.

32. *The Constitution of the Charleston Mechanic Society, Instituted at Charleston, South-Carolina, 1794* (James and Williams, Printers, 1858).

33. Summers, "A Prosopography," 24.

34. Summers, "A Prosopography," 34–38.

35. *Gazette*, July 25, 1794, September 22, 1794.

36. *Gazette*: September 24, 1796, advertisement for "house carpenter" who can manage a small gang of "negroes"; October 13, 1794, a carpenter advertises his new business, and offers "generous wages and punctual payments" to "good carpenter negroes"; November 2, 1796, three or four "negro" house carpenters wanted, good wages given; November 14, 1796, six carpenters and two "negro" sawyers wanted for good wages; December 2, 1796, "complete Negro Carpenter" for sale; May 16, 1796, two white men and three "negro" carpenters are working on a house in George Street. In 1795, commissioners appointed by the city council requested bids to build a new street. The commissioners expected that a white "workman" would supervise "six negro carpenters" and "twenty negro laborers, good axe men" (*Gazette*, March 31, 1795).

37. *Gazette*, April 19, 1794, Christopher Rogers, a tailor, offers to hire out his "negroes" to "make and mend by the month, week, or day, at the low price of negro wages"; *Gazette*, May 2, 1795, a "negro" shoemaker for hire by the month.

38. *Gazette*, February 18, 1796. However, there is no further indication that the journeymen were able to organize. The Mechanic Society had to call an "extra meeting" in February, in addition to its regular monthly meeting, which may be connected to the journeymen carpenters' agitation (*Gazette*, February 13, 1796).

39. *Gazette*, January 25, 1796.

40. *Gazette*, August 20, 1796.

41. Hart, *Building Charleston*, 146–47; Rauschenberg, "Evidence for the Apprenticeship System."

42. For more on how the problem evolved in the decades prior to the Civil War, see Keri Leigh Merritt, *Masterless Men: Poor Whites and Slavery in the Antebellum South* (New York: Cambridge University Press, 2017), chap. 9.

43. Barnes, *Artisan Workers*.

44. Summers, "A Prosopography," 45.

45. Francis Newton Thorpe, *The Federal and State Constitutions, Colonial Charters, and Other Organic Laws of the State, Territories, and Colonies Now or Heretofore Forming the United States of America*, vol. 6 (Washington, DC: U.S. Government Printing Office, 1909), 3258–59.

46. Summers, "A Prosopography," 19.

47. Jeff Strickland, *Unequal Freedoms: Ethnicity, Race, and White Supremacy in Civil War–Era Charleston* (Gainesville: University Press of Florida, 2015), 181.

48. Edna Bonacich, "A Theory of Ethnic Antagonism: The Split Labor Market," *American Sociological Review* 37, no. 5 (1972): 547–59.

49. Philip S. Foner, *Organized Labor and the Black Worker, 1619–1973* (New York: Praeger, 1974).

50. Theodore W. Allen, *The Invention of the White Race: The Origin of Racial Oppression in Anglo-America*, vol. 2 (London: Verso, 1994); Merritt, *Masterless Men*.

2

"Vagrant Negroes"

The Policing of Labor and Mobility in the Upper South in the Early Republic

KRISTIN O'BRASSILL-KULFAN

In 1864, George W. Sands, a delegate from Howard County, Maryland, stood before the members of the Maryland Constitutional Convention to discuss how free African Americans might be compelled to labor in the absence of slavery. He argued in favor of privileging the rights of former slaveholders in purchasing the indentures of forced laborers. The motivation for this, as Sands explained it, was to prevent vagrancy among the freedpeople:

> If they do not, now that they have an opportunity to labor for themselves[,] . . . become good, sober, honest citizens, or residents[,] . . . the law as it stands to-day and as I promise to embody it . . . will enable you to go into the orphans' court and require of the court that they apprentice to you in preference these children. That is right. We do not want vagrancy. I will go as far as any gentleman in this hall to guard against negro vagrancy. I never want to see it. I will be willing to resort to anything in the world to prevent it. But, in my humble opinion, the only way to prevent this class from becoming vagrants as a class, is to give them proper motives for exertion, labor, sobriety, and every virtue they ought to practice.[1]

Sands's speech was not an emergent reaction to the new freedom of African Americans at the close of the Civil War, as many historians have argued.[2] Rather, Maryland legislators, along with many authorities and average citizens in the Upper South, had been figuratively writing Sands's speech for decades prior to emancipation. The roots of the postbellum black codes—chief among them restrictive vagrancy laws—are not to be found in the emancipation era but in colonial and early republic legislation, poor laws, and other statutes governing free and particularly *mobile* free people of color.[3] This link stretches to far earlier than Reconstruction, and what some historians have referred to as the "lessons of emancipation employed against the poor" connect Elizabethan laws against vagabonds imported from England to twenty-first-century stop-and-frisk policies and riot curfews. The behavior of people classified as vagrants was policed in ways that were coded by both class and race.[4] The forms of legal regulation of the mobility of the poor throughout the eighteenth and nineteenth centuries demonstrate the lasting impact that labor and behavior coercion in the forms of slavery and indentured servitude had on the nation, most profoundly in the South.[5]

Laws regulating the movement, residence, employment, and labor of the poor, and especially of poor African Americans in states with burgeoning free populations, demonstrate how mobility, when enacted by the poor and by nonwhites, was classified as a criminal action in the eighteenth- and nineteenth-century United States. In the Upper South especially, these laws had the express goal of attaching to all people of color the potential consequences of enslavement. This essay will link these ideas by tracing mobility, and its construction as a classed and raced activity, as threats to existing labor regimes and social systems. This was most commonly and notoriously done through the policing of vagrancy. In so doing, it will argue that the power dynamics of the South can be read clearly in the classed and raced regulation of vagrancy and geographical mobility in the antebellum era.

At the dawn of the transportation and industrial revolutions, the experience of poverty was defined by transiency and its relief by persistence. Desires to curb the migration of indigents across international, state, and even municipal borders drove legislation relating to the poor for centuries: nearly all available poor relief was restricted to static residents of given districts.[6] Mobility was a central factor for determining how authorities viewed and, in turn, regulated the poor. From the very conceptualization of what a confederation of the former British colonies might look like, interstate travel by the poor and vagrant was banned. In the Articles of Confederation, article 4 clearly states that "the free inhabitants of each of these states, *paupers, vagabonds, and fugitives from justice excepted* . . . shall have free ingress and regress to and from any other state."[7] Following the Articles, states adopted their own legislation that excluded the poor and vagrant from crossing their borders or receiving poor relief.

Efforts to curb and punish vagrancy were ubiquitous throughout the nation until the mid-twentieth century. The ways in which such efforts were introduced and altered during this period was unique in the antebellum Upper South, where punishments were less severe than in the Deep South, but more distinctly racialized than in northern states. From the colonial era, Maryland had attempted to curb vagrancy by authorizing officials to, as a 1768 statute stated, "compel and oblige . . . the poor, beggars, vagrants, and vagabonds . . . to labour and work" against their will.[8] As some states began to allow for gradual manumission, however, concerns about the coexistence of enslaved and free people of color led authorities to seek to regulate the movement, behavior, and labor of the latter group. In 1796, the Maryland legislature had tightened earlier vagrancy legislation specifically for African Americans by adding to the vagrancy statute the possibility for sale into forced servitude as punishment.[9] Free people of color in Virginia after 1801 were effectively banned from leaving the county in which they resided without evidence of "honest employment," under threat of being "deemed and treated," and thus, punished, "as a vagrant."[10] Maryland's efforts to inhibit the movement of free people of color were similar in spirit and implementation to Virginia's 1801 law forbidding free people of color who lacked "honest employment" from being physically present in any portion of the state where they did not possess a legal settlement, on pain of a vagrancy conviction.[11] Free people of color were also required to carry passes stating they were free each time they travelled outside of their place of legal settlement.[12]

In Maryland, justices of the peace and constables were authorized to seek out the poor and monitor their movements to, as an 1811 law stipulated, "restrain poor people from going . . . from one county to another."[13] Those who did not comply with such laws were to be arrested as vagrants. The driving theme behind these laws and convictions was the transiency of the indigent. As Seth Rockman notes, northern vagrancy laws "polic[ed] people for the needs of a capitalist market system" as legal devices to force the idle or unemployed into economically productive activity.[14] Nonresidents—strangers, wanderers, and immigrants, especially, among these groups, African Americans and the Irish—were viewed as threats to the fiscal responsibility of communities, as they might draw on poor relief funds in an emergency without the ability or intention to ever pay back into community coffers as taxpayers.[15] To some extent in the North, but particularly in the labor-satiated Deep South, vagrancy laws were used, rather, to punish the illicit activities of the lower classes. The Upper South states of Maryland, Virginia, and Delaware, as well as Washington, DC, combined these efforts in ways reflective of their racially and economically mixed societies. Thus, indigent transiency was managed and, more pointedly, controlled, by authorities in the early nineteenth-century United States by punishing vagrancy for purposes of social, behavioral, and economic control.

Most northern states stipulated short periods of incarceration as punishment for vagrants, generally between thirty and sixty days.[16] The further south one traveled, however, the harsher the vagrancy sentences were. Baltimore's penalty for vagrancy stipulated the longest period of incarceration of any city in the Mid-Atlantic or Upper South. A city statute introduced in 1804 had penalized vagrancy, but an amendment in 1812 strengthened the punishment by stipulating that anyone convicted of vagrancy in the city of Baltimore was to be sentenced to incarceration in the penitentiary for a full year. Meanwhile, in the Deep South, sentences of up to four years were common.[17]

Justices of the peace in Baltimore were authorized to commit as vagrants "every person who has no visible means of maintenance from property or personal labor, and lives idle without employment; and any person who wanders about and begs in the street, or from door to door; and every person who wanders abroad and lodges in out houses, market places or the open air and cannot give a good account of the means by which he or she procures a living."[18] It is difficult to determine whether these laws functioned as actual behavior deterrents in any way, though it might be speculated that the subsistence-based nature of actions that most commonly led to vagrancy convictions (sleeping outdoors or begging for food) would have decreased the likelihood of that outcome. At least one contemporary argued that Baltimore's "rigid" treatment of paupers and vagrants had "the effect . . . of driving the idle, dissolute, vagrant class to other places."[19] In Maryland, between 1812 and 1819, only 186 individuals served the yearlong sentence in the state penitentiary that a vagrancy conviction required, suggesting there may be some truth to this interpretation. Many more individuals, of course, may have been held in city, county, or municipal jails.[20]

Vulnerability to vagrancy arrests was particularly problematic for free African Americans, who were frequent targets of local constables. Employment alone was not enough for black or even white vagrants to defend their status against a vagrancy charge; vagrancy was nearly always an externally assigned identity. As such, one's status as a citizen was determined not through an individual's own actions but by the ways one was viewed by the prosecutorial, political, and upper classes. As Paul Finkelman has noted, many whites held "a stereotyped belief that free people of color and fugitive slaves were less capable than whites of supporting themselves." This belief was codified in laws that particularly bound vagrancy, idleness, and poverty with blackness, to the point that this line of reasoning was used to prevent manumission.[21]

In the era of gradual emancipation, states in the Upper South repeatedly targeted poor transient people of color with punitive legislation that directly linked freedom with vagrancy. The city of Alexandria, Virginia, even dedicated a section of its vagrancy statute to making this point, stating that "all able-bodied persons" (read: all able-bodied white persons) "who not having wherewithal to maintain themselves, shall be found loitering or wandering abroad, without betaking themselves to some honest employment," as well as "all free negroes and mulattoes not entitled to residence, shall be considered and treated as Vagrants."[22] Washington, DC, achieved the same result from a mirror-image statute stipulating the removal of unregistered "free negroes and mulattoes" by including a section providing for the punishment of white and black 'vagrants' and idle and disorderly persons . . . who have no fixed place of residence."[23] Delaware, meanwhile, did not explicitly write vagrancy punishments into state law until several decades into the nineteenth century. But by the late 1830s, some citizens were outraged by this seeming oversight when, as gradual manumission was beginning to take effect, free black mobility blossomed. Dozens of petitions were made by concerned white residents, as will be detailed later, which led to the introduction of punitive racialized vagrancy laws in Delaware at a much later date than in the nearby states of Maryland and Virginia.[24]

In the Upper South in the 1840s, many contemporaries were attempting to parse out the distinction between idleness and industry at the individual level, to more clearly distinguish between paupers and vagrants as the deserving and undeserving poor. By emphasizing class distinctions, and drawing lines between real and false, and "great and small," vagrants, these commentators, such as the author of one editorial in the *Baltimore Sun* from 1841, argued that class and social standing were the characteristics that determined how a person's idleness was viewed: well-dressed idle men who lived "at the expense of a rich father" were not deemed vagrants, while "the forlorn widow," the destitute, and the ill were.[25] This distinction gave some contemporaries pause, especially for those classified as dependents, such as wives and children, whose destitution could likely be attributed to someone else's folly. But class still functioned as the primary metric for determining whether an individual's idleness was to be tolerated or punished. An 1844 editorial in the *Baltimore Sun* argued that the "majority" of vagrants arrested in the city were "white men who call themselves for lodgings." While a humanitarian impulse justified this allowance, it was argued, it would be preferable to have a "work-house, where loafers and vagrants might be placed and made to work," the result of which would be, the editorial argued, that "there would then be found fewer persons of that class amongst us."[26]

Legislators, constables, justices, and mayors held the primary responsibility for defining and prosecuting vagrant activities. But in important ways, their authority rested in part upon the involvement of the public. While constables had an occupational and legal "especial duty" to preserve order, the public was also charged with preserving the peace. In Washington, DC, for example, constables were asked to be proactive in their policing of vagrancy with the aid of the public. They were instructed to actively "endeavor to find out whether there be any such vagrants" within their jurisdiction, in addition to complying with a provision that declared it "lawful" for "any other person or persons" to compel any individual "they may esteem vagrants . . . before a justice of the peace for examination" so they "may be dealt with" appropriately.[27]

This sort of citizen vigilantism actually came with a monetary reward in Delaware, where individuals were incentivized by state legislatures to inform authorities about the presence of presumed vagrants, especially vagrant persons of color. In 1849, Delaware passed a law requiring county justices of the peace in the state to arrest any "free negro or mulatto, male or female . . . residing or staying" in his jurisdiction "without visible means of support"—effectively, any vagrant African Americans—for the purpose of forcibly binding them to an involuntary labor contract. Though individuals bound out under this law were considered servants, not slaves, the law created a de facto return to slavery for some. Successful informants who alerted justices to the presence of such persons were to receive a reward of three dollars for each report.[28] The integration of city and state denizens into the policing process suggests that vagrancy was perceived as a legible crime that the public could reliably identify, especially when the vagrant was African American.

From the colonial era, because indigent transients were feared as potential drains on public economy, children were a concern that was especially potent in relation to the possibility of future generations of vagrants growing up in early American cities. Authorities sought to limit the negative impact of widespread vagrancy among indigent transients and their children by forcing them into labor contracts, often without the consent of the parents or children. These were generally applicable to all poor persons, regardless of race, as Maryland law indicated. In 1808, however, Maryland had amended this law by introducing a requirement for justices of the peace to bring before the court "the child or children of any pauper or vagrant . . . lazy, indolent, and worthless free negroes, and bind them out as apprentices."[29] Several decades later, fears of the growing population of free people of color and heightened racial tensions in the Upper South led to careful clarification of the intent of the application of such laws. In 1839, Maryland began to require constables to take special oath to "take up vagrant blacks and their neglected children." Alongside this prevention of future generations of non-laboring African Americans, adult vagrants were vulnerable to resale into slavery: free African Americans who lacked "the necessary means of support and [were] not of good and industrious habits" were to "be sold at auction as a slave for the current year."[30] Such legislation, and the public discussions that promoted it, demonstrate the centrality of vagrancy to white authorities' efforts at economic, spatial, and behavioral control. These laws set a precedent that was expanded upon following total emancipation after the Civil War.[31]

Debates over how best to extract labor from both white and black vagrants, who were viewed as intentionally withholding their labor from the public economy, were quotidian in the antebellum Upper South. In regions facing chronic labor shortages, as in much of the Upper South throughout the nineteenth century, vagrancy laws provided a means to force laborers into employment contracts, thus ensuring a sufficiency of available workers.[32] Then General, later President William Henry Harrison argued in favor of "sell[ing] vagrants and persons who have been convicted of a crime and are unable to pay the fine and the costs."[33] Proponents of such practices used historical precedent to justify their arguments, claiming that there had been "scarce a state in the union where such laws did not exist before the erection of penitentiaries."[34] Bills introduced to the Maryland legislature from the 1830s through the 1850s repeatedly considered whether free African Americans ought to be forced to labor. Lengths of time were debated—the preference seeming to be for annual contracts, as a direct deterrent of vagrancy among people of color. One 1836 proposal suggesting compulsion of free African Americans into annual labor contracts was rejected solely on the grounds of its likelihood to bring free and enslaved people of color into close contact, a threat to the stability of the enslaved labor force. These laws clearly demonstrate not only that vagrants were viewed as a threat to social and economic order but also that black vagrants were deemed simultaneously more threatening and more deserving of control, given the perception that they were less capable of providing for themselves. Farther south, too, as in North Carolina, such measures were proposed as means of "reenslaving" the free black population, and of controlling white "vagabonds" and "idlers" lacking any "visible means of support" in the later antebellum period.[35]

Even outside of the law, public discussion about how the poor, especially poor people of color, were to participate in the labor force were couched in racially specific terms. In 1839, the *Alexandria Gazette* reported that "laborers on the wharf, that will work for fair prices, and do all the work, are wanted," because there was "a gang of lazy negroes, now on the wharves, who will only do such work as pleases them, and for which they ask double prices." The presence of these individuals necessitated not only the advertisement for more motivated laborers but also a call for punishment. "It is supposed," the article continued, "that if some of the 'gangs' on the wharf were thinned, by the operation of the 'vagrant' act, it would be as well."[36] Such comments document the absence of a sufficient workforce for the local market, while revealing a subtext of the perceived necessity of compulsion to extract labor from poor people of color.[37]

The introduction of more punitive legislation against African American vagrants in the antebellum era often prompted opposition from the targeted population themselves. One free black man, Henry Davis, was eighteen years old when he successfully presented a case for his freedom to the Orphan's Court of Baltimore County, Maryland, in 1848. He had been indentured as an apprentice to Thomas Knighton, according to Davis, "under the auspices of an act of 1793 that allowed 'the child or children of any pauper or vagrant, or the child or children of lazy indolent, and worthless free negroes' to be bound out as apprentices." Davis argued that Knighton was effectively forcibly stealing his labor, as he did not fall under the intention of that law, and he denied that he or his parents were vagrants, asserting that they were "regularly and industriously employed and earning a competent and sufficient livelihood." It appears that Davis's initial petition went unresolved in the spring of 1848, but by summer, Knighton had apparently sold Davis's services to a man named Dr. Benjamin Bird so that he might "more effectually conceal the fraud." Davis argued that this action was an admission of Knighton's guilt, and that as a result he ought to be "released from the unjust and oppressive servitude" in which Knighton held him. Davis's petition was granted on June 27, 1848.[38] The claim of personal industry was among the most common means utilized by convicted vagrants in contesting their sentences, thus reinforcing many authorities' views that in cases of "true" vagrancy, idleness and not strictly poverty rendered the individual a vagrant.

Engaged citizens sought to guide state legislatures' efforts in the Upper South by expressing concerns about growing populations of free African Americans, detailing the particular ways in which they wished to limit their movements and manage their engagement with the workforce. Delaware received numerous petitions from concerned residents to this effect in the 1840s that claimed that the absence of slavery among this group had led vagrant tendencies to run rampant amongst them. One petition claimed that "lazy, irresponsible, lawless, and miserable free negroes and mulattoes" had been "by their indigence rendered irresponsible to the obligations of a contract." The mobility that resulted from their impoverished and degraded status, they argued, precluded them from entering into long-term contracts for agricultural labor and thus needed to be curbed: "Our farmers," the petition read, "are deserted by the laborers they have employed in the cultivation of their crops, at the busiest season of the year." To remedy this problem, the petitioners requested that the legislature place vagrancy prosecution and labor contract management in the hands of "farmers and housekeepers to compel such as would otherwise be idle and worthless, to enter into engagements for the month or year, at the customary wages."[39] This argument was based on some employers' beliefs that mobility among laborers was to blame for the serious shortage of hands to bring in harvests annually, threatening the livelihoods of Delaware farmers.[40]

The shape of antebellum labor markets in the Upper South, where scarcity was common in both industrial and agricultural production, deeply impacted the economic and employment statuses of the poor, especially poor people of color, but it also influenced societal perceptions of the relationship among labor status, criminality, mobility, and racial identity. Antebellum residents of the Upper South employed the language of vagrancy statutes to argue against permitting African Americans to retain freedom of mobility. One petition described formerly enslaved and free African Americans as "a migratory tribe, without fixed abode, alternately roving from city to country, compelled to mete out a scanty subsistence." Others referred to the section of vagrancy laws that referenced visibility of means of subsistence, arguing for "more efficient" correction and restraint of "the idle and roving habits of the negroes and mulattoes" by mandating their entrance into longer-term wage labor contracts.[41] Some commentators even argued that the state legislature ought "to prevent our being overrun by vagrant negroes as well as slaves who are well known to be harboring among us . . . without any apparent business or means of support."[42] This conflation of vagrant tendencies with African American identity exacerbated the environment created by preexisting poor laws and other settlement laws that regulated the movement of the poor, thus racializing both poverty and mobility.[43]

Vagrancy laws had been used to control the movements and behavior of poor whites, "strangers," and people of color, both North and South, since the eighteenth century. Yet most American historians have tended to view vagrancy laws as an "inheritance" from early modern England that featured prominently in the colonial era, only to fade and resurface during the Civil War and Reconstruction, when vagrancy laws and compulsory contracts acted as tools "to mediate the transition from slavery to freedom."[44] But the examples laid out here suggest that this previous assessment elides the use of vagrancy laws to punish indigent transiency, unemployment, and other activities deemed "immoral" by authorities. Rather, white authorities had relied on vagrancy laws, as well as codified limitations of movement and residence based on race and class across the North since the eighteenth century.[45] Fear and the desire to "protect" communities from mobile free people of color drove the use of vagrancy statutes and laws limiting the geographical movement of recently emancipated slaves throughout the nineteenth century.[46] The gradual racialization of vagrancy laws in the Upper South during the antebellum era points to the influence of a shared conception of vagrancy laws as tools to regulate the behavior of the poor that stretched across geographical and socioeconomic borders.

The origins of the mobility restriction and labor compulsion of the Black Codes, the response to the "tramp scare" of the 1890s, to the rail-riding hoboes of the 1930s, and to the twenty-first-century urban homeless lie in early American poor laws and vagrancy statutes, and, even earlier still, colonial and British policies dealing with the poor and mobile. The potency and longevity of their impact can be seen, even in the present, in Baltimore officials' response to the unrest in that city in the spring of 2015, following the death of black Baltimore resident Freddie Gray at the hands of city police. There, as Robert Gamble has argued, the legacy of slavery and antebellum origins of laws limiting the mobility of African Americans were on full display as a curfew, upheld with "uneven enforcement for white and black protestors," was put in place to "curtail unlicensed movements" by African Americans. As twenty-first-century riot control harkened back to nineteenth-century efforts to "curb the nocturnal movements of African Americans," the "racially coded ways that movement has been defined and patrolled" in American cities is starkly clear.[47]

Curfews, of course, are not the only remnant of these antebellum efforts at mobility limitation of the poor and nonwhite. Loitering statutes and stop-and-frisk laws continue to echo the logic behind and language of vagrancy prosecution long after it was declared unconstitutional. Highly discretionary and overtly classed and raced, stop-and-frisk laws are viewed by some scholars as a direct replacement for vagrancy laws, for a nearly identical purpose. As Risa Goluboff has argued, since the 1960s, police have seen "stop and frisk and vagrancy (and similar) laws as alternative ways of apprehending suspects who had not given them probable cause to arrest for other crimes." [48] From the mid-twentieth century onward, vagrancy laws were replaced by stop-and-frisk policies that replaced the crime prevention aspects of the earlier statutes while policies prohibiting loitering addressed the mobility-curbing and stranger-punishing aspects.[49] The city police in Baltimore, as well as in, most prominently, New York City, have been investigated for aggressively targeting poor African Americans for random street searches. The minimal requirement that police perceive reasonable suspicion for stopping and frisking an individual based on visual cues harkens back clearly to the clause of vagrancy statutes that singled out visual presentations of vagrant behavior.[50] Now, as then, the targeting of the poor and the nonwhite through such legal apparatuses has led to excessive behavior-policing in these communities.

Notes

1. *Debates of the Constitutional Convention of the State of Maryland* (Annapolis, MD: Richard P. Bayly, 1864), 1597–99.

2. See Amy Dru Stanley, *From Bondage to Contract: Wage Labor, Marriage, and the Market in the Age of Slave Emancipation* (Cambridge: Cambridge University Press, 1998), 99, 132; and Mary Farmer-Kaiser, "'Are They Not in Some Sorts Vagrants?': Gender and the Efforts of the Freedmen's Bureau to Combat Vagrancy in the Reconstruction South," *Georgia Historical Quarterly* 88 (2004): 25–49. William Cohen is one of the few historians to acknowledge the full impact of antebellum racialized vagrancy legislation redeployed to punish recently emancipated slaves after the Civil War. He notes that "the prewar laws of North Carolina, Delaware, and Maryland dealing with free Negro vagrants bear a close resemblance to the southern vagrancy laws of 1865 and 1866" (*At Freedom's Edge: Black Mobility and the Southern White Quest for Racial Control, 1861–1915* [Baton Rouge: Louisiana State University Press, 1991], 34).

3. Ira Berlin made this assertion in "Southern Free People of Color in the Age of William Johnson," *Southern Quarterly* 43, no. 2 (2006): 10. See also Emily West, *Family or Freedom: People of Color in the Antebellum South* (Lexington: Kentucky University Press, 2012), 4–5.

4. This term adroitly illustrates the contextual nature of vagrancy convictions, where one's visual characteristics and geographical mobility contributed significantly to one's status as policed. See Sarah Nicolazzo, "Vagrant Figures: Law, Labor, and Refusal in the Eighteenth-Century Atlantic World," (Ph.D. diss., University of Pennsylvania, 2014), 94.

5. This legacy is found both North and South, in the antebellum and postbellum United States. See James D. Schmidt, *Free to Work: Labor Law, Emancipation, and Reconstruction, 1815–1880* (Athens: University of Georgia Press, 1998), 88–89.

6. Paul Finkelman, "Rehearsal for Reconstruction: Antebellum Origins of the Fourteenth Amendment," in *Facts of Reconstruction: Essays in Honor of John Hope Franklin*, ed. Eric Anderson and Alfred Moss (Baton Rouge: Louisiana State University Press, 1991), 8–9.

7. *Articles of Confederation and Perpetual Union between the States of New Hampshire, Massachusetts Bay, Rhode Island, and Providence plantations, Connecticut, New York, New Jersey, Pennsylvania, Delaware, Maryland, Virginia, North Carolina, South Carolina and Georgia* (Alexander Purdie: Williamsburg, VA), 1777; Records of the Continental and Confederation Congresses and the Constitutional Convention, 1774–1789, record group 360, National Archives. Emphasis added.

8. "An Act for the Relief of the Poor," in *Laws of Maryland, 1692–1785* (Baltimore: Nicklin, 1811).

9. Barbara Fields, *Slavery and Freedom on the Middle Ground: Maryland during the Nineteenth Century* (New Haven: Yale University Press, 1985), 35; Patience Essah, *A House Divided: Slavery and Emancipation in Delaware, 1638–1865* (Charlottesville: University Press of Virginia, 1996), 111.

10. Ellen D. Katz, "African-American Freedom in Antebellum Cumberland County, Virginia—Freedom: Personal Liberty and Private Law," *Chicago-Kent Law Review* 70, no. 3 (1995): 944. See Judith Kelleher Schafer, *Becoming Free, Remaining Free: Manumission and Enslavement in New Orleans, 1846–1862* (Baton Rouge: Louisiana State University Press, 2003), 1–6.

11. W. W. Hening, *The New Virginia Justice* (Richmond, VA: Johnson and Warner, 1810), 550.

12. Fields, *Slavery and Freedom*, 63–89; Essah, *House Divided*, 109–11.

13. "An Act for the Relief of the Poor," in *Laws of Maryland, 1692–1785* (Baltimore: Nicklin, 1811).

14. Seth Rockman, "Work, Wages, and Welfare at Baltimore's School of Industry," *Maryland Historical Magazine* 102 (2007): 572–607.

15. These groups were feared as economic burdens, interlopers who would degrade local communities, and threats to the physical and physiological well-being of others. See Kathleen M. Brown, *Foul Bodies: Cleanliness in Early America* (New Haven: Yale University Press, 2009), 284.

16. "An Act to Prevent the Increase of Pauperism in This Commonwealth," in *A Digest of the Laws of Pennsylvania* (Philadelphia, 1837); *Digest of the Laws of the State of New York* (New York, 1874), 116; "Act for the Settlement and Relief of the Poor," in *A Digest of the Laws of New Jersey* (Philadelphia: J. B. Lippincott, 1838).

17. Keri Leigh Merritt, *Masterless Men: Poor Whites and Slavery in the Antebellum South* (New York: Cambridge University Press, 2017), 183n8.

18. "An Act Relating to Vagrants in the City of Baltimore," in *The General Public Statutory Law and Public Local Law of the State of Maryland: From the Year 1692 to 1839*, vol. 141 (Baltimore: John D. Toy, 1840).

19. Artemas Simonds, *Boston Common Council—No. 15, 1835, Report on Almshouses and Pauperism* (Boston: J. H. Eastburn, 1835), 26.

20. Maryland Penitentiary Prisoners Record, 1811–1840, S275-1, Maryland State Archives, Annapolis, MD.

21. Finkelman, "Rehearsal for Reconstruction," 8–9.

22. This echoed an 1800 Virginia law, "An Act to Amend the Act Entitled, 'An Act to Reduce into One the Several Acts Concerning Slaves, Free Negroes and Mulattoes,'" in *The Statutes at Large of Virginia* (Richmond: Samuel Shepherd, 1835); *Alexandria Gazette*, March 23, 1827.

23. "An Act Concerning Free Negroes, Mulattoes, and Vagrants, and for Other Purposes," in *Acts of the Corporation of the City of Washington* (Washington, DC: A. & G. Way, 1813).

24. Joseph A. Ranney, *In the Wake of Slavery: Civil War, Civil Rights, and the Reconstruction of Southern Law* (Westport, CT: Praeger, 2006), 17; Essah, *House Divided*, 116; Jacqueline Jones, *American Work: Four Centuries of Black and White Labor* (New York: W. W. Norton, 1999), 110–11.

25. "Great and Small Vagrants," *Baltimore Sun*, November 15, 1841.

26. "Local Matters," *Baltimore Sun*, January 20, 1844.

27. "Laws of the District of Columbia," *Congressional Series of United States Public Documents*, vol. 231 (Washington, DC: Duff Green, 1832), 283.

28. Essah, *House Divided*, 116.

29. "A Further Supplement to an Act, Entitled, An Act for the Better Regulation of Apprentices," in *Laws of Maryland, 1801–1809* (Baltimore: Nicklin, 1811).

30. J. R. Brackett, *The Negro in Maryland: A Study of the Institution of Slavery*, vol. 6 (Baltimore: N. Murray, 1889), 219.

31. Ranney, *In the Wake of Slavery*, 17.

32. Ronald L. Lewis, *Black Coal Miners in America: Race, Class, and Community Conflict, 1780–1980* (Lexington, KY: University Press of Kentucky, 1987), xiii–xiv; Ronald L. Lewis, "Antebellum Industry," in *The New Encyclopedia of Southern Culture*, vol. 11: *Agriculture and Industry* (Chapel Hill: University of North Carolina Press, 2014), 230–31.

33. *Pilot and Transcript* (Baltimore), July 1, 1840.

34. *Pilot and Transcript*, July 1, 1840.

35. Jones, *American Work*, 202.

36. *Alexandria Gazette*, November 2, 1839.

37. This is similar to what Amy Dru Stanley has suggested regarding contract and compulsion in the postbellum period (Stanley, *From Bondage to Contract*, 132).

38. Petition of Henry Davis, Register of Wills, 1820–1851 (Petitions and Orders), Maryland State Archives, Annapolis, MD.

39. Records of the General Assembly, Legislative Papers, Petition 10383501, January 31, 1825, and Petitions 10384101-10384111, record group 1111, Delaware Public Archives, Dover (hereafter DPA); C. E. Hoffecker, *Democracy in Delaware: The Story of the First State's General Assembly* (Wilmington, DE: Cedar Tree Press, 2004), 102–3; William H. Williams, *Slavery and Freedom in Delaware, 1639–1865* (New York: Rowman and Littlefield, 1999), 195–96.

40. Essah, *House Divided*, 71.

41. Records of the General Assembly, Legislative Papers, Petition 10383501, January 31, 1825, and Petitions 10384101-10384111, record group 1111, DPA.

42. Records of the General Assembly, Legislative Papers, Petition 10384503, February 15, 1845, record group 1111, DPA.

43. This relationship between race and vagrancy continued into the Civil War itself, at which point, David Roediger notes, free blacks were seen as synonymous with vagrants. See David Roediger, *Seizing Freedom: Slave Emancipation and Liberty for All* (London: Verso, 2014), 28.

44. Roediger, *Seizing Freedom*, 99, 132. Jacqueline Jones, too, has noted that, immediately following the end of the Civil War, many plantation owners and overseers

prosecuted the formerly enslaved for exercising "liberty of locomotion" by leaving "the plantation without permission" (Jones, *American Work*, 245).

45. Stanley, *From Bondage to Contract*; Farmer-Kaiser, "'Are They Not'"; Cohen, *At Freedom's Edge*.

46. Finkelman, "Rehearsal for Reconstruction," 8–9.

47. Robert Gamble, "African Americans, Mobility, and the Law," *The Junto: A Group Blog in Early American History*, May 11, 2015, 2, https://earlyamericanists.com/2015/05/11/african-americans-mobility-and-the-law/.

48. Risa Goluboff, *Vagrant Nation: Police Power, Constitutional Change, and the Making of the 1960s* (New York: Oxford University Press, 2016), 209.

49. Goluboff, *Vagrant Nation*, 11.

50. Gloria Browne-Marshall, "Stop and Frisk: From Slave-Catchers to NYPD, A Legal Commentary," *Trotter Review* 21, no. 1 (2013); "City's 'Stop and Frisk' Oversight Criticized," *Baltimore Sun*, November 19, 2013.

3

Origins of the Prison-Industrial Complex

Inmate Labor in the Deep South, 1817–1865

BRETT J. DERBES

During the antebellum period, southern state legislators sought to create financially self-sustaining penitentiaries that encouraged inmate rehabilitation through silent reflection and physical labor. The European Enlightenment's influence on methods of punishment and technological innovation from the Industrial Revolution contributed to the rise of prison workshops and inmate labor in the Deep South. Convicts provided a captive, reliable, and inexpensive workforce, but also attracted criticism from local artisans and mechanics' organizations. The competition between private and forced inmate labor abated temporarily when demand for military supplies increased during the Civil War. Penitentiary workshops emerged in the antebellum years, thrived during the war, and developed into the modern prison-industrial complex. Inmate labor has swelled within an ever-expanding prison population and renewed public debate over wages, profits, and competition.

An examination of four state penitentiaries in the Deep South highlights a controversial aspect of free labor within an antebellum slave society. In 1817, the Georgia State Penitentiary in Milledgeville began accepting prisoners, whose days consisted of labor in workshops. The Louisiana State Penitentiary in Baton Rouge began holding prisoners in 1835. The legislature prohibited competition with local industry, but a lucrative textile mill and workshops operated nonetheless. In 1840, the Mississippi State Penitentiary opened in Jackson, where local artisans demanded that inmate labor be excluded from mechanical trades. The following year, the Alabama State Penitentiary in Wetumpka began employing prisoners in workshops that supplied goods to a private company in Montgomery. These four examples emphasize early public opposition to competition from inmate labor, as well as a public willingness to reconsider those viewpoints in times of crisis.

General studies of American penology provide essential overviews of the evolution of criminal justice, criminology, and facilities from the colonial era to the present day. Michael Ignatieff asserted that the economic, ideological, and social connections between prison reformers and new industrial employers led to the transformation of penitentiaries into well-ordered manufactories. Meanwhile, Edward L. Ayers confronted perceptions of honor and violence in the Old South by studying patterns of southern crime and punishment before and after the Civil War. Other, more specific studies of state penitentiaries and penal systems examine personnel, politics, budgets, and policy development. Yet the emergence and employment of inmate labor across the South in the decades prior to the Civil War remains vastly understudied, even in state-oriented works. Larry R. Findlay Sr. offered a concise overview of prison history from 1806 to 2007 but minimized the antebellum penitentiary workshops. Mark T. Carleton provided a broad study of the corruption and greed in the Louisiana penal system from 1835 through 1968 but abbreviated the war years. Robert David Ward and William Warren Rogers, meanwhile, produced a comprehensive examination of the Alabama penal system but devoted only limited attention to inmate labor during the Civil War. Finally, William B. Taylor explored the social factors, policymakers, and political tactics that generated the Mississippi penal system.[1]

Recent scholarship also investigates myriad social, legal, administrative, disciplinary, economic, gendered, and medical aspects of penitentiaries and inmates. Angela Y. Davis points out that profit-seeking corporations employ ever-increasing numbers of inmates across the prison-industrial complex as the national prison population has surpassed two million. Curtis R. Blakely insists that states have abandoned the rehabilitative emphasis of inmate labor at both state and private facilities. Examinations of state penitentiaries and penal systems largely compress the early history, minimize the implementation of inmate labor, and overlook nineteenth-century wartime production. Studies and scholars instead often identify the introduction of convict leasing across the South during Reconstruction as the genesis of the modern prison-industrial complex, even though widespread use of inmate labor began almost fifty years earlier.[2]

That development began in Georgia. On January 24, 1817, Governor David B. Mitchell proclaimed the Georgia State Penitentiary in Milledgeville suitable to accept prisoners. Legislators insisted that workshops provided vocational training for inmates that also would generate revenue to pay operating expenses. Regulations required inmates to work eight to ten hours every day except Sunday and permitted inmates thirty minutes for breakfast and one hour for meals. Public criticism of the penitentiary and inmate labor began almost immediately, and increased as the facility ran a two-year deficit of twenty-four hundred dollars. Editors of the *Georgia Journal* flipped from supporting the penitentiary to questioning the expenses, benefits of inmate labor, and possibility of rehabilitation. Another writer cautioned legislators against turning the facility into "a money-making machine."[3]

Throughout the 1820s and 1830s, the master mechanics of Georgia sought to protect their status as master craftsmen, as well as their system of apprenticeship, by forming and joining professional organizations. Still, organizations such as the Mechanics Society of Augusta in the 1820s fragmented from divisive politics and principles. Nonetheless, by 1831, inmates engaged in over twenty trades including cabinetmaking, cotton gin manufacturing, painting, spinning, and weaving. The General Assembly meanwhile adopted New York's Auburn System of Prison Management consisting of silence, solitary confinement, and labor in workshops.[4]

Louisiana followed the example of Georgia in the decision to build penitentiary workshops using inmate labor. On January 3, 1832, Governor Andre B. Roman led the call for a new house of correction. Following weeks of debate, the Act to Establish the Louisiana Penitentiary was passed in the state legislature on March 16, 1832. In June 1833 nearly one hundred convicts from the parish jail in New Orleans began construction of the state penitentiary in Baton Rouge. The following year, state inspectors initially recommended the manufacture of cotton bagging, and within a decade the inmates undertook textile production, tailoring, shoe shops, brick manufacturing, leather tanning, joinery, carpentry, forge work, cabinetmaking, painting, and blacksmithing.[5]

The expansion of the prison-industrial complex continued in Mississippi and Alabama. On February 26, 1836, Mississippi governor Charles Lynch signed an act to establish a state penitentiary in Jackson. The Mississippi Legislature appropriated seventy-five thousand dollars for construction of a facility capable of housing at least two hundred inmates.

A large prison yard allowed for the future expansion of workshops and factories. The exterior wall required over one million bricks to be manufactured with inmate labor, as mandated by section 6 of the Penitentiary Act.[6]

The Mississippi State Penitentiary opened on April 15, 1840, and initially housed twenty-eight inmates. A shoe, tailor, blacksmith, carpenter, and wheelwright shop, as well as a brickyard served as the main employs of prisoners. One inmate recalled, "The cells are not warmed. . . . The men can warm themselves by exercise, and some of the shops are comfortable." In the summer of 1843 the superintendent employed inmates at "rambling outdoors labor." Thus, experiments in convict leasing began in Mississippi nearly three decades before the brutal system employed across the South during and after Reconstruction.[7]

Meanwhile, the Alabama General Assembly approved construction of a state penitentiary on January 26, 1839, during the administration of Governor Arthur P. Bagby. The legislature appropriated thirty thousand dollars, and selected East Wetumpka as the location. On October 27, 1841, prison commissioners received the keys at a public celebration. The *Wetumpka Argus* described the red brick prison as "having some architectural beauty." In January 1842, the first inmates arrived at the penitentiary, where they engaged in wagon, shoe, cabinet, harness, and saddle making, as well as blacksmithing, coopering, tanning, painting, tailoring, and cooking.[8]

In Georgia, the Augusta Mechanics' Society still strongly opposed competition from inmate labor throughout the decade. In 1841 the legislature passed an act stipulating the time, place, and procedure for an annual auction of prison goods. In his annual message, Governor George W. Crawford acknowledged that the mechanics of Milledgeville had united in opposition against "convicts trained in skilled trades." By the early 1840s local artisans and mechanics in Jackson began petitioning the legislature for protection from damage "to their several mechanical and manufacturing trades which is caused by employing convict labor against and in competition with honest and unimpeachable labor." These petitions suggested the substitution of manufacturing coarse cotton fabrics, bale rope, and hemp and cotton bagging. On February 24, 1844, the Mississippi legislature appropriated fifteen thousand dollars to purchase a wool carding machine and construct an iron foundry.[9]

As production increased at the penitentiary workshops, competition with private industry led to increased public outcries against inmate labor. Milledgeville artisans protested the penitentiary store that saturated the market with far cheaper inmate-produced goods. In 1845, the Augusta Mechanics' Society—with support of other mechanics' societies—sent a public petition to the penitentiary charging the state with training and releasing "a corps of graduate villains, half skilled and half depraved, in most instances, to perform according to their ability, who will work at reduced prices."[10]

Local citizens in Jackson objected to competition from convict-artisans whose training occurred at a state facility financed by taxes. The introduction of prison goods into the consumer marketplace drove down prices, which led to unease from private manufacturers. On March 5, 1846, the legislature enacted a bill to change the labor of convicts in the state penitentiary and appropriated $4,000 to construct an industrial building within the prison yard. Additionally, the superintendent purchased a steam engine and the inmates constructed a textile factory capable of employing eighty workers. Completed in 1847, the three-story building cost a total of $8,115.75. The shift away from trade-oriented inmate labor appeased many artisans, and the transition to textile production attracted less public opposition.[11]

In the mid-1840s the Louisiana State Legislature similarly appropriated $53,000 to expand the textile factory and purchase additional machinery. By 1848 the prison population consisted of 172 inmates, which included thirteen African American female slaves and six children. Female inmates and their children lived in separate quarters and engaged in alternative forms of labor away from the workshops. On December 11, 1848, the Louisiana State Legislature passed a law stating that all children born to African American slaves incarcerated for life became the legal property of the state. The sheriff auctioned these children at the age of ten on the steps of the county courthouse, with the proceeds going to the state treasurer as part of the free-school fund. By October 1849, the Louisiana penitentiary included a bagging and rope factory, a cotton and wool factory, a foundry, a finishing shop, a shoemaker shop, and a brickyard.[12]

The textile mill at the penitentiary in Jackson required inmates to manufacture 250,000 bricks, while also supplying nearly 1 million bricks for the State Insane Asylum. Meanwhile, the state assigned inmate labor to build a brick wall around the capitol. In 1848 inmates built a "valuable and substantial brick residence" for the superintendent, and in 1851 they made substantial repairs to the front wall and the connected structures. Thus, thirty-five convicts worked constantly at the brickyard throughout the decade.[13]

On May 30, 1851, the *Alabama Daily Journal* reported of the state penitentiary in East Wetumpka: "Nearly every branch of industry is carried on within its walls, and the presumption is that the lessee is making money." Yet not all citizens were pleased with the productivity of the facility, and some suggested alternative uses for inmate labor. On July 4, 1851, the Georgia Mechanics Convention met in Atlanta, where the members called for a State Mechanical Institute, broader membership, and adherence to the traditional system of apprenticeship before addressing the "evil" of convict labor causing "pecuniary loss to the State." They opposed the instruction of convicts in mechanical trades that typically required five to six years of apprenticeship by free citizens. The speakers identified inmate labor as a major reason the South depended on northern manufacturing capital.[14]

The 1850s were a period of disaster, modernization, and expansion for the prison textile mills in Louisiana and Mississippi. An appropriation of $40,000 in 1853 allowed the Louisiana State Penitentiary to expand the textile factory to 2,300 spindles and 60 looms that produced 2,000 yards of cloth per day. A fire occurred on June 2, 1856, that provided an opportunity to modernize and expand the textile mill to the production levels reached during the war. The Louisiana State Penitentiary became a model institution, and the workshops produced annual sales of at least $117,624.[15]

In Jackson, public opposition to inmate labor renewed in 1851 as the penitentiary continued to sell goods at reduced prices. By 1855, 68 of the 82 convicts in the prison worked in the mill and annual sales totaled $32,372.89. On November 1, 1857, a fire in the wool and cotton factory completely destroyed the building. The legislature appropriated $40,000 to rebuild the factory as well as $30,000 for modern textile machinery. The new mill employed 150 inmates, and its equipment included 2,304 spindles, 24 carding machines, and 80 looms. In late 1858, a visiting journalist asserted, "no factory in the Southern States . . . can compete with it in size, durability, and the perfect system observed in all its parts."[16]

In Wetumpka, Dr. Meriwether Gaines Moore and Dr. Fleming Jordan coleased the Alabama State Penitentiary from May 18, 1852, until April 12, 1858. The new lessees focused inmate labor on the production of bagging, rope, and twine. The goods manufactured at the prison sold at the penitentiary and at Burrows, Holt & Co. in Montgomery. In 1860 the prison population reached 219, and the average inmate was thirty years old, male, and white. The most common offenses were murder, larceny, "negro stealing," burglary, robbery, manslaughter, and attempting to kill. Previous occupations ranged from "rat catcher" to physician but the most common were farmer, laborer, sailor, carpenter, shoemaker, and blacksmith. Skilled inmates with previous experience as blacksmiths, carpenters, shoemakers, coopers, machinists, millwrights, and wagon makers often became workshop overseers and trained fellow inmates.[17]

In Louisiana the inmate population rose steadily from 91 in 1835 to 343 by 1860. Inmates were overwhelmingly of twenty to forty years of age, of southern origin, convicted of violent crimes, and serving life sentences. The most common crimes committed included murder, larceny, robbery, manslaughter, and burglary. The cotton and wool factory required 240 inmates to operate at full capacity, while the engine room required 6 inmates to operate the two steam engines that powered the workshops. As in other southern states, the Louisiana Legislature urged the penitentiary to segregate workshops, but the lessees insisted the statute was "impractical" and would disrupt productivity.[18]

In 1860 the Georgia State Penitentiary housed 231 inmates. The average inmate was white, between twenty-one and forty years of age, and sentenced within the last four years for larceny, manslaughter, forgery, attempt to murder, or burglary. The vast majority had worked as common laborers, but their previous occupations ranged from physician and engineer to bricklayer and ditchdigger. By 1860, the penitentiary facility included over a dozen buildings inside and outside of the walls.[19]

On the eve of the Civil War, the Mississippi State Penitentiary held 181 male inmates, who were overwhelmingly sentenced within the previous four years. Most prisoners were between twenty and thirty-nine years old and convicted of larceny, manslaughter, or negro stealing. Prisoners hailed from twenty-seven locations across the world, with the highest numbers from Ireland, which was followed by Mississippi, Tennessee, and Georgia. The inmates held a wide variety of previous occupations from physician and watchmaker to stonecutter and upholsterer. The most common trades included farmer, laborer, and carpenter.[20]

The Civil War altered the history of prison manufacture by creating new state demands for inmate-produced goods. By June 1861, eleven states had seceded from the Union. Throughout the Civil War, inmates in Georgia operated brick, wagon, shoe, railroad car, harness, and blacksmith shops where they manufactured shoes, army tents, coats, mattresses, salt sacks, and other items. Tents became one of the most common items produced in the prison-industrial complex of the Confederacy. A sample of orders during the winter of 1861 demonstrates the successful conversion to manufacturing wartime supplies, especially tents. During the Civil War, the Mississippi State Penitentiary expanded to include a munitions factory and general production facility that produced other military supplies ranging from uniforms, belts, and tents to gun carriages and cartridge boxes.[21]

With the outbreak of the war, Louisiana's textile mill expanded to produce several varieties of finished cloth, including shirting, burlaps, and osnaburg. Confederate quartermasters in Louisiana purchased upward of two-thirds of the goods manufactured at the penitentiary during the war. In Alabama, Warden Burrows contracted with the Confederate Ordnance Department in Montgomery to provide knapsacks, tents, and wagon covers. The manufacture of canvas goods represented the most profitable items, and the total value of goods produced during 1861 amounted to $17,349.25. The initial steps toward establishing a state armory at the Georgia State Penitentiary began on December 9, 1861. The armory employed convict labor, and hired a master armorer and master artisans. The workshops located on the lower level of the penitentiary were converted into the state armory.[22]

The Louisiana State Penitentiary sold more than 2.5 million yards of cloth annually in 1861 and 1862 to supply soldiers in the Trans-Mississippi Department with uniforms, blankets, and tents. The workshops provided the Confederate Ordnance and Quartermaster Departments with $88,567.32 of prison goods from June 1861 to March 1862. Following the fall of New Orleans to Union forces on April 25, 1862, the Federal Army occupied Baton Rouge. Despite the prison officials' precaution of relocating workshop equipment to Clinton by river transport and railroad, Union forces located and destroyed a large portion of the textile machinery. The penitentiary was ultimately reduced to a charred brick shell after three years of fighting.[23]

As the war progressed, meanwhile, the Georgia General Assembly hoped to increase domestic production of cloth by manufacturing cotton cards with inmate labor. On December 6, 1862, the General Assembly appropriated $100,000, and Governor Brown contracted to relocate machinery to the penitentiary. The cotton card factory displayed a pair of Whittemore pattern cotton cards for inspection on December 20. Midway through the war, the Georgia penitentiary complex consisted of an armory, a cotton card factory, and various workshops.[24]

In the spring of 1863, Mississippi and Alabama demonstrated uncommon interstate cooperation as the Union Army under the direction of General William Tecumseh Sherman approached Jackson. State officials faced a crisis over relocating the convicts across state lines. On May 2, Governor John J. Pettus telegraphed Alabama governor John G. Shorter, "Twenty-three convicts in the Mississippi penitentiary disloyal and dangerous men. Will you receive them temporarily in your penitentiary?" Governor Shorter immediately responded, "Send your convicts here under guard I will receive them." The visiting inmates resided in solitary confinement for five months until the Alabama Legislature authorized the detention and supervision of convicts from other states. Due to the growing shortages of raw materials, the Mississippi inmates never labored in the Alabama workshops. In Jackson, the penitentiary accumulated $369,234.73 in sales and deposited at least $131,000.00 into the treasury during the war. On May 17, 1863, Federal troops commanded by Union general Ulysses S. Grant set fire to the cotton factory at the Mississippi State Penitentiary and the flames spread to the shoe and tailor shops.[25]

The Georgia State Penitentiary produced at least 448,866 items that resulted in at least $163,930.98 in net earnings during the war. In his memoirs, Union general Sherman admitted that he ordered the destruction of the "arsenal and its contents, and of such public buildings as could be easily converted to hostile uses." Union captain David P. Conyngham suggested that Union officers did not authorize burning the penitentiary, but he pointed out that the presence of an armory justified destroying it.[26]

Receipts from the Alabama State Penitentiary to the Montgomery Depot document at least 13,895 tents, 2,712 wagon covers, 1,272 knapsacks, and thousands of other items. Inmate labor manufactured at least

$299,565.58 of military supplies from 1861 to 1865. A skirmish that directly threatened the Alabama State Penitentiary on May 4, 1865, coincided with the surrender of the Confederate forces in the Department of Alabama, Mississippi, and Eastern Louisiana. The question of exactly which Union soldiers or subordinate officers of General James Wilson opened the doors of the penitentiary remains unanswered. As the war progressed, invading Union armies targeted Confederate state penitentiaries for occupation or destruction.[27]

Penitentiaries across the Deep South had operated workshops with inmate labor, and the outbreak of the Civil War forced manufactories in the Confederacy to adapt to wartime conditions. Southerners operated and endured dual systems of justice until 1865. The penal system incarcerated citizens and free blacks. Meanwhile, slave owners and overseers engaged in cruel forms of plantation justice and corporal punishment. The Civil War accomplished the goals of preserving the Union and emancipating the enslaved, but it is noteworthy that section 1 of the Thirteenth Amendment to the U.S. Constitution prohibited slavery and involuntary servitude, "except as punishment for crime whereof the party shall have been duly convicted." This explicit infringement on the rights of the incarcerated has since been characterized as a "loophole for slavery." Ultimately, the destruction of southern penitentiaries, postwar financial turmoil, vehement racism, and rapid growth of the African American prison population all contributed to the brutal convict leasing system that existed across the South for nearly fifty years.[28]

The Unites States currently incarcerates over two million prisoners, and debates regarding inmate labor, wages, and competition with private industry continue to rage. Advocates of inmate labor applaud rehabilitation, bemoan solitary confinement, and downplay the economic ramifications. Meanwhile, adversaries highlight recidivism rates, emphasize labor rights, and underscore the economic perils. By 2015, thirty-seven states permitted private corporations to contract inmate labor, which has resulted in a widespread "insourcing" of manufacturing jobs from the private sector. Federal Prison Industries, Inc. (FPI), also known as UNICOR, is a wholly government-owned corporation that employs over twelve thousand inmates in eighty factories to manufacture products purchased by the Department of Defense (DoD) and other federal departments, agencies, and bureaus. The modern prison-industrial complex evolved from experimental workshops established at southern state penitentiaries nearly two centuries ago. Clearly, inmate labor will continue to be utilized as long as it remains plentiful and profitable.[29]

Notes

1. Michael Ignatieff, *A Just Measure of Pain: The Penitentiary in the Industrial Revolution, 1750–1850* (New York: Pantheon Books, 1978); Edward L. Ayers, *Vengeance and Justice: Crime and Punishment in the Nineteenth-Century American South* (New York: Oxford University Press, 1984); Larry R. Findlay Sr., *History of the Georgia Prison System* (Frederick, MD: Publish America, 2007); Mark T. Carleton, *Politics and Punishment: The History of the Louisiana State Penal System* (Baton Rouge: Louisiana State University Press, 1971); Robert David Ward and William Warren Rogers, *Alabama's Response to the Penitentiary Movement, 1829–1865* (Gainesville: University Press of Florida, 2003); William Banks Taylor, *Brokered Justice: Race, Politics, and Mississippi Prisons, 1798–1992* (Columbus: Ohio State University Press, 1993).

2. Angela Y. Davis, *Are Prisons Obsolete?* (New York: Seven Stories Press, 2003); Curtis R. Blakely, *America's Prisons: The Movement toward Profit and Privatization* (Baton Rouge: Brown Walker Press, 2005).

3. James C. Bonner, "The Georgia Penitentiary at Milledgeville, 1817–1874," *Georgia Historical Quarterly* 15 (1971): 303, 306–8; Larry E. Sullivan, *Prison Reform Movement: Forlorn Hope* (Boston: Twayne, 1990), 9; Mary P. Walden, "History of the Georgia Penitentiary at Milledgeville, 1817–1868," (master's thesis, Georgia State University, 1974), 32, 36, 38–41, 59–60; Andrea N. Mitchell, "The Georgia Penitentiary at Milledgeville" (master's thesis, Georgia College and State University, 2003), 34–36, 39–40; *Georgia Journal* (Milledgeville, GA), March 11, 18, December 23, 1817, August 15, 1820, May 29, 1821; Leola Selman Beeson, *History Stories of Milledgeville and Baldwin County* (Macon: J. W. Burke, 1943), 86; George White, *Statistics of the State of Georgia Including an Account of Its Natural, Civil, and Ecclesiastical History* (Savannah: Thorne Williams, 1849), 85; Adiel Sherwood, *A Gazetteer of the State of Georgia* (Philadelphia: J. W. Martin and W. K. Boden, 1829), 146; *Milledgeville Reflector*, November 10, 1818; Findlay, *History of the Georgia Prison System*, 35; *Milledgeville Southern Recorder*, November 28, 1820, December 24, 1822.

4. Michelle Gillespie, *Free Labor in an Unfree World: White Artisans in Slaveholding Georgia, 1789–1860* (Athens: University of Georgia Press, 2004), 138, 142–44, 146, 151–52; Mitchell, "The Georgia Penitentiary at Milledgeville," 52; Walden, "History of the Georgia Penitentiary at Milledgeville, 1817–1868," 46, 73, 82; *Federal Union* (Milledgeville, GA), May 5, 1831; *Gettysburg (PA) Compiler*, May 4, 1831; Bonner, "The Georgia Penitentiary at Milledgeville, 1817–1874," 309.

5. Burk Foster, "Slaves of the State," *Angolite* 25 (2000): 42–45; Leon Stout, "Origin and Early History of the Louisiana Penitentiary" (master's thesis, Louisiana State University, 1934), 27, 29, 31–32, 35–36, 46–47; Thurston H. G. Hahn III and Susan Wurtzburg,

Hard Labor: History and Archaeology at the Old Louisiana State Penitentiary, Baton Rouge, Louisiana (Fort Worth: General Services Administration, 1991), 2–4; *Baton Rouge Gazette*, March 17, 1832; Acts of Louisiana, 10th Legislature, 2nd Sess. (New Orleans: Stroud and Pew, 1832), 110–12; *New Orleans Times Picayune*, January 15, 1843; Carleton, *Politics and Punishment*, 8; *Louisiana Times Picayune*, March 24, 1840, August 17, 1841.

6. Taylor, *Brokered Justice*, 15; Steve Sullivan, *Prison without Walls: A History of Mississippi's State Penal System* (n.p., 1978), Mississippi Department of Archives and History, Jackson, MS, 18, 20, 54; Paul B. Foreman and Julien R. Tatum, "A Short History of Mississippi's State Penal Systems," *Mississippi Law Journal* 10 (April 1938): 256–57; Mary Carol Miller, *Lost Landmarks of Mississippi* (Jackson: University Press of Mississippi, 2002), 115–16.

7. Taylor, *Brokered Justice*, 15–16, 21; William D. McCain, *The Story of Jackson: A History of the Capital of Mississippi, 1821–1951*, vol. 1 (Jackson: J. F. Hyer, 1953), 45, 47; Sullivan, "Prison without Walls," 30; Foreman and Tatum, "A Short History of Mississippi's State Penal Systems," 256; Sullivan, "Prison without Walls," 30, 42–44.

8. *Acts Passed at the Annual Session of the General Assembly of the State of Alabama* (Tuscaloosa: Hale and Eaton, 1838), 33; Elmore County Heritage Book Committee, *The Heritage of Elmore County, Alabama* (Clanton: Heritage Publishing Consultants, 2002), 204–6; Ward and Rogers, *Alabama's Response to the Penitentiary Movement, 1829–1865*, 45, 50–52, 60, 61–62, 64, 70–73, 86; *Wetumpka Argus*, February 22, 1843, May 15, 1839, June 19, 1839, December 11, 1839, January 15, 1840, March 4, 1840; Neeley, "Painful Circumstances," 4–6; *Acts of Alabama, 1846*, 9–13.

9. Walden, "History of the Georgia Penitentiary at Milledgeville, 1817–1868," 102; *Acts of the General Assembly of the State of Georgia, Passed at Milledgeville in an Annual Session, in November and December 1840* (Milledgeville: William S. Rogers, 1841), 164–66; *Journal of the Senate of the State of Georgia at an Annual Session of the General Assembly* (Milledgeville: William S. Rogers, 1842), 294–95; Mitchell, "The Georgia Penitentiary at Milledgeville," 43; *Acts of the General Assembly of the State of Georgia, Passed in November and December, 1843* (Milledgeville: William S. Rogers, 1843), 135; *Augusta Chronicle*, November 23, 1843; Foreman and Tatum, "A Short History of Mississippi's State Penal Systems," 257; Sullivan, "Prison without Walls," 55–56; Taylor, *Brokered Justice*, 23.

10. *Federal Union* (Milledgeville, GA), April 15, 1845; *Augusta Chronicle*, November 6, 11, 1845; Mitchell, "The Georgia Penitentiary at Milledgeville," 43; *Journal of the House of Representatives of the State of Georgia at an Annual Session of the General Assembly* (Milledgeville: William S. Rogers, 1845), 25; Walden, "History of the Georgia Penitentiary at Milledgeville, 1817–1868," 114, 118; *Journal of the House of Representatives of the State of Georgia at a Biennial Session of the General Assembly* (Milledgeville: Miller Grieve, 1848), 25; *Report of the Principal Keeper of the Georgia Penitentiary, 1847*, Board of Inspectors Reports, 1820–1873, RG21, SG1, 00-1015A, Georgia Archives, Morrow.

11. Taylor, *Brokered Justice*, 22–23; Charles C. Bolton, *Poor Whites of the Antebellum South: Tenants and Laborers in Central North Carolina and Northeast Mississippi* (Durham: Duke University Press, 1994), 111; McCain, *Story of Jackson*, vol. 1, 48; Sullivan, "Prison without Walls," 55–57.

12. Carleton, *Politics and Punishment*, 9–10; Foster, "Slaves of the State," 46; Stout, "Origin and Early History of the Louisiana Penitentiary," 45, 57–59; Hahn and Wurtzburg, *Hard Labor*, 5; *New Orleans Times Picayune*, February 21, March 15, 1843, October 2, 1844, January 10, 1845, May 1, 1846, April 30, 1845, April 22, 1846; *New Orleans Jeffersonian Republican*, May 1, 1846. Per Brett J. Derbes, "'Secret Horrors': Enslaved Women and Children in the Louisiana State Penitentiary, 1833–1862," *Journal of African American History* 98 (2013): 277–90, between 1842 and 1862 eleven children were auctioned with a total of $7,591 accumulated from their sale.

13. Taylor, *Brokered Justice*, 24–25.

14. *Daily Alabama Journal* (Montgomery), May 30, December 31, 1851; Neeley, "Painful Circumstances," 13; *Reports of the Inspectors of the Alabama Penitentiary to the General Assembly* (Montgomery: Brittan and de Wolf, 1851), 14–17, 24–25; *Savannah Republican*, July 10, 1851.

15. *Report of the Board of Control of the Louisiana Penitentiary to the General Assembly, January 1, 1852* (New Orleans: Emile La Sere, 1852), 2, 5, 6, 8; *Report of the Board of Directors of the Louisiana Penitentiary, January 2, 1854* (New Orleans: Emile La Sere, 1854), 4–6; *New Orleans Times Picayune*, June 6, 1856, May 12, August 10, 1859; Foster, "Slaves of the State," 46; *Annual Report of the Board of Directors, Clerk and Officers of the Louisiana Penitentiary, at Baton Rouge for the Year Ending December 31, 1854* (New Orleans: Emile La Sere, 1855), 22–23; *Message of Robert C. Wickliffe, Governor of the State of Louisiana Together with an Appendix Containing the Report of the Penitentiary Agents for the Year 1856* (Baton Rouge: Office of the Daily Advocate, 1857), 3, 9, 21–23, 27–32, 71; *Report of the Board of Control of the Louisiana Penitentiary to the General Assembly, December 31, 1859* (Baton Rouge: J. M. Taylor, 1859), 4–6, 15–16.

16. Taylor, *Brokered Justice*, 24–27; Sullivan, "Prison without Walls," 59; John Hebron Moore, *Emergence of the Cotton Kingdom in the Old Southwest: Mississippi, 1770–1860* (Baton Rouge: Louisiana State University, 1988), 226.

17. Ward and Rogers, *Alabama's Response to the Penitentiary Movement, 1829–1865*, 101–4, 109; *Reports of the Inspectors of the Alabama Penitentiary for the Years 1852–1853*, (Montgomery: Brittan and Blue, 1853), 3–4, 9, 24; Neeley, "Painful Circumstances," 14–15; Elmore County Heritage Book Committee, *Heritage of Elmore County*, 206; Mary K. Peck, "Moore Family History and Cain-Moore House History," Vertical File, Elmore County Museum, Wetumpka, AL; U.S. Bureau of the Census, *Seventh Census of the United States, 1850, Schedule 1, Free Inhabitants*, National Archives and Records Administration (hereafter NARA), roll M432_9, page 427a, image 478; Alabama Secretary of State, *Alabama State Census, 1850*, Government Records Collections, Alabama Department of Archives and History, Montgomery, AL (hereafter ADAH); Governor Andrew B. Moore Administrative File, SG6321, ADAH; *Alabama Daily Confederation*, February 17, April 10, 1860; U.S. Bureau of the Census, *Eighth Census of the United States, 1860, Schedule 1, Free Inhabitants*, NARA, roll M653_7, p. 115–20.

18. *Report of the Committee on the Penitentiary, 1858* (Baton Rouge: J. M. Taylor, 1858), 7, 18; *Report of the Board of Control of the Louisiana Penitentiary* (Baton Rouge: J. M. Taylor, 1858), 7; U.S. Bureau of the Census, *Eighth Census of the United States, 1860, Schedule 1, Free Inhabitants*, NARA, roll M653_408, p. 542.

19. U.S. Bureau of the Census, *Eighth Census of the United States, 1860*, NARA, roll M653_111, p. 163; *Augusta Chronicle*, November 13, 1860; *Annual Report of the Principal Keeper and Book Keeper of the Georgia Penitentiary, for the Fiscal Year Ending October 1st, 1860* (Milledgeville: Boughton, Nisbet, and Barnes, 1860), 3–5, 14–32; Leola Selman Beeson, *History Stories of Milledgeville and Baldwin County*, 86–88; *Milledgeville Union Recorder*, May 5, 1938.

20. U.S. Bureau of the Census, *Eighth Census of the United States, 1860, Schedule 1, Free Inhabitants*, NARA, roll M653_582, p. 521; Moore, *Emergence of the Cotton Kingdom in the Old Southwest*, 227; *Jackson Mississippian*, March 13, 1860.

21. Thomas F. Windsor, *Defense—Adjutant General—Ordnance Records, 1861–1864*, 022-01-017, folder 4636, Georgia State Archives, Morrow, GA; D. A. Jewell, *Confederate Papers Related to Citizens or Business Firms, 1861–65*, NARA M346, record group 109, roll 0505, document number 197; Green, James A., Folder, Records, Georgia Archives, Morrow, GA; Bolton, *Poor Whites of the Antebellum South*, 111; Moore, *Emergence of the Cotton Kingdom in the Old Southwest*, 22; Foreman and Tatum, "A Short History of Mississippi's State Penal Systems," 259; A. M. Hardin, *Confederate Papers Related to Citizens or Business Firms, 1861–65*, NARA M346, record group 109, roll 0404.

22. John D. Winters, *Civil War in Louisiana* (Baton Rouge: Louisiana State University Press, 1963), 60; *New Orleans Daily Picayune*, April 2, June 16, 1861, February 8, 28, 1862; *New Orleans Weekly Crescent*, February 8, 1862; Ward and Rogers, *Alabama's Response to the Penitentiary Movement, 1829–1865*, 110; Walter F. Fleming, *Civil War and Reconstruction in Alabama* (New York: Columbia University Press, 1905), 157; "A. Burrows," *Confederate Papers Relating to Citizens or Business Firms, 1861–65*, NARA M346, group 109, roll 0125; *Montgomery Daily Mail*, November 8, 1860; T. Conn Bryan, *Confederate Georgia* (Athens: University of Georgia Press, 1953), 25, 28; Allan D. Candler, ed., *Confederate Records of the State of Georgia*, 6 vols. (Atlanta: Charles P. Byrd, 1909), 2:266, 2:332–35, 2:354–55, 3:90; Walden, "History of the Georgia Penitentiary at Milledgeville, 1817–1868," 139; Mitchell, "The Georgia Penitentiary at Milledgeville," 44.

23. *Confederate Papers Relating to Citizens or Business Firms, 1861–1865*, NARA, M346, group 109, roll 632; *Times Picayune* (LA), September 11, October 3, 1861, November 26, December 4, 1864; Hahn and Wurtzburg, *Hard Labor*, 6–9; Brett J. Derbes, "Prison Productions: Textiles and Other Military Supplies at the Louisiana State Penitentiary in the Civil War," *Louisiana History* 55 (2014): 40–64; Edwin C. Bearss, "The Battle of Baton Rouge," *Louisiana History* 3 (1962): 77–128; Winters, *Civil War in Louisiana*, 123; Foster, "Slaves of the State," 41, 47–48, 50; Carleton, *Politics and Punishment*, 9; *Galveston Weekly News*, December 3, 1862; *Memphis Appeal*, May 16, 1863.

24. *Augusta Daily Constitutionalist*, December 2, 30, 1862, January 30, 1863; *Telegraph* (Macon, GA), December 3, 1862, January 9, 1863; Bryan, *Confederate Georgia*, 103–4; *DeBow's Review* 31 (1861): 556–57; Candler, *Confederate Records of the State of Georgia*, 4:450–53, 4:460–61, 4:666–67; *Confederate Union*, December 23, 1862, January 13, 1863; *Mobile Register and Advertiser*, December 28, 1862; *Southern Recorder*, December 23, 1862.

25. Sullivan, "Prison without Walls," 70–72; *Jackson Mississippian*, November 7, 1862; Jim Woodrick, *Civil War Siege of Jackson, Mississippi* (Charleston: History Press, 2016),

104–5; Bolton, *Poor Whites of the Antebellum South*, 111; Taylor, *Brokered Justice*, 27; *Brandon Republican*, May 18, 1863; Miller, *Lost Landmarks of Mississippi*, 116; Edwin C. Bearrs and Warren Grabau, *The Battle of Jackson, May 14, 1863. The Siege of Jackson July 10–17, 1863. Three Other Post-Vicksburg Actions* (Baltimore: Gateway Press, 1981); Buckley T. Foster, *Sherman's Mississippi Campaign* (Tuscaloosa: University of Alabama Press, 2006); *Penitentiary Accounting and Administration Records*, series 2678, box 30391, Mississippi Department of Archives and History, Jackson (hereafter MDAH); *Journal of the House of Representatives of the State of Mississippi, December Session of 1862, and November Session of 1863* (Jackson: Cooper & Kimball Steam Printers and Binders, 1864), 91, 96–97, 99.

26. James A. Green, "List of Military Equipment Made at Georgia Penitentiary and Sent Forward to Various Points," File Folder, Georgia Archives; *Macon Telegraph*, November 27, 1861; Mitchell, "The Georgia Penitentiary at Milledgeville," 44–45; *Annual Report of the Principal Keeper and Book Keeper of the Georgia Penitentiary, for the Fiscal Year Ending 1st October, 1862* (Milledgeville: Boughton, Nisbet, and Barnes, 1862), 2–6, 15–22; *Annual Report of the Principal Keeper and Book Keeper of the Georgia Penitentiary, for the Fiscal Year Ending 1st October, 1864* (Milledgeville: Boughton, Nisbet, Barnes, and Moore, 1864), 27–30; *Report of the Adjutant and Inspector General with Accompanying Papers, for the Year 1862–63* (Milledgeville: Boughton, Nisbet, Barnes, and Moore, 1863), 33–34; Lachlan McIntosh, *Defense—Adjutant General—Ordnance Records, 1861–1864*, 022-01-017, folder 2808, Georgia State Archives, Morrow, GA; *Augusta Chronicle*, December 22, 1864; James C. Bonner, "Sherman at Milledgeville in 1864," *Journal of Southern History* 22 (1956): 286–87; Walden, "History of the Georgia Penitentiary at Milledgeville, 1817–1868," 152–53; David P. Conyngham, *Sherman's March through the South* (New York: Sheldon, 1865), 255; *Frank Leslie's Illustrated Newspaper*, January 14, 1865; William T. Sherman, *Memoirs of William T. Sherman* (New York: D. Appleton, 1876), 190; *Milledgeville Southern Recorder*, December 20, 1864; *Federal Union* (Milledgeville, GA), December 6, 1864; *Journal of the Senate of the Extra Session of the General Assembly of the State of Georgia* (Milledgeville: Boughton, Nisbet, Barnes, and Moore, 1865), 21–22; Bryan, *Confederate Georgia*, 170.

27. "Mary G. Moore," *Confederate Papers Relating to Citizens or Business Firms, 1861–65*, NARA, M346, group 109, roll 0708; "Barnett, Micon and Co.," in *Confederate Papers Relating to Citizens or Business Firms, 1861–65*, NARA, M346, group 109, roll 0044; Brett J. Derbes, "The Production of Military Supplies at the Alabama State Penitentiary during the Civil War," *Alabama Review* 67 (2014): 131–60; "Mary G. Moore," *Confederate Papers Relating to Citizens or Business Firms, 1861–65*; "A. Burrows," in *Confederate Papers Relating to Citizens or Business Firms, 1861–65*; Ward and Rogers, "Mississippi Prisoners in the Alabama Penitentiary," 114; "Mobile Campaign: Summary of the Principal Events," *O.R.* (ser. 1), vol. 49, 87.

28. For more information on postwar convict leasing, see Douglas A. Blackmon, *Slavery by Another Name: The Re-enslavement of Black People in America from the Civil War to World War II* (New York: Doubleday, 2008); Matthew J. Mancini, *One Dies, Get Another: Convict Leasing in the American South, 1866–1928* (Columbia: University of South Carolina Press, 1996); Talitha L. LeFlouria, *Chained in Silence: Black Women and Convict Labor in the New South* (Chapel Hill: University of North Carolina Press, 2015);

Alex Lichtenstein, *Twice the Work of Free Labor: The Political Economy of Convict Labor in the New South* (New York: Verso, 1996); David M. Oshinsky, "*Worse Than Slavery*": *Parchman Farm and the Ordeal of Jim Crow Justice* (New York: Free Press, 1996).

29. Davis, *Are Prisons Obsolete?*, 84–104; Blakely, *America's Prisons*, 14–15; Frederick W. Derrick, Charles E. Scott, and Thomas Hutson, "Prison Labor Effects on the Unskilled Labor Market," *American Economist* 48 (2004): 74–81; Patricia A. Maulden, "Prisons in the United States: Inmates, Policies, and Profits" *S-Car News* 10 (November 2015), accessed August 14, 2016, http://scar.gmu.edu/newsletter-article/prisons-united-states-inmates-policies-and-profits, 1, 7; Department of Justice, Bureau of Prisons website, "FPI General Overview FAQs," accessed July 15, 2016, http://www.unicor.gov/FAQ_General.aspx.

4

To Carry That Burden

The Texas Cart War and the Place of Mexican Laborers in the Southern Landscape, 1854–1857

MARIA ANGELA DIAZ

The landscape of antebellum southern history is peopled with a particular cast of figures and narratives that come to encapsulate the experience of living and working in the South. Populated with African American slaves, poor whites, planters, and yeomen, it does not often include Texas or the diverse populations that lived there. For several months in 1857 whites in multiple Texas counties began attacking Mexican teamsters along the main road between the Gulf Coast and San Antonio. These attacks became known as the Cart War of 1857, and they culminated in the murder of several Mexican laborers in September and November of that year. Though bloody and violent, the incidents were few, resulted in no reported theft, and ended quickly when the state government called on militia and troops to stop the attacks and Mexican officials intervened. But the incident triggered debates about the nature of citizenship and the rights of nonwhite laborers in a slave state at the end of the antebellum era. The Cart War in Texas encapsulated a period in which the place of Mexican laborers—and, indeed, the Mexican people writ large—was defined by the limits of a black/white racial binary. In the aftermath of the U.S.-Mexican War more southerners migrated to Texas, slavery continued to take root, and Mexican Texans became entangled in a world not of their own making—one in which they were caught in between social classes and racial castes.

This essay will examine the place of these laborers in the increasingly paranoid and hostile environment of the southern borderlands in the years before the Civil War. It will also examine how a marginalized group such as Mexican Texans fought back against racist depictions and violent pressure. The process by which white elites sought to control Mexicans as a supplemental labor force to their slaves reveals much about the connections between race and class at this critical moment in southern history. This research is in conversation with a growing body of scholarship that seeks to understand southern society in a transnational and transcontinental context.[1] This context can expose the deep workings of socioeconomic class structure as well as race within antebellum southern society. When southern elite whites confronted Mexican society they viewed upper-class Mexicans as more like themselves, and Mexican laborers as little better than slaves. Working-class whites were forced to compete with them once they moved to Texas and were also hostile to them. The process by which Mexican laborers were racialized, as well as the competition between white laborers and Mexican laborers, resonates with today's issues concerning the place of immigrant labor in the American South. These issues have long roots and they are as much a part of the history of the antebellum South as they are of the history of immigration to the United States.

Examining the Cart War in Texas and its effects also sheds light on the usefulness of borderlands concepts in understanding the development of southern society and identity. The southwest borderlands collided with the American South in the Texas Gulf Coast region, and white southern notions of class and race met Mexican society. Additionally, examining the effects of the Cart War in Texas shows the impact of transnational forces on laborers living and working along the South's many borders. Recent studies reveal that the modern-day South is currently experiencing a population shift as Latin American immigrants move into the region, seeking work and new lives. Yet these recent movements and the reaction to them have a long history that dates back to the antebellum era as the slave South sought to expand into new territory previously owned by Mexico in the years before the Civil War.[2]

The hierarchical nature of southern society and racial perceptions colored white Texans' views of Mexican society. Both upper- and lower-class whites often referred to lower-class Mexican Texans as mixed-race "mongrels." In commenting on white Texans' continued hunger for more of Mexico's northern frontier, Frederick Law Olmsted revealed prevalent attitudes about Mexicans. "The Mexican masses," according to Olmsted, were "vaguely considered as degenerate and degraded Spaniards; it is, at least, equally correct to think of them as improved and Christianized Indians. In their tastes and social instincts, they approximate the African." The difference between Africans and Mexicans, he further noted, was "less felt" than those he saw between northern and southern Europeans. There were "many Mexicans of mixed negro blood," and Olmsted felt that thousands even "in respectable social positions [had a] color and physiognomy [that] would subject them, in Texas, to be sold by the sheriff as negro-estrays who cannot be allowed at large without detriment to the common wealth." For Olmsted, there seemed "between our Southern American and the Mexican, an unconquerable antagonism of character, which will prevent any condition of order where the two come together."[3] Learning in April 1855 that the Supreme Court had decided Asian immigrants would not be made full citizens in the United States, the *Texas State Gazette* complained that the "half-negro, half-Indian greaser who runs away from his master in Mexico and crossing into Texas, comes here among us claiming the same rights of citizenship as the best among us."[4]

Yet such stereotypes were primarily reserved for working-class Mexicans and those who were without land. A year earlier, a letter to the editor of the same newspaper, the *Gazette*, actually celebrated Mexican immigration, at least of wealthy migrants. "Many Mexicans of standing and owners of considerable wealth," the letter writer suggested, "have already commenced making arrangements to move out of the country all they have and settle with their families on this side of the river." Were Santa Ana to declare himself emperor of Mexico, the writer assured readers, "the really intelligent Mexicans who are lovers of true liberty will have cause to rejoice." While in Mexico, Olmsted called on the house of the *alcalde* (mayor) of the border town, Piedras Negras, and after noting his worn clothing and age, he commented that the supposedly upper-class Mexican was "quiet, self-possessed, gentlemanly and good-natured in his manner, and with a soft and winning voice."[5] White Texans' tentative approval of Mexicans of higher social status, coupled with their simultaneous denigration of Mexican migrant laborers, created a class aspect to the developing internal social boundaries and geopolitical borders in Texas. White Texans created images of "good" and "bad" migrants along class lines in the Mexican community. While riding through the countryside near San Antonio, Olmsted observed instances of elite Mexicans owning slaves who worked alongside Mexican laborers on their plantations.

Though Olmsted intended only to observe and record images of Texas slaveholding society, as a white American, he also participated in creating a distinction between Mexican social classes by conflating elite Mexicans with notions of "civilized" gentlemanly mannerisms and increased participation in slavery.[6]

Prior to 1861, the South relied heavily on river and ocean-going transportation to move its goods and agricultural commodities. Railroads had yet to penetrate effectively into the cotton South. Texas had even fewer railroads than did most other southern states. By 1857, there had yet to be a single significant railroad built in the entire state. Thus, the state depended on transportation such as ox carts to traffic goods from the coastal ports to cities such as San Antonio, one of the largest urban communities in the region. These teamsters were often Mexicans known as *arrieros*.[7]

From the 1820s to the 1850s Texas experienced constant immigration, primarily from the American South and Europe. The steady flow of new migrants destabilized the South's periphery. The racial and social diversity revealed much about rising tensions between Mexican and white laborers as well as between the white southern laboring class and the white southern elites that held sway over the state's political and economic power. The city of San Antonio figured prominently in the story of Mexican laborers in the quickly evolving southern society of Texas. By 1857 San Antonio was the largest city in Texas and, as one historian noted, aside from New Orleans was one of the most diverse cities in the South. Its population of roughly eight thousand included various European immigrants, whites, African Americans, and Mexican Americans, mostly from the surrounding areas of San Antonio. Economically, the city functioned in a way similar to that of the state's coastal ports. It was, as one historian called it, a distribution point for the entire region. Not only did cart drivers transport goods to and from the Gulf Coast to San Antonio, but they also transported goods and facilitated trade to Mexico, making them one of the southern frontier's first truly transnational workforces.[8]

In the area around San Antonio, Mexican Texans did some of the work that white yeoman and white laborers might have done elsewhere in the Old South. The 1850 census showed that Tejanos took up most occupations usually reserved for these other classes in the other southern states. The jobs that Tejanos listed as their occupations in the 1850 census demonstrate a diverse group of merchants and artisans. In San Antonio alone they worked as blacksmiths, masons, carpenters, cigar makers, and bakers.

Yet the most commonly cited work done by Tejanos was that of cart drivers. In fact, an astounding 58 percent of the heads of Tejano households in the city of San Antonio were cart drivers in the region between San Antonio and the Gulf Coast. In 1850 in the area surrounding the city of San Antonio there were 197 Mexican freighters.[9] Starting shortly after the U.S.-Mexican War, slaveholding white Texans in the state stepped up their efforts to assert their dominance over both the economy and politics. Local ordinances and expulsions in towns in central Texas sought to limit the power of Mexican Texans and German immigrants alike. Banding together to oppose political organizations such as the Know-Nothings that gained popularity in Texas during this same period, Germans and Mexicans asserted themselves despite native white efforts to silence them.[10]

By 1850, Texas had reached a total population of 212,000, and, a decade later, that number had grown to over 604,000.[11] Aside from population growth and favorable land policies aimed at keeping settlement rates high, Texas's political landscape underwent restructuring during the 1850s. Historians have noted that the multiethnic makeup of Texas and its large Catholic population fed nativism. At the local level, Know-Nothings, or the American Party, enjoyed a modest amount of success, gaining seats in city councils, yet when it came to ethnic strongholds such as San Antonio their anti-immigrant message was often times tempered. In fact, Know-Nothings wound up being allies during the Cart War that was to come in 1857.[12]

While the 1857 conflict was often described as a war, making it seem as though it was a singular incident, there were several disturbances in the years preceding it that were similar in tone and level of violence. It was amidst the rising nativist sentiment in the state that the first incidents of violence against Tejano teamsters began. The population growth of the mid-1850s brought white Americans, many of whom came from the South, into contact and competition with Tejanos who had already existed in the region for decades, sometimes even centuries. In 1855 one of San Antonio's Spanish-language newspapers, *El Bejareno*, reported that one of the city's Tejano citizens, Rafael de Herrera, was attacked while in southeast Texas. The paper described the attackers as highway robbers who had demanded corn for their horses before attacking the cart drivers. The attackers shot at three of his carts and robbed them. The violence surrounding the cart drivers was not solely about robbery. The *San Antonio Ledger* published a letter from a cart driver named Pedro Rodriguez in which he detailed a violent altercation with a white rancher named J. J. Golman. Rodriguez went to Golman's ranch looking to retrieve a team of oxen that a cart driver of his had left there on his trip through the South Texas region. Golman claimed that the cart driver owed him fifty dollars and that he was taking the oxen in payment. When Rodriguez protested, Golman, who claimed to be a justice, forced Rodriguez, who was surrounded by a mob threatening to lynch him, to sign a note for the money. Rodriguez wrote that Golman exclaimed, "He did not give a d[amn] for me or a hundred of my stripe, that it would do him no harm to stop up a creek with my body."[13]

Resistance against Mexican cart drivers throughout the 1850s also signaled an increasing need to limit the movement of Tejanos through central and eastern Texas. In 1854, some counties and towns along the rim of the expanding cotton belt expelled local Mexican populations. *El Bejareno* reported that the town of Seguin in central Texas had decided to expel all Mexican laborers from Guadalupe County, where Seguin was the county seat. White Seguin citizens created "Committees of Vigilance" to prevent the "peones" from living in or even entering the county. Vigilantes destroyed carts belonging to Mexican teamsters and drove Mexican families from the area. *El Bejareno* commented on the irony created by this situation. The expulsion of Mexicans may have preserved the stability of white mastery over the local slave populations, but it created a cotton transportation problem. Guadalupe's crop transportation depended on the Mexican teamsters that white citizens had expelled months before the harvest. Planters thus exchanged economic stability for social and racial stability. The situation created in the aftermath of the Seguin expulsions forced planters to transport their cotton crops to San Antonio, where Mexican teamsters were available to haul the crops down to Port Lavaca on the Gulf Coast.[14] White residents of the state's capital, Austin, also expelled Mexican families. Two decrees before 1855 permitted communities to forcibly remove Mexicans from Travis County, and yet another after 1855 targeted transient Mexicans, giving them ten days to permanently leave the area. Some Mexican families eventually migrated back to the city, but they were again violently expelled. When Mexican families moved back into Austin, they not only broke the law but also crossed a specifically demarcated racial boundary within the state.

Know-Nothings in San Antonio also worked to subvert the local power of Tejanos by enacting anti-Mexican ordinances. Bexar County supported both Mexican and German populations, and it was customary for all political documents to appear in English, Spanish, and German. In 1855, the San Antonio Know-Nothing government banned bull- and cockfights, which were part of the Tejano community's cultural practices. In addition to curtailing this expression of their cultural identities, the San Antonio Know-Nothings wanted to make it harder for Tejanos to participate in politics by discontinuing the practice of publishing government documents in Spanish and German. To curtail the freedom and political power of the Mexican community, the *San Antonio Ledger* suggested that unknown Mexicans visiting the city should be required to register with the mayor's office. The newspaper also proposed that unknown Mexicans should be forced to seek out special certificates in order to be permitted within city limits. In communities throughout the South free blacks fell under similar scrutiny during the antebellum period. In this way, Texas mirrored its older southern sister states in its dealing with both Mexican laborers and free African Americans. Prior to Texas's annexation into the United States in 1845, the Texas Legislature had attempted to rid the republic of all free blacks. At the same time, white Americans began pressuring Mexican land owners to leave their rancheros and farms and flee to Mexico.[15]

Resisting these ordinances, *El Bejareno* proposed to translate all government documents for the benefit of the Spanish-speaking community. Its editors argued that without Spanish translations the Tejano community would have no way of knowing the city's laws until they broke them. The editors argued that, according to the fundamental liberties of the U.S. Constitution, they had a right to preserve their culture, language, and religion while continuing to be citizens. Tejano children could learn English in public schools to fulfill their duties as American citizens, but, *El Bejareno* asserted, should not be forced to forget the language of Miguel de Cervantes—the language of their parents. In addressing the American nativist position on Roman Catholicism, the Spanish-speaking editors in San Antonio argued that that they had a right to practice their religion. Spanish speakers asserted the right to remain culturally Tejano while being American citizens.[16]

White ordinances and Mexican resistance to such decrees embodied a tug-of-war between the two groups in central Texas. The presence of slaves near the U.S.-Mexico border made it necessary to push unwanted groups away from eastern and central Texas. While in East Texas Olmsted was struck with a "peculiarity in the tone of the relation between master and slave." He described a warlike mentality on the part of the masters in regards to their slaves. "Damn 'em, give 'em hell," was said to be a frequent expression of the "ruder planters." Olmsted claimed that "whenever slavery in Texas has been carried in a wholesale way, into the neighborhood of Mexicans, it has been found necessary to treat them as outlaws. . . . The whole native population of county after county has been driven . . . from its homes, and forbidden, on pain of no less punishment than instant death, to return to the vicinity of the plantations." White Texans feared that lower-class Mexicans sympathized with the plight of enslaved African Americans and thus helped to funnel them across the Mexican border. Boundaries as lines of power remained important elsewhere in the Old South. Stephanie McCurry argued that in South Carolina fences symbolized white male political and social power. The boundaries that white Texans created using ordinances, violence, and expulsion functioned as symbols of the community's power to decide who would be permitted in the community.[17]

It was in this social milieu that the Cart War exploded across Texas and into the state legislature in 1857. With each attack, local and state leaders were forced to compromise and complicate their racial and class views when the economic lifeline of teamster transport was crippled by the cart attacks. The war was actually quite short lived, lasting only a few months. In five separate incidents from July to November attackers in the counties of Karnes and Goliad, which lay along the main roads between the coastal ports and the city of San Antonio, destroyed cart trains and injured drivers. The first attack occurred on July 3, 1857, when a small train of carts set off from San Antonio bound for the coast. Two cart drivers were wounded and several of the carts were destroyed in Goliad County. Indeed, nothing would be taken from any of the carts in the following months. The second attack, occurring almost two weeks later, happened in the same county, but was a much larger affair. The caravan of cart drivers, laden with goods, on its way up from the coastal town of Port Lavaca was set upon by some fifteen attackers. The attackers shot at the train of carts and cut the wheels off of them, though no one was harmed. Despite the fact that the *arrieros* were carrying goods with them, they claimed nothing had been stolen. Toward the end of the month a third attack occurred on yet another train of carts moving along the road between San Antonio and the coast. This time several men were injured, though again nothing was taken. One of the men wounded was a white man working with the Mexican cart drivers. Charles G. Edwards felt he had been specifically targeted for choosing to work with Mexican Texans. Choosing to work as a cart man meant that he had transgressed the racial boundaries of traditional southern society. The fact that nothing appeared to have been stolen from the carts gives clues to the attackers' motivations.[18] The crimes committed against Mexican laborers were not driven by theft, but were a blatant attempt to violently force Mexican cart drivers out of the transportation business in central Texas.

By November armed troops escorted wagon trains to the Gulf Coast. C. L. Pyron, a white cart train owner, believed that his carts would not be attacked due to his race. Yet his whiteness was not able to protect his transport team from yet another outbreak of violence. Pyron had also chosen to send his transport trains without any military escort. Two of Pyron's Mexican drivers were murdered, and Pyron's brother had to work to get the entire train back to the safety of a nearby Ranger camp. Yet due to the use of troops in between the coast and San Antonio, the attacks eventually stopped.[19]

The fear of being attacked quickly crippled the city's transportation services and economy. Cart service was not only responsible for bringing in goods, but also for distributing produce. Cart drivers became afraid of being caught out on the open roads in Karnes and Goliad counties, which resulted in a scarcity of drivers. The *San Antonio Herald* worried that with the attacks on Mexican cart drivers, hiring Mexicans would be tantamount to "signing the death warrant to the prosperity of San Antonio" because it would keep needed goods from being brought to the city. However, merchants in the city were reluctant to hire white traders because—as one letter to the editors noted—they required double the wages that Mexican cart drivers were paid. A woman from San Antonio wrote her brother and told him of the difficulties she was having. She could find no paint for her house and the price of flour had risen considerably. Thus, these workers remained the center of the burgeoning central Texas economy and yet they would not be paid the same as the white workers, putting them in a position in between African American slaves and white workers. Their racialization emphasized this "in-between" status.[20]

Aside from a stalling economy, another result was that class boundaries were further complicated when a prominent San Antonio citizen was murdered during an attack on the cart drivers in September. On

September 12, 1857, twelve Mexican cart drivers set off from San Antonio with loads of military supplies that were bound for the Gulf Coast ports. In Helena, located in Karnes County, the train of cart drivers encountered the largest group of attackers thus far. Some forty armed men wearing masks and painted faces surrounded the line of trains, pointed shotguns and handguns, and began firing on the group. One of the chief drivers who also partially owned the transportation company, Antonio Delgado, was shot fourteen times and killed. The train rushed for the safety of San Antonio. Two other Mexican drivers were wounded, the brothers of Delgado's partner, Nicanor Valdez. Delgado was not only a well-respected citizen, but a war hero who had fought in the Texas Revolution, and also under Andrew Jackson in the Battle of New Orleans during the War of 1812. The *Houston Weekly Telegraph* ran the obituary written for Delgado in the *San Antonio Ledger* and added that San Antonio civil authorities needed to take more steps to ensure the safety of their Mexican laborers, warning that without a sufficient plan to put down the attacks "all commerce must cease." In October, Governor Elisha Pease ordered a five-hundred-dollar reward for the capture of the attackers, and called on the militia to protect cart drivers on their routes. Delgado's gruesome death added to the terror and forced the state government to act.[21]

The public debate and the debate within the state legislature about how to address the Cart War also brought the complicated intersections of class, labor, and race together. Typically, newspapers in towns north of the state capital in Austin and farther east toward the Louisiana state line tended not to support the cart drivers, while those in San Antonio and on the Gulf Coast tended to be more supportive. Texans who did not support the cart drivers often blamed the drivers for the violence. Newspapers such as the *Belton Weekly Independent*, located in a small community north of Austin, published accounts claiming that the war had nothing to do with competition over prices and wages among the Mexican and white cart drivers, but everything to do with the "thieving of those greaser wagoners or cart-men on the road." The paper's informant said that cart drivers were responsible for killing a cow and stealing twenty to thirty pounds of meat and "many depredations of a like nature are committed by them in almost every trip." Such rumors originated in Goliad and Karnes counties, where local political and judicial leaders denounced the idea that their white wagoners were responsible for the assaults and murders. Recalling the common belief that Mexican peoples, especially working-class Mexicans, were suspicious figures, the Karnes County chief justice J. M. Lowrie stated that "to a man all the citizens along the road" wanted the Mexican cart drivers stopped and denounced them as "a race of murders, thieves, and vagabonds, who pollute the very soil upon which they tread."[22]

In "Address to the People of Bexar County," Goliad citizens refused to sympathize with Bexar County Mexican cart drivers. No cart drivers had been arrested for theft in either of the counties in which the attacks occurred, yet the address referred to Mexican teamsters as thieves. Another prominent citizen of Goliad, Martin M. Kinney, published a letter in the *Southern Intelligencer* explaining that "greaser means all that mongrel class of Mexicans who are slaves in their own country and vagabonds[,] . . . in short, the whole tribe of low flung Mexicans." Perhaps recalling that one of the murdered cart drivers was a well-respected citizen, he also took great pains to emphasize that there were also "Mexicans who are white men and gentlemen."[23]

Controversy over the Cart War united this much larger sphere of international politics with the local racial and class struggles taking place in San Antonio. In a testament to the transnational aspect of the Cart War and Mexican-white laborers' struggles, Secretary of State Lewis Cass sent Governor Pease a note on behalf of the Mexican minister Manuel Róbles y Pezuela reminding him that Mexican cart drivers were American citizens and encouraging him to take steps to stop the war. During the months that the cart drivers were attacked, Democrats and Know-Nothings in San Antonio worked to gain recognition of the problem from the state legislature. The vital role that cart drivers played in the local economy meant that even Know-Nothings, those people who had only two years before worked to subvert Tejano political power, were now supportive of protecting the cart drivers on the roads between the city and the coast. Democrats took up the mantle of supporting the efforts of cart workers and calling on the governor to get involved with plans to protect the roads. The city's leaders initially wanted to retaliate by forming a posse to hunt down the perpetrators. Citizens in Karnes County claimed that this group from San Antonio, which had been sanctioned by the commander of troops in the region, General David E. Twiggs, had committed acts of violence against them, though there is little evidence that this is true. A committee was also formed to determine whether there was a possibility of bringing the attackers to court. The findings of the committee were bleak. They reported that Karnes and Goliad County citizens were either entirely in support of their own local workers or afraid of testifying in court that they had seen anything. However committed to these efforts local leaders were, the state's leaders shied away from pledging large numbers of troops and the money needed to pay for them. Governor Pease did visit the city and region of the attacks, in addition to calling in the militia. Pease and local leaders had much difficulty in gaining enough people for the militia.[24] The war finally came to an end due to a combination of a show of force and foreign intervention on the part of Robles y Pezuela, but well into 1858 thoughts on the Cart War continued to crop up in Texas newspapers due largely to the efforts of residents in Goliad to assert their innocence in involvement in the attacks. In January 1858 attendants at a public meeting in Goliad passed resolutions denouncing both the government involvement in putting down the attacks and the focus on citizens of Goliad and Karnes Counties. Martin M. Kinney again took up the pen and wrote letters to the editors of the *Southern Intelligencer* and the *Colorado Citizen* in an attempt to exonerate Goliad County. Kinney warned the readers of the *Colorado Citizen* that the slaveholders of Texas believed that the Mexican "peons or greasers—forming about nine-tenths of the Mexicans—consort with negroes and continually incite them to murder their masters and escape to Mexico." Kinney went on to argue that the Mexican cart drivers were not only stealing slaves, but were themselves runaway slaves from Mexico. Through his retelling of the Cart War Kinney asserted that Mexicans only served to introduce chaos and undermine the system that kept that chaos at bay—that the presence of Mexican workers in Texas only served to worsen the problems that slaveholders and other southern whites faced from a mounting abolitionist protest.[25]

In these places where different ethnic groups converged, such as Texas, working-class whites attacked Mexican laborers for taking what in other parts of the South might have been their work, and upper-class whites denounced them as abolitionists threatening slave populations all the while exploiting their labor. Incidents such as the Cart War, then, demonstrated the fluidity, permeability, and uncertainty of life in the southern borderlands. Throughout the period of the Texas Republic and the early years of statehood, white Texans forcibly sought to claim land and political power from Mexican Texans. Those Mexican Texans willing to try to maintain their hold on trades and markets traditionally reserved for white workers in other parts of the South ultimately tested the entrenchment of white superiority in Texas. White southerners quickly found that they could not always do without the vital role that Mexican workers played in the state's burgeoning economy. Thus, the Mexican community could force the hand of white state power, which in turn changed the worlds of both, and Mexicans were ultimately able to carve out space for themselves in the antebellum southern landscape of the Texas borderlands.

The experience of the Cart War foretold the struggles that Mexican laborers would experience after the Civil War and in the twentieth and twenty-first centuries. Though Mexican Texans in the 1850s were most likely born in Texas, the hostility that they faced foreshadowed the anti-immigrant sentiment that Mexican immigrant laborers confronted at different times since the turn of the twentieth century. The repatriations and mass deportations of the 1930s and 1950s as well as the criminalization of undocumented immigrants and the policing of the U.S.-Mexico border have their foundations in these initial interactions within the antebellum South's borderlands. Likewise does the demand for Mexican laborers in the modern day. Through the most recent wave of immigration in the twenty-first century, Mexican workers as well as other Latin American workers began moving further into the South, recruited by chicken-processing plants and working in many other sectors of the modern southern economy. Their presence continues to alter the racial and class complexities of the South, and will for decades to come.[26]

Notes

1. Peter Kolchin, "The South and the World," *Journal of Southern History* 75, no. 3 (2007): 565–80; Robert E. May, *Southern Dream of a Caribbean Empire, 1854–1861* (Athens: University of Georgia Press, 1989); Walter Johnson, *River of Dark Dreams: Slavery and Empire in the Cotton Kingdom* (Cambridge: Harvard University Press, 2013), 17–20; Matthew Pratt Guterl, *American Mediterranean: Southern Slaveholders in the Age of Emancipation* (Cambridge: Harvard University Press, 2008).

2. Edward Baptist, *Creating an Old South: Middle Florida's Plantation Frontier before the Civil War* (Chapel Hill: University of North Carolina Press, 2002); Andrew J. Torget, *Seeds of Empire: Cotton, Slavery, and the Transformation of the Texas Borderlands, 1800–1850* (Chapel Hill: University of North Carolina Press, 2015); Christopher Morris, *Becoming Southern: The Evolution of a Way of Life, Warren County and Vicksburg, Mississippi, 1770–1860* (New York: Oxford University Press, 1999).

3. Frederick Law Olmsted, *A Journey through Texas: or, A Saddle Trip on the Southwestern Frontier* (Austin: University of Texas Press, 1978; first published 1857), 454–55.

4. *Texas State Gazette* (Austin), April 21, 1855.

5. Olmsted, *A Journey through Texas*, 321; *Texas State Gazette*, February 7, 1854; *Texas State Gazette*, February 13, 1854.

6. Robert W. Johannsen, *To the Halls of Montezuma: The Mexican War in the American Imagination* (New York: Oxford University Press, 1989); Louis A. Perez Jr., *On Becoming Cuban: Identity, Nationality, and Culture* (Chapel Hill: University of North Carolina Press, 1999); Louis A. Perez Jr., *The War of 1898: The United States and Cuba in History and Historiography* (Chapel Hill: University of North Carolina Press, 1998). These works all discuss similar trends in race and class in white outlooks toward Latin American peoples.

7. George C. Werner, "Railroads," in *Handbook of Texas Online*, accessed December 16, 2016, http://www.tshaonline.org/handbook/online/articles/eqr01.

8. Raul Ramos, *Beyond the Alamo: Forging Mexican Ethnicity in San Antonio, 1821–1861* (Chapel Hill: University of North Carolina Press, 2008), 207–10.

9. Ramos, *Beyond the Alamo*, 208.

10. William D. Carrigan, *The Making of Lynching Culture: Violence and Vigilantism in Central Texas, 1836–1916* (Urbana: University of Illinois Press, 2006), 23; Paul D. Lack, "Occupied Texas: Bexar and Goliad, 1835–1836," in *Mexican Americans in Texas History*, ed. Emilio Zamora, Cynthia Orozco, and Rodolfo Rocha (Austin: Texas State Historical Association, 2000), 35; David Montejano, *Anglos and Mexicans in the Making of Texas: 1836–1986* (Austin: University of Texas Press, 1987), 74–131; Randolph Campbell, *An Empire for Slavery: The Peculiar Institution in Texas, 1821–1865* (Baton Rouge: Louisiana State University Press, 1989), 156–57; Ramos, *Beyond the Alamo*, 167–73.

11. Robert Campbell, "Growth and Expansion, 1836–1861," in *An Empire for Slavery*, 50–66.

12. Walter L. Buenger, *Secession and the Union in Texas* (Austin: University of Texas Press, 1984), 91–94; Eric Foner, *Free Soil, Free Labor, Free Men: The Ideology of the Republican Party before the Civil War* (New York: Oxford University Press, 1995; first published 1970), 226–41.

13. *El Bejareno* (San Antonio), February 17, 1855; *El Bejareno*, July 7, 1855.

14. *El Bejareno*, April 28, 1855.

15. The article in the *San Antonio Ledger* was found in the *Texas State Gazette*, February 24, 1855; *Texas State Gazette*, October 14, 1854; *Texas State Gazette*, April 7, 1855; Ramos, *Beyond the Alamo*, 227–29.

16. *El Bejareno*, February 7, 1855; *Texas State Gazette*, June 23, 1855; *Texas State Gazette*, September 9, 1854; *San Antonio Ledger*, July 7, 1854; *El Ranchero* (San Antonio), July 28, 1856.

17. Stephanie McCurry, *Masters of Small Worlds: Yeoman Households, Gender Relations, and the Political Culture of the Antebellum South Carolina Low Country* (New York: Oxford University Press, 1997), 5–13.

18. Larry Knight, "The Cart Wars: Defining American in San Antonio in the 1850s," *Southwestern Historical Quarterly* 3, no. 109 (2006): 319–36.

19. Knight, "The Cart Wars."

20. Knight, "The Cart Wars."

21. *Houston Weekly Telegraph*, September 30, 1857; *San Antonio Texan*, October 8, 1857.

22. *Benton Weekly Independent*, September 26, 1857; *Southern Intelligencer* (Austin), October 28, 1857.

23. *San Antonio Ledger*, August 15, 1857; quotation in Knight, "The Cart Wars," 327.

24. *Southern Intelligencer*, December 12, 1857; *San Antonio Ledger*, December 26, 1857.

25. *Southern Intelligencer*, January 6, 1858; *Colorado Citizen*, January 23, 1858.

26. Miguel Antonio Levario, *Militarizing the Border: When Mexicans Became the Enemy* (College Station: Texas A&M Press, 2012); Natalia Molina, *How Race Is Made in America: Immigration, Citizenship, and the Historical Power of Racial Scripts* (Berkeley: University of California Press, 2014); Leon Fink, *The Maya of Morganton: Work and Community in the Nuevo New South* (Chapel Hill: University of North Carolina Press, 2003); George Sanchez, "Latinos, the American South, and the Future of US Race Relations," *Southern Spaces*, April 27, 2007, https://southernspaces.org/2007/latinos-american-south-and-future-us-race-relations.

2

Reconstruction and the Gilded Age

5

The Promise of Free Labor

Carl Schurz and Republican Conceptions of Labor within the Reconstruction South

STUART MACKAY

In 1865, a northern planter living in South Carolina complained to a local Union officer that "the free labor system can be managed much more easily in the lecture room or an editor's sanctum *theoretically* north, than in the field practically here." In the aftermath of the Civil War, many Republicans eager to see a free labor system implemented throughout the South were confronted with the difficulties of transforming their free labor ideology into a practical system. Extolling the virtues of free labor before the war, the complex and shifting political terrain of the South forced many to reevaluate their previously held positions. Carl Schurz, a key figure in the Republican Party, was asked by President Andrew Johnson in 1865 to survey conditions within the postwar South. Schurz's writings provide insight into how Republicans first saw the ideology of free labor; how these ideologies were challenged by the immediate political, economic, and racial disruptions of the postwar South; and how free labor was transformed from being considered as a "natural" process to one where political action would be necessary to implement it. Furthermore, his ideological transformation is a reminder that ill-defined theories and programs regarding labor must first take into account local and political factors.[1]

An enthusiastic supporter of the liberal German revolution of 1848, Schurz had emigrated to the United States in 1852, working as a lecturer and writer while seeking to establish a political career. Despite his enthusiasm for the democratic possibilities of his new country, the issue of slavery struck Schurz as a discordant element in American society. "The slavery question reveals itself in so many different aspects to him who has recently come to America that he finds it difficult to work his way through the confusion of considerations and interests," he declared to his former teacher and mentor Gottfried Kinkel, noting, "I have come to the final conclusion that . . . there can be but one question of freedom." In Germany, Schurz's antislavery beliefs had been nurtured by Kinkel, who admired British antislavery activists such as William Wilberforce, and whose relationship with American abolitionists corresponded with his liberal ideas. Seeking to establish himself politically in America, Schurz found his political options limited to the relatively new Republican Party. With the only other choices being a Democratic Party that was becoming increasingly identified with slaveholders and the nativist Know-Nothings promoting an anti-Catholic and anti-immigration platform, Schurz's antislavery politics found a home within an emerging Republican Party that opposed the extension of slavery and promoted the free labor ideal.[2]

Recruited to drum up support for the Republican Party amongst the German communities of the Midwest, Schurz threw himself into his work, developing a reputation as a superb orator while burnishing a professional image of himself as a liberal refugee from an undemocratic continent. Promoting the Republican message of "free soil, free labor, and free men," Schurz encouraged voters to support these Republican doctrines, while failing to articulate a definite ideology of free labor. His speeches held fast to the traditional tent poles of Republican speechmaking, decrying the proslavery doctrines of the Democratic Party, the antidemocratic and despotic nature of the slaveholders, and the supremacy of the northern free labor system. But Schurz's conception of how free labor would transform the South was hazy at best. To a Republican audience in Chicago, he suggested that slaveholders would eventually discover "that there are other more productive and far more honorable sources of wealth than laziness feeding upon slave-labor," and that they would soon "sacrifice old prejudices to a new spirit of enterprise." At a meeting ratifying Abraham Lincoln as the Republican nominee for the presidency, Schurz argued that Republicans would specifically promote the values and tenets of free labor everywhere, by "proposing to plant free labor in the Territories by the Homestead Bill, and to promote free labor all over the land by the encouragement of home industry." As a result, slavery would be "penned up" within the South, surrounded by a cordon of free states and free laborers.[3]

Schurz's floundering attempts at defining what exactly the Republican Party meant by free labor were understandable. In assembling a motley coalition of conservative and moderate former Democrats, Whigs, and Free Soilers, a broadly defined interpretation of what constituted free labor smoothed over ideological differences and partisan irritants. As Mark A. Lause has noted, the appeal of free labor was in its elasticity as a concept that could be neatly fitted into a variety of worldviews. While some Republicans saw free labor simply as morally superior to slave labor, others, especially wage workers, understood free labor in terms of cooperative ventures and full remuneration for labor. Some western Republicans emphasized that a free labor ideology should emphasize social mobility and economic growth coupled with land reform. Others, veterans of the Whig campaigns, encouraged a "harmony of interests" between labor and capital. Despite these ideological differences, this coalition saw the economic success of northern society as the finest argument for a free labor system. In 1859, during a speech to the Wisconsin State Agricultural Society, Abraham Lincoln articulated a free labor vision that would soon become the standard Republican position. Taking aim at James Hammond's "mud-sill" theory of labor, which argued that laborers, once hired, were trapped to that social position for life, Lincoln argued that given education, opportunity, and ambition, a laborer could rise to become independent. As result, the laborer in a slave society, without access to these elements, would remain dependent on a ruling class forever, and unable to improve his position in life. Therefore, it was in the best interest of Americans to support a political party that would exclude slavery from the territories and build a free labor empire across the West, thereby strengthening the social fabric of the nation.[4]

Lincoln's conceptualization of free labor resonated with Republicans, and provided an ideological weapon with which to attack slavery at its weakest points. Invited by the Republicans of St. Louis to help elect their candidates in the upcoming election, Schurz seized the opportunity to contrast a free labor system with a slave labor system to an audience living within a slave state. Drawing upon Lincoln's example, Schurz clarified how the ideology of free labor would assist the South, describing how southerners, wishing to match the economic and industrial superiority of the North, would eventually perceive free labor as superior. By recognizing this, slavery would gradually be worn away. Entitling his speech "The

Doom of Slavery," Schurz implored his audience to "cast your eyes over that great beehive called the Free States . . . see by the railroad and the telegraphic wire every village, almost every backwoods cottage, drawn within the immediate reach of civilization." Arguing that free labor was the "only safe basis of society," Schurz declared that it was necessary to "expand its blessings over all territory within our reach." All Americans, argued Schurz, must "recognize the right of the laboring man to the soil he cultivates, and shield against oppressive speculation," and ensure that all branches of labor be developed in concordance with one another in order to further national prosperity. To do this, Schurz argued, "we must adopt a policy which draws to light the resources of the land, gives work to our workshops, and security to our commerce." Schurz implored his audience in St. Louis to encourage their fellow citizens to adopt the Republican program of free labor and internal improvements in order to develop a middle class in Missouri that would challenge the political and economic power of the slaveholders. His speech, warmly received by his audience, was subsequently published in newspapers and circulated in pamphlets throughout the country. Schurz, never modest about his abilities as a public speaker, told his wife that he believed it to be the greatest speech of his life.[5]

Pressed by demands from state party committees for his talents, Schurz soon embarked upon a cross-country speaking tour, preaching the gospel of free soil, free men, and free labor to voters in Illinois, Pennsylvania, and New York. With the ability to speak clearly and eloquently in English and German while peppering his speeches with a forthrightness that belied his classical education, Republican power brokers soon began taking notice of Schurz's political potential. Even partisan newspapers grudgingly admitted that Schurz was an effective promoter of the Republican message. The *Louisville Journal*, whose editor had supported nativist candidates in the past, noted that despite his Republicanism, Schurz was "one of the most profound and most philosophical and powerful thinkers of the age. . . . He always gives utterance to his views in language remarkable for its clearness, its classical accuracy, and its eloquence." Furthermore, Schurz's notoriety and efforts for the party during the campaign were noted by Lincoln himself, who promised Schurz that his hard work would be rewarded should victory come to the Republican cause. When Schurz had returned home to Watertown, Wisconsin, he was exhausted but jubilant upon hearing the news that Lincoln had won New York and all other crucial northern states.[6]

The abstract debates over the contradictions and ambiguities of free labor that had consumed so much political oxygen during the 1860 campaign were quickly subsumed by the secession crisis that followed Lincoln's election. More concerned with both his strained financial situation and ensuring a patronage position in the Lincoln administration, Schurz refused to take secessionists' promises of disunion seriously. However, by the end of November, Schurz realized that "if the North remains firm," as he insisted to a friend, "the slave power is done for. We have to choose between a short and violent crisis and a long, exhausting, and dangerous one." By December 20, with South Carolina seceding from the Union, Schurz was convinced that the "the end of the political slave power is close at hand." Attempting to secure a position of influence within the new administration, Schurz lobbied Lincoln for a consular position. Acknowledging Schurz's efforts during the campaign, and not wishing to offend German-Americans who supported the Republican Party, Lincoln appointed Schurz as ambassador to Spain. While initially seen as unqualified for the post, Schurz succeeded in establishing friendly relations with the Spanish government, and in ensuring its neutrality during the war.[7]

Despite being pleased with his diplomatic appointment, Schurz soon found himself anxious to return the United States. Bored with the routines of diplomatic life, and disappointed with the languid, sun-baked atmosphere of Madrid, Schurz soon petitioned for a leave of absence from his duties. He believed that in order to advance his political career, he would have to involve himself in some sort of military capacity during the war. After numerous requests, Schurz found himself commissioned as a brigadier general with General John C. Frémont's forces in Virginia. Schurz's military campaigns had allowed him to see first-hand the economic disparity that a slave labor system had produced within the South. While stationed near Chattanooga, Schurz commented on the living conditions and the lack of education of the nonslaveholding whites in the backcountry. "You have no conception of the poverty which prevails here," Schurz wrote to his daughter, noting that slavery had produced a white population "who were kept ignorant" through a lack of schooling, and economically enfeebled by rich slaveholders. For these people, the war was "a genuine blessing," as they "became aware how miserable their condition is; their indolent habits are interfered with; they are compelled to help themselves and are thereby forced to turn their thoughts towards new things." Schurz observed that with the end of the war, northern men would have the opportunity to come to the backward regions of the South to make both the land and the people more industrious, wealthy, and happy.[8]

Schurz's vision of an economically prosperous free labor South was tested immediately by the ascension of Andrew Johnson to the presidency. Long devoted to the ideals of free labor, Schurz believed that the rebellious states should not be brought back into the Union until those states guaranteed the rights of freedmen and free labor. However, Schurz's subsequent meetings with Johnson underscored a growing disconnect between the president and the radical members of the Republican Party. Johnson urged a quick return of the states under prewar suffrage rules, with blanket amnesty for all southerners except for key members of the Confederacy. More important, the issue of free labor was barely mentioned in Johnson's presidential proclamations. Eager to repair the breach, Schurz repeatedly urged Johnson to slow down, consult with Congress, and formulate a Reconstruction policy amenable to both. Johnson ignored his requests.[9]

Instead, the president asked Schurz to undertake a fact-finding mission in the South. Johnson wanted Schurz to look into the results of the administration's Reconstruction policies, and to make recommendations. Despite wanting to play a role in Reconstruction, Schurz was surprised by the offer. He reminded Johnson that he felt the administration's policy "ill-advised and fraught with great danger," and that he would "consider it [his] only duty to tell the truth" about any shortcomings or failures of the president's policy. Johnson declared himself satisfied at the arrangement, and assured Schurz that he had an open mind. Schurz was further encouraged to take the assignment by other radical Republicans, including Charles Sumner, who urged him to provide an honest outlook on the status of the South in order for the radicals to defeat Johnson's plan for Reconstruction. Finally, Schurz, whose financial situation was shaky, arranged to have a series of letters about his travels throughout the South published in the *Boston Daily Advertiser*.[10]

On July 15, 1865, Schurz arrived in South Carolina. From the outset of his journey, Schurz reported that he was encountering resistance to the very idea of free labor. In his first letter to the *Advertiser*, Schurz managed to underscore the northern image of the aristocratic southern planter, the inefficient labor of the freedman, and the superiority of northern free labor systems. Conversing with a Georgia planter, Schurz was taken aback at how the planter could not comprehend the notion of making contracts with freedmen and paying them a fair wage. "You can't make a contract with any of them. . . . They don't know what a contract is. . . . They won't keep a contract," Schurz quoted the planter as saying. Schurz pressed further, affirming that the system of free labor worked well, and arguing that if the planter could not treat freedmen as free laborers, then the planter could cultivate a small farm by himself. The planter smiled at this, asserting, "I know how to manage a plantation with slaves on it, but I couldn't work. I never did a day's work in my life." Schurz concluded his encounter with the planter by remarking that "the introduction of a bona fide system of free labor is a thing wholly foreign to the Southerners' ideas. He does not know what free labor is." Schurz's conversation with his nameless Georgia planter, who figures prominently in his later reminiscences, represents a clear personification of the archetypical slaveholder whom Schurz had railed against while stumping for Lincoln throughout the Midwest. Schurz's Georgia planter was unwilling to labor himself, and saw emancipated slaves laboring freely as unfathomable.[11]

Traveling through the surrounding country, Schurz remarked on the difference between the small farms set up by freedmen and large plantations run by northerners. "Our way led us through fields cultivated by freedmen, mainly refugees who had arrived but a short time before," Schurz reported. "Some of the cotton and corn fields through which we passed were in a decidedly bad state of cultivation, others better, but hardly satisfactory." Suddenly, Schurz and his party arrived at a plantation managed by a man from Massachusetts. "The appearance of the crops suddenly changed," Schurz observed, noting that "the fields were free from weeds, the cotton plants healthy, and the corn fields promising a heavy yield. . . . Everything bespoke thrift and industry." Speaking to the lessee of the plantation only, Schurz saw this plantation as representing the culmination of the free labor ideal throughout the South, with workers, all of whom were former slaves, and all of whom are paid by the task, laboring with their only incentive being their own self-interest. Schurz concluded that "the evidence and prosperity all around, convinced me that a sensible, practical Yankee brought up under influence of free labor is better calculated to solve the great labor problem in the South." Despite this, Schurz failed to converse with any of the laborers themselves, instead relying on the assurances of the lessee that all of his workers considered this enterprise "a perfect success."[12]

Within this letter, Schurz emphasized two of the key components upon which Republican free labor ideology was centered. For Schurz, this Yankee-run plantation embodied the best elements of Republican political economic philosophy, and validated the goal of reshaping a southern slave society into the competitive capitalism of the North. The plantation described by Schurz represents the perfect embodiment of the "harmony of interests" between labor and capital that Republicans had adopted into their free labor ideology. Promoted by popular American political economists Francis Wayland and Henry Charles Carey, this belief in a harmony of interests heavily influenced Republican economic thought. Carey spoke of the necessity that "the interests of the capitalist and the laborer [be] in perfect harmony with each other, as each derives advantage from every measure that tends to facilitate the growth of capital, and to render labor productive." Wayland agreed, stating that "nothing . . . can be more unreasonable than the prejudices which sometimes exist between these different classes of laborers, and nothing can be more beautiful than their harmonious cooperation in every effort to increase production . . . and add to the conveniences and happiness of man." Schurz clearly saw this idea at work in South Carolina, saluting the lessee as "a man who is in possession of land and capital; he wants other men to labor for him [and] as inducement he offers fair remuneration. . . . It is a free transaction in which neither coercion nor protection is necessary." Schurz's free labor ideal, as described to the readers of the *Advertiser*, represented one example of what could be accomplished throughout the South if free labor principles were adopted.[13]

A trip to the interior of South Carolina, however, revealed to Schurz how the ideals of a free labor system came crashing up against the harsh reality of postwar southern society. Traveling around Orangeburg, Schurz discovered how the free labor ideal would be tested by planter and freeman alike. Noting that most planters had entered into agreements with freedmen, Schurz remarked that the military commanders of the district were reviewing and rejecting contracts to ensure that they were fair and proper. Examining one contract, Schurz noticed that it was "framed as to leave the freedmen only a very insignificant share of the crops [and] . . . subject to all sorts of constructive charges[,] . . . binding them to work for the indebtedness they might incur." Schurz felt that the ultimate success of the contract system rested upon the planters to carry it out in good faith, as well as the efficiency of freedmen as laborers. However, he was concerned that planters refused to accept an idea of free labor that saw capital and labor operating in harmony with one another, but rather pursued a free labor system where emancipated slaves were required to work. "The planter who has been taught from his childhood to look upon the system of free labor as intrinsically bad," writes Schurz, "jumps at the conclusion that the negro, who as a slave never worked except upon compulsion, will not work without compulsion now." For Schurz, the very basis of free labor that formed the foundation of his beliefs was being modified and twisted by planters who refused to accept its orthodoxy. The refusal of planters to accept black autonomy in matters of labor due to ingrained social and racial attitudes frustrated Schurz, who stood mystified at the planters' refusal to accept their new reality. His dawning realization that the ideals of free labor could be held together only by some sort of authority represents a significant leap in his thinking about the natural acceptance of free labor.[14]

Equally troubling for Schurz was the reaction of emancipated slaves to their new freedom. Surely, was it not the natural order of things for freedmen to happily accept their new roles as contracted wage laborers? In his article, Schurz reported that some freedmen were refusing to accept this new world of free labor. Stressing the fact that freedman struggled with "intricacies" of labor contracts, he noted that their "former condition was certainly not calculated to impress them with the idea that there exists a moral obligation to fairly exchange value for value." Even more worryingly, Schurz noted, freedmen have "got into their heads" the notion that "the land belongs to all of them." Additionally, Schurz stated that freedmen refused to work on Saturdays, the impression being that the "privilege not to work on Saturdays is one of the characteristics of a free man." Still, Schurz hoped that despite the "distracting influences" and the "confusion of ideas" that surrounded this new labor system, freedmen would eventually reach the standard of free labor in Ohio or Illinois. "I am sure the colored man will learn sooner what he has to do as a free laborer," concluded Schurz, "than the white man in these parts will learn how to treat a free laborer." The onus placed on freed slaves to neatly insert themselves in this new system represented a further transformation of Schurz's free labor philosophy.[15]

By the time Schurz reached Georgia, the illusions of quick conversion of a slave labor society into a free labor economy had vanished. Traveling through the state, Schurz encountered stories of former planters violently attacking ex-slaves and complaining to military authorities about the "insubordination" of many freedmen. Recounting the story of one Georgia planter who was incredulous that he could not sufficiently discipline his former slaves, Schurz concluded that planter simply could neither accept nor conceive of the idea that "a free laborer owes his employer no duty beyond the fulfillment of his contract. . . . They cannot get rid of the idea of that the man who works for them belongs to them." Therefore, in Schurz's opinion, only northern men could succeed in cultivating the South with free labor. Visiting a cotton planation run by an Iowa farmer, Schurz saw this in action. The lessee employed around thirty freedmen, all of whom were paid wages and had a regimented working schedule: start work in the field "about sunrise, stop a short time for breakfast at eight o'clock, stop again for dinner from twelve till two, and then work till after sundown." As a result of the system, noted Schurz, the "crops on this plantation, cotton as a well as corn, looked far better than any in the vicinity." He contrasted this productive plantation to several neighboring farms, which were cultivated by self-directed black labor, and where crops appeared to be in an "inferior condition." The reason for this, Schurz surmised, was that "their attention was perhaps a little too much devoted to the raising of articles which they could send to market and sell for ready cash. . . . These pursuits are not unprofitable, but they take away from the cotton and corn fields a considerable proportion of the labor force." By contrasting the efficiency and productiveness of the northern-run plantation, where freedmen operated simply as laborers and which relied on a rigidly scheduled workday, with the apparently disorganized, unprofitable farms led by autonomous freedmen, who chose instead to work independently, Schurz attempted to reinforce a more precise definition of free labor in the South, one where production and efficiency were privileged over autonomy and independence.[16]

Schurz's letters to the *Boston Daily Advertiser* reveal the ambiguity and inherent problems of northern free labor principles that Republicans would struggle with in the opening stages of Reconstruction. Northern Republican free labor ideology rested on the understanding that all classes in a free labor society shared the same interests. However, black and white southerners inherited from slavery contradictory views regarding work habits, and economic and social independence. In a postwar South, both groups attempted to carve out respective spaces where their views could succeed. Schurz's letters demonstrate that his northern free labor ideology assumed some sort of economic rationality, a belief that the "harmony of interest" between labor and capital would somehow transform the South into a free labor paradise. However, upon seeing how the ideals of free labor were being challenged within the South, Schurz attempted to form a system that somehow reconciled the contested spaces of labor within the South. In contrast to the free labor ideal of self-sufficient farmer, an ideal deeply rooted in the principles of western Republicans, Schurz tried to fuse a northern conception of free labor with southern racial realities, creating a southern free labor ideal that saw free black labor restricted to a laboring class, working under white supervision on a plantation.[17]

Schurz's modified system was destroyed by his experiences in Mississippi, which represented a turning point for him in his belief in the natural ascendency of free labor. In Mississippi, Schurz discovered a society in "a state of complete dissolution [that] can only be held in check by iron force." In the aftermath of the war, outlaw bands of Confederate deserters had become so widespread in parts of the state that Union and Confederate army units both attempted to suppress these groups. In addition, conditions in the state were exacerbated by politically and racially motivated violence between whites and blacks. Another one of Johnson's emissaries noted that "Mississippians have been shooting and cutting each other all [over] the state to a greater extent than in all the other states of the Union put together." In response to this violence, Mississippi governor William L. Sharkey sought to organize state militia units in order to keep the peace. The Union military commander of the Department of the Mississippi, Major General Henry W. Slocum, immediately forbade the formation of such units, declaring that he could not permit former Confederates to patrol counties that were now being garrisoned by black Union troops. By the end of August 1865, Johnson had rescinded Slocum's order, despite protests from Schurz that the militia was being used to oppress unionists and freedmen. Schurz saw in these actions and others that "the proslavery element is gaining the upper hand everywhere and the policy of the government is such as to encourage this outcome."[18]

Schurz was shocked by the conditions and attitudes of many of the white Mississippians, and their attitude contrasted with the behavior of the freedmen, forcing Schurz to reevaluate some of his earlier notions of free black labor. Toward the end of his journey through the South, and after encountering so much hostility toward the notion of free black labor, Schurz finally came to the conclusion that radical changes to southern society would be required. "This is the most shiftless, most demoralized people I have ever seen," Schurz complained to his wife, declaring that "the influence of slavery has confused their moral conceptions, their childish, morbid self-complacency has not allowed them to approach . . . a correct realization of their situation." Noting the increase in violence toward emancipated blacks, Schurz declared that in the South, the freedmen's life was "not deemed worth a wisp of straw." Nonetheless, in spite of the economic lethargy of the white population, and the violence inflicted on the free black population, Schurz noted that blacks were the only ones attempting to construct some sort of free labor system. "The negroes are unjustly accused of not wishing to work," Schurz wrote, emphasizing that "they are the only ones here who do work. . . . I have not seen one white man in the fields." Finally, Schurz noted that, economically, the freedmen were the only ones who had taken advantage of the new free labor system, as "they are the only persons who do not shrink from any sort of remunerative labor."[19]

This change of opinion over the future of free labor in the South influenced Schurz's final report to Congress. In comparison to his letters written for the *Advertiser*, which attempted to reshape a vision of a free labor society in the South that would be amenable to its Republican readers, Schurz's report emphasized both the monumental challenges and opportunities facing free labor in the South. Schurz repeated his claim that the majority of white southerners were trapped a mindset where it was impossible to fathom free black labor and that the small minority who grudgingly accepted free labor placed such onerous restrictions on black autonomy that it resembled a slave system in all but name. Furthermore, Schurz reiterated his belief that northern men were more capable of managing plantations, due to their familiarity with free labor systems. When discussing the situation of the freedmen, Schurz took a much more nuanced position regarding their possibilities than he had previously alluded to in his letters. Acknowledging that while some had been successful in working as wage laborers for planters, Schurz also recognized that many others had shown "thrift and industry" in independently managing crops and accumulating money. In addition to recognizing the economic independence of freedmen in his report, Schurz also made the bold suggestion that land ownership would help to stabilize the economic situation in the South. Noting that the "vagrancy and restlessness" of freedmen had become one of the key complaints of white southerners, Schurz suggested that land ownership may be the remedy. "Other emancipatory movements, for instance the abolition of serfdom in Russia, have resulted in little or no vagrancy," wrote Schurz, emphasizing that "it must not be forgotten that the emancipated serfs were speedily endowed with the ownership of land, which gave them a permanent moral and material interest in the soil upon which they lived." A similar program of land reform, he concluded, may help to stabilize the social and economic situation in the South.[20]

Schurz's report concluded with an admission that in order to develop a free labor society in the South, the government would have to take an active role in promoting and perpetuating it. White southerners, encumbered by hostility and prejudice toward both freedmen and free labor, were in no shape to govern a free labor society. "As long as the change from slavery to free labor is known to the southern people only by its destructive results . . . ," Schurz argued, "would it not be necessary that the movement of social reconstruction be kept in the right channel by the hand of power that originated the change, until that change can have disclosed some of its beneficial effects?" No longer acceptable were prewar conceptions of free labor gradually wearing away slavery, or Schurz's earlier belief that the "harmony of interests" between capital and labor would naturally transform the South into a free labor paradise. Instead, Schurz declared that the federal government itself must ensure that a free labor system take hold in the South. It is obvious, wrote Schurz, that "to every unbiased observer that unadulterated free labor cannot be had at the present, unless the national government holds its protective and controlling hand over it."[21]

Despite wrangling by Johnson's allies, Schurz's report was eventually presented to the Senate, where it was well received by radical Republicans as a "vivid, vigorous portraiture of the conditions of things in the rebel states." In the end, the Senate agreed to print more than one hundred thousand copies of Schurz's report, where it became an important weapon of radical Republican propaganda. Schurz, delighted at the reception of his report, wrote to his wife that Johnson himself was reported to have said that "the only great mistake I have made yet was to send Schurz to the South." The popularity of the report in radical Republicans circles, as well as the publicity the report afforded its author, would ensure that Schurz's political ambitions, as well as his impact on public policy, would continue in the near future.[22]

Schurz's writings demonstrate how his preconceived notions of free labor were transformed by his direct encounters with the changing social conditions within the postwar South. Many Republicans, Schurz included, struggled to transform their prewar free labor ideology into a coherent and permanent plan for reconstructing the South. With some underestimating the levels of racial antagonism by white southerners, and others beholden to an image of free blacks as a laboring class, and still others emphasizing the need for further government intervention, the incoherence of the Republican Party's early position on Reconstruction would lay the groundwork for later struggles during the era. Examining Schurz's writings provides a cautionary tale for those who wish to implement new labor systems in societies without fully understanding what Schurz discovered during his travels throughout the South: ideology is no sound replacement for practicality.

Notes

1. Eric Foner, *Reconstruction: America's Unfinished Revolution, 1863–1877*, updated ed. (New York: Harper Collins, 2014), 138.

2. Carl Schurz, *Speeches, Correspondence, and Political Papers of Carl Schurz*, ed. Frederic Bancroft (New York: G. P. Putnam's Sons, 1913), 1:5, 1:16 (hereafter cited as *SC*); Hans L. Trefousse, *Carl Schurz* (Knoxville: University of Tennessee Press, 1982), 59–60.

3. Schurz, *Speeches of Carl Schurz* (Philadelphia: Lipincott, 1865), 34–35, 108.

4. Mark A. Lause, *Free Labor: The Civil War and the Making of an American Working Class* (Urbana: University of Illinois Press, 2015), Kindle, introduction; Jonathan A. Glickstein, *Concepts of Free Labor in Antebellum America* (New Haven: Yale University Press, 1991), 11–16; Abraham Lincoln, "Address before the Wisconsin State Agricultural Society," in *Collected Works of Abraham Lincoln*, ed. Roy P. Basler (Rutgers, NJ: Rutgers University Press, 1953), 3:472–78; Heather Cox Richardson, *To Make Men Free: A History of the Republican Party* (New York: Basic Books, 2014), 16–18.

5. *SC*, 1:122–60; Schurz to Mrs. Schurz, *SC*, 1:121.

6. *Louisville Journal*, August 15, 1860; Trefousse, *Carl Schurz*, 91–94.

7. Schurz to J. F. Potter, November 30, 1860, *SC*, 1:165; Schurz to Mrs. Schurz, December 24, 1860, *SC*, 1:178; Trefousse, *Carl Schurz*, 95–97, 114; Barbara Donner, "Carl Schurz as Office Seeker," *Wisconsin Magazine of History* 20, no. 2 (1936): 135–36.

8. For an overview of Schurz's military career, see Trefousse, *Carl Schurz*, 115–49; Schurz to Agathe Schurz, November 9, 1863, in *Intimate Letters of Carl Schurz*, ed. Joseph

Schafer (Madison: State Historical Society of Wisconsin, 1928), 291–93 (hereafter cited as *IL*).

9. Schurz, *The Reminiscences of Carl Schurz*, 3 vols. (New York: McClure, 1908), 3:221–25; Trefousse, *Carl Schurz*, 150; Foner, *Reconstruction*, 183; Schurz to Andrew Johnson, June 6, 1965, *SC*, 1:260–63.

10. Schurz, *Reminiscences*, 3:157–59; Schurz to Charles Sumner, June 22, 1865, *SC*, 1:265.

11. *Boston Daily Advertiser*, July 17, 1865; Schurz, *Reminiscences*, 159–61. A useful collection of Schurz's letters, but one that remains affixed firmly within the Dunning School of Reconstruction historiography, can be found in Joseph H. Mahaffey, ed., "Carl Schurz's Letters from the South," *Georgia Historical Quarterly* 35, no. 3 (1951): 222–57.

12. *Boston Daily Advertiser*, July 17, 1865.

13. Heather Cox Richardson, *The Greatest Nation on Earth: Republican Economic Policies during the Civil War* (Cambridge: Harvard University Press, 1997), 19–22; Henry Charles Carey, *Principles of Political Economy* (Philadelphia: Carey, Lea and Blanchard, 1837), 141; Francis Wayland, *The Elements of Political Economy* (New York: Leavitt, Lord, 1837), 49–50; *Boston Daily Advertiser*, July 17, 1865.

14. *Boston Daily Advertiser*, July 25, 1865.

15. *Boston Daily Advertiser*, July 25, 1865.

16. *Boston Daily Advertiser*, August 8, 1865.

17. Foner, *Reconstruction*, 155–56.

18. Schurz to Margarethe Schurz, August 27, 1865, *IL*, 268; Dan T. Carter, *When the War Was Over: The Failure of Self-Reconstruction in the South, 1865–1867* (Baton Rouge: Louisiana State University Press, 1985), 21; George C. Rable, *But There Was No Peace: The Role of Violence in the Politics of Reconstruction* (Athens: University of Georgia Press, 1984), 27; Schurz to Agathe Schurz, September 12, 1865, *SC*, 350–51.

19. Schurz to Margarethe Schurz, August 27, 1865, *SC*, 268–69.

20. Schurz, *Report on the Condition of the South*, 39th Cong., 1st sess., December 18, 1865.

21. Schurz, *Report on the Condition of the South*, 39th Cong., 1st sess., December 18, 1865.

22. Charles Sumner to Schurz, December 25, 1865, *SC*, 375; Trefousse, *Carl Schurz*, 160; Schurz to Margarethe Schurz, January 23, 1866, *IL*, 359.

6

Haskins v. Royster and the Liberty to Be Unfree

Reconstructing North Carolina Labor Law

LINDA A. TVRDY

The Thirteenth and Fourteenth Amendments to the U.S. Constitution brought revolutionary legal change to the entire nation, not just to the South. While the legal history of Reconstruction tends to place federal law and federal actors at the center of the narrative, in fact, most of the work of implementing these new constitutional values fell to state legislators, lawyers, and judges applying them at the state and local level. The law governing the conditions of labor was no exception.

Slavery was not only a system of oppression. It was a system of labor supported by a thick tapestry of common law principles that had developed over hundreds of years. One of the most important and difficult problems that emancipation presented was how to disentangle laws designed to support a system of slave labor and reconstruct them on the basis of freedom. In the 1874 case *Haskins v. Royster*, the North Carolina Supreme Court had its first opportunity to articulate the law and policy that would govern labor in the state in the postwar era.[1]

Haskins v. Royster presented the North Carolina Supreme Court with the opportunity to reconstruct its law to promote an egalitarian system of labor, one that distributed power and economic advantage more evenly between employers and employees. Instead, the court's majority opinion resorted to long-standing ideas and practices embedded in local culture to preserve a hierarchical labor system with the propertied, white male continuing to occupy the seat of authority and power.

Legal scholar Reva Siegel has described a dynamic she calls preservation-through-transformation. This dynamic is one in which the legal system responds to reform efforts by changing rule structures and their justifications in a way that preserves preexisting status categories and relationships.[2] *Haskins v. Royster* was a pivotal step in the process of preserving the South's hierarchical system of labor by transforming the juridical space that surrounded and protected a master's property right in his servant from outside interference, to one that surrounded and protected an employer's contract with his employees from outside interference. By transforming the property-based tort (civil wrong) of enticement into the contract-based tort of tortious interference, the court defined freedom for workers to be the right to enter into an employment contract and nothing more. Entering into an employment agreement meant adopting the status of an employee and becoming subject to many of the common law prerogatives that antebellum masters had over their servants. In the postwar South, this preservation-through-transformation supported the continued existence of a race-based, caste-like system of labor under what legal authorities described as contract freedom and impeded workers' efforts to act collectively to improve their working conditions.

From the colonial era through the early nineteenth century, American labor relations existed within domestic status categories defined by the common law. Propertied, white, male heads of households controlled the labor of wives, children, servants, apprentices, slaves, and unrelated dependents through hierarchical status relationships. Most people who found themselves in a dependent domestic status category arrived there involuntarily. Children and slaves obviously had no choice in their status. Apprentices and wards frequently acquired their status through tragedy or hardship. Wives, servants, and voluntary apprentices entered into their domestic relationships by choice, but exercising that choice was the last act of volition the law allowed. No household member could opt to leave the relationship except at the expiration of a term of service or, for male children, when they reached majority age.[3]

The head of the household, whether in his capacity as husband, father, or master, derived his authority over his dependents from the property interest he possessed in their bodies. The common law of both England and the American states erected a zone of privacy and protection around a property owner and his property. A violation of that zone was a trespass. When a third party induced a wife, child, or servant to leave his or her husband or master that third party committed a trespass called "enticement." The rules against enticement applied equally to wives, children, servants, and slaves.[4]

Over the course of the nineteenth century, the nature of work and labor relationships changed. Northern states began to abolish slavery, and increasingly came to view long-term indentures as a form of unfreedom. Northerners came to understand servitude as a temporary life-stage for young people on their way to adult independence. Young men completed their apprenticeships or terms of service to become independent farmers, shop owners, or skilled craftsmen. Women completed their apprenticeships or terms of service to become the wives of independent householders.[5]

Yet economic independence became increasingly out of reach for many young people in the mid-nineteenth-century industrializing North. Rather than achieving independence, they continued to work for others for wages well into adulthood. As more adults remained wage laborers for longer periods, categorizing wage labor as a form of service contradicted the idea of America as a society of free individuals. American society required that adults be free and independent. If they were also wage laborers for long periods of their adulthood, then it was necessary to reconceptualize the social organization of work in a way that granted them that claim to freedom and independence. Free labor ideology offered a way for Americans to do this.[6]

Free labor ideology placed the contract at the center of the work relationship. The general law of contract had been evolving rapidly over the course of the nineteenth century. Before 1850, the common law defined a contract as an agreement for the exchange of tangible things. By mid-century, however, courts began to reconceive the contract as an exchange of promised obligations. This shift made it possible to conceptualize employment relationships as a subset of contract. Contracts, whether oral or written, created a relationship that was relatively equal and voluntary. In theory, neither party to the relationship was subservient to the other. Neither acquired a property interest in either the person or labor of the other. In contrast, in a common law status relationship, the higher-status person obtained a property interest in the lower-status person.[7]

Amy Dru Stanley has written about the broad, if not universal, attraction northerners felt toward the concept of contract as an organizing principle for social and civic relationships. Indeed, Stanley argues, Americans developed an ideology of contract as the embodiment of freedom in the civic sphere. In creating employment contracts, Americans could envision themselves as free and independent individuals organizing their economic lives without compulsion or interference from the state.[8]

In practice, however, the common law created what political scientist Karen Orren describes as a kind of jurisdictional sovereignty around the workplace. Common law master and servant rules migrated from the household to the workshop and factory, giving the employer a kind of sovereign authority over the terms and conditions of employment and physical control over their employees. Employees could exercise their freedom by entering into an employment relationship. But once they did, they acquired the status of employee and became subservient to the employer.[9]

The South did not participate in the development of free labor law during the antebellum period. Instead, southern intellectuals developed a proslavery ideology that held that slavery was more humane than free labor. Slaves occupied a position within the southern domestic hierarchy. Masters fed, clothed, and housed their enslaved workers. They provided for the workers even in their infancy or old age when they were unable to labor productively. The so-called free labor system produced an impoverished, permanent working class that received none of the protection or affection that enslaved workers purportedly received within the slave household.[10]

The slave state organization of labor, grounded on the proslavery ideology of hierarchy and social order, also included elite whites' authority to control nonelite whites and free blacks. Social order required everyone to be under the authority of a propertied, white householder. Southerners used poor laws and apprenticeships to bind poor adults and children to a head of household who could support them in exchange for their labor.[11]

North Carolina had a predominantly agricultural economy throughout the antebellum period. Enslaved workers performed virtually all the agricultural labor on plantations. On smaller farms, the landowner and his family performed the bulk of the labor themselves, occasionally purchasing or renting a slave or two in times of need.[12] Tenants and croppers could also perform both skilled and unskilled agricultural labor. Though the work of a "cropper" might have resembled wage labor, the law regulating both tenants and croppers grew out of the common law of landlord and tenant, not contract.[13]

At the beginning of 1871, North Carolina courts had yet to define the boundaries of the law governing labor relationships in the state. In this uncertain legal environment, a white planter named John Haskins entered into a yearlong agricultural labor agreement with a white man named Thomas Eastwood and a black man named Sam Wilkerson, who represented Jim Wilkerson and his family. The agreement specified the fields that Eastwood and Sam Wilkerson would farm, what they should plant, and what portion of each crop the parties would receive. Haskins was to provide Eastwood and Sam Wilkerson with all the tools necessary for farming and a team of two horses. Eastwood and Sam Wilkerson also agreed to feed all Haskins's livestock and to cut and haul wood for the entire plantation.

In addition to their own labor, Eastwood and Sam Wilkerson were to "'work' Elice Wilkerson as a full hand, Harriet and Lawyer Wilkerson together as one hand, and Horace Wilkerson as a half hand." They agreed to "work faithfully all the year and cause their hands to do the same." The workers had to follow Haskins's instructions at all times because Haskins retained "the privilege of discharging them at any time he may think proper." Haskins also claimed the right to discharge any of the hands he found to be insolent or disrespectful to himself or any member of his family. Any hand Haskins discharged forfeited all his (or her) labor and was required to leave the plantation immediately. The shares he would have been paid were to be retained by Haskins. The agreement required the workers to feed and clothe themselves at their own expense.[14]

It is unclear exactly what relationship, if any, existed between Sam and Jim Wilkerson. But the agreement refers to the hands Jim provided to Eastwood and Sam Wilkerson as Jim's family. The agreement also suggests that Jim Wilkerson's family lived somewhere on the plantation, and that housing was part of the labor agreement. Haskins drafted the agreement and Eastwood and the Wilkerson signed it with their marks, suggesting the men were not literate.

About two months after entering into this labor agreement with Haskins, the workers left to work for Fabian Royster on another plantation. Haskins sued Royster for two thousand dollars in superior court in Person County. Haskins's complaint alleged that the workers "bound themselves to serve the plaintiff as laborers" on his farm for the year 1871 and that Royster "did unlawfully entice, persuade, and procure" the workers to "unlawfully leave the service of the plaintiff."[15]

In the spring of 1873, superior court judge Albion Tourgée decided that, as a matter of law and public policy, the agreement between Haskins and the workers was too unfair to be legally enforceable.[16] Because there was no existing employment contract, the workers were under no obligation to Haskins and could work for whomever they pleased, including Royster. Royster could not be found liable for enticing the workers into breaking a contract that did not legally exist. Haskins appealed to the North Carolina Supreme Court.

It is evident that the lawyers and judges in this case understood its significance. William A. Graham, arguably one of North Carolina's most prominent elder statesman at the time, made a separate appeal on Haskins's behalf. Justice E. G. Reade broke tradition and filed a separate dissent in the case because, as he stated, "under the new regime, much of the labor of the country is performed under contract. This is the first case which has been before us in which the incidents of the relation of employer and laborer have been under discussion, and will probably be looked to as a precedent."[17]

It is also evident that the lawyers and judges involved in *Haskins* understood that the Thirteenth and Fourteenth Amendments protected the freedom of North Carolina's workers. A central question in the case was whether, under the new regime of freedom, a contract like the one Haskins created could or should be enforceable under North Carolina law.

The agreement required Eastwood and the Wilkersons to cede authority and control over their work to Haskins. But Haskins's control did not stop with matters related to their performance as workers. He also reserved the authority to fire any one of them for "insolence" toward Haskins or any member of his family. Furthermore, Haskins was to be the sole judge of what constituted "insolence." In the event Haskins decided to fire a worker, he had the right to turn him off the property and keep whatever wages the worker had earned. Because the contract did not pay wages until the workers produced a crop, Haskins could fire the entire group of workers just before harvest "for what he or any of his family may be pleased to consider disrespectful behavior to him, or to any of his family, in no way connected with their business—the mere flout of a child, it may be."[18]

Haskins's attorneys argued that consenting adults could, consistent with the new conditions of freedom, agree to create a master and servant relationship through contract. In support of this view, they echoed the proslavery ideology that governed labor relations before the war. "Society cannot long exist without grades, and the relation of master and servant springs from the earliest and always continuing needs of society, *without reference to the character of government*."[19] Status and hierarchy were not only consistent with freedom and free contract, but natural features of it. The agreement had to be voluntary and the intent to create the master and servant relationship had to be clear, but according to William A. Graham, this was an easy case. He argued that the terms of the contract indicated the intent to create a master-servant relationship because "the direction and control of the whole operations of the year are vested in the plaintiff, with stringent securities, not only for obedience, but for correct and respectful behavior towards him and his family, of all which he is made the judge."[20]

Haskins's lawyers attempted to preserve the structure of slave labor by transforming it into a legal right to enter a contract that approached slavery. Justice Reade, writing in dissent, said as much. According to Reade, if Eastwood and Wilkerson had contracted to be *slaves* the contract would surely have been against public policy. But he regarded the contract at issue to be worse than slavery. Under slave law, masters had the obligation to feed, clothe, and house their enslaved workers, even after their productive lives were over. Under this contract, the workers had to feed and clothe themselves and could be turned out of their homes at Haskins's whim. If anyone came along to offer better terms, that employer would have to pay damages, which cut off any avenue for the workers to escape their condition. To Judge Reade, contracts like the one in this case spelled disaster for both workers and employers: "There is no greater danger in any community than a dependent class upon whom is the hand of oppression bearing hard and who have nowhere to look for relief."[21]

Justice William B. Rodman's majority opinion in this case became the leading North Carolina law governing the employment relationship. He recognized that Haskins's lawyers' argument, which asked the court to conceptualize the employment relationship as a set of hierarchical status categories resembling slavery, was not consistent with a labor system based in equality and freedom. In his attempt to bring North Carolina in line with Reconstruction legal values, he looked north. Judge Rodman adopted the central holding of the 1871 Massachusetts Supreme Court decision in *Walker v. Cronin.*[22] This case represented the culmination of a process of preservation-through-transformation that preserved a master's property interest in his servant by transforming the trespass of enticement into a cause of action for tortious interference.[23]

In post-Reconstruction America, one man's ownership of another was constitutionally unacceptable. But even radical Republicans continued to believe that employers had an implicit right to wield authority over the workplace without interference from outsiders. The legal wrong of tortious interference preserved the employer's authority over his employees and his workplace by imposing damages on outsiders who encouraged workers to quit their employment agreements.

The move from enticement to tortious interference provided an intellectual justification for preserving incidents of mastery in the ostensibly free and equal contract relationship between employer and employee. Courts did this by relocating the source of an employer's authority over his employees, from his property interest in his employees to a general obligation to preserve the sanctity of contracts. Courts enforced this new norm by punishing those who encouraged others to break their contracts.

The process of transformation happened over a twenty-five-year span, beginning with an English case decided in 1853, *Lumley v. Gye.*[24] In *Lumley v. Gye* a famous singer named Johanna Wagner exchanged her promise to perform in Lumley's opera house for Lumley's promise to pay the singer for her performance. Wagner breached her agreement by performing in the establishment of Gye, the defendant, instead. Lumley could have sued the singer for breaching her contract. Instead he sued Gye for having enticed her to do so.

The singer's contract with Lumley did not fit within the concept of master and servant. The engagement was for a series of performances to take place at a specified time. It did not create a hierarchical status relationship, and the two parties had relatively equal bargaining power. Lumley could not have plausibly claimed a property interest in the labor of the famous singer. The court acknowledged this distinction, calling the contract one for personal services instead. The court held that a contract for personal services warranted protection from interference by third parties and found that Gye owed damages to Lumley.[25]

The dissent objected to this extension of enticement, pointing out that it had been a remedy that arose out of the Statute of Laborers, an ancient law governing masters and servants. The property interest masters had in their servants did not apply to a contract between more or less equal parties.[26]

Despite that foreign pedigree, in 1871 the Massachusetts Supreme Court followed the example of *Lumley v. Gye* and extended enticement beyond the bounds of master and servant law. In *Walker v. Cronin*, a Worcester shoe manufacturer sued the leaders of a labor union who had convinced a group of shoemakers to join a strike against the manufacturer. The manufacturer had recruited the shoemakers from a distance under contracts that advanced their travel expenses. The contracts required that the employees work off their travel expenses, but otherwise specified no length of time for employment. The defendants argued that the shoemakers had the "perfect right" to leave their employment and strike with the union if they wanted to. If the employer had any remedy for breach of an employment contract, it would be against workers, not union leaders who were third parties to the employment contract. The defendants warned that if the law expanded to protect employers from the acts of persons outside of the employer-employee contract relationship, "it would make any friend or neighbor who advised a party to a contract vulnerable to a third-party suit if his friend or neighbor breached his contract: So extensive a right of action . . . would be inconsistent with the rights of citizens under a free government."[27]

The Massachusetts Supreme Court acknowledged that enticement originated with master and servant, but saw no reason it could not be founded upon the legal right "derived from contract." The court further justified its decision, writing that "everyone has a right to enjoy the fruits and advantages of his own enterprise, industry, skill and credit. He has no right to be protected against competition; but he has a right to be free from malicious and wanton interference, disturbance or annoyance."[28] The court thus preserved the property right of masters to protect their servants from enticement, by transforming it into a tort that protected the sanctity of contracts.

By midcentury, the employment contract in the North had evolved into at-will employment. The fluid labor market that at-will employment created was a double-edged sword for employers. On the one hand, they could let go of unnecessary workers to suit the needs of their business cycles. On the other, workers' right to leave during periods of high labor demand left employers vulnerable. Tortious interference allowed employers to retain a kind of sovereignty around their workplace that protected them from outside interference. This zone of sovereignty did not just protect employers from business disruption. In delegating control over workers to employers, courts sought to preserve what they viewed as a stable economic and social order.[29]

Stability and social order were equally at stake in *Haskins v. Royster.* Justice Rodman cited *Walker v. Cronin* with respect and at great length, echoing the need to preserve social order, which he saw as necessarily hierarchical. Citing *Walker v. Cronin,* Justice Rodman explained that settled law protected a contract for personal service from enticement by outside parties and that nothing in that law was "inconsistent with personal freedom."[30] The law applied "impartially to every grade of service from the most brilliant and the best paid to the most homely. . . . It is not derived from any idea of property by the one party in the other, but is an inference from the obligation of a contract freely made by competent persons."[31] Rodman agreed with the reasoning and logic of the court in *Walker v. Cronin* that employers had no right to be free from competition for laborers, and that workers employed at-will could leave a job at their pleasure. But if the parties entered a contract for a term of service, the employer had the right to be free of "wanton and malicious" interference.[32]

Underpinning Rodman's opinion of what constituted "improper" interference with the employment relationship were his views that status relationships were necessary to a stable social order:

> There is a certain analogy among all the domestic relations, and it would be dangerous to the repose and happiness of families if the law permitted any man, under whatever professions of philanthropy or charity, to sow discontent between the head of a family and its various members, wife, children and servants. Interference with such relations can only be justified under the most special circumstances, and where there cannot be the slightest suspicion of a spirit of mischief-making, or self interest.[33]

The zone of protection Rodman placed around the employment relationship preserved much of the sovereignty that slave owners had as masters before the war. Rodman refused to consider the inequities of the contract and justified his refusal in terms of the workers' freedom. He recognized that the harsh terms of the contract might suggest an intent on the part of Haskins to take "some improper advantage" and to "exact from the employees a degree of personal deference and respect, beyond that civil and courteous deportment which every man owes to his fellow in every relation in life."[34] But without evidence of fraud or duress that might have compelled the workers to enter the agreement against their will, he refused to acknowledge the inequities of the bargain because to do so would require "an assumption inconsistent with [the workers'] freedom."[35]

Rodman may have borrowed his logic from the North, but his effort to preserve antebellum status categories expressed itself in white-supremacist terms in the postwar South. Black property ownership certainly existed in the postwar South, but it was always precarious.[36] Granting property owners a zone of authority around the people they employed returned a great deal of private power to whites that they exercised freely over black North Carolinians. An iconic example of this power, which extended well into the twentieth century, is the southern bloc of Democrats excluding agricultural and domestic workers from the benefits of New Deal programs attached to work. Because blacks in the South were concentrated in these two categories of work, a generation of black Americans were excluded from the economic safety net that white Americans enjoyed.[37]

In his dissent, Justice Reade tried to persuade the court to adopt a more egalitarian labor law scheme: "I think it of great importance that employers should make only just and reasonable contracts."[38] He tried to convince the majority that the contract at issue was not just and reasonable and should not be enforced under North Carolina law. He emphasized that the workers were ignorant, poor, and dependent. To Reade, the inequitable distribution of power between Haskins and the workers should have raised a presumption of fraud or duress, making the agreement unenforceable. He tried to convince the majority, as well, that Haskins's unfettered right to discharge any or all of the workers if their performance or behavior toward Haskins' family failed to suit him was against public policy. The workers risked forfeiting all their labor in the event of a breach, and the agreement made Haskins the sole judge of whether a breach had occurred. According to Reade, "no one can read the contract without being satisfied that the best interest of society forbid that it should be enforced or in any way countenanced in the Courts."[39]

But Justice Rodman's majority preferred to place nearly unfettered authority in the hands of employers to set the conditions of employment. Rodman recognized that the contract was "not to be commended" and that the terms suggested an intent "to take some improper advantage."[40] Nevertheless, Rodman upheld the employer's prerogative to exercise his power and authority without interference.[41]

The dynamic of preservation-through-transformation in the context of free labor law proceeded on different but overlapping tracks in the North and South, although each preserved a kind of property interest in workers' labor. Both northerners and southerners reexamined their employment law with an eye toward the freedom the post-emancipation Constitution required. Northern industrial capitalists needed a fluid labor supply that they could command if needed. Southern elites sought continued control at the plantation level over the labor of free blacks and poor whites. The transformation of enticement into tortious interference shows how courts could espouse the language of freedom and free contract while simultaneously preserving the preexisting status hierarchy in the master and servant relationship.

The decisions in *Haskins v. Royster* and *Walker v. Cronin* provided the logic and doctrine that empowered courts to block labor advocates from taking collective action to gain greater equality in the workplace and to improve their work conditions. Courts coupled tortious interference with conspiracy to impose tort damages on labor unions that persuaded workers to strike for better wages and hours.[42] Courts expressed a nearly hysterical fear that labor could tyrannize business if allowed to act collectively. On the other hand, the need for capital to consolidate itself raised no concern that it could tyrannize workers.[43] Consolidated capital did not upset the existing social and economic order. Empowered workers did.

The argument over what free labor entailed and required continued at the state level throughout the nineteenth century. But the Supreme Court of the United States also grappled with what role the Fourteenth Amendment gave the federal government to define freedom in the context of labor relations.

At about the same time that the North Carolina Supreme Court considered *Haskins v. Royster*, the United States Supreme Court decided the *Slaughter-House Cases*.[44] Historians have long regarded Justice Miller's majority opinion in the *Slaughter-House Cases* to have been the Supreme Court's first step toward dismantling Reconstruction. But historian Michael Ross has recently demonstrated that Justice Miller's overarching concern was that his conservative fellow justices, especially Stephen J. Field, would use the power of the Fourteenth Amendment to prevent states from regulating corporations and financial interests to protect their citizens from their predatory practices.[45]

Field's dissent in the *Slaughter-House Cases*, in which he praised the virtues of free labor, was an appeal to constitutionalize the inviolability of contracts necessary to free labor law. According to Ross, Miller believed that if the Supreme Court adopted Field's position, then "state legislatures that attempted to address the problems associated with industrialization, urbanization, and the concentration of capital would have to adjust their legislation to the views of conservative justices. Every piece of state regulatory legislation would be scrutinized by a Supreme Court that jealously guarded the interests of the propertied classes."[46] This included state legislation that would improve the condition of workers.

Eventually, with its decision in *Lochner v. New York*, that is exactly what the Supreme Court did. *Lochner* invalidated New York legislation limiting bakers' workdays to ten hours. The New York legislature justified the legislation on the grounds of health. Studies showed bakers suffered from respiratory ailments from the dust in the air, and from other ailments due to exhaustion from the long, odd hours the baking industry required. The majority opinion not only rejected New York's justification, but rejected the state's authority under the state police power to decide for itself what labor regulations were appropriate for its citizens. New York had previously rejected the *Haskins v. Royster* antireformist position in the 1891 case *Rogers v. Evarts et al.* But the Supreme Court in *Lochner* constitutionalized the hierarchical status relationship of *Haskins v. Royster* and *Walker v. Cronin*.[47]

The power structure that draws a protective line around the place of employment and grants employers control over the workspace is with us today. At-will employment is the dominant employment arrangement in the United States. In theory, employers and employees have the option to terminate the employment relationship at any time. But in practice, employers control virtually all aspects of the work environment, and many aspects that reach into their employees' private lives.[48] Because so much of our social safety net is tied to work (social security benefits, workman's compensation, health insurance, retirement benefits, to name a few) even an employee's right to quit is highly constrained. *Haskins v. Royster* presented a moment when employment relations could have taken on a more egalitarian cast. Instead, the case helped preserve hierarchies in the workplace that continue today.

Notes

1. 1874 N.C. LEXIS 295.

2. Reva B. Siegel, "'The Rule of Love': Wife Beating as Prerogative and Privacy," *Yale Law Journal* 105, no. 8 (1996): 2117, and "Why Equal Protection No Longer Protects: The Evolving Forms of Status-Enforcing State Action," *Stanford Law Review* 49 (1996–97): 1111.

3. Karen Orren, *Belated Feudalism: Labor, the Law, and Liberal Development in the United States* (Cambridge: Cambridge University Press, 1999; first published 1991).

4. "Tortious Interference with Contractual Relations in the Nineteenth Century: The Transformation of Property, Contract, and Tort," *Harvard Law Review* 93, no. 7 (1980), http://www.jstor.org/stable/1340608, 1510n; Christopher L. Tomlins, *Law, Labor, and Ideology in the Early Republic* (New York: Cambridge University Press, 1993), 283; and Christopher L. Tomlins, "Wifely Duties: Marriage, Labor, and the Common Law in Nineteenth-Century America," *Social Science History* 20, no. 1 (1996): 82–83.

5. Robert J. Steinfeld, *The Invention of Free Labor: The Employment Relation in English and American Law and Culture, 1350–1870* (Chapel Hill: University of North Carolina Press, 1991).

6. James D. Schmidt, *Free to Work: Labor Law, Emancipation, and Reconstruction, 1815–1880* (Athens: University of Georgia Press, 1998), 13; Christopher L. Tomlins, *Law, Labor, and Ideology in the Early Republic* (New York: Cambridge University Press, 1993), 229.

7. Robert J. Steinfeld, *Coercion, Contract, and Free Labor in the Nineteenth Century* (New York: Cambridge University Press, 2001).

8. Amy Dru Stanley, *From Bondage to Contract: Wage Labor, Marriage, and the Market in the Age of Slave Emancipation* (New York: Cambridge University Press, 1998).

9. Steinfeld, *Coercion*, 39, 255–64.

10. For slaves' place in the domestic sphere, see Peter W. Bardaglio, *Reconstructing the Household: Families, Sex, and the Law in the Nineteenth-Century South* (Chapel Hill: University of North Carolina Press, 1995). On proslavery ideology, see Mark A. Graber, *Dred Scott and the Problem of Constitutional Evil* (New York: Cambridge University Press, 2006).

11. Bardaglio, *Reconstructing the Household*; Karin L. Zipf, *Labor of Innocents: Forced Apprenticeship in North Carolina 1715–1919* (Baton Rouge: Louisiana State University Press, 2005).

12. Stephanie McCurry, *Masters of Small Worlds: Yeoman Households, Gender Relations, and the Political Culture of the Antebellum South Carolina Low Country* (New York: Oxford University Press, 1995), 82–84.

13. Harold D. Woodman, *New South-New Law: The Legal Foundations of Credit and Labor Relations in the Postbellum South* (Baton Rouge: Louisiana State University Press, 1995).

14. John R. Haskins against Fabian R. Royster, Supreme Court Original Cases, 1800–1900, North Carolina Division of Archives and History (NCDAH).

15. Civil Action Papers, Person County, Spring Term 1872, NCDAH.

16. 70 N.C., 601; Olsen, *Carpetbagger's Crusade*, 181. Tourgée was a radical Republican carpetbagger who moved from Ohio to North Carolina in 1865 and became deeply involved in North Carolina politics and law in 1867. North Carolina's 1868 constitutional convention selected Tourgée to serve on a three-person committee to convert all of North Carolina's laws, both statutes and common law rules, into a single written code. The committee managed to draft a well-regarded code of civil procedure before it was disbanded in 1873 by the newly elected conservative-controlled General Assembly. In 1868 Tourgée was elected superior court judge for the Seventh Judicial District. He remained committed to egalitarian principles throughout his life, even representing Homer Plessy in Plessy v. Ferguson, 163 U.S. 537 (1896). He nevertheless enjoyed the grudging respect of the overwhelmingly conservative North Carolina Bar for being the author of principled and well-reasoned legal opinions as a judge; see Otto H. Olsen, *Carpetbagger's Crusade: The Life of Albion Winegar Tourgée* (Baltimore: Johns Hopkins Press, 1965).

17. 1874 N.C. LEXIS 295, 2 and 20.

18. 1874 N.C. LEXIS 295, 28.

19. 1874 N.C. LEXIS 295, 5.

20. 1874 N.C. LEXIS 295, 5.

21. 1874 N.C. LEXIS 295, 31.

22. 1874 N.C. LEXIS 295, 6–11; Walker v. Cronin, 1871 Mass, LEXIS 246.

23. A tort is a civil wrong for which the person harmed can recover damages.

24. Lumley v. Gye, 2 El. & Bl. 216 (20 Eng. L. & E. R. 168). For more detailed discussion of the English cases, see Orren, *Belated Feudalism*, 129–44.

25. Lumley v. Gye.

26. "Tortious Interference with Contractual Relations in the Nineteenth Century."

27. 1871 Mass. LEXIS 246, 11.

28. 1871 Mass. LEXIS 246, 9–10.

29. Orren, *Belated Feudalism*, 118–35; Montgomery, *Beyond Equality*, 230–39.

30. Haskins v. Royster, 12–13.

31. Haskins v. Royster, 7.

32. Haskins v. Royster, 9, quoting Walker v. Cronin.

33. Haskins v. Royster, 19–20.

34. Haskins v. Royster, 7.

35. Haskins v. Royster.

36. See generally Robert C. Kenzer, *Enterprising Southerners: Black Economic Success in North Carolina, 1865–1915* (Charlottesville: University Press of Virginia, 1997).

37. Ira Katznelson, *When Affirmative Action Was White: An Untold History of Racial Inequality in Twentieth-Century America* (New York: W.W. Norton, 2006).

38. Haskins v. Royster, 36.

39. Haskins v. Royster, 33.

40. Haskins v. Royster, 17.

41. Haskins v. Royster, 18.

42. Orren, *Belated Feudalism*, 122–28.

43. Orren, *Belated Feudalism*, 122–28.

44. Slaughter-House Cases, 83 U.S. 36 (1873).

45. Michael A. Ross, *Justice of Shattered Dreams: Samuel Freeman Miller and the Supreme Court during the Civil War Era* (Baton Rouge: Louisiana State University Press, 2003).

46. Ross, *Justice of Shattered Dreams*, 206.

47. Lochner v. New York, 198 US 45 (1905).

48. For example, Burwell v. Hobby Lobby, 573 U.S., 134 S. Ct. 2751. ___ (2014) permitted the retail store Hobby Lobby to deny insurance coverage for birth control to its employees on the grounds of their employer's religious beliefs.

7

Unfaithful Followers

Rethinking Southern Nonunionism in the Late Nineteenth Century

DANA M. CALDEMEYER

In the late spring of 1894, western Kentucky miner Blackbird faced a dilemma. The United Mine Workers of America (UMW) had ordered miners to stop work in all bituminous coal districts.[1] No coal was to be hoisted until every mine operator in the United States agreed to pay their miners seventy cents for each ton of coal they mined. Strike supporters believed the suspension would dry up coal stockpiles, allowing coal prices and wages to increase, as long as no mine sold out early. Such a plan required cooperation from every mine in the nation and tested workers' faith in union strength, which grew increasingly unsteady as mine operators such as Blackbird's employer offered to pay the demanded wage rate if they returned to work early. Eager to feed their families, Blackbird's coworkers found the operator's offer tempting, especially as neighboring coal companies began importing strikebreakers that injured the strike's likelihood of success. "The men are getting restless now seeing all other mines working and we idle," Blackbird wrote to UMW officers via the *United Mine Workers' Journal*, noting that "it is useless for Bevier[, Kentucky,] miners to stay out any longer." Yet accepting the terms meant breaking UMW orders, a violation the Bevier miners did not take lightly. "I do not know what they are going to do," the Kentucky miner continued. "They want to work and are afraid to work, for they don't want to do anything wrong if they can help it."[2]

The curious part of Blackbird's statement was that his mine in Bevier was mostly nonunion. Miners in the western part of the state had never thoroughly unionized and the few feeble locals established in the late 1880s and early 1890s collapsed as the depression from the Panic of 1893 lingered. This lack of interest in unionism likely increased due to the growing racial divisions within the UMW that caused thousands of black miners who labored in western Kentucky mines to think twice before joining an order that did not always represent their interests. Still, Blackbird and his coworkers joined over 150,000 miners in the 1894 strike initiated by a union with only 13,000 members. Like the majority of the 1894 strikers, the Bevier miners were nonunion, but as Blackbird's dilemma demonstrated, they nonetheless cared deeply about having to violate the orders of an organization they refused to join.[3]

What caused such dedication from those unfaithful to the union? Many historians have attributed the ebb and flow of union membership to a younger generation of workers, many of whom were "new" immigrants, who had different outlooks on worker activism from those of the unionists of old. In some cases, this gave way to more conservative tactics as unionists tried to rein in radical elements, but, as Caroline Merithew and James Barrett observed, it also unleashed a wave of mob-like activism at the grassroots level.[4] According to Richard Oestreicher and others, this grassroots involvement provided the momentum for increased union activity and success. As more frustrated workers joined the effort, faith in collective action soared, making nonunion workers more willing to entertain the possibility of union success.[5]

In many respects, these analyses prove true in the late nineteenth-century South. One of the crucial events that galvanized organized labor originated in the southern states. The successful 1885 "Southwest Strike" that ultimately spurred faith in orders like the Knights of Labor throughout the nation originated because of workers' outrage over a new wage reduction. Their success caused thousands of workers to flock to organized labor, waging their own strikes. In most cases, these initial gains and membership increases were short-lived and unraveled quickly as additional strikes failed. In the South, ethnic divisions, hostile employers, unsympathetic government officials, and large numbers of strikebreakers (including convict laborers) all crippled attempts for collective gain and added to the disillusionment that caused union membership to wane.[6]

Daniel Nelson and others suggested that these factors influenced workers' own pragmatic decisions regarding union membership. Workers in industries difficult to regulate, like late nineteenth-century coal mining, were accustomed to operating with little managerial oversight and made independent decisions in the workplace daily. This autonomy, political theorist Timothy Mitchell argued, contributed to workers' sense of independence and democracy that allowed greater militancy in the coalfields, including the 1894 bituminous strike. Unlike the workers characterized in Julie Greene's *Pure and Simple Politics,* these workers made their decisions to join or reject unions not from falling prey to employer antiunion objectives, but from rational and strategic decisions based upon what was best for their individual situations.[7]

According to Nelson, worker autonomy combined with the economic hardship miners endured made union involvement lucrative to nonunion miners during the 1894 coal strike. His findings hold with other scholarly accounts of the strike that characterize it as an instance when the UMW learned to harness worker grievances to mobilize a national movement with an increasingly centralized bureaucracy at the helm. The strike, and nonunion worker support for it, is often credited as a sign of increasing UMW influence and strength.[8]

But neither union strength nor worker pragmatism fully explain why the nonunion men in Blackbird's mine were so conflicted in 1894. Their reluctance to return to work without the UMW officers' blessing indicates that at least some nonunion workers saw themselves as connected to a collective body whose bonds extended beyond union ties. Such viewpoints are often overshadowed when scholars focus first on labor organizations and occupational distinctions. While such studies add to our understanding of union development, they do little to explore the overlap between farmer and laborer or union and nonunion and ultimately obscure the sentiments of workers like Blackbird who did not quite fall into union ranks.[9] These overlaps, however, were crucial to Blackbird and many workers like him. They were pragmatic, but they also adhered to the values shared by their friends and neighbors, making their affiliation with unions and union objectives at times contradictory. Examining these connections and contradictions in detail and apart from the traditional union-focused analysis can add depth to our understanding of nonunionism in the late nineteenth century and shed light on why workers like Blackbird were followers unwilling to fully commit to labor's cause.

"Organization is simply a means to an end and not the end itself," one south central Indiana miner wrote two summers before the 1894 suspension.[10] At the time, the newly formed UMW had just come out of a failed national strike, crippling the order and causing thousands of the already low membership to abandon ranks. Those who remained disagreed over the best means to rebuild the broken union and what its new goals should be. Even as they remained in the order, the union miners had no delusions of grandeur for their organization and no real hope that this would change anytime soon. But, as the Indiana miner wrote, although a strong national union was desirable, it was not the miners' ultimate goal.

The miner's words reflected an outlook shared by thousands, both inside and outside labor organizations, who viewed organization as a tool to secure a desired outcome. Many miners fell into a distinct rhythm in organizing patterns that caused workers to join organizations when negotiating contracts but leave the order once the agreements were established. "The men out here remind me much of a little boy with a cup and pipe," Illinois miner Old Ninety-Sixer explained to the *United Mine Workers' Journal*. "He gets soap to make bells. He stirs awhile and then the bells come up and then disappear, to come up with a fresh blow." His parallel to a boy blowing bubbles fit with the ebb and flow of union membership throughout the South and Midwest: "In January they join the organization, then they stir till the end of March, they blow till April 30 and then disappear till next January, when they come up with a fresh blow."[11]

The blows and pops of union involvement were the product of the miners' strategic and informed decisions that they made on a regular basis. Many rural workers in the nineteenth century labored in multiple occupations throughout the year, depending upon seasonal demand and pay. Farmers and farm laborers found their way to coal mines, railroads, factories, and logging and turpentine camps when farm demand was low while laborers migrated to the farm fields during harvest time.[12] This occupational mobility enabled workers to build important workplace connections with laborers in multiple industries and develop a collective understanding of what was "fair" in the workplace.[13]

Workers' decisions regarding union membership and function mirrored this occupational fluidity. Unlike labor leaders who claimed unions were a protective force that defended workers in addition to fighting for them, many of the laborers acted according to what would best suit their immediate interests, allowing them to affiliate—or not affiliate—with organizations depending on what gave them a greater advantage. Hundreds of workers found union membership useful when negotiating contracts, but did not wish to pay dues to the UMW in the heat of summer when many of the smaller mines shut down and the farmers returned to their fields. Miners in eastern Tennessee flocked to the union to fight the influx of convict laborers in the mines in the mid-1890s. Such a trend continued into the twentieth century when miners in the West Virginia mine wars relied on aid from the Socialist Party to achieve their goals, even though few ascribed to socialist ideology.[14] Conversely, miners in Earlington, Kentucky, refused to affiliate with any miners' union in exchange for higher wages while hundreds of others who believed in union ideals refrained from joining for fear of losing their jobs.[15] These instances indicate that rural workers' strategic decisions to provide for their families often placed them outside traditional occupational or union and nonunion divides. Just as worker livelihoods extended beyond a single occupation, so workers' understandings of collective action extended beyond organized labor, at times making union membership unessential to securing their goals.

In the mining industry, this value in collective action without long-term organizational affiliation came from a long-standing tradition to negotiate differences with employers by electing a "pit committee" each time miners had concerns to be addressed. Committee members represented the miners' interests to the company not only negotiating agreements, but also leading strikes when agreements could not be reached. When regions unionized, these committee men typically became local officers, but in nonunion mines, committees formed and disbanded with each situation.[16]

Such an outlook allowed miners to value collective action even if they did not see merit in permanent union membership. As a result, when coal operators throughout the nation announced a new wage reduction that would go into effect on May 1, 1894, the miners' faith in the UMW's abilities factored little into their decisions to strike. Less than six months before the miners walked out, Missouri mine worker John Lumb wrote that the organization in his town "isn't dead yet, but right close to it." Hundreds of Missouri miners viewed national miners' unions like the UMW with contempt because the organizations demanded dues but rarely looked after the concerns of the miners west of the Mississippi River. Owned by railroads, mines in Missouri, Arkansas, Indian Territory, and Kansas did not compete in the national coal market or contribute to the coal surplus. The division between markets led UMW officials in Kansas to order its miners to *reject* the strike and remain at work.[17] Still, some western miners believed a national shortage of coal would raise prices everywhere, regardless of whether the coal went to the competitive market. Missouri miner Makeshift wrote that the miners in his town of Bevier, Missouri, needed no encouragement to join the strike. Unlike nonunion miners in typical strikes who joined only after the strike had commenced, Makeshift's coworkers voted to quit work *with* the UMW on the first day of the 1894 suspension. The willingness to answer the strike call, especially one by the UMW, was, as Makeshift described, "something unusual for Bevier to do."[18]

The Missouri miners were not alone in their mistrust for the UMW. The organization's past failures and seemingly endless membership hemorrhage made the organization particularly weak by the time officers called the strike. Even the most ardent union miners questioned the wisdom of calling for a national coal strike during a depression in the warm months when coal demand was low. Not only would the effort likely fail, they believed, but it would only further damage the UMW.[19] In Arkansas, where the UMW had yet to gain a strong foothold, the State Assembly of the Knights of Labor officially condemned the strike, claiming it was punitive to society and futile for miners. If the nonunion miners joined the strike out of some sort of organizing momentum or newfound faith in the power of organization, the inspiration did not come from the ranks of organized labor itself.[20]

But if the miners did not have faith in the union, they did have a working understanding of economics. The depression that crippled the nation hit the coal and agricultural industries particularly hard. As economists, currency reformers, and statisticians reviewed the data surrounding the depression, farmers and laborers put forward their own theories and ideologies for how to improve their situations. In 1894, most miners believed their wage trouble came more from depressed coal prices than from greedy employers. Coal, like the abundant crops, was stockpiled throughout the countryside, forcing prices and earnings ever lower. Consequently, charges like those from Populist reformer Mary Lease to challenge the market rather than abide by it resonated among rural farmers and laborers alike.[21]

Ideas of decreasing the supply while increasing demand, then, were part of a larger conversation among Gilded Age producers long before UMW leaders announced the 1894 strike. But mining less coal, like raising less corn, was a risky move to a rural worker struggling to keep his family fed. It required challenging the national market rather than any discernable entity. For the miners, it meant stopping production until the coal surplus dried up to affect the price of coal, a distinct change from previous strikes geared to pressure employers to raise wages out of their profits.[22]

To the miners who struck, it mattered little that the UMW was weak or that most of the nation's miners were outside of the order. "Let us . . . be like Mr. Coxey," one Illinois miner wrote of the coal strike. "Start out with the intention to get there, and we will find the people of the whole country will be with us." His statement referenced the march to Washington, DC, by Jacob Coxey and his "Industrial Army" that coincided with the strike and called attention to the commonalities between the two movements. Both centered their desired goals on regulating the economy. For the miners, this meant depleting the coal supply; for Coxeyites, this involved currency reform and more jobs. Yet as the miners' statement observed, neither effort was centralized. Coxey, though by far the most famous of the marchers, was but one of several reformers who led marches for reform. Although he was a figurehead, the industrial marches were decentralized movements of shared discontent, allowing for collective action without formal organizational membership. Such flexibility allowed Coxey to pull followers from beyond occupational and even political divides.[23]

The UMW played a similar role in the 1894 strike. Although the UMW was typically credited with initiating it, few miners saw the organization or its officers as the unequivocal leaders of the effort. Rather, the strike was more a collective and decentralized effort by miners to extend their local negotiation tactics to a national level. Just as miners joined unions in the spring to negotiate contracts or formed pit committees to settle disputes with employers, nonunion miners viewed the UMW as a tool to coordinate the national effort to dissolve the national coal surplus. As a result, although the UMW orchestrated the suspension, it tapped into widespread sentiments and traditions already embedded in mining communities, allowing support for the movement to extend beyond the UMW's base.[24] Such a surge in nonunion involvement caused the UMW to change its policy on national meetings, allowing nonunion regions and districts to send delegates to the meetings during the suspension to help determine the course of the strike. Although Arkansas had never established any strong connection to the UMW, its miners nonetheless participated in the suspension discourse and sent a delegate to the UMW national convention.[25]

This commitment to a cause rather than to an organization was critical in garnering nonunion support for the 1894 suspension. It caused miners like those in Blackbird's mine to express concern about acting against the UMW officers' orders regarding the strike. In Missouri, it prompted miners leery of the UMW to march to Kansas to encourage the miners there to honor the strike.[26] They were a part of a bigger movement, hoping to exact a larger change than simply organizing workers. Such interests extended beyond the miners or their strike, and aligned their interests with the other producer and worker reform efforts of the age, including the concurrent Pullman Strike and the Populist fervor gaining steam in the Midwest and South.[27] Indeed, on the same day Makeshift and his coworkers began the suspension in Bevier, Missouri, industrial workers and farmers gathered in a town less than ten miles to the east to join Coxey in his march to Washington. Their efforts were a testament to the fluidity of rural nineteenth-century workplaces, which were not limited to any consistent occupation or stance regarding union affiliation.[28]

Still, the decentralized nature of the 1894 coal strike and marches also made the efforts difficult to control. Diverse reform visions and political affiliations as well as a host of other divisions ultimately damned the Populists before they could secure many of their goals.[29] Striking miners met a similar fate as their own movement splintered, causing strikers' interests to diverge from those in UMW offices. Unable to convince all the miners in the nation to strike, UMW leaders called off the suspension after seven weeks and ordered the miners to return to work. Their decision marked a crucial point in the UMW's effort to centralize its authority and establish a precedent for workplace negotiations in a period when many reform groups became more centralized.[30] But to thousands of union and nonunion miners accustomed to mass meetings and votes, the officers' decision to settle the terms on behalf of all miners was unthinkable. To them, the strike movement was larger than the miners' organization, making the decision to cancel the strike beyond the authority of the UMW officers. Consequently, striking miners throughout the nation refused to acknowledge the settlement, instead opting to continue the suspension.[31] Even union miners believed the officers had acted beyond their official capacity by calling off the strike. At the 1895 UMW national convention, the officers who signed the 1894 settlement were tried and found guilty for overstepping their official duty by ending the strike without consulting the masses.[32]

The resentment over the settlement suggests that most miners in and outside of the union had an understanding very different from that of the UMW national officers regarding the UMW's role in the strike. Miners applied their localized understandings of temporary committees and local strikes to the national level, and viewed the UMW as the vehicle to navigate the movement. While the miners were willing to utilize the national structure the UMW provided, they did not wish to fully submit to its will. The UMW was but a means to coordinate the strike, but not the entity running it, as far as Missouri was concerned. They were not alone in these sentiments. The UMW's already low membership fell further, but such a decline in membership did not necessarily indicate a decline in faith in collective action. Although miners cursed the UMW and its officers, hundreds opted to join rival organizations, such as the Knights of Labor State Assemblies or one of the dozens of state or local unions that cropped up in the wake of the 1894 strike.[33]

Yet even as the miners broke from the UMW, they did not abandon the sentiments that, union leaders claimed, were characteristic of union men.[34] As the mines resumed work, miners in Jenny Lind, Arkansas, discovered that eight men were forbidden from returning to the mine. As local leaders of the miners, the company discharged them, seeking to quash unionism before it could gain a foothold. Although Jenny Lind was a predominantly nonunion region, most of the miners voted to resume the strike, this time on behalf of the discharged men. Their decision reflected the common tradition to use the local strike as a negotiating tactic with the company. But the strike was no more viable when defending discharged miners than it was to dry up a coal supply. Saddled with "an elephant on their shoulders," the miners were faced with a dilemma similar to the one faced by miners in Blackbird's Kentucky mine. The miners could not afford to strike any longer, despite the unfair treatment their coworkers received. Holding a mass meeting, the miners voted to return to work and give each of the eight displaced miners forty dollars. But ignoring the plight of their coworkers was an egregious wrong that, many Jenny Lind miners feared, made them "blacklegs," or dishonest laborers. The miners and their wives took this charge to heart, causing a miner named Fairplay from Jenny Lind to reach out to the *United Mine Workers'*

Journal for advice. "I should like to know . . . if the miners of Jenny Lind are blacklegging," the writer asked.[35]

Such concern indicated that nonunion miners could and did have a very clear understanding of fairness and a dedication to enforcing these fair practices in the local workplace through collective action. Long after union miners elsewhere had given up the strike, Fairplay and the Jenny Lind miners still felt guilty for not upholding a principle that they knew would be futile to defend. Like Blackbird seeking permission to break the strike, Fairplay appealed to the body of miners for approval of the Jenny Lind miners' own decisions to back down from their ideals of what was honest and fair. These situations indicate that nonunion men wrestled with difficult questions surrounding work and collective action, pragmatically balancing what they believed was fair to themselves and neighbors with the harsh realities of a depressed coal market. More importantly, their reliance on the UMW to help determine the answers to these questions indicates that nonunion miners did see use in a miners' organization, even if they did not join it.

The widespread nonunion involvement and the workers' connections forged outside union and occupational bounds are important to understanding politics and protest in the Gilded Age. During the final decades of the nineteenth century, producers in a host of industries faced harsh realities of a depressed economy and an ever-expanding national market. Workers and their unions alike struggled to cope with these dramatic changes and did so in ways that did not always correlate with union membership growth. Racism, employer hostility, public animosity, and a host of other factors contributed to workers' decisions to reject unions. The indecision Fairplay and Blackbird expressed on behalf of the miners suggests additional reasons that should also be explored. Their words and actions in 1894 indicate that they considered themselves dedicated to a cause even if they were not formal members of an organization and that this cause, and the collective action it demanded, extended beyond what any single organization could achieve. Making sense of the decisions miners like Fairplay and Blackbird made requires rethinking the dividing lines between union and nonunion action. The nonunion activism visible during the 1894 coal strike is but one example of how complicated nonunionism could be.

Notes

1. Bituminous coal was the most common type of coal and was mined in almost every mining district in the United States outside of Pennsylvania.

2. "Blackbird" to the editor, *United Mine Workers' Journal* (hereafter *UMWJ*), May 17, 1894 (quotation); Blackbird to the editor, *UMWJ*, May 24, 1894.

3. Maier B. Fox, *United We Stand: The United Mine Workers of America, 1890–1990* (Washington, DC: United Mine Workers of America, 1990), 45.

4. Herbert Gutman, "Labor in the Land of Lincoln," in *Power and Culture: Essays on the American Working Class*, ed. Ira Berlin (New York: Pantheon Books, 1987), 170–71; Caroline Waldron Merithew and James R. Barrett, "'We Are All Brothers in the Face of Starvation': Forging an Interethnic Working Class Movement in the 1894 Bituminous Coal Strike," *Mid-America* 83, no. 2 (2001): 121–54; Andrew B. Arnold, *Fueling the Gilded Age: Railroads, Miners, and Disorder in Pennsylvania Coal Country* (New York: New York University Press, 2014), 167–69.

5. Richard Jules Oestreicher, *Solidarity and Fragmentation: Working People and Class Consciousness in Detroit, 1875–1900* (Urbana: University of Illinois Press, 1986); James Green, *Death in the Haymarket: A Story of Chicago, the First Labor Movement, and the Bombing that Divided Gilded Age America* (New York: Pantheon Books, 2006); Susan E. Hirsch, *After the Strike: A Century of Labor Struggle at Pullman* (Urbana: University of Illinois Press, 2003); Kim Voss, *Making of American Exceptionalism: The Knights of Labor and Class Formation in the Nineteenth Century* (Ithaca: Cornell University Press, 1993).

6. Melton Alonza McLaurin, *The Knights of Labor in the South* (Westport: Greenwood, 1978); Elizabeth Sanders, *Roots of Reform: Farmers, Workers, and the American State, 1877–1917* (Chicago: University of Chicago Press, 1999), 45–51; Theresa Ann Case, "Losing the Middle Ground: Strikebreakers and Labor Protest on the Southwestern Railroads," in *Rethinking U.S. Labor History: Essays on the Working-Class Experience, 1756–2009*, ed. Donna T. Haverty-Stacke and Daniel J. Walkowitz (New York: Continuum, 2010): 54–81; Voss, *Making of American Exceptionalism*; Matthew Hild, *Greenbackers, Knights of Labor, and Populists: Farmer-Labor Insurgency in the Late-Nineteenth-Century South* (Athens: University of Georgia Press, 2007).

7. Daniel Nelson, *Shifting Fortunes: The Rise and Decline of American Labor, from the 1820s to the Present* (Chicago: Ivan R. Dee, 1997); Timothy Mitchell, *Carbon Democracy: Political Power in the Age of Oil* (New York: Verso, 2011), 20–21; James Green, *The Devil Is Here in These Hills: West Virginia's Coal Miners and Their Battle for Freedom* (New York: Atlantic Monthly Press, 2015); Julie Greene, *Pure and Simple Politics: The American Federation of Labor and Political Activism, 1881–1917* (New York: Cambridge University Press, 1998).

8. Nelson, *Shifting Fortunes*, 17–20; Maier B. Fox, *United We Stand*, 45–49; Arnold, *Fueling the Gilded Age*, 179–80; Merithew and Barrett, "'We Are All Brothers in the Face of Starvation'"; Jon Amsden and Stephen Brier, "Coal Miners on Strike: The Transformation of Strike Demands and the Formation of a National Union," *Journal of Interdisciplinary History* 2, no. 4 (1977): 583–616; Jörg Rössel, "Industrial Structure, Union Strategy,

and Strike Activity in American Bituminous Coal Mining, 1881–1894," *Social Science History* 26, no. 1 (2002): 1–32.

9. Joseph Gerteis, *Class and the Color Line: Interracial Class Coalition in the Knights of Labor and the Populist Movement* (Durham: Duke University Press, 2007); James Cobb, *Away Down South: A History of Southern Identity* (New York: Oxford University Press, 2005); Daniel Letwin, *The Challenge of Interracial Unionism: Alabama Coal Miners, 1878–1921* (Chapel Hill: University of North Carolina Press, 1998). An important exception to the frequent cross-occupational alliance is Hild, *Greenbackers, Knights of Labor, and Populists.*

10. "Old Residenter" to the editor, *UMWJ*, May 26, 1892.

11. "Old Ninety-Sixer" to the editor, *UMWJ*, July 9, 1891; P. H. Donnelly to the editor, *UMWJ*, December 31, 1891; M. J. Goings to the editor, *UMWJ*, October 22, 1891.

12. Frank Tobias Higbie, *Indispensable Outcasts: Hobo Workers and Community in the American Midwest, 1880–1930* (Urbana: University of Illinois Press, 2003).

13. Missouri labor commissioner Lee Meriwether, for example, conducted a nationwide survey of "scrip" payments in 1889, noting that laborers in nearly every rural industry did not receive their wages regularly. See Lee Meriwether report to Governor David R. Francis, *Eleventh Annual Report of the Bureau of Labor Statistics of the State of Missouri Being for the Year Ending November 5, 1889* (Jefferson City, MO: Tribune Printers and State Binders, 1889), 48, 51; "Fair Play," letter to the editor, and "Letter from Logan," *National Labor Tribune* (hereafter *NLT*), July 25, 1891; "Practical Christianity," reprinted from the *Farmer's Tribune* (Des Moines, Iowa), *NLT*, January 9, 1892; Richard Wilson testimony, The Cherokee & Pittsburg Coal & Mining Company v. Amelia Siplet, as the Administratrix of Alexis Siplet, deceased, case no. 10702, Supreme Court of the State of Kansas, 1896, Kansas State Historical Society, Topeka, 50–90; Alex Gourevitch, *From Slavery to Cooperative Commonwealth: Labor and Republican Liberty in the Nineteenth Century* (New York: Cambridge University Press, 2015).

14. Karin Shapiro, *A New South Rebellion: The Battle against Convict Labor in the Tennessee Coalfields, 1871–1896* (Chapel Hill: University of North Carolina Press, 1998); David Alan Corbin, *Life, Work, and Rebellion in the Coal Fields: The Southern West Virginia Miners, 1880–1922* (Urbana: University of Illinois Press, 1981). See also Nelson, *Shifting Fortunes*, 11–12.

15. "Incog" to the editor, *UMWJ*, November 21, 1895; "Vigo Kicker" to the editor, *UMWJ*, November 7, 1895; "Scot" to the editor, *UMWJ*, December 5, 1895.

16. Illinois Miners' Protective Association Official Report, "Illinois Miners," *NLT*, March 5, 1888; "Federation" to the editor, *NLT*, January 7, 1888; "Fifty Years a Union Miner" to the editor, *NLT*, July 9, 1887; "An Old Timer" to the editor, *NLT*, May 11, 1893.

17. S. T. Ryan to the editor, *UMWJ*, May 24, 1894; Philip Veal to the editor, *UMWJ*, June 28, 1894; James Bagnall to the editor, *UMWJ*, June 28, 1894.

18. John Lumb to the editor, *UMWJ*, December 28, 1893; "Makeshift" to the editor, *UMWJ*, May 3, 1894; "Justice" to the editor, *UMWJ*, July 5, 1894.

19. F. B. McGregor to the editor, *UMWJ*, July 19, 1894.

20. Hild, *Greenbackers, Knights of Labor, and Populists*, 176–78.

21. "The State of Trade," *Coal Trade Journal*, January 24, 1894; George A. Denison, "Suspension of Work in the Coal Mines," in *Work and Wages*, reprinted in *NLT*, January 1, 1887; Richard Jensen, *The Winning of the Midwest: Social and Political Conflict, 1888–1896* (Chicago: University of Chicago Press, 1971), 240–49.

22. "New Scheme," *St. Louis Post Dispatch* (hereafter *SLPD*), May 6, 1894; John Altgeld, *Live Questions* (Chicago: George S. Bowen and Son, 1899), 762.

23. "A Miner" to the editor, *UMWJ*, April 12, 1894 (quotation); "Sorehead" to the editor, *UMWJ*, May 10, 1894; "Addressed by Peffer," *Lawrence (KS) Daily Journal*, September 19, 1894; J. B. Bach, Ch'm, and Charles Bell to the editor, *UMWJ*, May 17, 1894; Charles Postel, *The Populist Vision* (New York: Oxford University Press, 2007); Benjamin F. Alexander, *Coxey's Army: Popular Protest in the Gilded Age* (Baltimore: Johns Hopkins University Press, 2015).

24. "Shorter Hours" to the editor, *NLT*, August 10, 1889; "J. D." to the editor, *NLT*, August 24, 1889; "Bob" to the editor, *NLT*, August 24, 1889; David Montgomery, "Workers' Control of Machine Production in the Nineteenth Century," in *Workers' Control in America* (New York: Cambridge University Press, 1979) 9–31; Herbert Gutman, "Work, Culture, and Society in Industrializing America, 1915–1919," in *Work, Culture, and Society in Industrializing America* (New York: Vintage Books, 1977): 3–78.

25. "Fairplay" to the editor, *UMWJ*, July 5, 1894; "The Poor Outcast Henry Flowerseed" to the editor, *UMWJ*, July 19, 1894; Hild, *Greenbackers, Knights of Labor, and Populists*, 178; Fox, *United We Stand*, 44; "Notice!" official UMW circular, *UMWJ*, May 10, 1894.

26. "Makeshift" to the editor, *UMWJ*, May 3, 1894; "Train Deserted," *Springfield (MO) Democrat*, April 28, 1894; "Threatened at Bevier," *SLPD*, May 9, 1894; "Working at Breeze," *SLPD*, May 9, 1894; "Out in Force," *SLPD*, May 9, 1894; "The Missouri Miners," *Pittsburg (KS) Daily Headlight*, May 18, 1894.

27. Chester McArthur Destler, "Consummation of a Labor-Populist Alliance in Illinois, 1894," *Mississippi Valley Historical Review* 27, no. 4 (1941): 589–602.

28. "The Macon Section," *SLPD*, April 22, 1894.

29. Destler, "Consummation of a Labor-Populist Alliance in Illinois, 1894."

30. Arnold, *Fueling the Gilded Age*; William A. Link, *The Paradox of Southern Progressivism, 1880–1930* (Chapel Hill: University of North Carolina Press, 1992).

31. "Justice" to the editor, *UMWJ*, July 5, 1894; "Blackbird" to the editor, *UMWJ*, July 12, 1894.

32. "Official Report," *UMWJ*, February 21, 1895.

33. "A Battle On," *SLPD*, May 25, 1894; D. H. Sullivan to the editor, *UMWJ*, August 22, 1895; G. W. Purcell to the editor, *UMWJ*, August 29, 1895; D. C. [name illegible] to the editor, *NLT*, August 29, 1895; "Cornfield Sailor" to the editor, *UMWJ*, November 28, 1895; D. E. Jones to the editor, *UMWJ*, July 18, 1895; Michael Ratchford to the editor, *UMWJ*, March 13, 1896.

34. "K of L" to the editor, *NLT*, February 19, 1887; Dan McLauchlan to the editor, *UMWJ*, May 21, 1891; "Mind Your Own Business" to the editor, *NLT*, June 15, 1893; "A Miner" to the editor, *UMWJ*, July 5, 1894; "A Miner" to the editor, *UMWJ*, August 9, 1894.

35. In an effort to become the miners' official mouthpiece (and make the UMW the miners' official organization) the *United Mine Workers' Journal* printed all letters submitted, creating a kind of forum open to union and nonunion miners and their wives. See "Fairplay" to the editor, *UMWJ*, July 5, 1894.

8

Southern Labor and the Lure of Populism

Workers and Power in North Carolina

DEBORAH BECKEL

Spreading across the country by the 1880s, the Knights of Labor (KOL) was the nation's largest, most inclusive labor union. It welcomed white and black, male and female workers, including industrial, domestic, and agricultural laborers, as well as craftsmen, small business owners, housewives, ministers, and teachers. At the same time, farmers' organizations, including black and white Farmers' Alliances, built massive national coalitions. As the United States became the world's leading industrial nation, corporations amassed wealth and power. Corporate lobbyists and the rich controlled the government, not the people who produced the wealth and goods. "We obtain in exchange for the most severe labor a salary which hardly prevents us from dying of hunger," the KOL charged, and demanded change.[1] Seeking to better their lives, millions of ordinary people became politicized. The KOL and the Farmers' Alliances provided organizational vehicles for grassroots leaders who felt that united action would bring economic fairness and political equality. By 1892 the KOL and farmers' organizations joined other national reform groups to create a new third party, the People's Party. Populists called for legislation, including the expansion of paper and silver currency supplies, short-term loans for farmers, and regulation of corporate privileges.

In 1894 and 1896, a biracial coalition of Populists and Republicans in North Carolina defeated the Democratic Party, which had ruled the post-Reconstruction South as the party of white supremacy. North Carolina was the only southern state to oust the Democrats from power in the

1890s. These victories occurred after Mississippi had pioneered the disfranchisement of most black and poorer white men in 1890.

As my research has shown, North Carolina's "Populist revolt" depended on collaboration with Republicans.[2] Founded in 1867 as an interracial organization, the state Republican Party promoted male political equality, workers' rights, educational opportunities, and free speech. African American men held about 70 percent of the Republican voting bloc. Women did not gain the vote in 1868, yet black families often considered the man's vote as a collective decision. Women participated in "parades, rallies, mass meetings, and conventions."[3] The party briefly held state power during Reconstruction. Republicans and their families suffered torture and murder perpetrated by Democrats, who reclaimed power in 1870. They passed laws restricting the rights of poorer blacks and whites. In the 1870s and 1880s, Republicans remained resilient by promoting coalitions with independent political factions (which they called "fusion"), but Democrats fought back with terror, electoral fraud, and gerrymandering. While black lawmakers in the General Assembly introduced bills to curtail abusive treatment of African Americans in landlord-tenant relations, apprenticeships, and prisons, these bills failed to pass.[4]

Using letters written by North Carolina's local KOL leaders to national KOL leaders in Philadelphia, this essay explores new ways of understanding the KOL and Populist coalitions.[5] It shows the complexities of labor-farm movements, their leaders, and the politics they advocated. The essay then explores race, class, and gender relations. Finally, it assesses the unique conditions in North Carolina and the consequences of the 1894–96 elections.

During the Gilded Age, American workers endured inhumane treatment and near-starvation conditions. Working twelve to sixteen hours a day in dangerous conditions, many laborers were paid when and how their employers chose. Often jobs were seasonal and unsteady. Many people traveled miles from home, looking for work. In eastern North Carolina most black workers labored on white-owned farms. They performed backbreaking work that contributed largely to the landowner's welfare. A KOL officer in Wilson County reported that wages for "Laber is verry lo here Mans get from $8 to $10 a monnth Woman get from $3 to $4 Dollars a monnth."[6] The KOL viewed this oppression as appalling.

The KOL vowed that changes would occur when workers educated themselves, united, and took political (but nonpartisan) action. Through traveling organizers, speakers, and publications, the KOL proclaimed that only adults should be employed, that they should receive a living wage for an eight-hour day in a safe environment, and that women should receive equal pay for equal work. Americans responded enthusiastically. The national KOL membership soared above seven hundred thousand by 1886. It rose so rapidly the officers could not track statistics. Consequently, local leaders organized KOL clubs, which national officers could authorize as official local assemblies ("locals") when time permitted. North Carolina KOL leaders promoted political action by 1886. The KOL represented both political parties, and advocates felt an influential mass movement could obtain prolabor legislation.[7]

Some Republicans and many old-guard Democrats tried to destroy the state KOL through sabotage, blackballing, evictions, vigilante terror, forceful prevention of voting, and racist accusations. KOL leaders conducted biracial state meetings, and some mixed-race KOL locals did exist. However, most white labor leaders advised organizers to form white Knights into separate locals before nearby black locals were founded. Opponents especially targeted the KOL organization of female African Americans, since black domestic workers had access to confidential information about whites. In addition, African American KOL women demanded freedom from their employers' sexual assaults, wage increases, and better working conditions.[8]

Some black KOL locals had to survive clandestinely, while others openly advocated labor rights. In 1886 Wilmington's black domestic servants and hotel waitresses organized KOL locals, but feared they would be fired if their identities were revealed.[9] Five years later, female Knights paraded through Wilmington's streets, wearing flower-adorned straw hats and long dresses with blue sashes. Dressed as ladies and riding in carriages, they "attracted much attention."[10] Whites decried such "uppity" behavior in blacks as a threat to southern civilization.

Family, church, and voluntary associations sustained activists. In 1889 in Edgecombe County, female members of St. Stephen's Colored Missionary Baptist Church and the Tarboro A.M.E. Zion Church held joint KOL meetings before church. The KOL women wore "holiday attire" and "white gloves," reflecting their respectability and the dignity of their cause. At the church service, the A.M.E. Zion minister enjoined everyone "to be faithful Knights, to be diligent in their duties, to be brotherly in their dealings with each other, to remember each other in the hour of need, and to discard forever the ways of traitors." Duties included labor and political action. After Republican Party and KOL leader F. U. Whitted offered a prayer, the choir sang "Work for the Night Is Coming."[11]

By the mid-1880s, labor and farm leaders were influential in North Carolina. They disseminated literature about their movements; listened to grassroots grievances; and built networks that extended across the state, the South, and the nation. Their motivations were complex and their organizational goals clashed. As a labor activist since the antebellum period and a postwar Republican, John Nichols became the head of the state biracial KOL in 1886. Enough black and white workers' votes were counted that year to elect him to Congress. Like many southerners who opposed the Democratic Party, he risked his life and endured frequent public censure. Nichols also gravitated to Republican patronage machines, state agricultural elites, and the fulfillment of his ambitions.[12] By contrast, L. L. Polk promoted a white farmers' movement in North Carolina before Farmers' Alliance agents arrived by 1887. Using his organizational connections, Polk became a state Alliance officer. In 1888 he announced in his popular *Progressive Farmer* newspaper that the black Farmers' Alliance was organizing. A well-known white supremacist who felt that black laborers received adequate wages, Polk warned that the Farmers' Alliances were segregated. His racial views were typical of white Alliancemen. Led by the prominent white Allianceman J. F. Payne in 1889, Democratic lawmakers passed a restrictive election law that Republicans charged would "reduce the blacks to a degraded position" and "disfranchise the laboring white man."[13]

For years Democrats had accused Republicans of advocating black rule. To prove their white-supremacist loyalties, many white Republicans claimed that Democrats were more "Negrophile" than they. During the 1888 campaign, white Republican Daniel Russell Jr. called blacks "largely savages."[14] Other white Republicans accused Democrats of appointing black officials and creating the "Black Second" Congressional District in eastern North Carolina through gerrymandering. This district then voted black men into Congress, they charged. In fact, four African Americans from the "Black Second" were elected to Congress from the 1870s to the 1890s, including the prominent Republican George Henry White, who introduced the first federal antilynching bill.[15] Black Republicans excoriated white Republican racism. By 1890 leading black men joined the national Afro-American League, which advocated race pride and solidarity, economic programs, and political agitation and action. State leaders of the League denounced both major political parties as "untrue" to African Americans, who must now unite as a race to gain their "constitutional rights."[16] However, elite blacks sometimes disagreed over political strategies and criticized "unworthy" (lower-class) blacks for causing negative images of the race.

In December 1889 L. L. Polk became president of the southern Farmers' Alliance at its St. Louis, Missouri, meeting. There the white Alliance and the biracial KOL joined forces with reform groups representing millions of Americans. They advocated passage of national laws to benefit farmers and workers. The black Farmers' Alliance preferred a more autonomous affiliation with the confederation, since they differed markedly on key issues. Black rights were badly compromised, not only by white political leaders, but also by white farm and labor leaders.[17] Yet some Knights and Alliancemen felt the St. Louis agreement authorized them to take political action to achieve their demands.[18]

By 1890 the North Carolina KOL and the two Alliances boasted a total membership of over 165,000. The KOL had lost members due to poverty, economic coercion, terror, and political losses.[19] However, with the number of voters in the state at about 300,000, the farmer-labor movements potentially had great influence. The KOL facilitated cooperation among the three organizations by arranging separate meetings with the black and white Alliances. They advocated state legislation increase public school taxes, since 25 percent of white North Carolinians were illiterate and black illiteracy was over twice that high.[20] About that time, the national KOL's top officer, Terence Powderly, told L. L. Polk that the KOL would soon vote on "independent political action."[21] This decision would plunge these divided movements into cutthroat party politics.

Meanwhile, eastern North Carolina KOL leaders had persuaded national KOL officer John Hayes to fund the work of their "much beloved" and charismatic organizer, Ellen Williams, by appointing her a KOL *Journal* subscription agent. In convincing Hayes (who was white), they referred him to George Tonnoffski, a longtime white state KOL officer who knew about Williams's legendary recruiting skills. Running for Congress in 1890, Tonnoffski met Ellen Williams that January at the state KOL assembly in Edgecombe County. She arrived as the exclusively male delegates were deliberating. Calling a recess, they granted her an audience and prominent black Knights took charge. F. U. Whitted introduced Williams.

She voiced optimism about the state KOL, provided that male leaders made "prudent and wise" decisions. George Scurlock, also a congressional candidate, took the floor. Widely known as a leader in the North Carolina Industrial Association (NCIA), one of the few state organizations under African American control, Scurlock successfully moved that the North Carolina KOL also fund Ellen Williams's work.[22]

As a KOL *Journal* subscription agent, Ellen Williams asked John Hayes to ship copies of the *Journal* to eastern North Carolina, where she was organizing men and women, including religious leaders, laborers, business owners, and farmers. In addition, Williams served as the top officer ("Master Workman") of her mixed-gender local in Wilson County. While she traveled, the local's other officers stayed busy, scraping together money for orphans and widows and to pay their KOL dues. They also aided striking workers.[23]

Leading white Farmers' Allianceman Elias Carr was one of the Edgecombe County plantation owners who faced striking workers who demanded subsistence wages. KOL leaders vowed not to "work for less than fifty cents per day and board, nor pick cotton for less than forty cents per hundred pounds." Visiting the county sheriff, W. T. Knight, who was also a plantation owner, KOL leaders stated that any non-striking KOL member would receive "a heavy penalty." When Sheriff Knight refused to raise wages, KOL leaders promised to "eat tadpoles and frogs before they would work for less." Strikers brought in a Pitt County activist to inspire them to stay determined, regardless of dangers. However, after other landowners refused to increase wages, some KOL members began working again. The county Democratic newspaper claimed that "pleasant relations" had characterized labor relations. In fact, planters demonstrated their power using threats, incarcerations, and evictions to break the strike.[24]

Alarmed, Elias Carr also witnessed massive emigration of black working families from North Carolina. The emigrations followed systematic discrimination and exploitation by elite Democrats like Carr, who seemed surprised by the exodus. He contacted a white Arkansas Agricultural Wheel officer, who explained that plantation owners were sending labor agents east. As for the black laborers in Arkansas, "Ninety nine Out of every one hundred are . . . pushed[,] driven[,] and worked harder than they were when we had them as slaves."[25] Carr may have thought that the black Farmers' Alliance would exert a better influence on black workers than the KOL could. After conferring with R. M. Humphrey, a white southerner who was head of the national black Farmers' Alliance, Elias Carr contacted W. A. Pattillo, the leading black Allianceman in North Carolina.[26] A former slave, Pattillo became an ordained minister and Shaw University graduate who developed extensive cross-class religious, educational, charitable, agricultural, and political networks in North Carolina. Rising to regional prominence in the 1880s as an Alliance leader, he issued the *Alliance Advocate* newspaper for North Carolina, Virginia, and Georgia.[27] Establishing cordial relations with Humphrey and other white leaders in the black Alliance, he became North Carolina's primary lecturer and organizer. Organizing across the state, Pattillo introduced himself to local white politicians and Alliancemen, which fostered his work and minimized repercussions from powerful whites.[28]

As a black female laborer, Ellen Williams was treated differently. In June 1891 Williams left the Wilson County plantation where her family lived. When the overseer spotted her on the road, he "ordered" her to stop. Officers at her KOL local reported the incident to John Hayes in Philadelphia and requested that he publish it in the national KOL *Journal*. The overseer demanded that Williams "take up her a hoe and go to the field" to work. She "stood up" to him "like a brave woman amid [his] oaths & curses" and told him "that she would suffer her head removed from her shoulders" rather than cease promoting labor rights, which were "for the good of all the people and Just honourable & right." After Williams refused to be "subdued to his will," the overseer evicted her family. Initially, she stopped organizing workers, but soon found "a shelter again." After risking her life, Ellen Williams again pursued her mission of helping "suffering humanity."[29]

Meanwhile, W. A. Pattillo expanded into national networks. He connected with T. Thomas Fortune, also a former slave, a newspaper publisher, and a National Afro-American Council founder.[30] North Carolina black leaders regularly contributed to Fortune's influential *New York Age* newspaper, where their opinions did not trigger southern white retaliation. Pattillo participated in the early national conventions that called for a third party and was a leader at the rousing 1892 St. Louis conference, when Populists issued a "Second Declaration of Independence" for Americans.[31] At St. Louis, Populists sought Albion Tourgée's help in writing resolutions on race relations. This indicated how expansive the movement had become theoretically. Tourgée had been a key white radical Republican in North Carolina during Reconstruction. But 1892 in St. Louis was not 1868 in Raleigh: reform leaders avoided addressing Tourgée's recommendations.[32] The KOL was strongly represented at the national People's Party's official organization in Omaha in July 1892, when Populists denounced the extremes of wealth and poverty in America. The national KOL endorsed the People's Party.[33]

As the People's Party emerged, southern Knights and Alliancemen considered whether to change parties. Most African Americans were loyal Republicans, while many whites were staunch Democrats. As national white Alliance leader L. L. Polk spoke before enthusiastic audiences across America, he became the likely Populist presidential candidate. Some North Carolina Populist leaders criticized Polk for failing to back the state People's Party initially, but many Alliance Democrats were outraged by his third-party advocacy.[34] Conservative Democrats saw party defections as threatening the social hierarchy that they maintained with coercion and violence. By May 1892 Polk crowed, "We will carry at least eight of the Southern states into the electoral college in favor of the People's Party ticket."[35] After he died that June, Populists selected as presidential candidate J. B. Weaver, who postponed his acceptance in order "to study the Southern situation."[36]

In North Carolina Marion Butler, president of the white state Farmers' Alliance, watched as Alliancemen split into combative Democratic and Populist camps. He supported Democrat Elias Carr for governor in 1892. Butler was surprised when Sampson County Populists informed him that they would win with him or without him.[37] Butler switched parties to lead his county's Populist convention that July. His fiancée, Florence Faison, soon warned him to repudiate the Democratic Party. After "the abuse you have received," she asserted "I will think you are crazy to vote for anyone they have," she asserted. As for herself, she said, "*I would die before I would vote for them*."[38] She told Butler that he should have supported "the people" initially. Keeping his options open, Marion Butler continued to associate with Democrats, including Alphonso Avery, a former Klan leader and state supreme court justice who opposed black voting rights.[39]

In 1892 Frank Johnson publicly announced that with Populist help, a Republican-led coalition could "whip" state Democrats. As a state KOL organizer, Johnson had once explained to Terence Powderly that when African Americans received unfair treatment, they suspected "a white man Trick."[40] The People's Party was not a white man's trick, Johnson reasoned, since some biracial county Populist conventions had nominated black candidates for office and the KOL was caucusing with Alliance Populists in some areas.[41] Coalition leaders had to attract African American voters in pivotal eastern counties, and one Knight correctly predicted that Populists did not have enough black support in 1892.[42]

Meanwhile, southern Knights had initiated new organizing drives.[43] Texas black Alliance leader, J. B. Rayner, a native North Carolinian, advised white national Alliance leaders that southern blacks would support a prolabor party if it were organized through the KOL. Alliance leaders put Rayner in touch with national KOL leaders.[44] Populism and Republican-Populist fusion became more popular in North Carolina by 1893, when the "free silver" fervor swept the country and people hoped that greater circulation of silver currency would revive the economy. By 1893 North Carolinians organized Silver Clubs and KOL officers collected signatures on "free silver" petitions. They sent them to national KOL leaders, who presented the petitions to Congressmen. A Pitt County KOL leader collected over one hundred names on one petition, stating that "all of the Citizens" in eastern North Carolina wanted free silver.[45] Voters' rage focused on the goldbug Democratic president Grover Cleveland as the country's worst economic depression hit.

In 1893 national KOL officer John Hayes visited North Carolina to encourage organization and political advocacy.[46] Hayes shipped copies of the People's Party platform to KOL leaders without access to newspapers. Ellen Williams and other KOL leaders told Hayes that they needed more organizers and Hayes authorized more appointments.[47] At that time J. R. Sovereign became the national KOL head. A craftsman from a farm background, he advocated KOL–Farmers' Alliance cooperation.[48] Marion Butler, the white national Farmers' Alliance president and a leading Populist, met with Sovereign to plan KOL-Alliance cooperation.[49] After the American Railway Union affiliated with the national KOL in mid-1894, Sovereign reported that KOL strength was growing throughout the country.[50]

In 1894 John Hayes contacted KOL leaders in twenty-two North Carolina counties that lay east of Raleigh, where Ellen Williams focused her organizing. He instructed them to choose delegates for a mandatory convention at Goldsboro on June 9. A national KOL representative would help them organize a district assembly. Hayes did not tell delegates to locate the national KOL leader, but instead he instructed them to find Populist Marion Butler.[51] The meetings between Butler and black KOL leaders occurred as the fusion campaign heated up. Hayes again contacted these leaders asking them to assemble on July 7, 1894, in James City, a primarily black coastal community. A large African American convention would not attract much attention in James City, where H. H. Perry, a minister and black Alliance leader, had built African American support for white Alliance political candidates. Ellen Williams had also organized the KOL in James City.[52] Hayes exhorted, "I should like so much to see North Carolina organized and prepared for the coming struggle [the election]."[53]

In 1894 the Populist state executive committee authorized Marion Butler to facilitate Republican-Populist fusion. The Populist platform called for fairer state election laws and local self-government. In an additional effort to gain black support, Populists endorsed a four-month public school term for all children. Other planks included free silver, abolition of national banks, direct election of U.S. senators, federal regulation of producers' interests, and restricted immigration. The grassroots crusade to defeat the Democrats overpowered state Populist and Republican leaders' efforts to direct the coalition. After their stunning upset victory, fusionists took control of the state legislature in 1895. Meanwhile, KOL organizers, including Ellen Williams, kept promoting the KOL. A Wilson County labor leader reported that the KOL was "on a boom."[54]

In 1895 fusionists passed new election laws and African American voting jumped to almost 90 percent. Interest rates were reduced to 6 percent. Elias Carr and many other state Democratic Party leaders endorsed "free silver," in an attempt to coopt or cooperate with Populists or bring them back to the Democratic fold.[55] By 1896 Carr stated that the politicization of the Farmers' Alliance had caused a "Stench in the nostrils of all good people."[56] His fears heightened as Republican-Populist fusionists proved victorious again in 1896 and elected Daniel Russell as governor. In the General Assembly, North Carolina's tobacco, textile, and railroad industries flexed their lobbying muscle, as did plantation owners. When black legislator William Henderson introduced indispensable legislation to redress the poverty and abuse of tenant farmers, laborers, and domestics during the 1896–97 legislative session, his bill did not pass.[57]

Determined to reclaim state power, Democrats demanded white-supremacist solidarity and the disfranchisement of African American men. Both demands were enforced by power, vigilante terror, and paramilitary violence. After Democrats won the 1898 state election, elite white Democrats forced a coup against Wilmington's fusionist government officials.

Wielding machine guns, these white insurrection leaders, followed by a white mob, burned black-owned businesses and houses. They murdered over thirty African Americans. At least fourteen black leaders and their families were banished from Wilmington, in addition to seven white fusion leaders.[58] State Democrats proceeded to study the most effective ways to disenfranchise African American men.

Historians have thought the state KOL became a black organization by 1887 and two years later "ceased to function as an effective organization in North Carolina."[59] I argue that the KOL was a remarkably resilient organization that included men and women, black and white, poor and middle-class North Carolinians. In 1890 the state KOL provided a connecting link between the segregated Farmers' Alliances. Working with national leaders, the KOL led organizational drives throughout the 1890s and collaborated with Populists and fusionists to effect political and economic change. In the process local labor leaders pushed state and national leaders to be more assertive in adopting a prolabor agenda.

Historians have believed that black Populist and fusion supporters in eastern North Carolina left "little written record of their Populist involvement" and found their "voice" only "with their votes."[60] I argue that black KOL leaders documented their lives, their grievances, their demands, and their contributions by writing to KOL officers at the national headquarters. KOL members documented their resistance to slavery-like exploitation. Female KOL members gained public attention when they became leaders, denounced sexual assaults, claimed public spaces, and dressed as they wished. Local labor leaders documented their petition drives, their educational and charitable contributions, and their attempts to buy land. They documented their support for KOL strikers. They recorded their connections with whites who were committed to the KOL cause. These leaders also reported to northern leaders and newspapers.[61] They urged white and black northerners to see their cooperative efforts toward change and how some southern whites were sabotaging free labor, representative government, and Christian values.

Populism found strength in North Carolina and Georgia in black-majority as well white-majority localities. Without black support, North Carolina Populists "would have amounted to merely a blip on the political scene," historian Joe Creech affirmed.[62] Populists in North Carolina and Georgia were stronger than those in South Carolina and Virginia,[63] but historians have thought that Marion Butler did not court African

Americans as Georgian Tom Watson did.[64] Butler maintained his white-supremacist credentials and did not publicly mention his meetings with black KOL leaders. Revealing those connections would have left him open to attacks.[65] Historians often portray Marion Butler as the key to fusion success.[66] But his power derived from his coalition-building and a network of dedicated Republicans and Populists of both races.

Charles Postel and Omar Ali describe "two separate Populisms—one black, one white."[67] Most white Populists and Republicans condoned racial discrimination and exploitation. Many whites were blind to their society's racism because they were immersed in it. Both black and white labor activists monitored the "color line," sometimes contesting it, at other times reinforcing it.[68] The conceptualization of racially distinct Populist movements dismisses the diverse, complicated interracial relationships in these movements and the complexities of class and gender. Black and white leaders made connections to facilitate their goals, although their goals differed. The labor and fusion movements mirrored societal hierarchies of race, class, and gender, but to varying extents. Ellen Williams's unofficial appearance at the all-male state KOL assembly provides one example. Elite and middle-class activists benefited from the exploitation of women and children.

The conditions that fostered the Democratic Party's defeat in 1890s North Carolina were unique to the state. Populism's success depended on the help of Republicans and labor rights activists. The postwar Republican Party had served as a vehicle for ambitious men of both races who had been excluded from traditional channels of power. It attracted more whites than did other southern Republican parties, which enhanced its legitimacy in a racist society. Republican leaders had honed cooperative arrangements with independent political factions opposed to Democratic Party policies. Their goals included fair elections and expanded voting rights, which became the core agenda of the 1890s fusionists. By 1892, when the People's Party was formed, many Republican Party leaders had over twenty years of coalition-building experience. Political and labor leaders knew that ordinary people were becoming engaged citizens, but race and class divisions rendered their coalitions fragile.[69] The fusionists did not champion a prolabor agenda. The repercussions of the Democratic Party's 1898 retaliation were devastating. Elite white Democrats held the weapons of power and re-enforced the social hierarchy according to their race, class, and gender dictates.

Notes

1. *Journal of United Labor*, in *Radical Reform: Interracial Politics in Post-Emancipation North Carolina*, by Deborah Beckel (Charlottesville: University of Virginia Press, 2011), 117. Thanks to Jim Hunt, Bart Shaw, Nancy Putzel, the editors, and the press's readers for their helpful comments.

2. Beckel, *Radical Reform*, 209–10.

3. E. B. Brown, "To Catch the Vision of Freedom: Reconstructing Southern Black Women's Political History, 1865–1880," in *Unequal Sisters: A Multicultural Reader in U.S. Women's History*, 3rd ed., ed. Vicki L. Ruiz and Ellen Carol DuBois (New York: Routledge, 2000), 129, 133; E. B. Brown, "Negotiating and Transforming the Public Sphere: African American Political Life in the Transition from Slavery to Freedom," in *Jumpin' Jim Crow: Southern Politics from Civil War to Civil Rights*, ed. Jane Dailey, Glenda Elizabeth Gilmore, and Bryant Simon (Princeton: Princeton University Press, 2000), 38–39.

4. Beckel, *Radical Reform*, 3, 97, 214n, 216n.

5. The papers of Terence Powderly and John Hayes, Catholic University of America, American Catholic History Research Center (CUA-ACHRC) (hereafter, respectively, Powderly Papers and Hayes Papers). The CUA-ACHRC Dorothy Mohler Travel Grant aided my research.

6. Amos Whittey to John Hayes, July 13, 1889, Hayes Papers.

7. Ellen Williams to John Hayes, October 22, 1890, Hayes Papers; Beckel, *Radical Reform*, 124–26.

8. *Journal of United Labor*, July 23, August 27, October 8, November 12, 19, 26, December 3, 10, 24, 1887; John Ray to Terence Powderly, November 9, 1886, John Nichols to Powderly, November 9, 1886, Powderly Papers.

9. Thomas Barnwell and Newel P. Davenport to Powderly, January 6, 1887, Hillard F. McNair and Powell Battle to Powderly, March 22, 1888, W. M. McCathern and others to Powderly, December 2, 1888, Powderly Papers; *Morning Star* (Wilmington), June 18, 1886.

10. *Wilmington Messenger*, September 4, 1891.

11. *Journal of United Labor*, July 11, 1889.

12. Beckel, *Radical Reform*, chs. 6 and 7.

13. Beckel, *Radical Reform*, 142–43, 150.

14. *Raleigh Signal*, June 21, July 19, 1888, in Beckel, *Radical Reform*, 148, 185.

15. John H. Haley, *Charles N. Hunter and Race Relations in North Carolina* (Chapel Hill: University of North Carolina Press, 1987), 71–72; Beckel, *Radical Reform*, 188.

16. *New York Age*, March 29, 1890.

17. R. H. Morehead to Elias Carr, April 26, 1889, Elias Carr Papers, East Carolina University, Greenville, NC (hereafter Carr Papers).

18. Moore County Farmers' Alliance Record Book (Meeting Minute Book), [1890?], Richard Street Papers, North Carolina State Archives, Raleigh.

19. *Tarboro Southerner*, January 30, 1890; Beckel, *Radical Reform*, 146.

20. Beckel, *Radical Reform*, 153–54, 245n.

21. Terence Powderly to L. L. Polk, October 11, 1890, Powderly Papers.

22. Robert Dawson to John Hayes, October 11, 1889, Hayes to Dawson, March 16, 1890, Hilliard Brasswell to Hayes, April 7, 1890, Resolutions, LA 10, 851, September 23, 1891, Hayes Papers; Beckel, *Radical Reform*, 146, 162; *Proceedings of the Fifth Annual Session of the State Assembly of North Carolina Knights of Labor* (Raleigh: E. M. Uzzell, 1890), 15, 19; Lala Carr Steelman, *The North Carolina Farmers' Alliance: A Political History, 1887–1893* (Greenville: East Carolina University Publications, 1985), 108.

23. Ellen Williams, Journal of United Labor Subscription List, June 16, 1890, Williams to John Hayes, August [?], September 1, October 22, 1890, Williams and Robert Dawson to Hayes, February 23, 1891, Dawson to Hayes, January 4, 1892, Hayes Papers.

24. *Tarboro Southerner*, September 12, 1889.

25. R. H. Morehead to Elias Carr, April 26, 1889, Carr Papers.

26. J. J. Rogers to Elias Carr, April 30, May 17, 1891, Carr Papers.

27. W. A. Pattillo to Elias Carr, April [10?], May 2, June [7?], 1891, Carr Papers; Beckel, *Radical Reform*, 142–46, 165.

28. W. A. Pattillo to Elias Carr, May 2, 1891 (see interlined word "white"), Pattillo to Carr, June [7?], 1891, Carr Papers.

29. Jesse Artis and others, notice for the *Journal of the Knights of Labor*, [June 1, 1891], Hayes Papers.

30. *New York Age*, December 22, 1888.

31. *New York Times*, December 16, 1890; Omar Ali, *In the Lion's Mouth: Black Populism in the New South, 1886–1900* (Jackson: University Press of Mississippi, 2010), 76, 87, 91.

32. W. E. Turner to Albion Tourgée, January 29, 1892, cited in Otton Olsen, *Carpetbagger's Crusade: The Life of Albion Winegar Tourgée* (Baltimore: Johns Hopkins University Press, 1965), 320.

33. Robert E. Weir, *Beyond Labor's Veil: The Culture of the Knights of Labor* (University Park: Pennsylvania State University Press, 1996), 15; Nick Salvatore, *Eugene V. Debs: Citizen and Socialist*, 2nd ed. (Urbana: University of Illinois Press, 2007; first published 1982), 126.

34. T. B. Lindsay to L. L. Polk, April 2, 1892, Polk Papers, Southern Historical Collection, University of North Carolina, Chapel Hill (hereafter SHC); S. B. Alexander to Elias Carr, May 23, 1891, Carr Papers.

35. L. L. Polk to Terence V. Powderly, May 24, 1892, in Powderly Papers.

36. Theodore Saloutos, *Farmer Movements in the South, 1865–1933* (Lincoln: University of Nebraska Press, 1960), 134.

37. James L. Hunt, *Marion Butler and American Populism* (Chapel Hill: University of North Carolina Press, 2003), 48.

38. Florence Faison to Marion Butler, September 18, 1892, in Steelman, *North Carolina Farmers' Alliance*, 230–31.

39. Alphonso Avery to Marion Butler, April 8, 1892, Butler Papers, SHC; Marion Butler to Alphonso Avery, May 18, 1896, Alphonso C. Avery Papers, SHC; Beckel, *Radical Reform*, 68, 172–73, 251n.

40. Frank Johnson to Terence Powderly, February 14, 1887, in Beckel, *Radical Reform*, 124.

41. *Raleigh Signal*, October 6, 13, 1892; *News and Observer* (Raleigh), Sept 1, 24, 1892;

J. Kelly Turner and Jonathan L. Bridgers Jr., *History of Edgecombe County North Carolina* (Raleigh: Edwards & Broughton, 1920), 295–97.

42. Turner and Bridgers, *History of Edgecombe County*, 300; John H. Battle to John Hayes, September 22, 1892, Hayes Papers; Jonathan Garlock, comp., *Guide to the Local Assemblies of the Knights of Labor* (Westport, CT: Greenwood, 1982), 355.

43. W. H. Mullen to Terence Powderly, March 3, 20, 1890, Powderly Papers.

44. J. B. Rayner to C. W. Macune, November 12, 1891, Powderly Papers.

45. M. C. Gorham to John Hayes, November 6, 1893, Freeman Wilson and L. E. Bass to Hayes, November 8, 1893, Hayes Papers.

46. John Hayes to George C. Young, [December 1891?], Hayes to John H. Battle, June 4, 1894, Gray Newsome to [Hayes], May 20, 1895, M. C. Gorham to Hayes, January 4, 1895, Hayes to M. C. Gorham, February 1, 1895, William Jolley Bell to J. R. Sovereign, 1895?, Ellen Williams to Hayes, July 17, 1893, Hayes Papers.

47. John Hayes to John H. Battle, October 7, 1892, Ellen Williams to Hayes, July 17, 1893, Hayes Papers.

48. J. R. Sovereign to Terence Powderly, January 20, 1891, Sovereign to Powderly, February 13, 1892, Powderly Papers.

49. *Caucasian*, May 17, June 7, 14, 1894.

50. Eugene V. Debs to Terence Powderly, November 12, 1891, Powderly Papers; Salvatore, *Eugene V. Debs*, 126; J. R. Sovereign to Powderly, January 29, 1894, John Hayes to Powderly, December 15, 1893, Powderly Papers.

51. John Hayes to Gray Newsome, June 4, 1894, Hayes to Howard Gray, June 4, 1894, Hayes to Marcus C. Gorham, June 4, 1894, Hayes to John H. Battle, June 4, 1894, Hayes to J. F. Hines, June 4, 1894, Hayes to James F. Foster, June 9, 21, 1894, Hayes Papers.

52. H. H. Perry to Elias Carr, September 22, 1890, in Steelman, *North Carolina Farmers' Alliance*, 106; Ellen Williams to John Hayes, October 14, 1890, Hayes Papers.

53. John Hayes to Gray Newsome, June 21, 1894, Hayes to Howard Gray, June 21, 1894, Hayes to Marcus C. Gorham, [June 1894], June 25, 1894, Hayes to John H. Battle, June 21, 1894, Hayes to J. F. Hines, June 21, 1894, Hayes Papers.

54. Ransom Howell to John Hayes, June 29, 1895, Gray Newsome to Hayes, April 18, 1896, Hayes Papers.

55. Marion Butler to Alphonso Avery, May 18, 1896, J. J. Mott to Alphonso Avery, May 25, 1896, Avery Papers, SHC.

56. Sol Reid to Elias Carr, January 27, 1896, Carr Papers.

57. Beckel, *Radical Reform*, 97, 153, 255n.

58. Beckel, *Radical Reform*, 199–200.

59. I. J. Ellis to John Hayes, August 29, 1891, April 15, 1893, Hayes Papers. For different views, see David Silkenat, "'Hard Times Is the Cry': Debt in Populist Thought in North Carolina," in *Populism in the South Revisited: New Interpretations and New Departures*, ed. James M. Beeby (Jackson: University Press of Mississippi, 2012), 113; Melton A. McLaurin, *The Knights of Labor in the South* (Westport, CT: Greenwood, 1978). Omar Ali, *In the Lion's Mouth*, states the southern KOL was part of Black Populism. But black Knights were prolabor Republicans and Independents in 1886–88 (*Journal of United Labor*, December 24, 1887).

60. Joe Creech, *Righteous Indignation: Religion and the Populist Revolution* (Urbana: University of Illinois Press, 2006), 136.

61. White Republican leader J.C.L. Harris wrote more candidly to northern than to southern newspapers.

62. Creech, *Righteous Indignation*, 136.

63. Barton C. Shaw, *The Wool-Hat Boys: Georgia's Populist Party* (Baton Rouge: Louisiana State University Press, 1984), 162. See also Matthew Hild, *Greenbackers, Knights of Labor, and Populists: Farmer-Labor Insurgency in the Late-Nineteenth-Century South* (Athens: University of Georgia Press, 2007); Joseph Gerteis, *Class and the Color Line: Interracial and Class Coalition in the Knights of Labor and Populist Movement* (Durham: Duke University Press, 2007).

64. Charles Postel, *The Populist Vision* (New York: Oxford University Press, 2007), 197.

65. See issues of Butler's *Caucasian* and Whitehurst [?] to Marion Butler, January 7, 1894, Marion Butler Papers, SHC.

66. Postel, *Populist Vision*, 197.

67. Postel, *Populist Vision*, 41–42; Ali, *In the Lion's Mouth*, 180.

68. Gerteis, *Class and the Color Line*, 202, states that the KOL and Populists thought the color line could be overcome.

69. Beckel, *Radical Reform*, 3, 6, 88, 100, 104, 209–10.

9

The Appalachian "Gunmen of Capitalism"

T.R.C. HUTTON

Thanks to PBS's 2016 broadcast of the *American Experience* miniseries "The Mine Wars," the labor struggles of World War I–era West Virginia have reentered the public imagination. The series' narrative stretched from the 1912 Paint Creek/Cabin Creek strike, the first major coal-related labor dispute in West Virginia's history, to the Battle of Blair Mountain in 1921, what some call the largest armed uprising in U.S. history save southern secession—although the New York Draft Riot (1863) and the nationwide railroad strike in 1877 may be more deserving of this honorific. Colorful figures like labor organizers Bill Blizzard, Frank Keeney, and Mother Jones were featured, and the producers made a special effort to include the voices of the rank-and-file miners who fought and died for the right to organize. The miniseries is the most comprehensive popular media presentation on this subject since John Sayles's theatrical *Matewan* (1987), and it was accompanied by the most thorough historical approach to Appalachian labor history in decades, *The Devil Is Here in These Hills*, by the late James Green.[1]

Among the constant antagonists in both book and miniseries were the hired guns of the Baldwin-Felts Detective Agency, an organization familiar, at least by name, to Americans with a cursory knowledge of labor history. Historians of the "mine wars" have rightly recognized the agency as the definitive tool of capital in Progressive-era West Virginia, while more than one have also acknowledged the agency's "legitimate" function as a peacekeeping entity.[2] As Richard Hadsell and William Coffey described it, Baldwin-Felts "functioned as a civilizing or at least stabilizing force in the absence of adequate public law enforcement," while it also "carried out policies of brutal repression which helped to incite some of the nation's most violent industrial conflicts."[3] The agency and its early years have gone largely unexplored, suggesting that the agency simply emerged from the proverbial foreheads of capitalists to oppose a worker-controlled minefield. Baldwin-Felts actually formed separately from its eventual industrial clients, and, unlike most of them, it was not an invasive outsider from the North or Midwest. In a sense, the Baldwin-Felts Detective Agency was somewhat the opposite, in that it infiltrated Appalachia *from the South.* It was a native species, founded by opportunistic members of the white southern middle class. Although it was an imitation of northern organizations like the Pinkerton agency, its tactics and motivations reflected the region's own peculiar pathway from an agrarian economy into an industrial one.[4] The primary services it provided, surveillance and violence, had been the primary means of labor control in the South since the days of slavery.

It was during this period that German sociologist Max Weber famously defined the state as whatever body monopolizes legitimate violence. But, as much as he considered the modern state and capitalism, Weber did not consider the cases in which states give up their capacity for violence to capitalists. In certain times and places, the state—be it a nation-state, an American state or perhaps even a rural American county (the state structure that affected American lives more than any other before the New Deal and arguably afterward)—has given up its control over violence and has allowed private interests to monopolize it on their own when profits were at stake. In the antebellum South, states ceded this capacity to the plantation system, in which the disciplining and punishing of labor required a constancy of violence. The nearness of planter and slave made it so that an intermediary was not always needed, and the overseer position was always a common wage-earning job but never a profession.

Baldwin-Felts offered a modern, professionalized version of what was once the domain of overseers and slave patrols before the Civil War, and Klansmen and state militias after Emancipation.[5] The detective agency was not simply a functionary of its industrial clients. It was a massive business enterprise that, at its height, employed hundreds—perhaps even thousands—of men hired from the same labor supply as were the workers they were used to oppress. The agency's role in the "Mine Wars" during the 1910s was its occupational apex, but nevertheless only a portion of a much longer story. In fact, as the name "Mine Wars" suggests something like a state of parity between adversaries, this period was somewhat exceptional in that workers put up a fight against the agency's authority. In decades before and after, a time when publicly funded law enforcement was limited to the county or municipal level in both states, this detective agency was arguably the most wide-ranging, and therefore most powerful, law enforcement agency in the South.

The organization that became Baldwin-Felts began with the career of William G. Baldwin, a Confederate officer's son born shortly before the Civil War in Tazewell County, Virginia. Baldwin was part of a commercial middle class in a section of the United States that had long nurtured "middling" farmers, but few other occupations that constituted what geographer Mary Beth Pudup has called an "indigenous vanguard class."[6] As most of the country was embarking upon the reckless financial adventures of the Gilded Age, mountaineers either fled their region or huddled into risk aversion.[7] By the end of the nineteenth century, many who chose the latter course were obliged to sell their homesteads to timber and coal companies that were finding more and more potential in places like Tazewell County. Like most of the Gilded Age middle class, Baldwin avoided these downfalls by finding his portion with capitalists. His predecessor whom he patterned himself after, Allan Pinkerton, had built his reputation as a sleuth from being Abraham Lincoln's spymaster during the Civil War. As the son of a rebel soldier, Baldwin probably considered himself a southern analog to the Unionist detective—though he was usually paid with northern capital.

The Baldwin family relocated, but not far. Baldwin's father moved at least part of the family to West Virginia in 1885, first to Charleston and then later back south to the state-line town of Bluefield.[8] At some point before 1890 William Baldwin began working for the Charleston-based Eureka Detective Agency, an organization run by Alfred Burnett, a colorful newspaperman who occasionally ran for local public office.[9] In 1888 Baldwin became a shareholder in Eureka and used his employer's company to form his own investigative concern after Burnett's death in 1892.[10] With Burnett, and after his tutelage, Baldwin discovered West Virginia's growing demand for the creation of a business-friendly disciplined landscape very unlike the sylvan farm and forest society that had existed in the southern part of the state until the Reconstruction era. Baldwin was an especial asset for Eureka since he grew up just across the state line from an area of West Virginia that had suddenly become valuable. Recently arrived businessmen relied on Burnett and Baldwin to hunt down moonshiners who exploited the demand for distilled spirits in new timber camps and mine villages.[11]

Eureka's greatest triumph was the capture of Cap Hatfield, a local "feudist," who represented to many the old, precapitalist order of the mountains.[12] Although Hatfield probably did not constitute a "social outlaw" in Eric Hobsbawm's famous phrasing, many observers considered his presence a barrier to enlightenment and industrial progress (his surname's association with the so-called Hatfield-McCoy feud inflated his significance but also proved to many Americans that West Virginia's natural resources could not be properly harnessed until its native population was tamed). It was not the sort of urban labor discipline perfected by the Pinkerton agency since the 1860s. It was an attempt to prepare southern West Virginia for its industrial future by eliminating whatever small amount of preindustrial resistance stood in its way.[13] Along the way, Baldwin and his agents solved property crimes and created a well-known public brand with help from newspapers in Virginia and West Virginia, all intent on boosting the latter's coal fields as a land of potential that simply needed taming. In 1895 Virginia's *Roanoke Times* commended him for being "a powerful factor in the development and civilizing of the West Virginia coal region," and decades later a former West Virginia attorney general remembered Baldwin's agency as "a great civilizing influence in the southern mountains."[14]

Baldwin learned from Burnett the risky but potentially lucrative practice of hiring operatives who were themselves on the fringes of the law, and thus the record of crimes by reported Eureka agents is lengthy, ranging from forgery to murder.[15] As Baldwin grew his business he favored employees willing to skirt the law and resort to violence with little concern for ramifications or due process. With so many mountaineers in both Virginias recently on the skids because of economic calamity, the supply of desperate men willing to make money with gunfire was plentiful. Baldwin-Felts was an Appalachian organization, and its chief strength was almost exactly the same as that enjoyed by its industrial clients: a seemingly endless supply of ready, cheap, and often desperate labor. By technically not being "law officers," his agents could avoid public censure while still being attached to a cause largely understood as "law and order." Around 1893 William Baldwin hired Thomas Felts, a younger man who was also from southwestern Virginia who eventually became his business partner.[16] As Baldwin had under Burnett, Felts (a "mild-mannered Terror" with "grit") demonstrated boldness in the face of danger and ruthlessness with firearms and, as Baldwin's leading field agent, was erroneously reported dead on at least two occasions.[17]

Around the same time he enlisted Felts, Baldwin took on the N&W as one of his largest and most long-lasting clients, thus initiating a second phase in the lifespan of his agency. The N&W was among the largest railroads of the New South, and it distinguished itself by connecting the coal fields of West Virginia and southwestern Virginia to the Atlantic coast. It also contributed to one of the most dramatic demographic changes in the region's history: the movement of thousands of black southerners from the lowland and piedmont to the West Virginia coal mines. (Booker T. Washington stands as the most famous person to take part in this migration.)[18] The presence of African Americans in an area of the South that was historically vastly white created an atmosphere of social unrest that frequently resulted in white-supremacist violence. Beginning in the 1890s, southwestern Virginia's rate of lynching was disproportionately higher than that of any other part of the state. In what was probably the largest mass lynching in Virginia history, five black N&W employees were lynched for robbery in Tazewell County in 1893.[19] Baldwin personally attempted to prevent mob justice, and was frequently successful, although West Virginia governor William Glasscock found his services in investigating a state-line lynching of a black teenager lacking.[20] But his agency was better known for its ability to capture and extract confessions from black suspects. The N&W's primary task for Baldwin, Felts, and their agents was capturing, and often killing, illicit "rail tramps" using rolling stock for free transportation between the coal fields and the larger South. Black tramps bore the brunt of their attention, as did N&W employees who were victims of mistaken identity (leading, in at least one case, to a fatal shooting).[21] No doubt the carelessness of Baldwin's guards was as much a cautionary tale to tramps and workers as their actual assignments or authority. Their unpredictability was perhaps their most effective weapon. As Walter Johnson has recently illustrated, slave societies of the Deep South needed not sustain themselves purely by rational means. Slaves became capital through a process of rationalization, but slavery was also maintained by irrational means. Wealth was protected or created by the animal savagery of a hound attack on an escaped field hand, or in the form of the offspring created by the forced coupling of a chambermaid and a planter rapist.[22]

Baldwin and Felts were themselves were put on trial after the former shot the father of a suspected black forger during a botched arrest, and was swiftly acquitted by a judge who reportedly ignored the prosecution.[23] Baldwin's knowledge of black crime was also noticed by Secretary of War William Howard Taft, who sent Baldwin to Texas in 1908 to gather evidence to support the summary discharges of 167 black soldiers for allegedly shooting up a border-town saloon.[24] At a time when Progressive northerners deemed white southerners as "race experts," Baldwin's expertise was integral to what many historians consider the federal government's greatest sin of commission against African Americans since the Civil War.[25]

It is likely that Baldwin-Felts's ability to rise above the law in arresting and punishing black criminals was a reflection of Virginia's preexistent white supremacy. "No influence is so subtle and overwhelming," said one black-owned newspaper after the detectives' acquittals, "as that which accompanies a white skin."[26] Perhaps, also, the dozens of items in Virginia newspapers detailing the detectives' ensnarement of black criminals (who, unlike white miscreants, were always identified by their race) promoted the already-popular image of the African American criminal, and contributed to Virginia's proliferation of Jim Crow legislation after 1900.[27]

Baldwin retired from fieldwork soon after his Brownsville investigation, and under Thomas Felts's leadership the agency initiated the third phase of its existence, its aforementioned expansion of "mine guard" management.[28] While focusing on patrolling the N&W, Baldwin had maintained agents in coal towns since the 1890s, spying on mine employees and evicting prounion miners and other malcontents at company behest. Before eventually rebranding his organization as "Baldwin-Felts Detectives, Incorporated," he had originally chartered it as the "West Virginia Coal and Iron Police," inspired by the Pinkerton-associated Pennsylvania Coal and Iron Police founded in the last months of the Civil War.[29] It is likely that Baldwin anticipated the labor uprisings of the North would soon come south. West Virginia governor William Dawson had lambasted Baldwin-Felts as early as 1907 for their brutal tactics against miners, and it is very likely that the agency's intimidations were a major factor in keeping mines in southern West Virginia from taking part in at least three national strikes between 1894 and 1902.[30] Beginning in 1912, the United Mine Workers of America (UMWA) began making semi-successful organizing campaigns as far south as Charleston, leading to the famously violent strikes at Paint Creek and Cabin Creek in 1912–13.[31] The agency proved itself adept in its first real test of strike suppression, and it was hired by subsidiaries of the Rockefeller organization to patrol its mine towns in southern Colorado. Thus, Baldwin-Felts became a central player in events leading up to the 1914 Ludlow, Colorado, massacre, described by one historian as the "deadliest strike in the history of the United States."[32] Six years later the agency became nationally known when six Baldwin-Felts operatives (including one of Thomas Felts's brothers) were killed while trying to force evictions in Matewan, West Virginia, a town the agency had patrolled for decades.[33] Sid Hatfield, the town policeman who allegedly shot them, was assassinated by Baldwin-Felts agents the following year, and all involved were acquitted.[34] The narrative of the Baldwin-Felts Detective Agency has heretofore centered around only this third phase of its existence, when workers resisted their iron hand en masse. Its quieter moments were its more lucrative ones, such as in 1931 when it organized an arrestees-for-sale system with a North Carolina prison warden, an arrangement that, unlike the Matewan massacre, escaped public knowledge.[35] The agency crumbled ignominiously a half-decade later, when its founders died of natural causes within eighteen months of each other, just as the agency was coming under congressional investigation. But both men died very wealthy amid the permanent poverty of Appalachia.

In the early twentieth century, white southern booster Newcomb Frierson Thompson proclaimed repeatedly that the South was a model of industrial harmony since its rich and poor, black and white, had come to a mutually self-beneficial accord in the years after Reconstruction. Organized labor and the "closed shop" were therefore unnecessary as, he believed, northern workers would eventually realize.[36] The hundreds, perhaps thousands, of worker uprisings all over the former slave states between 1870 and 1930 suggest Thompson's disingenuousness, but he did have cause to proclaim a strike-free South; the fact remained that worker organization, and the ability to bargain collectively and strike, were distinctively stifled in his time and, indeed, remain so to this day. Thompson refused—and given his past as a member of the Ku Klux Klan in the 1860s, it should not be surprising—to acknowledge that the South's open-shop status quo was mortared with the blood of workers, most of them former slaves and their descendants. The lifespan of the Baldwin-Felts Detective Agency presents us with a force that controlled both black and white bodies in an industrial setting, clad in the robe of economic progress even as leftists recognized them as mercenary "gunmen of capitalism."[37] Their work was nothing new under the southern sun, nor the American one. As David Montgomery has shown, the "policing" of industrial workers was an antebellum invention that became overt only after the Civil War, when organizations like Pinkerton's used violence to suppress worker movements and preserve the new post-guild regime of the "free market," a role formerly played by the state.[38] Even though William Baldwin (dubbed "the Pinkerton of the [S]outh" during a 1905 policemen's convention) patterned his business after Pinkerton's, Baldwin-Felts was actually granted more police powers in its time and place, in settings such as Progressive-era railroad depots and coal company towns, than its larger, more famous northern predecessor was.[39] Professional law enforcement in Virginia and West Virginia was capital enforcement and, unlike state militias and national guards, a privately owned, for-profit enterprise. William Baldwin was a prime example of the New South's native-born capitalists fueled by northern investment after the South's "Redemption," as described in C. Vann Woodward's *Origins of the New South.*[40] Like the owners of textile mills, railroads, and coal mines, Baldwin gained his wealth through exploiting extraordinarily cheap labor, although his adventures in his younger years "civilizing" the mountain landscape and enforcing Jim Crow in the rails gave him greater evidence for "self-made" status than most southern middle-class men-made-good had. In his later years, he invested far less time into his detective agency than he did into his mortuary, candy factory, and three bank directorships.[41] Meanwhile former Baldwin-Felts agent C. E. Lively (one of the trio behind the assassination of Sid Hatfield) was destitute by 1927, begging for help to feed his eight children after having returned to mining after his detective career.[42]

The history of private police in the New South speaks to twenty-first-century concerns. Baldwin-Felts was essentially a domestically operating version of the current-day U.S.-based private military industry, its most famous representative being Academi (formerly known as Blackwater), a company also headquartered in Virginia. Like Baldwin-Felts, Academi provides contractual corporate security, and (most notably in Iraq) has shown a penchant for forcible interrogation.[43] Closer to home, the detective agency's police enforcement of white supremacy on Virginia's railroads is echoed by the continuance of pronounced police brutality against black men, in the South and elsewhere. Finally, the recent mania for privatization of public services on the civic and state level may one day create demand for the services of new organizations like Baldwin-Felts, especially since growing furor over police violence could act as a "shock" (in reference to Naomi Klein's concept of the "Shock Doctrine") in that direction.[44]

More immediately, however, the study of professional antiworker violence presents labor history with a special challenge. Over the last five decades, the vast majority of labor historians have followed E. P. Thompson's lead in creating histories "from below," in the interest of demonstrating the agency of the working class. The emphasis on worker agency in times of conflict and resistance has inadvertently led to the under-examination of the forces against which workers contend. The enemies of organized industrial workers must be examined as well. Workers had moments of victory (moral or material), but capital has its obvious advantages as well, and far more often, especially when it monopolized the usage of "legitimate" violence. Southern antilabor practices were successful, and Baldwin-Felts was no exception.

Notes

1. James Green, *The Devil Is Here in These Hills* (New York: Atlantic Monthly Press, 2015).

2. Only a few writers have concentrated articles or books solely on the Baldwin-Felts Detective Agency; see Richard M. Hadsell and William E. Coffey, "From Law and Order to Class Warfare: Baldwin-Felts Detectives in the Southern West Virginia Coal Fields," *West Virginia History* 40 (1979): 268–86; For nonscholarly apologiae for Baldwin and his agency, see John A. Velke III and Richard Mann II, *The True Story of the Baldwin-Felts Detective Agency* (Richmond [?]: self-pub., 2004); and John A. Velke III, *Baldwin-Felts Detectives, Inc.* (Richmond: self-pub., 1997). See also Meg Hewes, "The Effects of Mis-memory and the Tragedy of the Hillsville Courthouse," *International Social Science Review* 73, nos. 1/2 (1998), 22–36; Randal L. Hall, "A Courtroom Massacre: Politics and Public Sentiment in Progressive-Era Virginia," *Journal of Southern History* 70 (May 2004): 249–92, esp. 266–67, 27n; and Robert P. Weiss, "Private Detective Agencies and Labour Discipline in the United States, 1855–1946," *The Historical Journal* 29 (1986): 96.

Although few historians have concentrated attention on the Baldwin-Felts agency itself, its vicious roles in the Paint Creek/Cabin Creek Strike (1912–13) and southern Colorado's Ludlow Massacre (1914) are well documented in various labor history monographs: Evelyn L. K. Harris and Frank J. Krebs, *From Humble Beginnings: West Virginia*

State Federation of Labor, 1903–1957 (Charleston: West Virginia Labor History, 1960), 72–76, 150–53; Howard B. Lee, *Bloodletting in Appalachia: The Story of West Virginia's Four Major Mine Wars and Other Thrilling Incidents* (Morgantown, WV: Mcclain Printing, 1969), 17–47; George S. McGovern and Leonard F. Guttridge, *The Great Coalfield War* (Boston: Houghton Mifflin, 1972); John A. Williams, *West Virginia and the Captains of Industry* (Morgantown: West Virginia University Press, 1976), 251–52; Richard D. Lunt, *Law and Order vs. the Miners: West Virginia, 1907–1933* (Hamden, CT: Archon Books, 1979), 94, 97–99; Rebecca J. Bailey, *Matewan before the Massacre: Politics, Coal, and the Roots of Conflict in a West Virginia Mining Community* (Morgantown: West Virginia University Press, 2008), 1–6, 12–13, 126, 134–36, 168, 185, 188, 215–18, 224, 238–39, 259; Anthony DeStefanis, "Violence and the Colorado National Guard: Masculinity, Race, Class, and Identity in the 1913–1914 Southern Colorado Coal Strike," in *Mining Women: Gender in the Development of a Global Industry, 1670 to the Present*, ed. Laurie Mercier and Jaclyn Gier (New York: Palgrave MacMillan, 2010), 195–212; Thomas G. Andrews, *Killing for Coal: America's Deadliest Labor War* (Cambridge, MA: Harvard University Press, 2010), 233–86; David Alan Corbin, *Life, Work, and Rebellion in the Coal Fields: The Southern West Virginia Miners, 1880–1922* (Urbana: University of Illinois Press, 1981), 87–136; Stephen H. Norwood, *Strikebreaking and Intimidation: Mercenaries and Masculinity in Twentieth-Century America* (Chapel Hill: University of North Carolina Press, 2002), 133–40; Frederick A. Barkey, *Working Class Radicals: The Socialist Party in West Virginia, 1898–1220* (Morgantown: West Virginia University Press, 2012), 85–86; and Green, *The Devil Is Here in These Hills*, 49–50, 81–89, 103–14, 205–14, 222–25, 342, 350.

3. Richard M. Hadsell and William E. Coffey, "From Law and Order to Class Warfare," 268.

4. Until recently, few historians have taken a direct interest in the internal operations of detective agencies in the late nineteenth, and early twentieth, centuries. Three recent studies of the subject demonstrate a new flowering of study: Robert Michael Smith, *From Blackjacks to Briefcases: A History of Commercialized Strikebreakers and Unionbusting in the United States* (Athens: Ohio University Press, 2003); Jennifer Fronc, *New York Undercover: Private Surveillance in the Progressive Era* (Chicago: University of Chicago Press, 2009); S. Paul O'Hara, *Inventing the Pinkertons; or, Spies, Sleuths, Mercenaries, and Thugs: Being a Story of the Nation's Most Famous (and Infamous) Detective Agency* (Baltimore: Johns Hopkins University, 2016).

5. Among the more significant studies of the relationship between violence and New South labor: David M. Oshinsky, *Worse Than Slavery: Parchman Farm and the Ordeal of Jim Crow Justice* (New York: Simon and Schuster, 1997); Scott Reynolds Nelson, *Iron Confederacies: Southern Railways, Klan Violence, and Reconstruction* (Chapel Hill: University of North Carolina Press, 1999); Gilles Vandal, *Rethinking Southern Violence: Homicides in Post–Civil War Louisiana, 1866–1884* (Columbus: Ohio State University Press, 2000); and William A. Link and James J. Broomall, eds., *Rethinking American Emancipation: Legacies of Slavery and the Quest for Black Freedom* (Cambridge: Cambridge University Press, 2015).

6. Mary Beth Pudup, "Land Before Coal: Class and Regional Development in Southeast Kentucky," (Ph.D. diss., UC Berkeley, 1987), 127. Pudup's conception of class in

nineteenth-century Appalachia depends upon E. P. Thompson's dictum that class is not only defined by economic relationships but is also formed according to the dictates of very specific historical contexts. Essentially, class relations in the most sparsely populated areas of Appalachia were defined according to the parameters of the immediate vicinity, involving factors such as land ownership, profession, and kinship that may not have corresponded directly to other parts of the Upper South or the United States as a whole; see E. P. Thompson, *Making of the English Working Class* (New York: Vintage Books, 1966), 11. For a close examination of antebellum Tazewell County, Virginia, see Ralph Mann, "Mountains, Land, and Kin Networks: Burkes Garden, Virginia, in the 1840s and 1850s," *Journal of Southern History* 58 (1992): 411–34.

7. Altina Waller, *Feud: Hatfields, McCoys, and Social Change in Appalachia, 1860–1900* (Chapel Hill, 1988), 37–52, 98–101.

8. D. B. Baldwin to Sallie W. Baldwin, undated, D. B. Baldwin to Sallie W. Baldwin from Camp near Cotton Mountain (WV), October 31, 1861, D. B. Baldwin to Sallie W. Baldwin from Wabash Camp Ground (Giles Co. VA?), June 2, 1862, D. B. Baldwin to Sallie W. Baldwin from Wabash Camp Ground (Giles Co. VA?), June 2, 1862, and O. H. Barns to Sallie W. Baldwin from Fort Delaware, Delaware, January 23, 1865, Baldwin Family Letters, 1861–1897, Special Collections, Newman Library, Virginia Tech, Blacksburg, VA.

9. *Maysville (KY) Bulletin*, June 15, 1883; *Wheeling Intelligencer*, May 30, 1884, July 9, 1888; *Point Pleasant (WV) Weekly Register*, November 8, 1892.

10. *Washington National Tribune*, April 11, 1889; *Point Pleasant (WV) Weekly Register*, April 17, 1889.

11. *Washington Evening Star*, February 28, 1889; *Wheeling Intelligencer*, April 4, 1889.

12. *Wheeling Intelligencer*, July 9, 1888, October 17, 1888; *Washington Evening Star*, January 21, 1889; *Washington Times*, August 16, 1897.

13. Gordon McKinney, "Industrialization and Violence in Appalachia in the 1890s," in *An Appalachian Symposium*, ed. Joel W. Williamson (Boone, NC: Appalachian Consortium Press, 1977), 131–44; James Klotter, "Feuds in Appalachia: An Overview," *Filson Club Historical Quarterly* 56, no. 3 (1982): 290–317; Waller, *Feud*; Dwight Billings and Kathleen Blee, *The Road to Poverty: The Making of Wealth and Hardship in Appalachia* (Cambridge: Cambridge University Press, 2000); Dwight Billings and Kathleen Blee, "Where 'Bloodshed Is a Pastime': Mountain Feuds and Appalachian Stereotyping," in *Confronting Appalachian Stereotypes: Backtalk from an American Region*, ed. Dwight Billings, Gurney Norman, and Katherine Ledford (Lexington: University Press of Kentucky, 1999), 119–37. For a very good summation of Appalachian history's "revisionist" generation, see Mark T. Banker, *Appalachians All: East Tennesseans and the Elusive History of an American Region* (Knoxville: University of Tennessee Press, 2010), 2–5.

14. "Baldwin's Detective Agency," *Roanoke Times*, January 3, 1893; Lee, *Bloodletting in Appalachia*, 11, 190.

15. *Wheeling Intelligencer*, October 21, November 1, 25, 1887; *Roanoke Times*, October 9, 1890; *Wheeling Intelligencer*, February 7, July 18, 1891; *Roanoke Times*, April 3, 1894.

16. *New York Sun*, August 6, 1892; *Roanoke Times*, April 14, 1893; *Roanoke Times*, April 3, 1894.

17. *Richmond Planet*, February 17, 1900; *Washington Suburban Citizen*, February 17, 1900; *Big Stone Gap (VA) Post*, February 22, 1900; *Staunton (VA) Spectator and Vindicator*, February 16, March 23, 1900; *Richmond Dispatch*, November 17, 1901.

18. Charles Phillips Anson, "A History of the Labor Movement in West Virginia" (unpublished diss., University of North Carolina, 1940), 63–71.

19. W. Fitzhugh Brundage. *Lynching in the New South: Georgia and Virginia, 1880–1930* (Urbana: University of Illinois Press, 1993), 143–44.

20. *Richmond Times Dispatch*, February 13, 1904; *Roanoke Times*, February 17, 1904; *Richmond Times Dispatch*, February 17, 1904; *Shenandoah Herald*, February 19, 1904; *Monterey (VA) Highland Recorder*, February 19, 1904; *Roanoke Times*, March 17, 1904; *Roanoke Times*, March 18, 1904; *Richmond Times-Dispatch*, March 18, 1904; *Alexandria Gazette*, March 18, 1904; *Roanoke Times*, March 19, 1904; *Clinch Valley News* (Jeffersonville, VA), March 25, 1904; *Monterey (VA) Highland Recorder*, March 25, 1904; *Alexandria Gazette*, June 16, 18, 1900; *Washington Post*, June 19, 1900; *Richmond Times*, June 20, 1900; *Richmond Dispatch*, June 20, 1900; *Alexandria Gazette*, June 21, 1900; *Washington Post*, June 19, 26, September 18, 1900; *Roanoke Times*, June 21, 1900; *Richmond Times*, August 15, 1900; *Alexandria Gazette*, August 15, September 17, 1900; *Tazewell Republican*, August 16, 1900; *Richmond Dispatch*, September 15, 1900; *Richmond Times*, September 18, 19, 1900; Gary Jackson Tucker, *Governor William E. Glasscock and Progressive Politics in West Virginia* (Morgantown: West Virginia University Press, 2008), 146–47.

21. *Richmond Times*, August 26, 1900; *Richmond Dispatch*, August 26, 1900; *Washington Post*, August 28, 1900.

22. Walter Johnson, *River of Dark Dreams: Slavery and Empire in the Cotton Kingdom* (Cambridge: Harvard University Press, 2013).

23. *Richmond Dispatch*, September 17, 1898; *Washington Evening Times*, September 17, 1898; *Washington Times*, September 17, 1898; *Richmond Times*, September 17, 1898; *Alexandria Gazette*, September 17, 1898; *Richmond Dispatch*, September 18, 1898; *Richmond Times*, September 18, 1898; *Richmond Dispatch*, September 20, 1898; *Alexandria Gazette*, September 20, 25, 1898; *Alexandria Gazette*, October 19, 1898; *Richmond Planet*, October 29, 1898; *Richmond Times*, September 20, October 18, 1898; *Richmond Dispatch*, September 20, October 13, December 23, 1898; *Richmond Times*, October 18, 1898; *Alexandria Gazette*, October 19, 1898; *Baltimore Sun*, October 19, 1898; *Richmond Planet*, October 29, 1898; *Richmond Dispatch*, November 20, 1898; *Richmond Dispatch*, November 23, 1898; *Richmond Dispatch*, November 24–27, 1898; *Richmond Planet*, December 3, 1898; "Virginia News," *Alexandria Gazette*, November 28, 1898; *Tazewell Republican*, December 1, 1898; *Clinch Valley News* (Jeffersonville, VA), December 2, 1898 (quotation); *Richmond Planet*, December 3, 1898.

24. "Letter from the Secretary of War . . . ," in *Congressional Series of United States Public Documents*, vol. 5407 (Washington, DC: Government Printing Office, 1908), 2 (quotation); "General Report," in *Congressional Series of United States Public Documents*, vol. 5407 (Washington, DC: Government Printing Office, 1908), 9–12; *New York Sun*, December 15, 1908; *New York Tribune*, December 15, 1908; *Washington Evening Star*, December 17, 1908; *Washington Bee*, December 19, 1908; *Washington Herald*, January 6, 1909; *New York Tribune*, January 6, 1909; *New York Sun*, January 13, 1909; *Nashville Globe*,

January 15, 1909; *Washington Evening Star*, January 21, 1909; "General Report," 9–12, 13, 28–30; "Companies B, C, and D, Twenty-Fifth United States Infantry . . . ," 133–72, 198–210, 212–52, 250–71, 414–61, 478–81.

25. K. Stephen Prince, *Stories of the South: Race and the Reconstruction of Southern Identity, 1865–1915* (Chapel Hill: University of North Carolina Press, 2014), 226–35. See also George C. Rable, *But There Was No Peace: The Role of Violence in the Politics of Reconstruction* (Athens: University of Georgia Press, 1984), 18.

26. *Richmond Planet*, December 3, 1898.

27. A 1901–2 constitutional convention broadened the quantity and quality of crimes that resulted in a citizen's permanent disenfranchisement to include forms of forgery and petty larceny that were more likely to result in convictions of black men. See William C. Pendleton, *Political History of Appalachian Virginia* (Dayton, VA: Shenandoah Press, 1927), 429–501; Andrew Buni, *The Negro in Virginia Politics, 1902–1965* (Charlottesville: University of Virginia Press, 1967), 16–19; Jane Dailey, *Before Jim Crow: The Politics of Race in Postemancipation Virginia* (Chapel Hill: University of North Carolina Press, 2000), 161–65; and John Dinan, *The Virginia State Constitution*, 2nd ed. (Oxford York: Oxford University Press, 2014), 89–90, 89n46, 90n47. For black male criminals in the New South, see Lawrence W. Levine, *Black Culture and Black Consciousness: Afro-American Folk Thought from Slavery to Freedom* (New York: Oxford University Press, 1977); Edward Ayers, *Vengeance and Justice: Crime and Punishment in the 19th Century American South* (New York: Oxford University Press, 1984), 231–32; John W. Roberts, *From Trickster to Badman: The Black Folk Hero in Slavery and Freedom* (Philadelphia: University of Pennsylvania Press, 1989); and Billy Jaynes Chandler, "Harmon Murray: Black Desperado in Late Nineteenth-Century Florida," *Florida Historical Quarterly* 73 (1994): 184–99.

28. Edward Levinson, *I Break Strikes: The Technique of Pearl L. Bergoff* (New York: Arno Press, 1969), 26.

29. *Point Pleasant (WV) Weekly Register*, November 8, 1892; *Acts Passed by the Legislature of West Virginia at Its Twenty-Third Regular Session, Beginning January 3, 1897* (Charleston, 1897): 149; *Tazewell Republican*, March 31, 1910; *Richmond Times-Dispatch*, February 18, 1911. For Pennsylvania's coal and iron police, see Kevin Kenny, *Making Sense of the Molly Maguires* (New York: Oxford University Press, 1998), 107–9; and Norwood, *Strikebreaking and Intimidation*, 4, 120–27; Spencer J. Sadler, *Pennsylvania's Coal and Iron Police* (Charleston, SC: Arcadia, 2009).

30. Anson, "A History of the Labor Movement in West Virginia," 116.

31. *Conditions in the Paint Creek District, West Virginia, before a Sub-Committee of the Committee on Education and Labor in the Senate of the United States, Senate Resolution No. 37* (Charleston, WV: Lovett Printing., undated), Printed Ephemera Collection on the United Mine Workers of America, collection PE.010, box 1, folder 6 (Conditions in the Paint Creek District, West Virginia: Hearings), Tamiment Library and Robert F. Wagner Labor Archives, New York University; *New York Tribune*, June 17, 1913; William Leavitt Stoddard, "Confessions of the 'Gunmen of Industry,'" *Pearson's Magazine* 32, no. 1 (July 1914): 147–57; Lawrence R. Lynch, "The West Virginia Coal Strike," *Political*

Science Quarterly 29 (1914): 626–63; Anson, "A History of the Labor Movement in West Virginia," 220–25.

32. Andrews, *Killing for Coal*, 1. See also Statistical Department, UMWA, *Lawson Case: A Brief History Based on Court Records and Incontrovertible Facts* (Cheyenne, WY: Smith-Brooks Press, 1915); *Militarism: What It Costs the Taxpayers* (Denver: Williamson-Haffner, n.d.), pamphlet; and John R. Lawson's Reply to Judge Hillyer, Printed Ephemera Collection on the United Mine Workers of America, collection PE.010, box 1, folder 17 (Lawson, John R. Case [District 15]), Tamiment Library and Robert F. Wagner Labor Archives, New York University.

33. *Richmond Times-Dispatch*, May 20, 1920; *Big Stone Gap Post*, May 26, 1920; John A. Williams, *West Virginia and the Captains of Industry*, 251–52; Bailey, *Matewan before the Massacre*, 1–6, 12–13, 126, 134–36, 168, 185, 188, 215–18, 224, 238–39, 259; Green, *The Devil Is Here in These Hills*, 49–50, 81–89, 103–14, 205–14, 222–25, 342, 350.

34. "The West Virginia Miners' War," *Christian Century*, June 30, 1921, 19; *Duluth (MN) Labor World*, September 3, 1921; *Fairmont West Virginian*, September 10, 1921.

35. Velke and Mann, *The True Story of the Baldwin-Felts Detective Agency*, 259.

36. Chad Pearson, *Reform or Repression: Organizing America's Anti-Union Movement* (Philadelphia: University of Pennsylvania Press, 2016), 182–215, 221–22.

37. "The Open and Closed Shop Controversy in Los Angeles," *Final Report and Testimony Submitted to the Commission on Industrial Relations, Created by the Act of August 23, 1912*, Senate Journal, 64th Congress, 1st sess., document no. 415, vol. 6 (Washington, DC: Government Printing Office, 1916), 5852.

38. David Montgomery, *Citizen Worker: The Experience of Workers in the United States with Democracy and the Free Market during the Nineteenth Century* (Cambridge: Cambridge University Press, 1993), 52–114.

39. *Washington Evening Star*, May 24, 1905.

40. C. Vann Woodward, *Origins of the New South, 1877–1913* (Baton Rouge: Louisiana State University Press, 1971), 107–41.

41. *Roanoke Times*, April 1, 1936.

42. John A. Williams, *Appalachia: A History* (Chapel Hill: University of North Carolina Press, 2002), 272.

43. Ward Churchill, "The Security Industrial Complex," in *The Global Industrial Complex: Systems of Domination*, ed. Steven Best, Richard Kahn, Anthony J. Nocella II, and Peter McLaren (Plymouth, UK: Lexington Books, 2011), 43–96. S. Paul O'Hara has similarly compared the Pinkerton Detective Agency to Academi/Blackwater; see O'Hara, *Inventing the Pinkertons*, 11, 160–61, 167.

44. Naomi Klein, *The Shock Doctrine: The Rise of Disaster Capitalism* (New York: Metropolitan Books, 2007).

3

The Twentieth Century and Civil Rights

10

Rooted

Black Railroad Shopmen, the 1922 Strike, and Southern Civil Rights Struggles

THERESA A. CASE

Popular thought and academic literature usually associate African American railroad workers with geographical movement. Pullman porters "rode the rails." "Boomer" railroaders followed expanding railroad lines in the nineteenth century, and trackliners drove spikes and shored up rails across hundreds of miles of track, bringing John Henry songs with them. George Swanson Starling, featured in Isabel Wilkerson's Pulitzer Prize–winning *The Warmth of Other Suns*, labored as a coach attendant, shepherding southern black migrants north.[1] Shop work, the maintenance and construction of engines and cars, is less remembered and investigated, and the few excellent resources on black shopmen do not follow this workforce out of the shops into their larger communities.[2] Yet while whites held the vast majority of railroad shop positions, in numerous southern towns and cities—like Louisville, Kentucky; Mobile and Birmingham, Alabama; Fort Worth, Texas; Vicksburg, Mississippi; and Bluefield, West Virginia—black shop workers' numbers and presence were significant.[3] The history of World War I–era and postwar Texas shop towns attests to this. In Marshall, Texas, particularly, a grassroots story of black shopmen emerges from the historical record. One central event that permits reconstruction of this history was the 1922 nationwide shopmen's strike. Black shop workers participated on both sides of the strike divide, and in doing so took exceptional risks at a time when the prospect of progress was fast receding. Their actions reflected the influence of black wartime protest and activism, the unique aspects of race relations in the shops, and the rooted life of many black shopmen and their families. The connection that many had to Marshall raises questions about how, in the decades following the 1922 walkout, black shop workers related to each other, to white shopmen, and to the developing civil rights movement.

In 1922, nationally, over 400,000 shopmen on over fifty railroads went on strike. This was part of a tidal wave of labor protest between 1919 and 1922 that engulfed the coal mines and steel mills and included a general strike in Seattle. In 1919 alone, an astounding 4 million plus American workers struck.[4] Texas industries, too, saw episodes of labor rebellion, involving 1,600 longshoremen in Galveston in 1920, for example, and 2,000 Fort Worth packinghouse workers the following year.[5] An estimated 8,000 to 10,000 shop workers across Texas struck in 1922, including 2,500 in Houston, 1,400 in Fort Worth, 1,100 in San Antonio, 1,000 in Marshall, 1,000 in Denison, 1,000 in El Paso, 900 in Cleburne, perhaps 400 in Texarkana, and 278 in Wichita Falls. Railroad companies' assaults on pay and work rules propelled even conservative unionists to action.[6]

The Railway Employees Department of the American Federation of Labor issued the strike order. It represented the "lily-white" shopcraft unions of machinists, blacksmiths, boilermakers, electricians, sheet metal workers, and railway carmen. These workers built, painted, and repaired railroad locomotive and freight and passenger cars. Most black shop workers were relegated to semiskilled and unskilled positions, often as helper, with no chance of advancement, regardless of skill or experience. Those black shop workers who joined trade unions were, historian Eric Arnesen explains, forced into a "subordinate affiliation with the AFL and its constituent craft unions."[7] This meant that "black locals could not negotiate with the railroads, but were instead 'represented' by the white local General Chairman." Whites further blocked black access to the crafts with work rules that specified which tasks different race-typed classes of employees could undertake.[8]

The tradition of rigid racial exclusivity among white craft workers had long encouraged black strikebreaking. While some white unionists correctly assumed that railroad companies lured black laborers to break strikes "under false pretenses," for many others, Arnesen contends, "strikebreaking was nothing less than a form of working-class activism"—often a collective, concerted effort that "afforded black workers the means to enter realms of employment previously closed to them and to begin a long, slow climb up the economic ladder."[9] One striking white Texas shopman understood the logic: "Our ranks are holding tight, but the management invites the negro to grasp an opportunity to advance himself in mechanical lines."[10] Material and social gains alone did not motivate black workers to apply for striking workers' positions. Some black strikebreakers justified the act of crossing the picket line as a nativist and patriotic deed; for many others, strikebreaking lodged a protest of racial inequities.[11]

That said, reports of significant black strike participation in 1922 surface in the newspaper coverage. Initially, a white unionist claimed that one hundred strikers in Dallas were African American, many of them upset about the proposed wage cut. Another boasted that sixty black workers answered the union's daily roll call and that "no friction" existed "between them and the white men." An appeal to the black community to back the walkout seemed to confirm this characterization. Black carman Ollie Williamson wrote to the *Dallas Express* that one hundred black shop workers were "among the 500 Dallas railroad strikers." African American strikers purportedly beat other African American strikebreakers in Texarkana, San Antonio, and Marshall. In Denison, once the state militia intervened, Texas guardsmen fired their guns in the railroad yards at three black men whom they suspected of sabotage. One report hints at broader black community support for the strike in Denison: black members of two churches sang "old time songs" and "a few religious numbers" before a mass meeting of federated shop crafts early in the conflict. In Longview, federal officials charged four black strikers with intimidation of new black employees, and, well into October 1922, fifty-five white and thirty-one black workers remained out, because they opposed returning to work on the railroad's terms.[12]

Why did some black shop workers throw their lot in with white unionists? Possibly, the lack of overt racial hostility in white unionist rhetoric tipped the balance. Even as the walkout neared collapse, unionists in Fort Worth and Dallas consistently cast their struggle as a peaceable, unified one.[13] Black strikers probably recognized the opportunism behind these appeals and bristled at the insistence that black workers blindly follow the strike order. Still, the calls for solidarity on the basis of shared, harsh "on-the-job realities" hit a chord with some, as shopmen together faced a crisis after World War I in the form of "intensified exploitation and harsher discipline."[14] Ollie Williamson explained to Dallas's black citizens, "[We] are part of the union, just as white workers. The union has bound us up together. A raise for them has meant a raise for us, and cut for them has meant a cut for us." Moreover, management's efforts came in the midst of the Texas Open Shop Association's attack on state labor laws that had "established a minimum wage and eight-hour workday for some workers, outlawed blacklisting," and regulated child labor and safety in mines and on the railroads. Concern about the broader antilabor mood may have persuaded black shopmen to strike.[15]

Perhaps the relatively less overtly hostile racial climate in the shops, too, played a role. Generally, white shopmen controlled entry into apprentice and craft positions. Their hold on white supremacy in the workplace was mostly assured. Within this context of white dominance, African American shopmen at times petitioned to "use the limited organizational room that the AFL had provided them through so called federal labor unions, to push for a greater degree of influence within the Federation." While the line between skilled and semiskilled shop work was more porous by 1922, the situation in the shops stood in stark contrast to that in train service, where "there was no clear distinction of skill or craft" and white trainmen's brotherhoods waged bloody race strikes to drive black workers out of all positions except porter.[16]

While an untold number of black shop workers cooperated with white unionists, the majority of black shop workers in Marshall openly defied the strike order. Having initially walked out en masse, 216 black workers returned to work and reportedly signed their names to a petition addressed to the Texas & Pacific general office at Dallas and to the United States Labor Board in Chicago. They were presumably among the roughly 250 men who had returned to work shortly after the strike began. The petition stated that "union men" had threatened that "they would be banked" if they did not join the strike. They feared for "their families and homes" and for "themselves and their property."[17] By this point, a pattern of violence had emerged against strikebreakers. In Fort Worth, while pickets had remained peaceable during the conflict's first week, beginning on July 8, attacks on strikebreakers grew more frequent. [18] In Temple and Greenville, strikebreakers met with beatings. In Houston, over 60 workers testified that strikers showered them with rocks, knocked them unconscious, and smashed the windows of the train carrying them to work. A black strikebreaker, William McClure, died after a striker's brick hit his temple. Hundreds of Denison unionists laid siege to strikebreakers and U.S. marshals making their way home from the Katy shops. Sixteen unarmed guards were abducted and flogged near a river bottom. Strikebreakers met with floggings in various locales.[19]

Black strikebreakers risked much more than whites. Only seven months prior, during a walkout by Fort Worth packinghouse workers, an angry crowd of white strikers assailed three black strikebreakers. One of the three, Fred Rouse, took out his pistol and shot wildly into the advancing throng, wounding two white men. The enraged mob closed in on him, pounded him senseless, and left him for dead. Within a day or two, thirty unmasked men dragged Rouse from his hospital bed. His eyes still swollen shut, he was too weak to resist. His body was soon found hanging from a tree, "riddled with bullets."[20]

The lynching of Fred Rouse made plain once again the price of black self-defense in a context of racial terror. Black Texans met with news of unthinkable atrocities everywhere they looked—in the public burnings of Bragg Williams in Hillsboro in 1919, two black men in Paris, Texas, in 1920, and three black victims in Kirvin in 1922; the 1918 assault of white mobs on the black community of Huntsville, Texas, which ended in the murder of an entire black family; and the 1919 Longview riot—only twenty odd miles away from Marshall. Long descriptions of the mass race violence in East St. Louis and Houston in 1917, Chicago and Elaine in 1919, and Tulsa in 1921 filled Texas newspapers.[21] Marshall, once a major Confederate operations center and site of intense Reconstruction-era struggles, was "notorious for frequent and particularly barbaric lynching," recalled NAACP field secretary William Pickens, who taught college there between 1914 and 1915. It was "one of the worst sections in all this round World . . . for any Negro to live in."[22]

Under such circumstances, black strikebreakers broke with Marshall's white citizens, who generally favored the strike. The *Marshall News Messenger*'s editor characterized strikers as men of "good character" and as stable, home-owning "citizens" and pledged to provide striking men with free editions of the newspaper for six months. The local American Legion applauded shopmens' "lawful" and "dignified" fight. A large town dance raised strike funds. On July 8, 1922, striking railroad workers "packed" city hall to hear Earle Mayfield, a champion of white labor and also the candidate for governor most closely tied to the Klan. Introduced by the head of the federated shop crafts in the city, Mayfield enjoyed a "hearty greeting" and was "frequently cheered."[23] The paper remained silent regarding the black workers' petition.[24]

The Marshall petition, then, was a remarkable attempt to expose white strikers' coercion to the wider world. The signatories hoped that improvement locally might come through a direct, collective appeal for federal intervention. World War I had encouraged such expectation. Wartime demand for industrial goods had necessitated government management of the roads with the aim of labor peace through collective bargaining. To this end, the U.S. Railroad Administration's General Order no. 27 had raised wages, required overtime pay, imposed an eight-hour day, and called for equal pay for equal work. The USRA had pushed unions to organize the unorganized. The federal government had not intervened so directly and substantially to improve black lives since Reconstruction. However, railroad companies often resisted these mandates, federal enforcement was uneven, and Jim Crow practices were entrenched. Black workers often had to push hard for implementation. Incidents of independent black labor protest on the railroads multiplied nationally.[25] The gap between federal law and railroad practices also spurred African American workers to "correspond directly with high ranking officials" of the USRA. Trainmen "took courage . . . to dispatch a flood of letters and petitions that collectively expressed a confidence they previously lacked, especially in the South, where they seldom had access to higher authorities than local supervisors and managers who generally shared oppressive Southern racial norms."[26]

Just as "circuits of communication" among "kin, neighbors, and friends," in churches and benevolent associations, and along railroad lines via itinerant black workers, "helped facilitate the Great Migration," the 216 signatories quite likely were connected to networks of information and organizations and therefore conscious of the protests and appeals that came in the wake of an enlarged federal role during World War I. Some may have even taken part. Although shopmen labored in town, other railroad workers rode the rails into rural and industrial areas, bringing information with them. Federal involvement had not always brought better conditions, but the memory of its relative responsiveness to labor protest surely emboldened the Marshall petitioners to take such a dramatic step.[27]

Conceivably, news of the wider black protest movement prompted petitioners to act. Epidemic racial violence, the Great Migration of black southerners north and west, and the enlistment and return of black soldiers from a "war for democracy" abroad had inspired grassroots black militancy nationally, including in Texas. One measure of this new militancy was the rise of the NAACP. As Steven Reich observed of the Texas NAACP, "janitors, laborers, letter carriers, housekeepers, laundresses, seamstresses—even the butler at the governor's mansion—joined the ranks of the NAACP. . . . Given the size of some of these branches and the occupational profile of the African American population, the Black working class likely constituted the core of the membership."[28] Houston NAACP records confirm Reich's supposition. From the list of 425 persons in the Houston membership rolls, 134 individuals can be identified in the 1918 Houston city directory. That list teems with the names of shop workers, railroad laborers, porters, barbers, and hairdressers.[29] Likewise, in Marshall, the head of the NAACP in 1919 was not a professional or business person but a bricklayer, E. C. Cooper, who, along with two other bricklayers, wrote the national office about the city's failure to protect them from white bricklayers' attacks and threats.[30] Additionally, in 1920 NAACP supporter and black brakeman Rufus Reed of Arkansas traveled to San Antonio, with stops in Texarkana and Longview, to meet with black trainmen. Although class differences existed within the Texas NAACP, it possessed a strong working-class base that may have inspired petitioners.[31]

Waves of white terror took their toll on the Texas NAACP. Membership fell precipitously between 1919 and 1921, from 267 to 0 in Fort Worth, from 606 to 280 in Houston, from 1,152 to 278 in Dallas, and in Marshall, from 97 to 0. Reich concludes, "The campaign of terror . . . did not defeat black activism entirely. . . . Resistance and struggle continued, just as it had before the war, in countless ways, at the subterranean level."[32] The Marshall petition suggests that white violence did not drive black protest entirely underground. What was it about Marshall itself that might explain the petitioners' decision to openly, collectively resist white society? Was it simply the philosophy that one has the right to strike but not to "prevent a fellow workman from plying his trade?" Or was it that African Americans have a right to "scab" against only Jim Crow unions?[33]

Considering events in 1916, the latter seems more probable. On September 23, 1916, the Marshall shop superintendent reported a walkout of a broad spectrum of the black shop workforce. Wages were at issue, and also the firing of individual workmen. When the white boilermakers' committee complained that its apprentices had received an order to perform the work of striking helpers, the superintendent replied that he would ensure the apprentices' load was light. He asked the committee to inform the strikers that, unless they returned to work, he would replace them. "This seemed to be agreeable to mechanics," he noted. The white mechanics and the car repairmen and car builders agreed "to do the best they could until help was furnished them." In the end, the perhaps four hundred black strikers resumed their places for the usual 19 to 26 cents per hour with the hollow promise of a possible future wage increase.[34] White unionists' collaboration with management likely was not forgotten or forgiven by black shop employees.

An additional factor in the petitioners' decision may have been the commitment many black shopmen had made to life in Marshall. These shopmen resembled not the lone, wandering Black Ulysses of lore but flesh-and-blood southern lumber workers of the 1920s, '30s, and '40s. While boogie-woogie probably originated in the piney woods surrounding Marshall among itinerant black workers in logging camp barrelhouses, by the 1920s more than two-thirds of southern black lumber workers were married and lived in settled sawmill communities. Similarly, about three-quarters of the 307 black shopmen in Marshall were married (regardless of skill). Most lived with family members, the majority with dependent children but some with parents or extended family. Only 10 percent boarded. About one-third of semiskilled and skilled black shopmen, and 39 percent of unskilled laborers, owned their home. Given this social profile, one might reasonably suppose that petitioners rejected support for a walkout that, if successful, would mostly benefit white workers and, if defeated, would jeopardize their resources and family life.[35]

One resident of Marshall, whose grandfather was a railroader during the 1920s, remembers that the town was a magnet for African Americans who aspired to send their children to school or attend school themselves. Her grandfather's children attended college in Marshall. Marshall boasted two black institutions of higher education, Wiley College and Bishop College, with roughly five hundred and four hundred students in 1919, respectively. During this time (up until 1974), the town's only library was Wiley College's Carnegie Library. In the 1910s, Marshall's first black public school grew fivefold to reach one thousand students in 1919, and included, by 1916, Central High School. A 1932 study of African Americans in Marshall indicates that shopmen and their families had a reputation for seizing the town's educational opportunities whenever possible. The study lays out four case studies—two involving destitute, unstable families and two of families that enjoyed some modern conveniences and sent their children to public schools and Wiley College. The latter two families were those of Texas & Pacific shopmen.[36]

Black shopmen's economic situation was not necessarily an enviable one. The 1932 study does not list the shopmen's occupation. Laborers received lower wages than helpers did, and seasonal layoffs ate into most railroaders' incomes. For many, it was wives' and children's wages, often for low-paid domestic work, that afforded shopmen's families some greater resources and status. The McDonald family is a case in point. In 1921 washerwoman Callie McDonald won election as PTA officer at Central High School. Her spouse, Robert, labored in the Texas & Pacific shops in town. Their three children and nephew attended school and could read and write. A cousin, also a washerwoman, contributed to the household income.[37] Similarly, in Houston, shop workers' families living in the Fifth Ward typically relied on a two-family income (or more). Without this, they "struggled to make ends meet."[38]

To send one's children into Marshall's educational system then meant a good deal. That same system helped to produce Clifton F. Richardson—the son of a railroad laborer, a 1909 graduate of Bishop College, and founder and editor of the *Houston Informer*, the pages of which blistered with condemnations of lynching and substandard housing and city services. Rebecca D. Buard, a local historian and teacher, was initially educated by her mother in a neighborhood school in Marshall, graduated from Pemberton High School in 1925, and went on to Bishop College. More famously, Wiley College professor and poet Melvin Tolson coached Henrietta Pauline Bell Wells and others to compete in the first interracial college debate in 1930, a milestone event depicted in the 2007 film *The Great Debaters*, starring Denzel Washington. Long before the "Freedom Rides," James Farmer Jr. returned to his home town of Marshall to attend Wiley College and join the debate team. The astrophysicist Walter Samuel McAfee's parents brought him and a legion of siblings to Marshall from the rural town of Ore City when he was an infant. His father was a college-educated minister but labored as a mechanic, carpenter, and housebuilder in Marshall, while his mother taught at Wiley College Normal

School. After graduating with honors from Wiley in 1934, McAfee went on to win recognition for his contributions to the Moon Radar Project and radiation detection. Marshall represented an educational oasis, and one of its chief leaders took steps to make this so. Historian Gail Beil recalled that longtime Wiley president Matthew Dogan rented a private car for black students on their way to various destinations in order to shield them from the humiliation of a Jim Crow railway car.[39]

In these fraught but hopeful circumstances, 216 of Marshall's black shopmen organized. Their identities and fate are unknown, because the petition itself remains undiscovered. A comparison of the 1920 census and 1924 city directory records hints that a substantial number stayed in Marshall. Of the 307 black shopmen in the 1920 census, 275 could be clearly identified as having persisted or not. Fifty-four percent of those 275 black shopmen remained in 1924—most employed at the T&P shops. Homeowners were almost twice as likely to stay as renters were. The degree to which outmigration from Marshall resulted directly from the strike is unclear, but shop management probably fired a number of black strikers. By 1924, 46 percent of black shop workers no longer lived in Marshall. Additionally, 23 black shop workers who remained at the T&P shops suffered, perhaps as a result of the roles they had assumed in 1922, demotion from semiskilled or skilled work to unskilled while 11 were promoted.[40]

How did the shop workforce in Marshall reconstitute itself in the wake of the strike's defeat? How did black shopmen carry on, despite some divisions within their ranks over the walkout, and in the face of white resentment? Public memory in Marshall offers few clues about shopmen, white or black. While older residents recall how the shop whistle structured town life, and a historic railroad depot still stands, the sprawling, mammoth shop complex is gone. The Texas & Pacific Railway Museum displays items such as fittings, tools, maps, and railroad tickets but nothing to remind visitors of powerful railroad brotherhoods, or labor upheavals such as in 1922, or black and white railroad employees' relationship to their work, managers, each other, or unionism. One collection of oral histories on African Americans in Marshall concentrates on professional classes; railroad work appears fleetingly as mere prelude to stories of social and economic advancement.[41]

One possibility is that, after the divisive 1922 strike, black shop workers cooperated with management and dedicated their energy to building institutions outside the workplace to improve, quietly and steadily, their lives and the prospects of their children. Some indirect support for this exists. In late March of 1960, energized by the nonviolent protests in Greensboro, North Carolina, seventy-one students from Wiley and Bishop Colleges sat in at local lunch counters and the bus station. Hundreds of black citizens rallied to their cause in Marshall's main square. The protests received national attention and were the largest sit-ins in the state. The former teacher of many of the students drew a straight line between the demonstrations and the town's tradition of black education.[42] Alternatively, perhaps labor turmoil continued, exposing and aggravating fissures within the black shop workforce and the larger black community, and between black and white railroad employees. It could be that the civil rights movement in Marshall drew lessons from such workplace discord, over economic and racial issues, and, like the 1963 March on Washington, linked "jobs" and "freedom."

Black shopmen were clearly relevant to the World War I–era history of shop towns. In the early 1920s, most were not ramblers but were instead anchored, with their families, in Marshall. The desire for stability, the recent experience with federal policies, and the memory of whites' wartime betrayal of black strikers strengthened the resolve of petitioners to organize independently of whites for their collective benefit, despite threats of racial violence. The potential for some measure of protection from the white shopmen's unions, which were at once rigidly exclusive and relatively less hostile, in a context of reinvigorated corporate control, pulled others toward a prostrike position. The fact that black shop workers were a vital presence in Marshall during the World War I era, and until well after World War II, invites exploration of possible linkages between labor and civil rights struggles, there and in shop towns across the South.

* * *

The author appreciates the anonymous reviewers' advice to make one more push with the primary and secondary sources. She is also indebted to James Maroney and Michael Botson, scholars of Texas working-class history, for their insightful commentary on earlier drafts, and also to Mr. Jack Canson, Ms. Gail Beil, and Ms. Glenda Clay of Marshall, Texas, for sharing their knowledge of the town's history.

Notes

1. Scott Reynolds Nelson, *Steel Drivin' Man: John Henry, The Untold Story of an American Legend* (New York: Oxford University Press, 2006), 112–15; Isabel Wilkerson, *The Warmth of Other Suns: The Epic Story of America's Great Migration* (New York: Random House, 2010).

2. Eric Arnesen, *Brotherhoods of Color: Black Railroad Workers and the Struggle for Equality* (Cambridge: Harvard University Press, 2002); Joseph Kelly, "Organized for a Fair Deal: African American Railroad Workers in the Deep South, 1900–1940" (Ph.D. diss., University of Toronto, 2010); Colin Davis, *Power at Odds: The 1922 National Railroad Shopmen's Strike* (Urbana: University of Illinois Press, 1997); Theodore Kornweibel Jr., *Railroads in the African American Experience: A Photographic Journey* (Baltimore: Johns Hopkins University Press, 2010).

3. Kornweibel Jr., *Railroads in the African American Experience*, 304–9.

4. David Joseph Goldberg, *Discontented America: The United States in the 1920s* (Baltimore: Johns Hopkins University Press, 1999), 66.

5. Jackie S. Gabriel, "Unionizing the 'Jungle': A Century of Meatpacking Strikes," in *Encyclopedia of Strikes in American History*, ed. Aaron Brenner, Benjamin Day, and Immanuel Ness (London: Routledge, 2009), 378; *Dallas Morning News* (hereafter *DMN*), December 6, 7, 1921; *Fort Worth Star-Telegram* (hereafter *FWST*), December 3, 5, 1921; Joseph Abel, "Opening the Closed-Shop: The Galveston Longshoremen's Strike of 1920–1921," *Southwestern Historical Quarterly* 110 (2007): 317–47.

6. Davis, *Power at Odds*, 13 (table 1), 59–63; *FWST*, July 3, 1922; *DMN*, July 2–5, 1922.

7. Davis, *Power at Odds*, 11, 22–23, 27, 61; Ernest Obadele-Starks, *Black Unionism in the Industrial South* (College Station: Texas A&M University Press, 2000), 54; Arnesen, *Brotherhoods of Color*, 58 (quotation).

8. Kornweibel Jr., *Railroads in the African American Experience*, 305 (quotation), 307.

9. Eric Arnesen, "The Quicksands of Economic Insecurity: African Americans, Strikebreaking, and Labor Activism in the Industrial Era," in *The Black Worker: Race, Labor, and Civil Rights since Emancipation*, ed. Eric Arnesen (Chicago: University of Illinois Press, 2007), 44.

10. Davis, *Power at Odds*, 118–19 (quotation).

11. Arnesen, "The Quicksands of Economic Insecurity," 57–59.

12. *Dallas Express*, July 6, 8 (second quotation), September 9, 1922; *DMN*, July 8 (first quotations), 12; August 3, 10 (third quotations), 1922; *FWST*, August 4, 1922; *Wichita Daily Times*, July 12, 1922; *Longview News-Journal*, September 11, October 13, 1922; Davis, *Power at Odds*, 69.

13. *DMN*, July 4, 7–9, 31, 1922; *FWST*, July 3–6, 9, 18, 24, 1922.

14. Davis, *Power at Odds*, 48–63, 69–70; Kelly, "Organized for a Fair Deal," 73.

15. George N. Green with Michael R. Botson Jr., "Looking for Lefty: Liberal/Left Activism and Texas Labor, 1920s–1960s," in *The Texas Left: The Radical Roots of Lone Star Liberalism*, ed. David O'Donald Cullen and Kyle Wilkison (College Station: Texas A&M University Press, 2010), 113; Joseph Kelly, "Showing Agency on the Margins: African

American Railway Workers in the South and Their Unions, 1917–1930," *Labour / Le Travail* 71 (2013): 127, 133; *Dallas Express*, July 8, 1922.

16. Kelly, "Showing Agency on the Margins," 134; Kelly, "Organized for a Fair Deal," 7–8 (quotations), 11.

17. *DMN*, July 7, 1922; *Dallas Express*, July 1, 1922.

18. *FWST*, July 4–5, 7–8, 1922; *DMN*, July 5–6, 12, 18, 1922; City of Marshall, *Marshall News Messenger* Archives (hereafter *MNM*), July 1–8, 1922, http://www.marshalltexas.net/visitors/archived_articles.

19. *DMN*, July 8–9, 12, 14, 17, 19, 29, August 3, December 14, 1922; *FWST*, July 9, 20, 28, August 5, 1922.

20. *FWST*, December 8, 1921, January 22, 1922; *DMN*, January 9, 23, February 23, 1922.

21. *Dallas Express*, January 25, 1919; *DMN*, July 4, 1917; July and October 1919; July 8, 1920; *Houston Informer*, June 7, 1919; July 10, 1920; Part 7, May 12, 1922, Papers of the NAACP (Fondren Library, Rice University, Houston, TX); Ken Durham, "Longview Race Riot of 1919," Handbook of Texas Online (hereafter HTO), http://www.tshaonline.org/handbook/online/articles/jc102.

22. Quoted in Will Guzmán, *Civil Rights in the Texas Borderlands: Dr. Lawrence A. Nixon and Black Activism* (Urbana: University of Illinois Press, 2015), 28–29.

23. *MNM*, July 4, 8, 21, 22; *Shreveport Times*, July 8, 1922 (quotations); Michael Phillips, *White Metropolis: Race, Ethnicity, and Religion in Dallas, 1841–2001* (Austin: University of Texas Press, 2005), 121. The Klan did not always back white labor. In Mobile, Alabama, for example, the organization allied with "open shop" forces to help undermine a tenuous post–World War I alliance among black and white waterfront workers. The Klan, for example, kidnapped Ralph Clemmons, a leading black labor figure who was active among Mobile's longshoremen and laundry workers. See Robert H. Woodrum, "Race, Unionism, and the Open-Shop Movement along the Waterfront in Mobile, Alabama," in *Against Labor: How U.S. Employers Organized to Defeat Union Activism*, ed. Rosemary Feurer and Chad Pearson (Urbana: University of Illinois Press, 2017), 104–28.

24. As was the case in Mobile, it was typical for the Marshall paper, and area papers such as the *Longview-News Journal*, to ignore black life outside of reports on crime and lynching. (Issues of Texas black newspapers are limited for this period.) Mention of African American participation in labor protests, union activity, or workplace issues was rare in Texas newspapers. In Mobile, during times of labor turmoil, this seemed quite deliberate. See Woodrum, "Race, Unionism, and the Open-Shop Movement," 110, 116.

25. Arnesen, *Brotherhoods of Color*, 48–54.

26. Kelly, "Showing Agency on the Margins," 128.

27. Steven Hahn, *A Nation under Our Feet: Black Political Struggles in the Rural South from Slavery to the Great Migration* (Cambridge: Harvard University Press, 2003), 467–68 (quotations); Arnesen, *Brotherhoods of Color*, 43, 49–50, 65–73; Bernadette Pruitt, *The Other Great Migration: The Movement of Rural African Americans to Houston, 1900–1941* (College Station: Texas A&M University Press, 2013). Joseph Kelly observes that African American railroad workers' organizations general opposed dissolution of the

Railway Labor Board while white unionists tended to condemn the board as a tool of management. See Kelly, "Organized for a Fair Deal," 175–76.

28. Steven Reich, "Soldiers of Democracy: Black Texans and the Fight for Citizenship," *Journal of American History* 82, no. 4 (1996): 1490 (quotation).

29. Houston Branch Membership Rolls, July 1918, part 12, reel 19, Papers of the NAACP; *Houston City Directory 1917* (Morrison & Fourmy Directory Co., 1917); Pruitt, *The Other Great Migration*, 226.

30. Letter from E. C. Cooper, J. Honore, and G. Nelson to John Shillady, February 24, 1919, and Memorandum from John Shillady, March 28, 1919, part 10, reel 9, Papers of the NAACP.

31. Refund Claim from Rufus Reed to unnamed railroad superintendent, August 20, 1920, part 1, reel 5, Papers of the NAACP.

32. Reich, "Soldiers of Democracy," 1502, 1503 (table 2). Garveyism did not possess much in the way of organized expression in Texas, probably in part due to this tidal wave of postwar white violence. When UNIA commissioner to Texas R. B. Mosely visited rural northeast Texas in 1922, whites attacked and beat him brutally. See Mary G. Rolinson, *Grassroots Garveyism: The Universal Negro Improvement Association in the Rural South, 1920–1927* (Chapel Hill: University of North Carolina Press, 2012), 90. The fates of E. C. Cooper and his bricklayer compatriots may have discouraged activism around the NAACP in Marshall for some time. Inexplicably, NAACP national secretary John Shillady sent their letter to the Marshall newspaper and protested their treatment in a communication to Marshall's mayor. The 1920 census does not list the men's names. Shillady himself met with mob terror when he visited Austin in August 1919 on NAACP business. See Letter from John Shillady to E. C. Cooper, J. Honore, and G. Nelson, April 8, 1919, and Letter from John Shillady to the Mayor of Marshall, Tex., April 8, 1919, part 10, reel 9, Papers of the NAACP; Reich, "Soldiers of Democracy," 1500.

33. *Chicago Defender*, August 12 (quotation), September 2, 1922. Marshall, of course, was not the only site of black labor protest in a Texas railroad town. While the outcome is unknown, in Texarkana, Texas, black cooks and waiters together left the premises of five hotels in the city after managers, under pressure from the local Klan, fired all black bellhops. See *Marshall News Messenger*, August 6, 1921.

34. Report of J. J. Carey, Superintendent in Marshall Texas & Pacific Shops, September 24, 1916, Harrison County Historical Museum, Marshall, TX (hereafter HCHM); *MNM*, September 25, 29, 1916.

35. William P. Jones, *The Tribe of Black Ulysses: African American Lumber Workers in the Jim Crow South* (Urbana: University of Illinois Press, 2005), 52–56; Dave Oliphant, *Texan Jazz* (Austin: University of Texas Press, 1996) 74–75; "Marshall, Texas: The Birthplace of Boogie Woogie," accessed May 2016, http://boogiewoogiemarshall.com/about/; 1920 United States Census, Harrison County, TX, Marshall, HeritageQuest online.

36. Glenda Clay, interview by author, Marshall, TX, May 12, 2016; Gail Beil, "Wiley College," HTO, accessed August 2016, http://www.tshaonline.org/handbook/online/articles/kbw17; *Sketches Drawn from Marshall and Vicinity, Past and Present* (Marshall, TX: Prices's Print, 1919), 44–46; *Annual Report of the Missouri, Kansas & Texas Railway to the Railroad Commission of the State of Texas*, 1920, 1922, Texas State Library Archives,

Austin, TX; Cyrus Wilson LaGrone, "A Sociological Study of the Negro Population of Marshall, Texas" (master's thesis, University of Texas at Austin, 1932), 21–28.

37. LaGrone, "A Sociological Study"; *MNM*, October 8, 1921; 1920 United States Census, Harrison County, TX, Marshall.

38. LaGrone, "A Sociological Study," 61–64; Pruitt, *The Other Great Migration*, 37.

39. Mary M. Cronin, "C. F. Richardson and the Houston Informer's Fight for Equality in the 1920s," *American Journalism* 3, no. 3 (2006): 84–86; Jennifer Bridges, "Buard, Rebecca D.," HTO, http://www.tshaonline.org/handbook/online/articles/fbuca; Robin Roe, "Wells, Henrietta Pauline Bell," HTO, http://www.tshaonline.org/handbook/online/articles/fwe87; Gail K. Beil, "Farmer, James Leonard, Jr.," HTO, http://www.tshaonline.org/handbook/online/articles/ffa19; Robert Johnson Jr., "McAfee, Walter Samuel," in *African American National Biography*, ed. Henry Louis Gates Jr., Oxford African American Studies Center, accessed June 2017, http://www.oxfordaasc.com/article/opr/t0001/e3302; Gail Beil, interview by author, Marshall, TX, May 12, 2016.

40. 1920 United States Census, Harrison County, TX, Marshall; *City Directory for Marshall, Texas* (Springfield, MO: C. B. Page, 1924).

41. "The Black Citizen and American Democracy: Black Culture in Harrison County, Past, Present, and Future," 1976, HCHM.

42. Gail Beil, "Four Marshallites' Roles in the Passage of the Civil Rights Act of 1964," *Southwestern Historical Quarterly* 106 (2002): 12–14.

11

African American and Latino Workers in the Age of Industrial Agriculture

ERIN L. CONLIN

Industrial agriculture is destroying the environment.
It's destroying the health of our people.

Tirso Moreno, cofounder, Farmworker Association of Florida[1]

Southern farmworkers have been largely invisible to the American public, from African Americans laboring in the fields during slavery and the Jim Crow era to more recent generations of Latino farmworkers who entered southern farming operations as predominantly undocumented, migrant labor. Scholarly accounts of farm labor tend to treat the African American and Latino experiences separately, but there is real value in considering overlap and interconnections.[2] Extensive pesticide and chemical exposure in the post–World War II period highlight shared encounters with coercive labor structures, state hostility, economic marginality, racial discrimination, and bleak working conditions. Drawing directly on workers' lived experiences this chapter opens a window into the modern labor and environmental history of southern farmwork. Oral histories with men and women associated with postwar farming in Apopka, Florida, provide a lens through which we can analyze the related histories of African American and Latino workers.[3] Understanding the deep history of exploitation and negligence enables us to understand the challenges facing the South's new working class.

Oral testimonies, archival documents, and secondary sources all highlight pesticide exposure as one of the greatest threats to farmworkers both historically and today. It affects workers, their families, and the environment. Chemical usage increased exponentially in wake of World War II, as civilians began looking for ways to use wartime chemicals in domestic pursuits.[4] Insecticides, herbicides, and fungicides helped farmers eliminate many of the elements that could damage or destroy an entire crop. Until the 1980s, however, there was little definitive data regarding the unintended consequences of pesticide usage on plants and animals, including their effects on humans.[5] Even as information emerged, politicians largely ignored workers' concerns, favoring agricultural producers because the latter wielded substantial political power, especially in states like Florida. For example, what little regulation existed in Florida occurred under the auspice of the Department of Agriculture—the agency tasked with promoting agricultural development.[6] Unsurprisingly, the department put most of its efforts into supporting the interests of its clientele, Florida growers, over those of the workers who regularly came into contact with pesticides. With limited political protections and no sufficient union representation, workers are often exploited.

Federal and state legislation has made it difficult for agricultural and private-sector workers to unionize historically and today. For example, the 1935 Wagner Act granted industrial unions basic federal protections but excluded fieldworkers and domestics. Furthermore, Florida adopted "Right to Work" language in its 1944 constitution.[7] Many southern states followed suit and remain right-to-work states. During World War II, state and federal government officials also undermined workers by conceding to grower demands. As Cindy Hahamovitch demonstrated in *The Fruits of Their Labor,* the importation of Bracero, Bahamian, and British West Indians displaced American farmworkers, drove down wages, and solidified an agricultural labor system reliant on foreign, low-wage, migrant workers. Americans had to accept lower wages or face replacement by foreign workers. Guest workers who attempted to express dissatisfaction over wages or working conditions, much less strike or try to unionize, were deported.[8] Given these circumstances, Florida farmworkers have rarely organized successfully. There are two exceptions to this trend.

The United Farm Workers of America (UFW) hired Tirso Moreno, cofounder of the Farmworker Association of Florida (FWAF), to help unionize citrus harvesters for the Minute Maid division of Coca-Cola in 1972.[9] Although these efforts were successful, the company did not renew the union contract the following year.[10] The second successful unionization effort occurred in 1999, when the UFW helped mushroom harvesters at Quincy Farms secure an eighteen-month contract.[11]

The failure of formal labor unions to take hold in Florida and throughout much of the Southeast explains why advocacy groups like the FWAF or the Coalition of Immokalee Workers (CIW) are vitally important to fighting for workers' rights. The CIW is a worker-run human rights organization founded in 1993. It successfully organized the "Penny per Pound" campaign and "Fair Food Program" to raise wages and improve working conditions for tomato harvesters.[12] The CIW has used union-like tactics—marches and boycotts—to force major retailers utilizing large quantities of tomatoes to negotiate plans with farm owners and farmworkers to increase the amount they pay for tomatoes so that the extra money supplements workers' wages. The CIW's efforts have proven successful but they remain largely limited to tomato workers.[13] Additionally, although the organization addresses pesticide issues, they are not primary concerns.

Tirso Moreno has dedicated his life to fighting unjust working conditions, focusing explicitly on pesticide exposure. The FWAF advocates for more stringent federal and state pesticide restrictions and employer compliance. It also provides training for workers and health care providers to diagnose and prevent pesticide exposure, which was and remains a threat to worker welfare. The experiences of Florida's historically black agricultural workers highlight the many challenges facing the new predominantly Latino workforce.

Apopka, Florida, headquarters of the FWAF, provides a useful case study for examining the impact of pesticide exposure and the power of oral histories to understand how farmworkers themselves experienced pesticide exposure and dealt with the consequences. Documentary evidence provides data around pesticide application and the possible impacts of exposure, but it does not teach us about the lived experience of navigating a landscape fraught with potential toxins. As Jean Lucner Millien, a Haitian American activist and former farmworker, pointed out, he and the other workers "were not stupid"—they knew they were being exposed to chemicals but they had few real options for mitigating the situation.[14] Dorceta E. Taylor's *Toxic Communities: Environmental Racism, Industrial Pollution, and Residential Mobility* examines how communities marginalized by race, class, or both suffer significant environmental injustices and are often unable to move to healthier locations.[15] Within this broader framework of environmental injustice, the Apopka oral testimonies reveal the difficult decisions economically and racially marginalized people made in order to survive and thrive in a given situation. Facing an onslaught of industrial pollution, these farmworkers' testimonies reveal the complex intersection of employment, health, and the environment.

An Environmental History

Apopka is a small city located roughly twenty miles northwest of Orlando, situated along a lake that bears its name. For generations, local community members harvested foodstuffs from the lake and its surrounding habitat. The history of this small community changed dramatically during World War II when it became one of the state's leading agricultural communities. Federal and state government officials worked together to drain off large portions of Lake Apopka, along the northern edge, to make the rich "mucklands" of the former lake available for farming to meet food demands generated by the war. Government agencies helped private companies convert over twenty thousand acres of the lake's wetlands into large-scale farming operations, subsequently referred to as the Zellwood Drainage District.

Farm operations in the Zellwood Drainage District and those just outside it, like A. Duda & Sons, profited immensely, but it came at a high cost to the environment.[16] For nearly fifty years, area farms engaged in a system of flooding and draining the mucklands to irrigate and prepare the land, resulting in a constant transfer of pesticide and fertilizer-laced water between the lake and the fields. Eventually phosphorus discharge from the farms led to algae blooms that destroyed the lake's habitat. Waste discharge from local citrus processing plants and burgeoning local communities also increased the lake's toxicity. A 1980 chemical spill of a substance similar to DDT, by Tower Chemical Company, resulted in the Environmental Protection Agency (EPA) declaring the area a Superfund site in 1983.[17]

The state began restoring the devastated wetlands in the mid-1980s and purchasing and closing the area's "muck farms" in 1996 in an effort to rehabilitate the environment after decades of toxic chemical exposure.[18] Although a positive change for the area's flora and fauna, this action displaced approximately twenty-five hundred (predominately African American) farmworkers who had previously worked the muck farms.[19] Government assistance went mainly to addressing environmental concerns. Former farmworkers were left with few alternative employment or job retraining opportunities, and virtually no money was spent investigating how long-term pesticide exposure affected former farmworkers' and community members' health. Workers had faced direct exposure through their jobs and, like the area wildlife, residual exposure by eating contaminated food from the lake.

Pesticide Exposure

> We didn't have any pesticide education. The bosses knew the pesticides were dangerous and they would fly a plane and spray it over the fields like a mist. In the fields we wore big straw hats to stop it from spraying us in the face.
>
> Earma Lee Carey Peterson, former farmworker

Florida, with its temperate climate and copious insects, provided both opportunities and challenges for farmers.[20] The climate suited agricultural production, but countless rodents, insects, and fungi threatened crops. From the 1940s onward, then, chemicals became a staple in industrial agriculture. Few regulations existed and little was known about the impact pesticides could have on people or the environment, so growers applied chemicals freely.

Geraldean Matthew and Linda Lee, Apopka residents and former farmworkers, recalled how pesticides would "rain down" on them while they worked in the fields.[21] Betty Jean Dubose explained how they felt "all messed up" and "sticky" when the crop dusters sprayed them from overhead.[22] Dubose and Johanna Collins both recalled being sprayed every few days even though the two women worked in different agricultural industries. Dubose worked on the muck (vegetable) farms. Collins worked in the ornamental plant nurseries. Collins estimated she and fellow workers were sprayed about three times a week, and this occurred regularly for the five to six years she worked there.[23] Outdoor exposure often resulted from crop dusters flying directly overhead or pesticide clouds drifting over from neighboring fields.[24] Jean Lucner Millien, working in the 1980s, recalled running across the fields trying to stay out of the blowing toxic pesticide drift.

Millien explained that workers "felt something" and although they were not sure what exactly made them feel poor at the time, they knew something was making them sick. He said this was particularly true in the orange groves, where workers could "see something dark on the leaves."[25] He recalled one friend who broke out in a rash all over his arms, a common reaction to pesticide poisoning. Other citrus workers reiterated Millien's assessment that orange groves were among the more toxic work environments. Robert Griffin grew up in a farmworking family and reported his father lost his sight after spraying citrus groves with the toxin pyridine. He remained blind for the rest of his life.[26] William Gladden recalled Temik as the worst chemical he worked with as a citrus grove manager. Although designed to kill nematodes, he argued, "it'd kill everything else, including you." This assessment may have been somewhat hyperbolic, but there was enough concern over the use of Temik that it was temporarily banned in 1984 after it was linked to groundwater contamination. The *Port St. Lucie News Tribune*, which investigated the pesticide issue in the county's citrus industry in 1988, reported that Temik was a carbamate and its active ingredient, aldicarb, was "at least 250 times more deadly for mammals than DDT."[27] Eventually, growers reincorporated Temik into the pesticide regimen, but it could be applied only during the dry season and it could not be used within three hundred feet of a well, with the restriction increased up to one thousand feet depending on the type of soil.[28]

These types of restrictions protected some people, but not farmworkers living in unregulated employer-owned camps or cabins. A 1971 report estimated 22,276 out-of-state workers and their family members lived in private housing, often in nonpermitted camps.[29] Florida legislation required labor camps meet health and sanitation requirements, but the state lacked sufficient funds or manpower to regularly inspect the facilities. As a result, many camps were unlicensed operations run by private farm owners or crew leaders. In 1973, the Department of Health and Rehabilitative Services identified 407 labor camps in Florida, only 259 of which were permitted.[30] Individual employers usually built these unlicensed camps in rural, isolated areas close to the fields or groves where workers labored. Local activist Sister Gail Grimes recalled in the 1970s they did not know where the Latino farmworkers in Apopka lived because they rarely saw them around town. Over time they discovered many workers and their families living in "horrible conditions . . . in the middle of orange groves" in employer-provided labor camps or housing.[31]

This housing arrangement elevated one's risk of exposure. Homes could be directly sprayed or indirectly affected by toxins drifting over from recently sprayed adjacent fields. Most pesticides have a regulated minimum "reentry" time, meaning the amount of time—usually measured in hours or days—that must pass before people are allowed into a treated field. The more toxic the chemical, the longer the reentry period. If workers and their families lived in the fields or groves, they likely would not be able to wait the appropriate amount of time before reentering the treated area. Additionally, most of these informal labor camps would not have certified wells for drinking water, so there were no guarantees the water was potable and toxin free.

Children and families faced exposure in other ways as well. Many of the Apopka interviewees related stories about accompanying their parents to the fields as children, or bringing their children with them, unaware of the possible exposure to pesticides.[32] Children both played and worked in the fields. Working children faced the greatest risks because they had direct contact with the pesticide-covered plants, fruits, and vegetables they touched while tending or harvesting crops. Chemicals also reached children's bloodstreams in utero.

Women often worked in the fields throughout their pregnancies, potentially exposing their fetuses to harmful toxins. A study in the 1980s found that fetal blood samples collected from pregnant women exposed to DDT contained about half the amount found in maternal blood.[33] Chemicals the mother is exposed to and life-sustaining nourishment alike pass through the placenta. Scientists, however, generally lack hard data that specifically link pesticides and birth defects. The reasons are twofold: one, it can be difficult to test subjects immediately for exposure since workers may not seek, or be allowed to seek, immediate medical assistance; and two, a variety of factors can complicate fetal development, and it is difficult to isolate pesticides as the sole causal factor. Consequently, many scientists and activists have relied on anecdotal evidence in addition to lab test results on mammals to make their arguments that pesticides may cause birth defects.

In 1988 the *News Tribune* in Port St. Lucie, Florida, reported the story of Maria and Ruben Cienfuegos, farmworkers in Indiantown, who lost their baby during the eighth month of pregnancy. The fetus had no hands or feet and one side of his face was smooth because the eye never formed. Mr. Cienfuegos recalled working with the chemicals captan, paraquat, and parathion as a pesticide sprayer, and Mrs. Cienfuegos had hoed trees in a citrus grove throughout her pregnancy, where she likely interacted with trees that had been sprayed.[34] Even if organophosphates like parathion were not "acutely toxic," they might cause cancer or birth defects from chronic effect.[35] Since the 1970s, scientific research began linking chemicals like parathion to congenital deformities and genetic mutations, and a 1988 crop sheet from the Texas Department of Agriculture noted parathion is "suspected of causing birth defects, [and] reproductive effects" among other health issues.[36] Neither of the Cienfuegoses knew about the potential severe negative effects of pesticide exposure to a developing fetus, and although there was no conclusive proof that pesticides caused their son's deformities, incidents like this sparked intense concern over the potential harm pesticide exposure could cause pregnant women and children.

Similar events occurred in 2004 and 2005, in which three children born within three months of each other suffered severe birth defects. One child was born without any limbs, another suffered from Pierre Robin syndrome, and the third child, who died a few days after birth, was born missing facial features like her nose and ear and lacked visible sexual organs. The mothers all worked in the same tomato fields during their pregnancies and lived in the same labor camp in Immokalee, Florida.[37] The investigation yielded no conclusive proof pesticides caused the birth defects, but lab tests showed that some of the chemicals caused birth defects in mammals. Ag-Mart, the company that owned the fields, eventually quit using chemicals linked to birth defects, but it stopped short of claiming responsibility for the babies' birth defects.[38]

Although researchers have not been able to declare a direct link, several studies conducted in the 1990s and early 2000s "showed an association between DDT exposure and miscarriage or preterm birth."[39] Researchers found both DDT and DDE disrupted "placental detoxification machinery," which they believed might "lead to an increased susceptibility of the fetus to environmental toxins and may be a risk factor for recurrent pregnancy loss."[40] Some Apopka residents were exposed to DDE in the fields and after the 1980 Tower Chemical Company spill. Many interviewees noted they, or people they knew, had miscarriages or gave birth to low-birthweight babies.

Apopka resident Leroy Bell expressed concern that other toxins could also be negatively affecting the community. In particular, he was nervous about the landfills, wastewater treatment plant, and medical waste incinerator situated in his neighborhood, which was predominantly African American. In an approximately two-block radius he pointed out at least seven households with low-birthweight babies, at least five of whom died shortly after birth.[41] These incidents may or may not have resulted from pesticides or exposure to other toxins, but the data points to the need for further investigation.

In addition to absorbing toxins in the womb and via a mother's milk, children face indirect pesticide exposure in other ways, like fabric or dermal contact. To prevent exposure, work clothes must be washed separately from the rest of the family's clothes. Likewise, children should not have physical contact with someone who is still wearing work clothes. The EPA and many farmworker advocates, both historically and today, provide literature to farmworkers illustrating how best to avoid exposing other people after working with toxic chemicals.[42] Nevertheless, people are sometimes exposed, and this highlights another critical problem for farmworkers and their families.

Pesticide poisoning is not common among the general population, so few doctors are prepared to recognize symptoms, run appropriate tests, and diagnose exposure. Since mild exposure also tends to have fairly generic symptoms like rash, fatigue, nausea, and so on, they are easily and often attributed to other possible health conditions. Finally, the body eliminates low levels of organophosphates in three to six days, so health care providers must test immediately for the toxins, and this rarely occurs. As a result, many cases go unreported.

Employment and community pressures exacerbate underreporting issues. In some cases workers know they have been exposed to pesticides but refuse to visit a doctor because they fear retaliation from their employer.[43] They also avoid going to the doctor because they cannot earn money if they are not working.[44] Furthermore, some doctors felt pressure from local agricultural employers not to diagnose possible pesticide poisoning because it was detrimental to the employer's business.

Historically, pesticide poisoning was significantly underreported in Florida. Even in 1980, when exposure was becoming a matter of public concern, the EPA Pesticide Monitoring System was voluntary. Between 1982 and 1988, Florida reported 160 incidents.[45] In contrast, California, which experts identified as having the most rigorous and successful reporting procedures, had 1,779 cases that were "either confirmed or suspected pesticide exposure" incidents in 1985 *alone*.[46]

Conclusions

Scientists and farmworkers alike may not have known, or been able to prove unequivocally, the potential impacts of pesticides; but, as Jean Lucner Millien argued, farmworkers knew something was harming them even if they did not know the specific details about the causes and effects.[47] In the absence of effective public health surveillance systems, both scientists and activists have had to rely on anecdotal evidence and the testimony of individual farmworkers in making policy decisions and determining future research topics. As the evidence indicates, Florida routinely failed to report pesticide cases. This quantitative failure highlights the need to utilize qualitative data that can point to areas for further investigation and inquiry, like the impact of pesticide exposure on pregnancy and fetal development. Oral histories are central to this mission. Not only do they alert us to potential problems, but they also illustrate the ways in which farmworkers attempted to adapt or adjust their routines to limit risk and harm.

Mary Tinsely and other interviewees expressed concern about accidentally exposing their children to pesticide residues by repurposing the containers the pesticides came in for household use. She recalled rinsing the containers and then using them for household chores like soaking clothes when doing laundry.[48] Geraldean Matthew described how they would store foodstuffs, like sugar and flour, or children's clothes in the containers. Lacking sophisticated knowledge about pesticides and their residues, workers would take home the empty containers, rinse them with soap and water, and then put them to use in a variety of ways. She explained how low-income people do not have the luxury of buying many nonessentials, so they make use of available resources. Looking back, Matthew reflected that children often had rashes and broken skin, but that no one, including the doctor, knew what caused the problems. She now wonders whether the pesticides were to blame.[49] Like most Americans at the time, the mothers had no idea pesticide residues could permeate the container walls, slowly releasing their poison over time. The women were not thoughtless or irresponsible—in Jean Lucner Millien's words, "not stupid." Facing real economic limitations, they made the best choices they could with the information and opportunities available at the time.

If we are looking for connections between past and present workers in the American South we need only to talk to farmworkers today, since they face the same challenges as their black counterparts did in the mid- to late twentieth century. Negligent pesticide application practices continue today, causing the issue to persist as a major concern for modern farm labor advocates.[50]

As Joan Flocks notes, both *historically* and today, legislation often fails to fully protect agricultural workers.[51] This is due to the system of "agricultural exceptionalism," which long exempted farmworkers from many regulations that could afford some measure of protection. For example, labor laws introduced in the 1930s exempted agricultural workers for political reasons.[52] President Franklin Delano Roosevelt excluded African American farmworkers from New Deal labor legislation in order to shore up his political support amongst southern white Democrats. Since African Americans throughout the South were disfranchised, Roosevelt found it politically expedient to cater to power-holding white supremacists. This meant excluding agricultural and domestic workers from most labor protections so that they remained economically dependent upon white employers.

Employers today often utilize labor practices like hiring labor contractors or temporary workers, which enables the employer to shift the burden of risk to the workers.[53] In 1947, the government enacted the Federal Insecticide, Fungicide, and Rodenticide Act (FIFRA) to regulate pesticides entering the marketplace after World War II. In 1970, the U.S. government created the EPA and moved the FIFRA administrative staff from the U.S. Department of Agriculture to the EPA. The EPA also developed the Worker Protection Standard in 1974 to regulate pesticides, but both this measure and FIFRA have fallen short. The power to enforce pesticide restrictions was transferred to states, and as the evidence here and elsewhere indicates, states like Florida routinely failed to adequately regulate exposure and protect workers.[54]

The large number of undocumented, non–native English speakers working in agriculture makes it more difficult to promote pesticide awareness among workers. Undocumented workers are less likely to raise concerns about workplace conditions, because they fear deportation. Additionally, documentation about pesticides (labels on the packages, signs posted in the fields, or literature distributed by state agencies or local advocacy groups) may prove insufficient if the workers cannot read it. Many contemporary workers speak Spanish, Haitian Creole, and a variety of indigenous languages found in Mexico and Central America. Pesticide literature usually incorporates images to get the main points across, but this does not help workers who have already been exposed to chemicals. Their inability to easily communicate with others and marginal status in society makes them easy to exploit.

Industrial agriculture has long capitalized on the traditional model of southern labor by taking advantage of impoverished workers with few available alternative opportunities. In the past, farmworkers were typically black workers subjected to Jim Crow segregation and coercive labor practices. Today, most farmworkers are individuals born in Mexico or Central America who accept high-risk positions in agriculture because they "are low-income, ethnic minorities who often feel they have little control over their workplace."[55] Regardless of their backgrounds or the periods in which they worked in American agriculture, workers' stories teach us that only when we move away from an agricultural system based on the exploitation of low-wage and now predominantly undocumented workers with few alternative employment opportunities will we see significant social and economic improvements for workers in the American South.

Notes

1. FAF 004 Tirso Moreno. The oral histories in this article come from the Farmworker Association of Florida Collection, housed at the Samuel Proctor Oral History Program and in the University of Florida Digital Collections (hereafter FAF).

2. Pete Daniel, *The Shadow of Slavery: Peonage in the South, 1901–1969* (Urbana: University of Illinois Press, 1972), focuses on the African American experience. Ella Schmidt, *The Dream Fields of Florida: Mexican Farmworkers and the Myth of Belonging* (Lanham, MD: Lexington Books, 2009), examines Latino experiences. Charles D. Thompson Jr. and Melinda F. Wiggins, *The Human Cost of Food: Farmworkers' Lives, Labor, and Advocacy* (Austin: University of Texas Press, 2002), discusses the shared experiences of black and Latino migrant laborers, though most chapters focus on the latter. David Griffith, *American Guestworkers: Jamaicans and Mexicans in the U.S. Labor Market* (University Park: Pennsylvania State University Press, 2006). Cindy Hahamovitch, *The Fruits of Their Labor: Atlantic Coast Farmworkers and the Making of Migrant Poverty, 1870–1945* (Chapel Hill: University of North Carolina Press, 1997), and Cindy Hahamovitch, *No Man's Land: Jamaican Guestworkers in America and the Global History of Deportable Labor* (Princeton: Princeton University Press, 2012), include both black and Latino labor but mainly focus on guest worker programs and experiences.

3. In summer 2013, partnering with the Farmworker Association of Florida (FWAF),

my students collected twenty-six interviews with residents of Apopka, Florida, who were all associated with farmwork in some capacity. Roughly two-thirds of the interviewees identified as African American. Of the remaining one-third, one interviewee identified as white, two as Haitian American, and five as Latino. Several participants' oral histories also appear in Dale Slongwhite, *Fed Up: The High Cost of Cheap Food* (Gainesville: University Press of Florida, 2014).

4. The Germans created chemicals like organophosphate nerve poisons to use during the war. See Pete Daniel, *Toxic Drift: Pesticides and Health in the Post–World War II South* (Baton Rouge: Louisiana State University Press, 2005), 2, 5.

5. Rachel Carson first introduced Americans to the deadly effects of DDT in her groundbreaking work *Silent Spring* (New York: Houghton Mifflin, 1962). She explained how America's unfettered use of persistent chemicals like DDT was destroying the natural world. It took decades, however, for people to grasp the full implications of pesticide exposure.

6. Florida Rural Legal Services, *Danger in the Field: The Myth of Pesticide Safety* (1980), 24, RG 100 Office of the Governor. series 1423 Florida. Governor's Advisory Council on Farmworker Affairs, box 2, folder Correspondence, October 6, 1988, S1423, State Archives of Florida, Tallahassee (hereafter SAF).

7. Article 1, section 6 of the Constitution of the State of Florida "prohibits union shop and agency shop arrangements, which require workers to belong to a union or support union activity." See Talbot D'Alemberte, *The Florida State Constitution*, 2nd ed. (New York: Oxford University Press, 2016), 43.

8. Hahamovitch, *The Fruits of Their Labor*.

9. FAF 004 Tirso Moreno.

10. "Florida Farm Strike a Lesson in Organizing Problems," *New York Times*, April 20, 1978. Coca-Cola, however, did ban the use of several major chemicals in its fields, including parathion, DDT, and Temik (1981) to name a few. It continued to use other toxic chemicals, but implemented a testing system to try to protect workers. See Bill Maxwell, "Coca-Cola, Union Join to Protect Workers," *Port St. Lucie News Tribune*, March 31, 1988, H11. RG 200 Florida Department of Agriculture and Consumer Services, series 1911 Assistant Commissioner of Agriculture Martha Rhodes Administrative Support File, box 2, folder S1911 ("Pesticides-1988, box 2, FF7"), SAF.

11. Steven Greenhouse, "Picking and Packing Portobellos, Now with a Union Contract," *New York Times*, July 21, 1999.

12. As a human right organization, the CIW focuses explicitly on "social responsibility, human trafficking, and gender-based violence at work" ("About CIW," Coalition of Immokalee Workers website, http://www.ciw-online.org).

13. "About CIW." The Fair Food Program expanded into tomatoes in several states as well as Florida strawberries and peppers in 2015.

14. FAF 007 Jean Lucner Millien. Virtually no interviewees revealed the names of the farms they previously worked on. In one instance, a participant revealed the name of a farm and later asked to have it removed from the interview and transcript. She did not reveal the reason for this request, but it may be because she still lives in Apopka, where many of the former farm owners remain powerful community members.

15. Dorceta E. Taylor, *Toxic Communities: Environmental Racism, Industrial Pollution, and Residential Mobility* (New York: New York University Press, 2014).

16. A. Duda & Sons owned much of the nine thousand acres of farmland just north of Lake Apopka, outside the Zellwood Drainage District. See "A to Z: Zellwood Drainage and Water Control District Brochure," photocopy of original fifteen-page brochure by Henry Swanson, binder 1962, drawer 1938–1987, Friends of Lake Apopka Archives, Ginn Museum, Oakland Nature Preserve, Oakland, FL, https://richesmi.cah.ucf.edu/omeka/files/original/91963639374e2b65ddd7ca96bdbba321.pdf.

17. Nano Riley, *Florida's Farmworkers in the Twenty-First Century* (Gainesville: University Press of Florida, 2003), 137–38. The company released dicofol, an organocholorine in the DDE/DDT pesticide family, into an unlined percolation pond that overflowed and eventually passed into the lake. See Associated Press, "Lake Apopka Worse Off Than Previously Thought," *Ocala Star-Banner*, August 5, 1994; Susan O'Reilly, "Researchers Seek Answers to Gator Plight," *Gainesville Sun*, July 12, 1993. Information about Lake Apopka's history is available through the website of the St. Johns River Water Management District (SJRWMD), the Florida state agency tasked with the lake's restoration.

18. The state passed the Lake Apopka Restoration Act of 1985 followed by Florida's Surface Water Improvement and Management Act in 1987. Between 1998 and 2001, the U.S. Department of Agriculture and the SJRWMD purchased nearly all of the muck farms on the lake's north shore. Subsequent legislation further restricted the amount of phosphorous farms could release into the lake. Physical reclamation began in 1998. See Riley, *Florida's Farmworkers in the Twenty-First Century*, 140.

19. Most job loss estimates range from twenty-five hundred to three thousand. Riley places the estimate closer to five thousand. See Riley, *Florida's Farmworkers in the Twenty-First Century*, 138.

20. FAF 009 Earma Lee Carey Peterson (Earma Lee Carey Peterson quote in epigraph).

21. FAF 008 Geraldean Matthew; FAF 013 Linda Lee.

22. FAF 014 Betty Jean Dubose.

23. FAF 014 Betty Jean Dubose; FAF 021 Johanna Collins.

24. For more information see Daniel, *Toxic Drift*.

25. FAF 007 Jean Lucner Millien.

26. FAF 012 Robert Griffin and William Gladden. Pyridine is used to make the herbicide paraquat.

27. "A Chemical Chronology: EDB and Temik," *Port St. Lucie News Tribune*, March 31, 1988, H17. RG 200, series 1911, box 2 ("incl. dates 1984–1989"), folder S1911 ("Pesticide-1988, box 2, FF7"), SAF. The article did not provide corroborating evidence for this statistic, but it did note that although no known deaths were attributed to Temik the product is related to a chemical that killed thousands of people in Bhopal, India, in 1984. The newspaper put the death toll around two thousand, but subsequent research places it close to fifteen thousand. Additionally, many survivors bore children with significant birth defects and disabilities. See Alan Taylor, "Bhopal: The World's Worst Industrial Disaster, 30 Years Later," *Atlantic*, December 2, 2014, accessed November 16, 2016, http://www.theatlantic.com/photo/2014/12/bhopal-the-worlds-worst-industrial-disaster-30-years-later/100864/.

28. Bill Maxwell, "Coca-Cola, Union Join to Protect Workers," *Port St. Lucie News Tribune*, March 31, 1988, H11. RG 200, series 1911, box 2, folder S1911 ("Pesticides-1988, box 2, FF7"), SAF.

29. "Report: Migrant Farmworker Problem Areas and Agencies, Legislative Committees, and Other Organizations Involved in Alleviation Thereof," July 24, 1973, RG 855 Migrant Labor Program, box 2, series 568 Department of Community Affairs, Div. of Community Services, Migrant Labor subject files, 1970–1978, folder Community Affairs-Migrant Labor subject files [Legislative Committee-Migrant Labor Advisory Committee] S. 568 #41, SAF.

30. Department of Health and Rehabilitative Services, Division of Health, June 1, 1973, RG 800 Dept. of Health and Rehabilitation, series 595 Health programs subject files, 1969–1975, box 2, series 595, H.R.S. Office of the Sec. Div. of Health, 1974–1975, folder Health, Division of Migrant Labor Camps, 1973, SAF.

31. FAF 017 Sister Gail Grimes.

32. Little scientific data existed in the 1980s when the general public first became concerned about residual pesticide exposure. Congress did not take action until 1996, when it passed the Food Quality Protection Act in response to public concern following the 1993 National Academy of Sciences' report "Pesticides in the Diets of Infants and Children."

33. Bill Maxwell, "Birth Defect-Pesticide Link Difficult to Establish," *Port St. Lucie News Tribune*, March 31, 1988, H6. RG 200, series 1911, box 2, folder S1911 ("Pesticides-1988, box 2, FF7"), SAF.

34. The National Academy of Sciences issued a report in 1987 identifying pesticides whose residues carried the "greatest oncogenic [cancer-causing] risk." Captan was on the list. See Confidential Memo: on foods with oncogenic risk, From Florida Department of Agriculture and Consumer Services, Martha E. Rhodes, PhD, to Commissioner Conner, May 4, 1987, RG 200, series 1911, box 1, folder S1911, Pesticide Residues, box 1, FF9, SAF. It identified paraquat as an organic groundwater pollutant and a teratogen, or "chemical that acts during pregnancy to produce a physical or functional defect in the developing offspring." See M. P. Rao and P.S.C. Rao (student assistant and professor), "Soil Science Fact Sheet, Organic Pollutants in Groundwater: 1, Health Effects," Soil Science Department, Institute of Food and Agricultural Sciences, University of Florida, Gainesville, RG 200, series 1911, box 2, incl. dates 1984–1989, folder S1911 Pesticides-1988 (2 of 4), box 2 FF13, SAF.

35. "Soil Science Fact Sheet, Organic Pollutants in Groundwater: 1, Health Effects"; "Farm Workers, Children May Carry 'Body Burdens,'" *Port St. Lucie News Tribune*, March 31, 1988, H5. RG 200, series 1911, box 1, folder S1911, Pesticide Residues, box 1, FF9, SAF.

36. "Public Service Handout, Crop Sheet," Texas Department of Agriculture, 1988, RG 100 Office of the Governor, series 1423 Florida, Governor's Advisory Council on Farmworker Affairs, box 1, incl. dates 1984–1989, folder S1911, Pesticide Residues, box 1, FF9, SAF.

37. John Lantigua, "Why Was Carlitos Born This Way?" *Palm Beach Post*, March 13, 2005, accessed July 2016, http://www.mypalmbeachpost.com/news/carlitos/.

38. Christine Stapleton and Christine Evans, "Ag-Mart Produce Says It No Longer Will Use Chemicals Linked to Birth Defects, Asserting There Is 'Nothing in the Investigation That Will Say We Should Do This,'" *Palm Beach Post*, October 1, 2005, accessed July 2016, http://www.mypalmbeachpost.com/news/carlitos/.

39. Ezra J. Mremba, Federico M. Rubino, Gabri Brambilla, Angelo Moretto, Aristidis M. Tsatsakis, and Claudio Colosio, "Persistent Organochlorinated Pesticides and Mechanisms of Their Toxicity," *Toxicology* 307 (2013): 80.

40. Mremba, Rubino, Brambilla, Moretto, Tsatsakis, Colosio, "Persistent Organochlorinated Pesticides and Mechanisms of Their Toxicity," 80.

41. FAF 025 Leroy Bell. See Taylor's *Toxic Communities* for more information about why communities that are low-income, minority, or both most often suffer from environmental injustice and cannot easily remedy or escape their circumstances.

42. An example of an illustrated English-language EPA pamphlet is Association of Farmworker Opportunity Programs, "How Can We Protect Our Families from Pesticides?" https://www.epa.gov/sites/production/files/2015-05/documents/afop-brochure-fl1002.pdf.

43. Bill Maxwell, "Silence Shrouds Worker Illnesses," *Port St. Lucie News Tribune*, March 31, 1988, H6, H9. RG 200, series 1911, folder S1911, Pesticide Residues, box 1, FF9, SAF.

44. In the past, employers exploited loopholes in workers' compensation legislation and denied workers coverage by claiming the crew leaders were the employers, not the growers. See Maxwell, "Silence Shrouds Worker Illnesses."

45. Roger Inman, "Use Violations," 1986, RG 100, series 1423, box 2, folder Pesticide Sub-Handouts-Correspondence, November 3, 1988, S1423, SAF.

46. Initially there were 2,499 reported cases of possible poisoning. Eventually, 611 were found to be unrelated to pesticides, and 109 were nonoccupational incidents and therefore outside the scope of the California Department of Food and Agriculture's purview. See Inman, "Use Violations," and California Department of Food and Agriculture, Division of Pest Management, Environmental Protection, and Worker Safety, "Summary of Reports from Physicians of Illnesses That Were Possibly Related to Pesticide Exposure during the Period January 1–December 31, 1985, in California," RG 100, series 1423, box 2, folder Pesticide Sub-Committee-Work Group, Nov. 3, 1988, S1423, SAF.

47. FAF 007 Jean Lucner Millien.

48. FAF 022 Mary Tinsley.

49. FAF 008 Geraldean Matthew. At one point Matthew had a rash for six weeks, but the doctor never asked what kind of work she did, so potential pesticide exposure never entered the conversation.

50. Advocacy groups like Farmworker Justice, National Farm Worker Ministry, Farmworker Association of Florida, and Worker Justice Center continue to address pesticide exposure issues among workers. In 2015 the EPA revised its agricultural Worker Protection Standards (WPS), first adopted in 1992, to try to better protect workers from pesticide exposure. The EPA estimates that ten to twenty thousand workers annually suffer pesticide exposure, and advocacy groups believe there may be even more cases. See Michelle Faust, "EPA's New Farmworker Pesticide Standards

Leave Unanswered Questions," *WXXI*, November 19, 2015, http://wxxinews.org/post/epa-s-new-farmworker-pesticide-standards-leave-unanswered-questions.

51. Joan Flocks, "The Environmental and Social Injustice of Farmworker Pesticide Exposure," *Georgetown Journal on Poverty Law & Policy* 19, no. 2 (2012): 264.

52. Flocks, "The Environmental and Social Injustice of Farmworker Pesticide Exposure," 269. Examples of these laws include the National Labor Relations Act (the Wagner Act) and the Fair Labor Standards Act.

53. Flocks, "The Environmental and Social Injustice of Farmworker Pesticide Exposure," 264. The crew leader system and guest worker programs dominated the latter half of the twentieth century and persist to the present. Under the crew leader system, responsibility for occupational safety falls on the labor crew leader, rather than on the farm owners. Guest worker programs cause problems because their temporary, and competitive, nature make it difficult for workers to unionize. See Flocks, "The Environmental and Social Injustice of Farmworker Pesticide Exposure," 270–71.

54. Flocks, "The Environmental and Social Injustice of Farmworker Pesticide Exposure," 268.

55. Joan Flocks, "Pesticide Policy and Farmworker Health," *Reviews on Environmental History* 24, no. 4 (2009): 297, http://scholarship.law.ufl.edu/facultypub/640; C. Austin, T. A. Arcury, S. A. Quandt, J. S. Preisser, R. M. Saavedra, and L. F. Cabrera, "Training Farmworkers about Pesticide Safety: Issues of Control," *Journal of Health Care for the Poor and Underserved* 12, no. 2 (2001): 236–49.

12

The Freedom Labor Union

Economic Justice and the Civil Rights Movement in Mississippi

MICHAEL SISTROM

One evening in January 1965, in the dusty little Delta town of Shaw, in Bolivar County, Mississippi, a small group of black farm laborers sat in a Freedom School class discussing their assigned reading—Communist author Howard Fast's polemical novel of southern Reconstruction, *Freedom Road*. The discussion soon turned from the fictional travails of the freedmen to their own real-life suffering. They complained to each other of the long hours spent under the hot sun chopping and picking cotton for below-poverty-level wages. A witness to the meeting recalled that the mood turned exciting when one person stood up and said, "We have worked all of our life for nothing. It look like there ought to be something that we can do to get more for our work." The observer related that "then somebody said something about the unions up North."[1] In the next few months the black community in Shaw sought the advice of local Mississippi Freedom Democratic Party (MFDP) members, Delta Ministry staff, and the few Student Nonviolent Coordinating Committee staff left in the state after the fall of 1964. Together, the veteran activists and the aggrieved local farmworkers created the Mississippi Freedom Labor Union (MFLU) and went out on strike.

The Freedom Labor Union and related attempts to gain a voice in the local application of federal antipoverty programs and to establish communal housing for displaced workers were part of the larger evolution of black activism in Mississippi in the mid- and late 1960s. The MFLU and its offshoots embodied this mutation: first, in strategy, from a focus on demonstrations to capture the attention of a national white audience to awakening and organizing the poor black community in the South; and second, a shift in goals from requesting civil rights from the country's lawmakers to demanding a share of political and economic power. After a series of plantation strikes in the summer of 1965, the members of the MFLU and other black Mississippians left behind the borrowed tactics of organized labor. In 1966 and beyond, they helped open new skirmish lines in the War on Poverty and experimented with new types of separatist self-rule that were part of the maturing and varied philosophy of Black Power.

The story of the MFLU's shortcomings and of its related initiatives, like that of other Freedom Party progenies, is significant for its revelations about economic racism's overwhelming resilience and resistance to change and about the human costs of agricultural modernization. The lessons to be gleaned, however, are not all pessimistic. The unrealized potential of this black labor activism also demonstrates the courage, imagination, and patience of organizers and local people who were willing to try almost anything, but did not expect dramatic, immediate progress. As an attempt to organize farmworkers, the MFLU echoed the earlier struggles of the Southern Tenant Farmers' Union and paralleled the contemporary action of California's Chicano migrant fieldworkers and of black urban labor in Memphis, Charleston, and elsewhere. Black Mississippians' efforts to bring national attention and federal support for food, jobs, and housing were as important as more familiar struggles over Head Start or Dr. Martin Luther King's Poor People's Campaign.

With little industry or urbanization, few independent black farms, and not even much sharecropping remaining by the 1960s, about the only way left for Delta black residents to make any kind of a living was as day labor on the huge cotton plantations. Women and children tended the plants and picked the crop from sunup to sundown for $2.50 to $3.00 a day, at a time when the federal minimum wage was $1.25 an hour. Men drove the tractors, fixed the machines, and hauled work gangs to and from the fields for $5.00 a day, six days a week. With the exception of tractor drivers and mechanics, workers could not even count on these meager wages beyond the spring and summer. In the six long, cold months between growing seasons, the average black family had to live on $12.00 a week, even though the federal government had determined in 1964 that any amount under $75.00 a week fell below the poverty line.[2]

Before black workers could glimpse the possibility of change, however, they saw the employment situation worsen heading into the 1965 season. Planters had been accelerating the use of farm machinery and chemicals so much since the 1950s that by the mid-1960s they required less than half the land to produce more cotton. Federal agricultural policies that encouraged cotton growers to reduce their acreage further compounded the process. As a result, the Mississippi State Employment Security Commission estimated that by the spring of 1966 the pool of tractor drivers, mechanics, and crew haulers in the Delta would decline by 25 percent while the number of choppers and pickers would be slashed by 50 percent.[3]

By April 1965, the MFDP had reached conclusions that made the bold and dramatic actions of a strike seem necessary, but also potentially desperate and foolhardy. On the one hand, a movement on behalf of black workers could not take its time getting under way. The activists would have to act quickly to organize a dwindling black labor pool. Upstart cotton choppers also stood little chance of succeeding on their own against the power of white planters. More generally, the local white elite's ability to warp well-intentioned new federal agricultural and welfare policies to their advantage had to be dramatically revealed to the nation before progress could occur. On the other hand, SNCC veterans, Delta Ministry staff, and Freedom Party leaders thought that the MFLU could serve an important inspirational and educational function for black Mississippi and America, much as the Freedom Democrats had with their 1964 Democratic National Convention credentials challenge and 1965 seating challenge against Mississippi's congressional delegation. A well-publicized strike, combined with boycotts and other protests for food, jobs, and housing could dramatize the economic plight of rural black Mississippians in the eyes of the nation. At the same time, however, farm laborers might within a few months discover what voting rights activists were also discovering by the summer of 1965: that the national white power structure was well aware of black economic and political oppression in Mississippi, but was unwilling or unable to effectively confront it.

With these goals in mind, the Mississippi Freedom Labor Union grew rapidly. In early April 1965, as the young cotton began to sprout, a group of Freedom Democrats, Delta Ministry staff, and other local black leaders officially unveiled their new creation at a statewide meeting attended by 350 delegates from counties around the state. The delegates did not, however, officially call for any immediate action. Meanwhile, in Bolivar County, workers on five plantations had already pledged to strike. The next day, ten of the new union's members on one farm in Shaw boldly dropped their hoes and stopped their tractors and walked away from the fields where they worked just outside town.[4]

The strikers then presented a list of demands to their incredulous boss that became a blueprint for all future Freedom Union members. These black rebels called for the following: a $1.25 per hour minimum wage, an eight-hour day, an end to work for those under sixteen and over sixty-five, free medical coverage, federal unemployment compensation, employer-provided accident insurance and Social Security, and racial equity in hiring and wage decisions. Local police quickly arrested the original cadre, but after two weeks of organizing the MFLU boasted one thousand members in Shaw, which was over half the black population of the town, and two hundred of those unionists had gone on strike.[5] Over the course of the summer, more and more black field hands would put down their tools and take up the banner of the MFLU.

In June 1965, the Freedom Union added another 325 workers to its ranks from around Bolivar County and 150 more laborers had refused to work.[6] By July 1965, the new gospel of unionism had spread to eight other Delta counties and across state lines into Louisiana and Tennessee. The male tractor drivers and their families often called the strikes, but they drew in other male and female workers from ages seventeen to seventy-five.[7]

On balance, though, MFLU disciples found it a daunting task to get the majority of rather cautious black farm laborers even to *listen* to the union sermon, let alone join the choir, stand up to their employers and walk off the job. A year earlier, many of these same workers might have blanched at the risks in registering to vote, let alone joining the Freedom Party. Even if they did support the MFDP and its political challenge, a labor union and a strike may have been too bold an economic attack against their white employers. By late May 1965, one white Freedom Summer veteran turned MFLU booster concluded glumly that his audiences were "afraid of the *word* 'strike.'" He found he had no choice but to keep pushing the notion of unionizing and to inculcate a strike mentality more gradually.[8]

Other segments of the black community were skeptical about the merits of a union and a strike, just as they had been and continued to be about the MFDP as a black third party and protest movement. The black male labor haulers were especially hostile. They were paid a commission based on the number of workers they delivered to the fields each day. In the short run, striking workers meant no pay for the drivers. They might also face the wrath of their white bosses for failing to keep the workers in line. In the long run, the bus drivers would get no immediate benefit out of a wage hike for choppers and pickers, unless they were family members. Not surprisingly then, there were at times tense and even violent confrontations between black haulers and angry young black picketers trying to turn the buses back at the plantation gates. These fracases also aired the larger movement-related grievances between the young MFDP "radicals" and the so-called NAACP Toms that Mississippi movement historians have well recorded.[9]

The Mississippi state AFL-CIO and most national labor unions, with the exception of the United Auto Workers, adopted a wait-and-see attitude toward contributing financially to the Delta strikes for much of the summer.[10] As with all other civil rights activity, however, the greatest impediment to the MFLU came not from skeptical black citizens or white moderates, but from violent white repression and severe economic intimidation. The white planters in Bolivar County provided an example for their brethren elsewhere with their swift and sure response to the April strikes. First, the landlords evicted the black dissidents from their plantation shanties and brought in convict labor to remove all the possessions from the houses and throw them onto the highway. Small groups of the displaced erected tent homes in Tribbett, which later evolved into Tent City. White employers also hired white families off the county relief rolls as replacement field labor.[11] Then the owners secured a court injunction to limit picket lines outside plantation gates so black and white scab labor could get through.[12] The sheriff's deputies also began escorting replacement workers to the fields, often in county-owned trucks if the black drivers refused to cooperate.[13]

Some beleaguered white employers resorted to violence: shooting at the union leaders and spraying the picketers with ammonia. Predictably, when the local police arrived, they arrested the strikers. Finally, white thugs applied the old tactic of firebombing Freedom Houses to the new local MFLU headquarters.[14] Justice Department officials were sympathetic to the union and promised to investigate the violence, but they felt powerless to intervene since no federal law had been broken.[15] Mississippi State Sovereignty Commission agents felt no such restraint in intervening.

They infiltrated MFLU and MFDP meetings and carefully documented the white counterinsurgency in Bolivar so that white planters under siege elsewhere could emulate it.[16]

Whatever the eventual outcome of the strikes might have been by the end of the summer, the MFLU had helped to energize and educate even more poor black Mississippians and bring them into the larger struggle for civil rights and economic justice. From the outset, the members and local leaders of the Freedom Labor Unions did not make organizational distinctions. Most of them were also active Freedom Democrats. Strikers took their time off from work to engage in desegregation protests, voter registration drives, and lobbying in Washington in support of the MFDP's congressional challenge, the minimum wage law, and job training.[17]

By the end of the summer, however, outside observers' predictions that the Freedom Labor Union was too impractical a project to last seemed proven correct. With few resources to sustain them, all of the Delta strikes had been broken by the end of September. Workers on some plantations received raises to their daily wages of around fifty cents to a dollar when they returned to the fields, though most of the strikers were never hired back.[18]

Former strikers and other displaced black farm laborers were in desperate need of food, housing, and other resources heading into the winter of 1965–66. This became another battle in the larger War on Poverty in Mississippi. To form a battle plan, MFLU members, Delta Ministry staff, and Freedom Party executives convened the Poor People's Conference (PPC) in January 1966 at Mount Beulah. The seven hundred black participants shared frustration at the lack of action from Washington and futility of continued traditional lobbying and nonviolent protest efforts in forcing some action from either the Office of Economic Opportunity (OEO) or the Department of Agriculture. One MFLU and MFDP member complained, "Last year I talked with the house of congressmen. I [told] them what it was like to be a Negro in Mississippi. And I wonder today, why have we got to keep on tellin' them and tellin' them; cause they keep on sayin' they haven't got the story. I know they got the story."[19] After vigorous debate, the conference officially settled on a plan to occupy the abandoned U.S. Air Force base in Greenville.

At the crack of dawn on January 31, 1966, a group of sixty black and white invaders swept past bewildered guards at the entry gate and rushed to occupy a few of the three hundred empty buildings on the two-thousand-acre property. The score of Delta Ministry (DM) veterans, like DM director Art Thomas and staff member Thelma Barnes, and Freedom Party leaders, like Unita Blackwell, on hand never expected to take permanent possession of all of the grounds. Instead, they hoped, among achieving other things, to persuade the Farm Home Administration to offer the PPC a self-help-housing grant on a small portion of the base.[20] Not all of the one hundred poor, homeless black squatters and former strikers who eventually arrived, however, viewed the storming of the gates as a symbolic gesture. Many of them truly believed they could settle at the base and find employment. They went so far as to hang a sign at the front entrance that read, "This is Our Home. Please knock before entering."[21] Air force major general R. W. Puryear, sent in on February 1 to end the crisis, tried to negotiate with the hostile occupiers by promising to deliver their "demands" to federal officials if they would depart within the hour. When Isaac Foster, MFLU chair, asked for another day and for commitments to convert the base for community use, air force police dragged the black interlopers biting, kicking, and screaming off the base. (County and city officials had refused to evict the group for fear of negative publicity. In the midst of the occupation, they had also offered to, but never did, open an integrated public school on the grounds.) Outside the gate, the PPC issued a terse public statement: "Now we are our own government—government by poor people. . . . No part of the system has any authority or control over us."[22] Despite the revolutionary rhetoric, the PPC and other black organizations were very interested in how the state and especially the federal government would react to the air base sit-in. Isaac Foster, the MFLU chair and one of the PPC's elected spokespersons, assured reporters as the protesters left that "we had got [*sic*] our message across."[23]

Lyndon Johnson's administration took the air base occupation very seriously, more so than it had the short-lived Freedom Labor Union activism, and did not assume that removing the squatters with federal troops had ended the problem. Attorney General Nicholas Katzenbach feared the situation was "explosive" and that Mississippi could become "the Selma, Alabama of 1966."[24] Katzenbach, however, was not nearly so convinced as the Mississippi congressional delegation that radical black agitators had led the charge. To Katzenbach, the real blame for any detonation lay with the "unwillingness of the white community to attempt to deal with" the genuine suffering and discontent of poor black Mississippians. The attorney general concluded that the solution was not to pillory the Freedom

Democrats and former MFLU members but to address the "problem expeditiously and directly through surplus food distribution, crash employment problems, and as many poverty programs as we can fund."[25]

Various agents of the federal government set to work on Katzenbach's agenda over the next year. The secretary of agriculture pledged to reform Mississippi's commodity system. The state soon received a new grant in order to reach more hungry people and to allow counties to hire the poor to help administer the service and distribute the food.[26] By 1966, Mississippi was already the second most federally subsidized state in the nation, even though Mississippi politicians regularly criticized wasteful government welfare.[27] In the summer of 1967, the OEO and the Department of Labor jointly funded two small-scale job-training services, the Mississippi Research and Development Center (MRDC), run by the state Department of Labor, and the Systematic Training and Redevelopment (STAR) program, run by the Catholic archdiocese of Mississippi.[28] STAR quickly opened eighteen adult literacy and vocational training centers across the state, serving a majority-black student body and hiring many black staff members.[29] More important than funding the STAR program was Congress's decision in February 1967 to bring agricultural labor under the coverage of the new minimum wage of $1.25 per hour.

Even the minimum wage extension, however, proved to be a hollow victory. Rather than boosting the wages of black workers, it gave white employers another reason to accelerate the process of mechanization and crop reduction. By the spring of 1966, twelve thousand tractor drivers and choppers had already lost the jobs they had held the season before. In 1967, another twenty-five thousand field hands were thrown out of work, at least in part because of the minimum wage law.[30] One planter made the link explicit: "Hell," he said. "[1967] was the first time we really found out what labor efficiency could mean. We knew we couldn't use any more casual labor because of the minimum wage and now we're finding we don't need as much specialized labor either."[31] Only half of those laid off left the state that year, which meant the other half were left to wander the Delta in search of sustenance and shelter.[32]

As 1967 wore on, therefore, it became clear that none of these reforms would dramatically ease the suffering of poor black Mississippians, and in some cases, the new federal policies worsened the problems of hunger and homelessness. A new federal surplus commodities program was less than a year old when white-controlled county governments began to hand out less food. They disguised some of the cutbacks by shifting from direct distribution of commodities to dispensing USDA food stamps. Planters did not object to the loss of the commodities, because as the demand for field hands diminished, they no longer needed a source of free food to tide their labor pool over in the wintertime. The switch to food stamps cut the percentage of poor who received aid by over 25 percent. The scrip also gave white employers and officials a new source of leverage over the black community. The Delta Ministry and the MFDP lobbied the White House to intervene. President Johnson's men refused, however, for fear of rousing the ire of Mississippi congressmen. Senator John Stennis had already used a threatened blockade of the president's new Teacher Corps bill to keep the federal government from reneging on a promise to turn the air base property over to the city of Greenville.[33] And Representative Jamie Whitten might have used his control over the House agricultural committee to wreak havoc on the president's farm policy unless Johnson let the food stamp program be.[34]

Thus, in 1966 and 1967, poor black Mississippians were desperate about their economic plight and frustrated with the ability of the state to blunt the force of federal antipoverty efforts. In response, their activist mentors began to pay less attention to demanding action from the state and federal governments and devoted more of their energies to setting up self-sustaining black communities. This paralleled the Freedom Democrats' resolve to put more emphasis on building independent political power at the local level in 1966 and 1967, while forging ahead with their bid for recognition as Democrats, culminating at the 1968 Democratic National Convention.

Former Mississippi Freedom Labor Union members and their Delta Ministry and Freedom Democratic allies had long sought out new ways to aid struggling black farmers (especially displaced field laborers), and their efforts continued through the mid-1970s. One radical alternative to the union was to create new all-black communities. The uncertain venture into separatist self-rule took the form of two distinct settlements: "Strike City" and "Freedom City."

The two experiments in community-building had difficult beginnings, but they also exhibited promise. Both of the "cities" were Delta Ministry projects. The MFDP was never an official sponsor, but local Freedom Parties and individual Freedom Democrats were important supporters, and former MFLU members were among the leaders and residents.[35] As its name implied, Strike City sprang up during the MFLU's summer strikes as a cluster of tents to house 140 evicted tractor drivers, mechanics, and other skilled farm laborers. By the summer of 1966, the refugees were building permanent homes for nearly seventy black families, finding jobs in and around Greenville, and setting up a Head Start center and a job training program.[36] Meanwhile, another group of forty squatters from the air base sit-in, along with one hundred additional exodusters, traversed the Delta for nearly three months in the cold and rain, searching for a home. In early April 1966, they found a promised land on a four-hundred-acre farm near Greenville, which they christened "Freedom City."[37] In the surrounding fields, residents raised soybeans and wheat, which they managed to sell to local white buyers.

Strike City and especially Freedom City were designed to be model communities governed by the poor, but serious external and internal problems hampered their progress. Mississippi's secretary of state postponed granting nonprofit status to the two entities, in order to deny them the chance to apply for state funding. In April 1966, the OEO was on the verge of awarding Freedom City a substantial self-help housing grant when Senator Stennis sabotaged the effort.[38] Without federal subsidies, the projects faced large deficits that they could not erase with the meager profits from crop sales.[39] Delta Ministry staff nudged their fellow clergymen across the country for donations, while the Freedom Democrats included Strike City and Freedom City in their national fundraising appeals.[40]

The most vexing task for the Freedom City organizers was getting poor, abused, black farm laborers truly to take charge of their own lives for the first time and in short order. Isaac Foster recalled what he faced at Freedom City: "With few exceptions, we were dealing with the discarded ruins of the plantations; it was really tough to rebuild enough spirit to get them to accept any responsibility. . . . It was because they had never done anything for themselves, they thought they had to have someone to tell them what to do; in that sense they had never done anything for themselves, but always for the 'boss man.'" Families received a low-interest loan to build their simple dwellings. Some residents, however, wanted to keep receiving government aid and "free" housing, rather than becoming self-sufficient. Still others gave up their houses after paying off the initial loan, because they did not want the burden of long-term home ownership.[41] By 1967, there were only eleven demoralized families left at Strike City.

Freedom City persisted for a while longer, but by 1968, all but thirty-five families had abandoned the settlement. Freedom City eventually closed in the mid-1970s.[42]

The Mississippi Freedom Labor Union, the Greenville air base sit-in, and Strike City and Freedom City created a good deal of excitement, if few fundamental changes, in the economic life of the Mississippi Delta. None of them really could have been expected to reverse the slide of farm labor in the Delta and the subsequent rise in rural black unemployment and poverty in the later 1960s and early 1970s. The outcry of poor black workers and their allies did keep the attention of the federal government on Mississippi and turned its Black Belt into a major skirmish line in the Johnson administration's War on Poverty. The protests also shook thousands of blacks out of their timidity for a time and made them a more vigorous part of black activism in Mississippi from the mid-1960s through the early 1970s. In the final analysis, then, the Mississippi Freedom Labor Union ultimately bears a measure of responsibility for shaping the evolution of the civil rights movement in Mississippi from a struggle for political power and voting rights to one that included economic justice and black self-empowerment as well.

Notes

1. Aaron German, "MFLU," n.d. [1965], Student Nonviolent Coordinating Committee Papers (hereafter SNCC Papers), 1959–1972, subgroup A, series 16, reel 43; "The Mississippi Freedom Democratic Party, 1960–1967," Davis Library Microfilm Collection, University of North Carolina, Chapel Hill.

2. Patricia Gail Noble, "The Delta Ministry: Black Power, Poverty, and Politics in the Mississippi Delta" (master's thesis, Cornell University, 1969), 33; "Background on Refugees' Use of the Greenville AFB," n.d. 1966, SNCC Papers, MFDP records, reel 38, item 119, p. 404, University of North Carolina at Chapel Hill.

3. Gene Roberts, "Delta Area of Miss. in Turmoil," *New York Times*, February 7, 1966.

4. Douglas Blackmon, "Strike City," *Atlanta Journal-Constitution*, June 4, 1995.

5. Interview transcript #0142, 3, and "MFDP Chapter 24, Orientation," July 7, 1965, Project South, Summer 1965, Stanford University, Department of Special Collections, Stanford University Libraries, Palo Alto, CA (hereafter PS); "Shaw, Miss.: New Sounds in the Delta," April 1965, reel 40, item 44, SNCC Papers; German, "MFLU."

6. Joanne Grant, "Wave of Strikes by Negroes," *National Guardian*, June 26, 1965.

7. It is difficult to estimate the total number of MFLU members and strikers in Mississippi because all of the unions were local ventures and there was little statewide organization or record-keeping. It is not likely, however, that MFLU members or strikers ever reached the proportions they did in Shaw or in Bolivar County. There were a handful of

strikes in the ten counties, ranging from one hundred plus people in Shaw at any given time down to seven people in one county. See "MFLU State Office," n.d. [1965], reel 43, item 20, SNCC Papers.

8. Interview transcript #0323, "FLU, Chapter One, Discussion," n.d. [1965], 1, PS.

9. Investigation reports, June 11–13, 1965, 2-153-0-3, Mississippi State Sovereignty Commission Records, Mississippi State Archives, Jackson, MS; Owen Brooks, interview with author, November 3, 1999, Jackson, MS, tape 1, side A. For more on the general attitude of young Delta blacks toward older farmers and laborers, see Hodding Carter III, "The Negro Exodus from the Delta Continues," *New York Times Magazine*, March 10, 1968, 15–20.

10. The various branches of the MFLU did secure $14,600 in general donations, and another $8,000 from the UAW. See "MFLU Report from George Shelton," SNCC Papers. See also Claude Ramsey, "A Report on the Delta Farm Strike," August 16, 1965, box 1602, folder 132, AFL-CIO, Civil Rights Department, Southern Office Records, 1964–1979, Southern Labor Archives, Georgia State University, Atlanta, GA.

11. Grant, "Wave of Strikes," 1; Handwritten notes, n.d. [1965], and A. L. Andrews to James Green, May 31, 1965, box 21, folder 49, Delta Ministry Papers, Martin Luther King Jr. Center for Nonviolent Social Change, Atlanta, GA (hereafter DMP).

12. Subpoena issued to Rev. Larry Walker in A. L. Andrews et al. vs. James Green, et al., June 9, 1965, box 21, folder 49, DMP. Ironically, a district court judge later refused to lift the injunction on the grounds that the strike was a traditional labor dispute, which could be enjoined, not a civil rights protest. See "Judge Rules Farm Strike Not Racial," *Clarion-Ledger*, June 17, 1965.

13. "Why Are the Farm Laborers Poor?" June 7, 1965, reel 3, SNCC Papers; Interview transcript #0323, 3, PS.

14. "Freedom Now," n.d. [1965], box 8, folder 25; Handwritten affidavit, Issac Foster, et al., August 9, 1965, box 21, folder 49, DMP; Interview transcript #0303, 5, PS.

15. John Doar to Lawrence Walker, July 8, 1965, box 21, folder 49, DMP.

16. Investigation report, June 11–13, 1965, File memo, Earle Johnston, "Mississippi Labor Party," July 1, 1965, 2-153-0-5, and Investigation report, July 10–13, 1965, 2-153-0-6, Mississippi Sovereignty Commission Records, Mississippi State Department of Archives and History, Jackson.

17. Interview transcript #0484, "FLU, Chapter 7, Discussion," n.d. [1965], 3, PS; "Letters from Shelby," November, 1965, reel 38, item 151; "MFLU Report from George Shelton," SNCC Papers.

18. "MFLU Report from George Shelton," SNCC Papers.

19. Charles Cobb, "Report on the Poor People's Conference, Mount Beulah, Mississippi," [n.d.] 1966, reel 40, item 208, SNCC Papers.

20. Rims Barber, interview with author, November 4, 1999, tape 2, side A; Brooks interview, tape 2, side B.

21. "Why We Are Here at the Greenville AFB," January 31, 1966, and "Now Is the Time to Do Something Else," n.d. [1966], reel 38, item 119, SNCC Papers.

22. "We Have No Government," February 1, 1965, reel 40, item 15, SNCC Papers.

23. Gene Roberts, "Air Force Ejects Negroes Occupying a Mississippi Base," *New York Times*, February 2, 1966.

24. Nicholas Katzenbach, "Memorandum for the President: Civil Rights, Mississippi," February 14, 1966, WHCF Ex HU 2/St 24, AG7, WE 9, Lyndon Baines Johnson Presidential Library and Archives, Austin, TX (hereafter LBJ).

25. Katzenbach, "Memorandum for the President."

26. James Gaither to Joseph Califano, August 17, 1967, Presidential Task Force, Subject File, box 31, folder Starvation in Miss., LBJ.

27. John Herbers, "Mississippi Scores U.S. in Spite of Aid," *New York Times* [n.d.] 1966, in box 12, folder 635, Ed King Papers, Tougaloo College Archives, Tougaloo, MS (hereafter EKP).

28. "STAR Reopens," December 28, 1967, box 5, folder 259, EKP; Carter, "The Negro Exodus from the Delta," 25; Cobb, "'Somebody Done Nailed Us on the Cross': Federal Farm and Welfare Policy and the Civil Rights Movement in the Mississippi Delta," *Journal of American History* 77 (1990): 930; Leon Howell, *Freedom City: The Substance of Things Hoped For* (Richmond: John Know Press, 1969), 32; Jill Quadagno, *The Color of Welfare: How Racism Undermined the War on Poverty* (New York: Oxford University Press, 1994), 41–42.

29. "STAR Reopens"; Carter, "The Negro Exodus from the Delta," 25; Cobb, "'Somebody Done Nailed Us on the Cross,'" 930; Howell, *Freedom City*, 32; Quadagno, *The Color of Welfare*, 41–42; Brooks interview, tape 4, side A.

30. Roberts, "Delta Area of Miss. in Turmoil"; Cobb, "'Somebody Done Nailed Us on the Cross,'" 921.

31. Carter, "The Negro Exodus from the Delta," 25.

32. Carter, "The Negro Exodus from the Delta," 25.

33. Wilbur J. Cohen, "Memorandum for the Honorable Jake Jacobsen," July 6, 1966, Ex Hu 2/ST 24, box 9, LBJ, and "To: Files. From: Marion E. Wright. Re: Greenville Air Force Base," August 1, 1966, box 24, DMP.

34. Joseph Califano to Lyndon Baines Johnson, April 17, 1967, WHCF, ST 24, box 11, LBJ.

35. Brooks interview, tape 3, side A; Edwin King interview with author December 21, 1999, Chapel Hill, NC, tape 3, side A.

36. Warren McKenna to Richard Fernandez, October 19, 1965; McKenna to Paul Schulze, February 15, 1966, box 17, folders 35 and 42, DMP; "Sharecroppers Declare Own Government," February 2, 1966, reel 38, item 119, SNCC Papers; Noble, "The Delta Ministry," 93–94.

37. "From the Greenville Air Force Base to Mount Beulah," March 26, 1966, box 9, folder 4, DMP; "This Land is Our Land," n.d. [1967], box 5, folder 224, EKP.

38. Mary Ann Pardue, "Stennis Is Assured of Study before Handouts," *Jackson (MS) Clarion-Ledger*, April 8, 1966; Billy Skelton, "OEO Says Pressure Ignored," *Clarion-Ledger*, April 8, 1966; Wilbur Cohen, "Memorandum for the Honorable Jake Jacobsen," July 6, 1966, Ex HU 2/ST 24, WE 9, LBJ; Cobb, "'Somebody Done Nailed Us on the Cross,'" 931.

39. "Delta Ministry Staff Meeting," February 23, 1967, box 5, folder 224, EKP.

40. McKenna to Bruce McSpadden, January 27, 1966, box 16, folder 31, DMP.

41. Howell, *Freedom City*, 45, 49; Barber interview, tape 2, side A; Brooks interview, tape 2, side B.

42. A handful of the original Strike City families still occupied their homes in the 1990s. See Delta Ministry Reports, November 1967, January 1968, roll 11, box 26, folder 15, Fannie Lou Hamer Papers, Amistad Research Center, Tulane University, New Orleans, LA; Noble, "The Delta Ministry," 93; Blackmon, "Strike City" N4–5; and Brooks interview, tape 2, side B.

13

"A Threshold Moment"

Public-Sector Organizing and Civil Rights Unionism in the Postwar South

JOSEPH E. HOWER

On a late April morning in 2011, eight aging black men arrived at the White House. Forty-three years after the historic Memphis sanitation strike, the surviving members of American Federation of State, County, and Municipal Employees (AFSCME) Local 1733 had the opportunity to spend a few moments in the Map Room with the country's first African American president. It was the first in a series of events connected to their induction into the Department of Labor Hall of Honor—the first time that a group of union members, rather than an individual labor leader, cabinet officer, or public official, had been so recognized.[1] As Republican governors launched ambitious efforts to roll back government employees' right to collective bargaining in states like Wisconsin and Ohio, the Memphis sanitation workers were honored for their "distinctive contributions to the quality of life of America's working families."

The Memphis sanitation strike of 1968 has long been recognized as a crucial turning point in postwar southern labor history. Historians like Joan Beifuss, Laurie Green, and Michael Honey have shown how the city's thirteen hundred black sanitation workers drew on a long, rich history of local civil rights activism to challenge the racial structure of political power in Memphis.[2] Even before Martin Luther King's fateful visit to the city, the struggle had drawn unusually wide-ranging support from the city's black community. It was, Reverend James Lawson later reflected, a "threshold moment," when the working and middle classes connected "the question of economic exploitation and rapaciousness" and built a genuine, organic alliance that could challenge the political and social status quo.[3]

While Memphis was a landmark moment in civil rights unionism, it was also part of a longer struggle by public workers for union recognition in the postwar South.[4] Though in some respects driven by the same grievances and concerns that galvanized organizing drives in state and local governments all across the country during the second half of the twentieth century, the southern public-sector labor movement took on a distinctive form because of its integral ties to the black freedom struggle. Though alliances between labor and civil rights were most evident in Memphis, they had precursors elsewhere and survived thereafter, allowing public workers to cut through long-standing opposition to unionism and win beachheads throughout the South. Though these gains were strained by the onset of the fiscal crisis in the mid-1970s, they survived into the late twentieth century, bolstering black political power in southern cities and providing a model and foundation for the revival of civil rights unionism in the early twenty-first century.

Though teachers, firefighters, and federal employees had unionized sporadically during the first half of the twentieth century, the first sustained foray into southern organizing in the public sector came in the early postwar era.[5] In 1946, the United Public Workers of America (UPWA), an affiliate of the Congress of Industrial Organizations (CIO), launched an ambitious organizing drive among state and local government workers alongside the CIO's far-better-known "Operation Dixie." At the organization's founding convention, UPWA president Abram Flaxer identified the South as one of the union's "principal targets" and it openly tied its organizing efforts to a broader vision of racial egalitarianism. The UPWA enjoyed initial success, carving out small but significant strongholds among black sanitation and service workers and forming thirty-eight locals in eight southern states by the late 1940s, when turmoil over the union's acceptance of Communists thrust it into crisis. The UPWA declined following its expulsion from the CIO in 1950, but remnants of the organization eventually found their way into other unions.[6]

AFSCME was perhaps the most direct beneficiary of the CIO legacy. Founded in 1932 by a small group of state employees desperate to defend Wisconsin's civil service system, AFSCME soon spread through state governments in the Upper Midwest. In the decade after World War II, the union expanded into East Coast cities like Philadelphia and New York and, somewhat later, into the South, where it had approximately eight thousand members by the mid-1950s. Building on this modest base and absorbing the remnants of old CIO locals, AFSCME tripled its membership in the region over the next decade.[7] Excluded from New Deal labor laws, the unions' growth rested on a tenuous legal landscape, particularly in the South.[8] Denied both the right to strike and legally protected collective bargaining, much of the union's growth in the region came well within the confines of its traditional model: early inroads in Arkansas, Delaware, and Texas, in particular, featured a strong emphasis on expanding coverage of the merit system in state and local employment.[9]

Dedicated to improving the operation government and dominated by white-collar and administrative employees, AFSCME gave only modest attention to issues of racial justice in its early years. While it lobbied for both state and federal antidiscrimination laws and supported civil rights demonstrations, the union failed to seriously tackle the thorny issues of racial discrimination at the public workplace, particularly in the South.[10] While partly reflecting the union's tradition of local autonomy, AFSCME's cautious position on civil rights was consistent with its collaborative approach with public employers. While some within the union argued for a more proactive stance, the national leadership feared that forcing an integrated union on a segregated workforce risked alienating both workers and local government officials, and thus imperiling its position in the region.[11] As a result, the union rarely challenged the dictates of Jim Crow. As late as 1964, it maintained dual locals for black and white workers in parts of Georgia, Florida, and Louisiana.[12]

AFSCME's civil service model came under increased pressure in the 1960s. A younger generation of rank-and-file members and union activists pressed the national office to abandon its emphasis on genteel lobbying for a more militant style of trade unionism. Often moved by their personal experiences with civil rights activism, they pushed beyond the union's original white-collar and professional base to organize the growing ranks of low-paid, blue-collar, and service-sector workers who filled state and local government in the decades after World War II. Evident as early as the mid-1950s, these tensions erupted into a full-fledged political contest after 1960 and culminated in 1964, when Jerry Wurf, a former socialist and head of the union's largest council in New York City, successfully unseated AFSCME's founding president, Arnold Zander, signaling a broader shift in the history of public-sector unionism.

The union's new emphasis on winning power and dignity through an aggressive model of unionism made state and local government a crucial site of civil rights unionism.[13] State and local government had long served as one of the most promising sources of employment for African Americans and women, but mostly in a narrow range of occupational categories.[14] A 1969 study by the U.S. Commission on Civil Rights found that arbitrarily high job and education requirements, narrow recruitment efforts, and subjective oral and written examinations all combined to limit black workers' access to better-paying administrative and supervisory positions and concentrate them in the lowest-paid, most menial positions.[15] Nowhere, perhaps, was this clearer than in public sanitation and sewer departments, where 40 percent of all employees were African American by the late 1960s.[16] The number of sanitation strikes doubled during the second half of the decade, as mostly black workers demanded both bread-and-butter gains and dignity at the workplace, regardless of legal restrictions.[17]

At a time when the elected leadership of most southern cities was still white, these workplace confrontations quickly took "racial overtones," as one public official lamented.[18] Perhaps the first major on-the-ground breakthrough came in Savannah, Georgia. After a decade of informally representing eight hundred city workers through lobbying and political agitation, Local 342 won the first certification election ever held in the state by an overwhelming margin in June 1966.[19] Negotiations proceeded smoothly until a city manager intervened to block the bilateral agreement as "unconstitutional." Despite an injunction and threat of mass terminations, the workers struck in August 1967. Crucially, they had the support of not just the local labor movement but also the local black community. Facing unrelenting criticism from local civil rights leaders, the city government relented after ten days. "This marks the first time that an SCME municipal local union located south of the Mason-Dixon line has obtained a settlement with decency for its employees," director of field staff P. J. Ciampa told the union's newspaper. "We hope to repeat this performance in every major city in the South in the near future."[20]

In some respects, Savannah foreshadowed the dynamics that played out in Memphis. While both public officials and the press later claimed that city was "being used" by the union as the starting point for a broader southern campaign, the national office was largely oblivious to mounting tensions in the Memphis Public Works Department.[21] Navy veteran and Memphis native T. O. Jones had been trying to form a union for the sanitation workers for half a decade by the time AFSCME put him on staff as an organizer in late 1964. With modest support from the national office, Local 1733 struggled to gain recognition in a city still deeply enmeshed in the paternalistic racism of the Mississippi Valley plantation.

Two events in the winter of 1968 changed the landscape in the city. On January 30, two dozen black sewer workers were sent home from the yards after rain interrupted their work, dismissed with two hours' wages, while their white counterparts were allowed to remain until the storm passed and paid for a full day's shift. Two days later, a pair of black sanitation workers were crushed when the hydraulic ram of their aging truck malfunctioned as they sheltered in the truck during an icy-cold rainstorm—a dramatic reminder of the daily dangers of their work. The latest in a series of indignities and grievances that stretched back decades, the city's indifferent response pushed the members of the struggling local union to a breaking point. On the morning of February 12, the black sanitation workers struck.[22]

To the national office, the strike initially seemed destined for disaster. "You are stupid if you have a garbage strike in January or February," Wurf later recalled of his reaction to the news. "It doesn't stink as much as if you have it in the middle of the summer." Still, AFSCME's policy was to allow local organizations full autonomy in calling and ending strikes, and Wurf harbored no doubts that another failed action would doom the union in Memphis. "I didn't call the strike and I would have advised anybody against it," he remembered of his initial reaction, "but now that they're out, it's got to be."[23] The union immediately dispatched several high-ranking field staff to the city—a show of strength for the workers and a signal to the city that it was eager to secure a quick settlement.[24]

Memphis city officials missed the hint. Mayor Henry Loeb, a white fiscal conservative who had won election in 1967 with almost no support from the city's black community, refused to recognize the union representatives even as he invited individual workers to discuss their concerns through his "open door" policy. At one point, the administration agreed to participate in talks brokered by the city's clergy, but not to negotiate directly with AFSCME. Instead, city officials presented their positions to the ministers, who in turn repeated them for the union sitting across the table. For ten days, talks devolved further into spectacle and demagogy. By late February, the union finally gave up on Loeb and shifted its focus to the city council.[25]

The city's fusion of legalistic objections and traditional paternalism united much of the black community behind the strikers. Initially carried out though mostly ad-hoc arrangements, this support was later formalized in the Community on the Move for Equality (COME), which included 150 ministers (mostly black) and was chaired by Rev. James Lawson. For a union that lacked a strike fund, the daily donations of food and money were particularly important. Beyond tangible contributions, the visible, vocal backing of the black clergy reinforced a broader sense of moral clarity and purpose. At the same time, the strike functioned as a focal point to bring the broader community together around a wider range of grievances, including police brutality, housing, jobs, and schools.[26] Though often obscured in contemporary accounts, black women played a crucial role in the Memphis movement—marching, picketing, collecting cash, and distributing aid. A younger generation of black militants often found themselves on the outside of these formal institutional arrangements, but nevertheless added their support through demonstrations, including a mock funeral for "freedom" on the steps of city hall. The workers were the glue that held together a fractious and fragile coalition, a community movement that was, as one observer put it, "open at both ends."[27]

Though the strike had begun as a self-conscious labor dispute, by the end of February, it was much broader. Staffers Jesse Epps and Bill Lucy played crucial roles as brokers between the union local, the black community, and the national office. The daily routine of the strike—a strategy meeting in the morning, a union meeting in the afternoon, and a mass meeting each evening at a different church, with two separate marches in between—was designed to maximize the involvement of the community.[28] The union recognized that the concerns transcended the workplace. Rather than providing a weekly stipend, it made a much more open-ended, need-based commitment to the workers early in the strike. Essentially operating on an honor system, the union paid medical bills, mortgages, and rent, intervened with merchants to defer payments, and even bought groceries for striking families. Though almost ruinously expensive, the approach nevertheless gave the national staff a much more intimate picture of working-class life in the southern city. For Lucy, this made Memphis the most significant event in postwar American labor history. "It focused all the things that the labor movement ought to be and is," he reflected. "You had the civil rights aspects of the strike, you had the human rights aspect, you had the economic goals, you had the very basic question of equality and relationship to the employer."[29]

It was this combination of labor and civil rights that drew the attention of national movement leaders like Bayard Rustin, Roy Wilkins, and, of course, Martin Luther King. For King in particular, the Memphis movement seemed to embody his vision for the Poor People's Campaign, announced in late 1967 and scheduled for the summer of 1968.[30] For the union, the visits by major figures in the black freedom struggle helped to nationalize the local struggle, put political pressure on recalcitrant city officials, and boost morale. After appearing at a rousing rally in mid-March in which he called for a general strike in the city, King agreed to return to Memphis to lead a mass march. When that demonstration broke up in chaos on March 22, it made national headlines. Under growing pressure from other civil rights leaders as well as the nation's press to prove that his nonviolent philosophy was still viable, King returned to the city on April 3, where he delivered a rousing speech to three thousand rain-soaked Memphians at Mason Temple. He spent much of the next day preparing for the April 8 march—briefly pausing to step out onto the balcony of the Lorraine Motel just after 6:00 p.m., where he was struck dead by an assassin's bullet.

King's death drew national attention to the local strike, and eventually proved the critical turning point in the dispute. The Johnson administration, which had previously shown little interest in the local stoppage, dispatched Undersecretary of Labor James Reynolds to Memphis to mediate a settlement. Federal pressure combined with growing concern among white Memphis businessmen that the assassination and strike might permanently damage the city's reputation to soften the city council's stance, but the Reynolds-brokered talks dragged on through Easter weekend. Finally, on April 16, after sixty-five days, the union reached an agreement with the city that granted recognition, allowed for dues check-off, guaranteed benefits and color-blind hiring and promotion, established a grievance procedure, and included an extensive nondiscrimination clause.[31] Built on in the decades that followed, the settlement helped to transform sanitation work into a vehicle for a poorly educated, overwhelmingly black workforce to push into the lower reaches of the urban middle class. It also spurred additional organizing drives in the municipal housing authority, board of education, and public hospitals.[32] By the early 1970s, Local 1733 became the largest union in Memphis, and, for a time, the state of Tennessee.[33]

The importance of the strike soon transcended the banks of the Mississippi River. It gave visibility to the union at a time when its membership was still well under five hundred thousand nationally. It also helped AFSCME challenge and change popular perceptions of government employees. Picketing black sanitation men fit far more comfortably into existing conceptions of exploited workers than desk-bound bureaucrats, police officers and firefighters, and teachers.[34] By linking the union to the black freedom struggle, Memphis provided moral credibility for AFSCME's organizing drives and workplace demands throughout the country.[35] The union nurtured the connection. Each April, it commemorated the anniversary of King's death with memorial marches, and all across the country, locals bargained for King's birthday as a paid holiday even before it was marked as such at the national level.[36] Later, AFSCME played a key role in raising funds to purchase and preserve the Lorraine Motel as a memorial to King.[37]

As AFSCME surged to the forefront of the labor movement in the decade that followed, it adopted and embraced a broader social vision that, as Wurf memorably put it, demanded "something more than 'more.'" The union increasingly turned its considerable resources toward issues that ranged from civil rights and public housing to tax reform and military spending. Institutional concerns fused with a broader social-democratic impulse to transform AFSCME into a leading advocate for the social benefits of expanded government. "The need for ever greater and more costly services," Wurf told a congressional committee in late 1971, "is one price we pay for attempting to improve the quality of life in our increasingly urbanized society."[38]

While AFSCME captured national attention as a model vehicle for labor liberalism, the Memphis experience also reshaped its approach to public-sector organizing, particularly among poor black workers in the South. "We said that before the strike was ended that we were going to have a wave of these things around the country," Lucy noted just months after the strike ended, "because the conditions . . . in Memphis [were] not unique to Memphis."[39] For union and civil rights activists, the "Memphis formula" seemed to promise a new path forward in the South. "While they might be able to beat the union on the one hand or the community on the other," Jesse Epps told interviewers in November 1969, "they can't beat the community and the union in a combination effort."[40] Bayard Rustin suggested that the strike represented a turning point in the broader black freedom struggle. "As Montgomery was for the beginning of the struggle for equality in public accommodations," he told the *Los Angeles Times*, "Memphis is the beginning of the struggle for economic equality through trade union development."[41]

Across the country, but particularly in the South, black sanitation workers became "the militant vanguard" of the new public-sector labor movement that soon swelled to include a wide range of blue-collar and service sector jobs.[42] The "I Am a Man" signs used in Memphis appeared in Atlanta, Baltimore, and Washington, DC, in the five years that followed.[43] It carved out significant strongholds in Florida and Louisiana and made inroads into Arkansas, Alabama, Mississippi, and North Carolina.[44] Other unions soon seized on the community-centered approach. Building on earlier breakthroughs in New York City hospitals, Local 1199 (later 1199 Service Employees International Union [SEIU]) transported its own model of "union power, soul power" to Charleston, South Carolina. Though the workforce was overwhelmingly female, their demands for dignity and equity as well as bread-and-butter benefits paralleled those of the Memphis sanitation workers in important ways. Also similar to the situation in Memphis was the close and crucial partnership between the fledgling union and the local black community. A two-month strike in 1969 featured a similar synthesis of labor rights and civil rights, complete with marches, demonstrations, and boycotts. The subsequent settlement helped to position Local 1199 to push into cities like Baltimore, Pittsburgh, and Philadelphia. It also accelerated organizing drives by unions like SEIU, the Teamsters, and the American Federation of Teachers, and helped spur the American Nurses Association to more fully embrace the trappings and tactics of a trade union.[45]

More than any other union, AFSCME successfully fused the economic grievances of state and local government workers with the broader protest movements of the late 1960s and early 1970s. On the federal level, the union pushed for the extension of the Civil Rights Act to state and local government and demanded the implementation of affirmative action programs. While initially focused on racial discrimination, the union eventually emerged as a crucial advocate for working women, adopting a far-reaching program that included paid paternal leaves, pregnancy disability, and pay equity. In the late 1960s and early 1970s, the union began actively recruiting women and racial minorities for its staff and leadership ranks. AFSCME activists and leaders also played founding roles in the formation of both the Coalition of Black Trade Unionists and the Coalition of Labor Union Women. Mostly, though, AFSCME organized. Largely driven by the influx of women and racial minorities, the union quadrupled its membership between 1964 and 1978, when it topped a million members for the first time.

Beyond simply raising wages, AFSCME used collective bargaining to upgrade the most difficult and degrading jobs. Working in conjunction with both local officials and the Departments of Labor and Health, Education, and Welfare, AFSCME developed a pioneering career development program designed to provide men and women trapped in low-paid public employment with the training and education needed to advance to higher-paying positions in the civil service system. Initially focused on public hospitals in Boston, Cleveland, and Milwaukee, the program eventually expanded to Baltimore, Houston, Memphis, and Washington, DC, and grew to include sanitation, motor vehicle, corrections, and social work departments.[46] By the late twentieth century, state and local governments composed the single most important source of decent-paying, well-benefited jobs for African American men and women.[47]

Yet in crucial respects, the success of unions like AFSCME masked an underlying vulnerability that became apparent during the mid-1970s, when soaring inflation and stagnant growth put public workers and anxious taxpayers on a collision course. The product of decades of deindustrialization, suburban white flight, and overleveraged public debt, the fiscal crisis erupted onto the front pages of American newspapers in the summer of 1975, when New York City teetered on the edge of bankruptcy.[48] All across the country, public officials, many with strong liberal credentials, balanced budgets by dramatically cutting public services and demanding concessions from public workers.[49]

Emerging at the moment when a generation of African American leaders were finally breaking through into the highest ranks of local government, the fiscal crisis exposed a complicated blend of class, racial, and political dynamics that threatened to disrupt the communal alliances that had first helped unions like AFSCME break through in the South.[50] Nowhere were these tensions more apparent than in Atlanta. Maynard Jackson, a former labor and civil rights attorney who had supported the union during a thirty-six-day strike in 1970, was elected with AFSCME's support as the city's first black mayor in 1973. Jackson came into office at the very moment the broader fiscal crisis was beginning to garner attention from the nation's press. Over the next three years, Jackson struck a complicated pose, pledging his personal support for raising the wages of the city's lowest-paid workers while opposing additional budget outlays—and supporting the rights of public-sector workers to unionize, but stalling on efforts to create a more formal bargaining relationships. Union leaders struggled to channel the growing militancy of a rank-and-file membership caught between inflated costs and stagnant wages. After months of unproductive discussions and a pair of one-day demonstrations, the members of Local 1644 voted to strike in late March 1977.[51]

On the surface, the Atlanta strike marked a bookend to the first wave of community unionism in the postwar South. Jackson responded by firing the strikers and hiring replacement workers—resurrecting a tactic that had lain mostly dormant since the late 1960s. Much of the city's middle-class black community backed Jackson's stand. Local chapters of the NAACP and Urban League both announced their support for the mayor, as did the city's main black newspaper. Most damning for the union, though, was the vocal opposition of many black ministers, including Martin Luther King Sr. A massive national publicity drive failed to change the local dynamics, and the strike collapsed a month after it began. The defeat sent a signal to public employers throughout the country, and, combined with the New York City fiscal crisis and onset of the tax revolt, radically altered the political landscape on which public-sector unions operated.[52]

At the very moment that public-sector unions grabbed a foothold and helped transform low-paying government jobs into entryways into the middle class, they came under fire. Under increasing pressure from antitax politics, elected officials turned to privatization and contracting out jobs to reduce costs, often regardless of their impact on the quality and extent of services. Automation and mechanization eased the physical burden and mitigated the dangers of garbage collection, but it also reduced the demand for labor and number of jobs. More broadly, the precipitous decline in private-sector union density robbed government employees of labor allies, while the combination of deindustrialization, mass incarceration, and voter disfranchisement undermined the economic and political power of the black community. By the time conservative governors targeted basic human rights like collective bargaining in the wake of the Great Recession, there was seemingly little basis for opposition. Just months after the veterans of the 1968 strike appeared at the White House, the Memphis City Council held public hearings on privatizing the sanitation department.[53]

Yet the blend of civil rights and community unionism that had thrived in Memphis, Charleston, and other southern cities during the late 1960s and early 1970s proved more resilient than most contemporary observers recognized. The Justice for Janitors campaign of the 1980s and 1990s fused older traditions of trade unionism with the innovations of the midcentury Farm Workers to improve the lives of millions of custodians, including in southern cities like Miami, Houston, Atlanta, and Washington, DC. Unions like AFSCME and SEIU have gained significant ground in organizing home health care workers all across the country.[54] More recently, major unions have consciously committed to incorporating community groups (and concerns) into the fundamental process of contract negotiation—"bargaining for the common good."[55] The Chicago Teachers Union strike of 2012 highlighted how organized labor's oldest tactic could still be viable in the twenty-first century if rooted in a broader community struggle.[56] The Moral Monday movement is perhaps the best-known manifestation of a new birth of inclusive collaboration among labor, community, and civil rights. Launched in response to cuts to earned-income tax credits, Medicaid coverage, unemployment benefits, and public education funding by the fiscally conservative state legislature in 2013, the weekly protests in Raleigh, North Carolina, have since expanded to include issues that range from voter suppression to hydraulic fracking. The Fight for $15 movement that began among fast-food workers and has since expanded into a national effort to win a living minimum wage reflects a similar convergence. Circumventing the dilatory processes of American labor law, the campaign has sought to organize the working poor through community mobilization, public demonstrations, and workplace action.

The national fortunes of labor have long been tied to its fate in the South, and that seems unlikely to change in the twenty-first century. By 2015, roughly half of all union members were public employees, and African Americans were the most likely racial demographic to be unionized. Yet these rates remained lower in the region than the national average. As activists seek new ways of grappling with the political and economic perils of organizing in the postindustrial era, they can draw on the rich, visible, but not yet fully developed histories of civil rights unionism in the postwar South.

Notes

1. Bartholomew Sullivan, "Memphis Sanitation Workers Honored by Obama," *McClatchy Tribune Business News*, April 29, 2011.

2. Joan Turner Beifuss, *At the River I Stand: Memphis, the 1968 Strike, and Martin Luther King* (Brooklyn: Carlson, 1985); Laurie B. Green, *Battling the Plantation Mentality: Memphis and the Black Freedom Struggle* (Chapel Hill: University of North Carolina Press, 2007); Michael Honey, *Going Down Jericho Road: The Memphis Sanitation Strike, Martin Luther King's Last Campaign* (New York: W.W. Norton, 2007).

3. James Lawson, "Forty Years since King: The Memphis Sanitation Strike," *Labor: Studies in Working Class History of the Americas* 5, no. 1 (2008): 11–12.

4. Robert Korstad, *Civil Rights Unionism: Tobacco Workers and the Struggle for Democracy in the Mid-Twentieth Century* (Chapel Hill: University of North Carolina Press, 2003).

5. On public-sector labor prior to the 1950s, see David Ziskind, *One Thousand Strikes of Government Employees* (New York: Columbia University Press, 1940); Sterling D. Spero, *Government as Employer* (New York: Remsen Press, 1948); and Wilson R. Hart, *Collective Bargaining in the Federal Service: A Study of Labor-Management Relations in United States Government Employment* (New York: Harper Brothers, 1961).

6. William P. Jones, "The Other Operation Dixie: Public Employees in the New Deal Order," paper presented at Beyond the New Deal Order Conference, University of California at Santa Barbara, September 24–26, 2015, in possession of the author.

7. Arnold S. Zander, "A Union Grows in Dixie," *Municipal South*, February 1959, 24–26.

8. Henry T. Wilson, "Where We Stand Legally," *Public Employee*, March 1958, 13–16; "The Laws against Us," *Public Employee*, March 1960, 12–14. On public-sector labor law through the early 1960s, see Joseph E. Slater, *Public Workers: Government Employee Unions, the Law, and the State, 1900–1962* (Ithaca: Cornell University Press, 2004), 72–94. In at least one case, AFSCME locals used southern right-to-work laws to overturn universal prohibitions on union membership. See "Arkansas Council Uses 'Right to Work' Law," *Public Employee* 31, no. 12 (1966): 1, 4.

9. "Spoils Systems Still Control Half of State Jobs Despite Civil Service," *Public Employee* 7 (June 1963): 1, 5.

10. "Union Members Help Swell Freedom Marches' Ranks," *Public Employee*, September 1963, 5; "Union Launches Vigorous Civil Rights Campaign," *Public Employee*, March 1964, 5.

11. This issue erupted to the surface in 1957 over the issuance of a charter in Jacksonville, Florida. See Minutes, executive board meeting, November 15, 1957, box 1, vol. 10, AFSCME International Executive Board Records (hereafter AIEBR), Walter P. Reuther Library of Labor and Urban Affairs, Wayne State University, Detroit, MI (hereafter WPRL).

12. Civil rights report, October 26, 1964, box 2, folder 21, AIEBR, WPRL.

13. On the alliance between public-sector labor unions and the social movements of the 1960s, see Paul Johnston, *Success While Others Fail: Social Movement Unionism and*

the Public Workplace (Ithaca: Cornell University Press, 1994); and Stanley Aronowitz, *From the Ashes of the Old: American Labor and America's Future* (New York: Basic Books, 1998).

14. Thomas J. Sugrue, *The Origins of the Urban Crisis: Race and Inequality in Postwar Detroit* (Princeton: Princeton University Press, 1996), 110.

15. U.S. Commission on Civil Rights, *For All the People . . . By All the People: A Report on Equal Opportunity in State and Local Government* (Washington, DC: Government Printing Office, 1969).

16. Joseph N. Cayer and Lee Sigelman, "Minorities and Women in State and Local Government: 1973–1975," *Public Administration Review* 40, no. 5 (1980): 443–50.

17. As late as 1970, only twenty-one states offered general protection for organizing in the public sector, and only fourteen obliged public officials to bargain with their employees. See Joseph P. Goldberg, "Changing Policies in Public Employee Labor Relations," *Monthly Labor Review* 93 (1970): 5–14.

18. Vice Mayor Don Jones of St. Petersburg, as quoted in Joseph A. McCartin, "'Fire the Hell Out of Them': Sanitation Workers' Struggles and the Normalization of the Striker Replacement Strategy in the 1970s," *Labor: Studies in Working Class History of the Americas* 2, no. 3 (2005): 73.

19. "AFSCME Wins First Public Employee Certification Election in Georgia," *Public Employee*, July 1966, 10.

20. "Settlement Ends Strike in Savannah, Ga.," *Public Employee*, September 1967, 3.

21. "Memphis Is Being Used," *Memphis Commercial Appeal*, February 18, 1968, 6.

22. "1,300 Members Participate in Memphis Garbage Strike," *Public Employee*, February 1968, 3.

23. Quoted in Joseph C. Goulden, *Jerry Wurf: Labor's Last Angry Man* (New York: Atheneum, 1982), 148.

24. Interview with Jerry Wurf, February 3, 1972, Memphis Search for Meaning Committee (MSMC), Mississippi Valley Collection, University of Memphis, Crossroads to Freedom Project.

25. "Memphis Strikers Stand Firm," *Public Employee*, March 1968, 1–4.

26. J. Edwin Stanfield, "In Memphis: More Than Just a Garbage Strike," special report, Southern Regional Council, March 22, 1968, box 2, folder 43, AFSCME Local 1733 Records, WPRL.

27. Rev. Henry Starks quoted in Honey, *Going Down Jericho Road*, 252–53.

28. Honey, *Going Down Jericho Road*, 224.

29. Interview with William Lucy, November 1, 1968, MSMC.

30. Thomas F. Jackson, *From Civil Rights to Human Rights: Martin Luther King, Jr., and the Struggle for Economic Justice* (Philadelphia: University of Pennsylvania Press, 2007).

31. Beifuss, *At the River I Stand*, 328–50; Honey, *Going Down Jericho Road*, 483–96.

32. "AFSCME in Action," *Public Employee*, December 1969, 5.

33. "Memorial Service Conducted," *Public Employee*, April 1973, 5.

34. Jon Shelton, "Letters to the Essex County Penitentiary: David Selden and the Fracturing of America," *Journal of Social History* 48, no. 1 (2014): 135–55.

35. Jerry Wurf and Mary L. Hennessy, "The American Federation of State, County and Municipal Employees," in *Collective Bargaining Government* (Englewood Cliffs, NJ: Prentice-Hall, 1972), 63.

36. "AFSCME Honors King, Calls for Economic Justice," *Public Employee*, April 1978, 7.

37. "Group Buys Site of Rev. King's Slaying," *Chicago Tribune*, December 14, 1982.

38. Testimony of Jerry Wurf, Hearings on "The Employment and Manpower Act of 1972," before the Select Subcommittee on Labor, Committee on Education and Labor, House of Representatives, 92nd Cong., 1st sess., November 3, 1971, 177–83.

39. Interview with William Lucy, November 1, 1968, MSMC.

40. Interview with Jesse Epps, November 1969, MSMC.

41. "Civil Rights, Labor Find Unity Pays," *Los Angeles Times*, May 6, 1968.

42. McCartin, "'Fire the Hell Out of Them,'" 72.

43. John Nordheimer, "Atlanta Union Cool to Attack on Mayor," *New York Times*, March 30, 1970; Robert F. Levey, "Sanitation Dispute Becomes Polarized," *Washington Post*, May 20, 1970; Alex Ward, "Trashmen Vote Strike Unanimously," *Washington Post*, May 20, 1970.

44. "Pascagoula, Miss. Local 1944 Stoppage Wins Pay Increase," *Public Employee*, May 1968, 8; "Exclusive Recognition Won by Newly-Chartered Local," *Public Employee*, September 1968, 11; "New Orleans Sewer, Water Employees Win Recognition, Pact," *Public Employee*, October 1968, 3; "Sanitation Men Win SCME," *Public Employee*, September 1969, 3.

45. Leon Fink and Brian Greenberg, *Upheaval in the Quiet Zone: 1199SEIU and the Politics of Health Care Unionism*, 2nd ed. (Urbana: University of Illinois Press, 2009).

46. "SCME Operation Upgrade," *Public Employee*, January 1969, 6–7; "Job Upgrading Program Extended," *Public Employee*, Jul. 1971, 16; "Career Ladders Grant Extended," *Public Employee*, March 1975, 15.

47. Michael B. Katz and Mark J. Stern, *One Nation Divisible: What America Was and What It Is Becoming* (New York: Russell Sage, 2007), 86–101.

48. Kim Phillips-Fein, *Fear City: New York's Fiscal Crisis and the Rise of Austerity Politics* (New York: Metropolitan Books, 2017).

49. "Fiscal Distress in State and Local Government," memorandum from AFSCME Research Department, n.d. [1975], box 13, folder 10, AFSCME Program Development Department Records, part 2, WPRL.

50. For an influential analysis of class dynamics in African American politics, see Adolph L. Reed Jr., *Stirrings in the Jug: Black Politics in the Post-Segregation Era* (Minneapolis: University of Minnesota Press, 1999). Also see the symposium on Reed's work, including his response, in *Labor Studies Journal* 41, no. 3 (2016): 233–91.

51. On the background to the 1977 strike, see Joseph A. McCartin, "Managing Discontent: The Life and Career of Leamon Hood," in *The Black Worker: Race, Labor, and Civil Rights since Emancipation*, ed. Eric Arnesen (Urbana: University of Illinois Press, 2007), 271–300.

52. On the history and legacy of the 1977 strike, see McCartin, "Striker Replacement Strategy in the 1970s."

53. Linda S. Wallace, "Budget Wars: If Blacks Lose Ground, Can Memphis Make Progress?" *Tri-State Defender*, June 23, 2011.

54. Eileen Boris and Jennifer Klein, *Caring for America: Home Health Workers in the Shadow of the Welfare State* (New York: Oxford University Press, 2012).

55. Joseph A. McCartin, "Bargaining for the Common Good," *Dissent*, Spring 2016, 128–35.

56. Tom Alter, "Social Movement Unionism and the Chicago Teachers Union Strike of 2012," *Labor: Studies in Working Class History of the Americas* 10, no. 3 (2013): 11–25.

4

The Modern South

14

Pens, Planes, and Politics

How Race and Labor Practices Shaped Postwar Atlanta

JOSEPH M. THOMPSON

In September 1963, union leaders from the International Chemical Workers Union (ICWU) distributed handbills around the Scripto, Inc., factory in downtown Atlanta, Georgia, that practically shouted the need to regulate the private sector: "SCRIPTO IS NOT BIGGER THAN THE UNITED STATES GOVERNMENT! THEY WILL OBEY THE LAW!"[1] Scripto employed about one thousand workers at the time, approximately 85 percent of whom were African American women, who labored for poverty wages manufacturing mechanical pencils, pens, and cigarette lighters. With a vote on unionization looming, these women, only six of whom worked as skilled labor, could have used the government's help.[2] Being black and female in the South during the death of Jim Crow meant still dealing with a double burden that placed them at the bottom of the South's political economy. Indeed, Scripto had long relied on this marginalized labor force to maximize profits, while providing steady employment for Atlanta's black working class. In search of assistance, the women voted for the union and were striking in the streets a year later with the help of Martin Luther King Jr., demanding an end to racial discrimination that trapped them in low-skill, low-wage positions.[3]

Twenty miles northwest of the Scripto plant in the town of Marietta, the few African American workers at Lockheed-Georgia, almost all of whom were male, also looked for the government's help in fighting shop-floor white supremacy. Of course, the government was never far away in Marietta. Lockheed received unprecedented funding from the Cold War growth of what historians deem the associational state, that mode of governance that greatly expanded the state by filtering it through private enterprise.[4] Opened in 1951 to build aircraft for the Korean War, Lockheed-Georgia employed 10,500 workers by 1961 with a $100 million payroll, making it the largest industrial employer in the South. But the plant's African American employees, who numbered fewer than 500, labored in segregated spaces and could join only the all-black local of the International Association of Machinists (IAM). In March 1961, President Kennedy issued Executive Order 10925, allowing the government to punish contractors found guilty of racial discrimination. The NAACP then filed over two dozen affidavits against Lockheed, leading to the integration of the factory and making the company an unlikely ally of black capitalism in the Sunbelt South.[5]

Within two years and twenty miles of each other, two groups of African American laborers combated southern white supremacy with the best means at their disposal. But the tale of these two factories uncovers the stark contrasts between the ways race, gender, and government intervention shaped different sectors of the Sunbelt economy. Although situated within close geographical proximity, these factories helped create disparate racial, political, and cultural worlds. Federal defense contracts practically built modern-day Marietta and made its surrounding Cobb County one of the most economically prosperous areas of the country by the 1990s. In this way, Lockheed's workers essentially functioned as government employees, occupying a valuable position in the political economy. Yet the county's political culture fostered antistatist ideologies that obscured the hand of the government in its economic ascendancy.[6] And while Washington built places like Marietta, the urban communities that supplied Scripto with its workers experienced the removal of the factory's jobs, first to suburban Doraville, then to California, and then to Mexico.[7] A comparative study of these factories reveals the federal government's sometimes unintended role in the maintenance of Sunbelt white supremacy and exposes the way organized labor, the black freedom struggle, and the military-industrial complex shaped the political economy of the postwar South.

Many of the disparities between these factories stemmed from their common management history found in the career of attorney, businessman, and civic leader James V. Carmichael. A native of Marietta, Carmichael had proven instrumental in bringing the aircraft industry to his hometown, as well as transforming Scripto from a local company to the leading manufacturer of writing implements in the 1950s global market. His involvement in the aircraft industry began during World War II. Under the influence of Georgia's Senator Walter George, the government selected Marietta as the site of a Bell Bomber factory, where workers began building B-29s in 1943.[8] Carmichael took on the role of assistant general manager in 1944, and by February 1945 the factory reached its peak employment of 28,158 laborers, about 2,000 of whom were African American.[9]

The Bell factory closed in 1945, but its wartime achievement poised Carmichael for greater successes down the road. He ran for governor the next year, basing much of his campaign on denouncing opponent Eugene Talmadge's race-baiting. In a radio address on Atlanta's WSB, Carmichael cautioned against the economic repercussions of a Talmadge win, believing that "no one is going to invest money in industry when you have in the governor's office a man who is continually stirring up race and class hatred and creating unrest in labor's ranks."[10] These warnings resonated with voters, and Carmichael won the Democratic primary's popular vote yet lost the race due to Georgia's county unit election system.[11]

While considered a moderate for the time, Carmichael's politics of racial and labor harmony did not translate into a practice of racial equality or sympathy for unions. At Bell, African Americans had tried in vain to gain employment numbers proportional to their population, and the war ended with the plant in violation of the Fair Employment Practices Committee's racial policies. Carmichael blamed Bell's majority-white workforce, whom he described as the "undeveloped hill-billies of Georgia with deeply entrenched prejudice."[12] Still, the factory had created jobs for blacks and fulfilled its contracts while never crashing a test flight. For Carmichael, preserving this efficiency overruled seeking to challenge the disproportionate hiring of white workers or the practice of segregation.[13] His tenure at Bell would prove formative to the management style that Carmichael used at Scripto, when he went from producing planes to pencils but maintained a tight control over who worked for him.

Founded in 1919 by Monie Ferst, Scripto first occupied the pencil factory where Leo Frank allegedly raped and murdered Mary Phagan in 1913.[14] The company relocated in 1931 to the black business district of Sweet Auburn, and by the 1940s Scripto's workforce consisted almost entirely of African American women, supervised by both black and white male superiors. As Ferst's daughter-in-law recalled, Scripto employed so many working-class black women that white women bemoaned how "you couldn't get a good cook in Atlanta."[15] The United Steelworkers of America (USW) tried to unionize this workforce in 1940 but found their efforts blocked by the few white workers.[16] In 1946, the USW as well as the IAM competed for worker loyalties. After the first election on February 1, 1946, proved inconclusive, the rival unions held another vote that gave the election to the USW, which Scripto disputed.[17]

Nevertheless, the USW persisted as Local 3748, winning certification in May 1946. With a union but no contract, organizer W. H. Crawford called a strike on October 7, 1946, for "vacations with pay, eight hour day, wages, and union security," and over five hundred of Scripto's six hundred employees, all African Americans, took to the streets.[18] Immediately, the company tried to cast this organized walkout as a wildcat strike and issued a statement to its employees, apologizing "that an effort was made this morning to cause a strike at the factory by a few outsiders and a small group of employees." They concluded by expressing their "hope that you will not get involved in any improper activity." The letter included a postcard addressed to the company with the statement "I want to return and am ready to return to work at Scripto" with a space for the employee's signature at the bottom.[19]

These company overtures did little to deter the union, and the strike continued in spite of violence from the Atlanta Police Department. The USW described how the police "were anxious to break the strike. Two of the policemen in particular were known to be Klansmen and one in particular had a record for shooting several Negroes." The police also functioned as paid guards for strikebreakers in their off-duty hours.[20] After nearly six months and with approximately four hundred employees, many of them mothers, still on the picket line, the USW faced waning financial support and called an end to the strike on Saturday, March 22, 1947. When work resumed on that Monday, Scripto returned only nineteen workers to their jobs, leading the USW to file charges with the NLRB.[21] By July 8, 1947, the NLRB delivered its ruling on the alleged violations, finding the company free of wrongdoing, and the union's efforts dissolved with no contract.[22]

Carmichael had started at Scripto in November 1946, bringing his ambivalence to organized labor with him. Yet he also recognized the extent to which good management, like his moderate politics, hinged on maintaining the peace among business, government, and labor. During a speech at

Emory University, Carmichael lamented that in the current political climate, "if you are in business some man from Washington walks into your office. . . . He starts off on the presumption you are out to beat the government, that you are a crook!" In the same speech, he admitted that "much of the labor trouble in this country was brought on by management itself" and could be avoided by enlightened bosses. By Carmichael's estimation, successful management, like his, "has a consciousness of its obligation to its workers; a consciousness of its obligation to pay a fair wage."[23] But not all employees would profit equally from this sense of obligation, as white supremacy and government action influenced the distribution of wages and benefits at his factories.

In 1952, Carmichael endured unionization at the Scripto plant as well as the Lockheed factory, where he had served as general manager for a year starting in January 1951, after this California-based company reopened the Marietta facility built by Bell Aircraft. Just before the plant began production, local coverage heralded Carmichael and Lockheed's corporate president Robert E. Gross as "1951-style '49ers who have reversed the gold rush to California."[24] By courting this type of investment, Carmichael pioneered the kind of conservative politics based in military Keynesianism that supplied Lockheed contracts, enriched Cobb County, provided jobs for a majority-white workforce, and led to the area's unprecedented suburban growth. Ironically, he bemoaned the government's ability "to whittle" away at the ostensibly free enterprise and praised Georgia's legislators "for stemming the tide of socialism," all while benefiting from taxpayer funding and growing the federal government via the military-industrial complex.[25] For Carmichael, Lockheed employees represented a vital link in this global fight against communistic threats to what he imagined as free-market capitalism. In a Christmas speech to the Marietta plant, he reminded workers that "all freedom loving peoples of the world are looking to the Georgia Division of Lockheed to turn out these bombers in quantity."[26] Carmichael considered Lockheed's cold warriors as extensions of the nation's battle against socialism and communism, even as the federal government paid their salaries and blurred the line between private business and state-sponsored industry.

Fears of communism pervaded the unionization efforts at Lockheed as well. The International Association of Machinists and Aeronautical Industrial Lodge 1996 had drafted an agreement with management that took effect on April 2, 1951.[27] This American Federation of Labor (AFL)–affiliated union soon faced a challenge from the Congress of Industrial Organization (CIO), which the IAM characterized as Communist sympathizers. By 1952, the IAM had reorganized as Local 33 and busily promoted anti-CIO propaganda, alleging that the House Un-American Activities Committee had exposed the CIO's use of Communist tactics. In contrast, the IAM presented itself as an all-American union, even sponsoring the "I.A.M. Melody Parade" on Marietta's WFOM.[28] The CIO countered that a majority of Lockheed workers had signed cards with their more progressive union, which included an African American trustee.[29] The IAM-AFL Local 33 ultimately won out and negotiated a two-year contract with Lockheed on December 22, 1952, ensuring wage rates that started at $1.25 and capped at $2.50 per hour.[30] With the federal minimum wage at $0.75 an hour, Lockheed's least-paid employees of this virtually all-white workforce could enjoy the fruits of Cold War armament with the assurance of powerful union backing.[31]

With the IAM in place, Lockheed-Georgia gained an ally in preserving segregation. In September 1951, Carmichael had assured his white workers that "Lockheed will live the Southern tradition here" and that black workers "will not be mixed on the assembly line with whites." Elaborating on this practice, Carmichael expressed his belief that "all the colored people want is the opportunity to earn a living . . . and the right to be citizens. That is all they want here in the South. I have talked to them and their leaders. I know that is all they want." However, the African American newspaper *Atlanta Daily World* noted how Lockheed's employment record stood in contradiction to federal policy on racial segregation in defense contracts.[32] The NAACP recognized the potential for black employment at Lockheed and expressed its dismay at Carmichael's disregard for the law. The Atlanta chapter president, C. L. Harper, and chairman of the Military and War Mobilization Committee, C. W. Greenlea, argued that continuing to discriminate played into Communist propaganda and gave the nation's foes "a cold war weapon more powerful than guns, planes, or battleships."[33] In a public rebuttal, Carmichael claimed that the press had misrepresented his statements and that the company welcomed all qualified applicants for any job.[34]

Racial bias influenced this ostensibly colorblind rhetoric of qualifications since Carmichael knew African Americans possessed fewer of the educational opportunities needed for employment in high-skill jobs. In

November 1951, the *Chicago Defender* reported that of the five thousand employed at the Marietta plant, only three hundred were black maintenance workers and only one held a white-collar staff position.[35] In a conference with the Atlanta Urban League (AUL), Carmichael reused his "hill-billies" excuse, stating that "the employment of Negroes in skilled and technical jobs would be resented by other plant personnel."[36] The AUL persisted and, in partnership with the company, began recruiting educated blacks for skilled positions at the plant in 1952, including Harry L. Hudson, a veteran and graduate of Morehouse. He would go on to serve as the first black supervisor of an all-black crew in 1953, the first black supervisor of an integrated crew in 1958, and the first black purchasing agent in 1961.[37]

But Hudson, along with a small cohort of other well-educated, middle-class black employees, proved the exception to the rule when it came to Lockheed's hiring in the 1950s. By 1956, African Americans counted only 1,350 of Lockheed's 17,350 workers, and only 7 of those black workers were female. To make matters worse, as NAACP labor secretary Herbert Hill reported, "one has only to walk through the plant to witness the total pattern of racial segregation in every phase of the Company's operation."[38] The NAACP helped win significant advances for these employees in 1957, including greater access to skilled jobs and seniority rights.[39] Despite these gains, the IAM continued to relegate black members to Local 2016, which met at Frazier's Café Society in Atlanta, while white members met at the District 33 lodge building in Marietta.[40]

Back in Atlanta, Scripto's black women workers tried again to gain economic agency through unionization. In January 1952, Carmichael had stepped down as general manager of Lockheed but stayed on as a vice president, which, according to the Atlanta press, allowed "him to give more time to another phase of defense in a government contract which Scripto, Inc., has undertaken."[41] Perhaps inspired by the "gold rush" at Lockheed, Scripto expanded its operations to create an ordnance plant that assembled shell boosters for the U.S. Army beginning in 1951.[42] This plant offered a new opportunity for union organizers to secure a foothold at Scripto. In a repeat of 1946, the USW and IAM competed for worker loyalties, while Carmichael reportedly intimidated workers if they voted for either union. Employee Wilma E. Guice recalled that he threatened to "let the machinery rust out before he would allow the union to come in."[43]

However, in an attempt to practice the enlightened management he preached, Carmichael allowed USW's W. H. Crawford to "give the Union's side of the story," but made plain that he and the company held "no preference between the CIO and the AFL. We just don't want any union."[44] The election proceeded on December 4, 1952, but the NLRB overturned these results due to the evidence of Carmichael's interference.[45] With the help of the NLRB, the workers tried again on May 7, 1953, and a majority voted to reinstate Local 3748. After seven months, the black women of Scripto's ordnance division had organized in the face of pressure by one of the leading businessmen in Atlanta's white establishment, demonstrating courage that belied the marginalized status of their race and gender.

Scripto's retribution came in the swift and strategic firing of the women most involved with unionization. The USW charged Scripto with NLRB violations and gathered affidavits from these women that detailed the intimidation used to discourage collective action at the hands of Carmichael, personnel manager Janie Sappington, and the floor supervisors.[46] Even when these allegations were resolved, the company refused to cooperate with the union, and, according to Carmichael, the employees petitioned to decertify the USW representation.[47] Despite the union's intentions of helping these black women laborers, it could not compete with the power management held, and Scripto ended its ordnance division in 1954.[48] With little power in the southern political economy, Scripto's workers found themselves cast aside as a disposable resource, and what little recourse was offered by the NLRB and the union proved weak in the face of capital's strategies.

If Scripto's black women workers represented the bottom of the southern political economy, Lockheed's workers ranked near the top as producers of Cold War national defense. As a result, even the company's African American workers could benefit from the company's intimate relationship to the federal government. When the Kennedy administration established the President's Committee on Equal Employment Opportunity (PCEEO) in March 1961, the NAACP and Lockheed's African American workers easily built a case against the company's discriminatory practices. Black employees like Nathaniel Billingsley, an Atlanta resident hired in 1953, stepped forward to accuse the company of discrimination. Although Billingsley worked as an aircraft mechanic in the armed forces and had taken 160 hours of in-plant training, he experienced a narrowing of opportunities that blocked him from higher-waged "white" jobs. "From my estimation," Billingsley argued, "Lockheed has been and will remain segregated unless there is some follow up on the President's segregation order."[49]

With the government threatening to cancel the first billion-dollar contract granted to a single company for the C-141 Starlifter, Lockheed complied. Lockheed's director of industrial relations denied any intentional wrongdoing, and the company instituted a nondiscrimination code on April 2, 1961, just days before the PCEEO took effect that led to the removal of white and colored signs from the factory facilities. He did admit that the company's social activities remained segregated but believed this racial division continued "by voluntary association."[50] The IAM integrated soon after on April 23, and on May 25, President Kennedy and Vice President Johnson welcomed Lockheed's corporate president Courtlant S. Gross to the White House to sign a nondiscrimination agreement that became the "Plans for Progress," a blueprint for what would evolve into affirmative action. With this ceremony, Lockheed became the first defense contractor to refute the South's culture of segregation and adhere to federal equal employment policy.[51] At the same time, Cobb County's political leaders took steps to insulate its residents from encroachment by an increasing population of black Atlantans. In 1961, they created a ten-foot-wide, thirty-mile-long nominal city called Chattahoochee Plantation on the border of Atlanta, taking advantage of a law that blocked Atlanta from skipping over one city to annex another, essentially stopping any future annexation of Cobb County.[52] Lockheed's relationship to the federal government might include the hiring of black workers, but Cobb County politics made it so that those workers would live, shop, and send their children to schools in Atlanta.

Scripto's workers would receive no such federal intervention on their behalf, and Carmichael's political views certainly did not align with Kennedy's executive action. Since the early 1950s, the Scripto chief had opposed the "dealerism" of Democratic presidents, and he had introduced and endorsed Richard Nixon on a 1960 campaign stop in Atlanta. Throughout these partisan realignments, Carmichael maintained a racial philosophy characteristic of Sunbelt conservatism and viewed Scripto's history of black employment as an act of corporate responsibility that made a union unnecessary. On September 11, 1963, two days before the plant voted on representation, Carmichael reminded his employees of his reputation as "one of the truest friends the Negro has ever had in

Georgia and in the entire South." In spite of Carmichael's assurances, Scripto workers voted to organize with the ICWU, which used the issue of civil rights as a basis for unionization and equated Martin Luther King Jr.'s nonviolent protests for social equality with the economic agency of collective bargaining. Carmichael said that one was employing a "Red Herring . . . [if one claimed] that if you want to help the Negro to secure his civil rights and equal economic opportunities that the way to do it is to join the Union." Carmichael's pleading could not dissuade his employees, even as he argued, "I know the Negroes of Georgia and they know me. . . . I have never—no not once—turned my back on the struggle of the Negro Race to improve its economic opportunities and make secure its civil rights."[53] Nevertheless, one month after the March on Washington for Jobs and Freedom, the Scripto employees voted to organize with the ICWU on a wave of civil rights activism.

Scripto's attorney argued that the ICWU's conflation of unionism and racial solidarity invalidated the vote, citing precedents in two NLRB rulings, which struck down union appeals to "racial prejudices."[54] But these cases overturned votes when unionization had strengthened white supremacy over interracial organizing. The strategy of turning black solidarity into a "racial prejudice" negated the way Scripto's black female workers had understood economic and civil rights as inherently related since the 1940s. Furthermore, Scripto's attempt to turn black solidarity into "racial prejudice" appears as one of the first charges of reverse discrimination, which would become a rallying cry for the Silent Majority of the early 1970s, as well as Cobb County conservative leaders like Newt Gingrich in the 1990s.[55]

The union persevered through these legal maneuvers, as well as Scripto's delay of the negotiation process. Tired of having no contract, workers stormed into ICWU office on the day before Thanksgiving in 1964 and insisted on striking for wage increases, union dues checkouts, and better working conditions.[56] The strike caught the attention of civil rights leaders, including King, who had recently received the Nobel Peace Prize. King joined the seven hundred picketers in December 1964, making national headlines as the strike proceeded for six weeks. As Christmas approached, King's Southern Christian Leadership Conference encouraged a worldwide boycott of Scripto products. Student Nonviolent Coordinating Committee chairman John Lewis also wrote to the PCEEO, describing how Scripto workers averaged "$400 less than the nationally defined poverty level." Scripto held two government contracts for writing instruments valued at $514,000, meaning that its racial discrimination placed it in violation of Kennedy's executive order.[57]

The combination of the boycott and the threat of losing federal contracts proved enough to move Scripto to the bargaining table. Profits had sagged in the early 1960s, and Carl Singer had replaced Carmichael in September 1964, although the ex-president stayed on as chairman of the board of directors. On Christmas Eve, Singer and King held the first of four meetings unbeknownst to the ICWU and reached a settlement in which the workers received union recognition, their Christmas bonus, and a four-cent across-the-board raise. Although this secret arrangement angered the ICWU leadership, who felt King settled for too little too soon, the agreement went into effect January 9, 1965, bringing an end to the strike and boycott.[58] The company signed a three-year contract with the ICWU and renewed it for another three years in 1968.[59]

By the 1970s Scripto had reached an all-time low after a series of missteps that included the brief ownership of Dalton, Georgia's Modern Carpeting, Inc.[60] Near the end of 1977, the company moved its assembly and distribution to suburban Doraville. This departure left the ten-acre site in downtown vacant and ended Scripto's investment in the city's black working-class community.[61] In November 1984, the Japanese company Tokai Seiki bought Scripto and took the new name Scripto Tokai. Although Tokai Seiki's president, Tomio Nitta, claimed he wanted to expand the Atlanta-based facilities, the company fired its Doraville workers in 1986, moving operations to Southern California and then to Tijuana in 1988, making it a pioneer in the transnational production that proliferated following the passage of NAFTA.[62]

In 1995, the Tokai Company helped pay for the abandoned plant's demolition, making the space into a parking lot for the Martin Luther King Jr. Museum. According to the *Atlanta Constitution*, the site had developed a reputation after Scripto's departure as "both an environmental hazard and a hangout for drug dealers and prostitutes."[63] Atlanta's leadership targeted such blighted sites to improve the city's image ahead of the city hosting the 1996 Olympics. These predominantly African American areas located within the perimeter created by Atlanta's freeways were marked by poverty and industrial pollution, representing the antithesis of New South suburbia. Atlanta certainly contained an economically diverse black population that included politicians, an educated middle class, and young professionals from the top schools in the nation. But the flight of capital represented in industrial departures like Scripto gutted the city's working-class communities, leaving them to search for work in the Sunbelt's service economy.[64]

Just across the Chattahoochee River, Cobb County offered a vision of white prosperity, famously described by Republican Newt Gingrich, its Seventh District congressional representative from 1979 to 1999, as a "Norman Rockwell world with fiber optic computers and jet airplanes." Cobb County's population had exploded since 1950, when it counted just over sixty thousand, to nearly five hundred thousand in the 1990 census, only 10 percent of whom were African American. Lockheed had functioned as the foundation of this boom, ensuring an unprecedented accumulation of wealth delivered by defense contracts. The company had weathered scandal in 1972 over the mishandling of billions of federal dollars with the contract for the C-5A. The fallout from this disgrace led to the cutting of the Lockheed workforce from thirty-three thousand to nine thousand, while the corporation survived thanks to a $250 million bailout approved by the Nixon administration.[65] Additionally, the company endured a seventy-day strike in 1977, when workers won a 13 percent wage increase over three years and ensured their seniority system, all on the verge of Lockheed winning a $129.5 million contract to make fourteen cargo planes for Egypt.[66]

Regardless of these challenges, Cobb County owed its affluence and political culture to Lockheed and James Carmichael. Together, a corporation and a business booster established a channel for the associational state to build the county's economy dating back to 1951. In the process, these forces created an enclave of white conservatism that defined itself in opposition to Atlanta's blackness. The labor and political histories of Scripto and Lockheed offer an origin story at the heart of this phenomenon. While Lockheed's predominantly white workers sat at the top of the political economy as an extension of the military-industrial complex, Scripto's black workers represented the bottom of this hierarchy, susceptible to corporate strategies and the unremitting fluctuations of the market. For these black women, race and gender doubled the weight of economic oppression. Meanwhile, Lockheed's relationship to the federal government made it a pioneer of workplace integration based on racial compliance standards that, though it was for only a small number of black workers, importantly established opportunities to partake in the wealth of defense contracts. Yet the overall impact of Lockheed's tenure in Cobb County strengthened white supremacy by disproportionately delivering its economic benefits to the predominantly white county. When placed together, the tale of these two factories reveals whose labor and communities attained value in the South's political economy and whose ultimately suffered during the region's ascendancy.

Notes

1. ICWU flyer, Union Handbills, 1963, Scripto Strike Records, L2003-01, Southern Labor Archives, Special Collections and Archives, Georgia State University, Atlanta (hereafter Scripto Strike Records).

2. "The Biggest Little Strike in the USA," *People's World*, January 2, 1965, folder 8, box 1, Scripto Pen Company Records, 1964–1965, Strike publicity (national), MSS 1013, Kenan Research Center at the Atlanta History Center.

3. Hartwell Hooper and Susan Hooper, "The Scripto Strike: Martin Luther King, Jr.'s 'Valley of Problems' in Atlanta, 1964–1965," *Atlanta History: A Journal of Georgia and the South* 43, no. 3 (1999): 5–34.

4. Brian Balogh, *The Associational State: American Governance in the Twentieth Century* (Philadelphia: University of Pennsylvania Press, 2015).

5. Hugh Davis Graham, *The Civil Rights Era: Origins and Development of National Policy* (New York: Oxford University Press, 1990), 47; Bruce J. Schulman, *From Cotton Belt to Sunbelt: Federal Policy, Economic Development, and the Transformation of the South, 1938–1910* (New York: Oxford University Press, 1991); Thomas Allan Scott, *Cobb County, Georgia and the Origins of the Suburban South: A Twentieth-Century History* (Marietta, GA: Cobb Landmarks and Historical Society, 2003), 341–48; Jennifer Delton, *Racial Integration in Corporate America, 1940–1990* (Cambridge: Cambridge University Press, 2009), 178.

6. Matthew D. Lassiter, "Big Government and Family Values: Political Culture in the Metropolitan Sunbelt," in *Sunbelt Rising: The Politics of Space, Place, and Region*, ed. Michelle Nickerson and Darren Dochuk (Philadelphia: University of Pennsylvania Press, 2011), 82–109.

7. Sallye Salter, "Scripto Quits Downtown for Doraville 'Economy,'" *Atlanta Journal-Constitution*, March 17, 1978; Chris Kraul, "Japanese Firm's U.S. Unit Plans Plant in Mexico," *Los Angeles Times*, August 6, 1988; Jefferson Cowie, *Capital Moves: RCA's Seventy-Year Quest for Cheap Labor* (Ithaca: Cornell University Press, 1999).

8. Merl E. Reed, "Bell Aircraft Comes South: The Struggle by Atlanta Blacks for Jobs during World War II," in *Labor in the Modern South*, ed. Glenn T. Eskew (Athens: University of Georgia Press, 2001), 102; Scott, *Cobb County*, 134.

9. Scott, *Cobb County*, 136, 159; Randall L. Patton, introduction to *Working for Equality: The Narrative of Harry Hudson*, ed. Randall L. Patton (Athens: University of Georgia Press, 2015), 7. For more on Carmichael's role in courting federal investment, see Brent

Cebul, *The American Way of Growth: Business, Poverty, and Development in the American Century* (Philadelphia: University of Pennsylvania Press, forthcoming).

10. WSB Broadcast, May 11, 1946, James Vinson Carmichael Papers, Stuart A. Rose Manuscript, Archives, and Rare Book Library, Emory University (hereafter Carmichael Papers).

11. Scott, *Cobb County*, 207.

12. Quoted in Reed, "Bell Aircraft Comes South," 125.

13. Reed, "Bell Aircraft Comes South," 126.

14. Scott, *Cobb County*, 207.

15. Quoted in Hooper and Hooper, "The Scripto Strike," 8.

16. Charles Mathias to the White Employees of Scripto Manufacturing, Inc., October 14, 1946, Correspondence, Scripto Manufacturing Co., 1946–1952, United Steelworkers of America, District 35 Records, 1940–1974, L1975-21, Southern Labor Archives, Special Collections and Archives, Georgia State University, Atlanta (hereafter USW Records).

17. Case no. 10-R-1610, Exceptions to Report on Objections, Correspondence, Scripto Manufacturing Co., 1946–1952, USW Records.

18. W. H. Crawford to USW District Directors, October 24, 1946, Correspondence, Scripto Manufacturing Co., 1946–1952, USW Records.

19. Scripto Statement to Employees, October 7, 1946, Correspondence, Scripto Manufacturing Co., 1946–1952, USW Records.

20. W. H. Crawford to USW District Directors, October 24, 1946, Correspondence, Scripto Manufacturing Co., 1946–1952, USW Records.

21. Report on Conferences with Scripto Plant, Correspondence, Scripto Manufacturing Co., 1946–1952, USW Records.

22. A. C. Joy to Charles C. Mathias, July 8, 1947, Correspondence, Scripto Manufacturing Co., 1946–1952, USW Records.

23. "Good Business Management—What It Takes!" 1952 Spring, folder 24, box 62, Carmichael Papers.

24. "California Gold Rush Hits Georgia; Gross, Carmichael Strike Bonanza," *Cobb County Times* (Marietta), January 15, 1951, OBV 10, Carmichael Papers.

25. Clark Howell Jr., "Korea Policy Denounced By Carmichael," *Atlanta Journal-Constitution*, n.d., OBV 11, Carmichael Papers.

26. "Employees Hear Carmichael's Christmas Message," *Lockheed Southern Star*, January 4, 1952, OBV 11, Carmichael Papers.

27. Agreement between Lockheed Aircraft Corporation and the International Association of Machinists and Aeronautical Industrial Lodge 1991, folder 6, box 275, Atlanta Urban League Papers, Archives Research Center, Atlanta University Center Robert W. Woodruff Library (hereinafter AUL Papers).

28. *The Aircrafter*, May 8, 1952, folder 6, box 275, AUL Papers.

29. *CIO Lockheed News*, May 12, 1952, folder 6, box 275, AUL Papers.

30. IAMAW Contracts, Lockheed Aircraft Corporation and Local 33 (Marietta, GA), December 22, 1952, ICW Agreements, International Association of Machinists and Aerospace Workers Contracts Collection, Archives of the International Association

of Machinists and Aerospace Workers, Special Collections and Archives, Georgia State University, Atlanta.

31. U.S. Department of Labor, "Minimum Wage—Chart 1," https://www.dol.gov/featured/minimum-wage/chart1.

32. "Carmichael to Follow Southern Tradition at Bomber Plant," *Atlanta Daily World*, September 14, 1951, folder 7, box 275, AUL Papers.

33. Harper and Greenlea to Carmichael, November 24, 1951, folder 7, box 275, AUL Papers.

34. "Carmichael Says Plant Will Not Discriminate," *Atlanta Daily World*, November 5, 1951.

35. "Segregation Isn't Discrimination! Indignant Lockheed Boss Explains," *Chicago Defender*, November 21, 1951.

36. Atlanta Urban League Memo, Lockheed Conference, January 24, 1952, folder 1, box 276, AUL Papers.

37. Patton, *Working for Equality*, 1–2.

38. Hill to Wilkins, December 18, 1956, folder 1, box 276, AUL Papers.

39. Hill to Wilkins, June 18, 1957, folder 1, box 276, AUL Papers.

40. Willie T. Elkins affidavit, folder 33, box 7, Gordon, Kruse, Wentzel Collection, Dept. of Museums, Archives & Rare Books, Kennesaw State University (hereafter Gordon, Kruse, Wentzel Collection).

41. "Lockheed Operations Are in Good Hands," *Atlanta Journal-Constitution*, January 11, 1952.

42. "Comparison of Sales 1947 thru 1962," folder 12, box 31, Carmichael Papers.

43. Guice affidavit, December 13, 1952, Scripto, Inc. Legal Documents, Affidavits, 1952–1956, Charles Mathias Collection, L1973–31, Southern Labor Archives, Special Collections and Archives, Georgia State University, Atlanta (hereafter Mathias Collection).

44. Crawford to Carmichael, October 22, 1952; Thrasher to NLRB, January 19, 1953, Scripto, Inc. Correspondence, 1952–1954, Mathias Collection.

45. NLRB report, March 16, 1952, Scripto, Inc. Correspondence, 1952–1954, Mathias Collection.

46. Scripto, Inc. Legal Documents, Affidavits, 1952–1956, Mathias Collection.

47. Carmichael speech to Scripto employees, folder 12, box 63, Carmichael Papers.

48. "Comparison of Sales 1947 thru 1962."

49. President's Committee on Equal Employment Opportunity—Complaints—Lockheed-Georgia Co. (GELAC)—Affidavits, Employee—A-M, 1961, folder 3, box 7, Gordon, Kruse, Wentzel Collection.

50. E. G. Mattison affidavit, May 1, 1961, folder 35, box 7, Gordon, Kruse, Wentzel Collection.

51. Graham, *The Civil Rights Era*, 48, 49.

52. Stephannie Stokes, "How Atlanta Was Kept Out of Cobb County by a 10-Foot Wide City," *90.1 FM WABE*, April 27, 2015, http://news.wabe.org/post/how-atlanta-was-kept-out-cobb-county-10-foot-wide-city.

53. Carmichael remarks, September 11, 1963, folder 10, box 63, Carmichael Papers.

54. Hooper and Hooper, "The Scripto Strike," 5–9.

55. On reverse discrimination, see Matthew D. Lassiter, *The Silent Majority: Suburban Politics in the Sunbelt South* (Princeton: Princeton University Press, 2006); Jennifer L. Hochschild, "The Strange Career of Affirmative Action," *Ohio State Law Journal* 59, no. 3 (1998): 997–1038.

56. Harmon G. Perry, "Strike Said Based on 'Maltreatment,'" *Atlanta Daily World*, November 29, 1964; Hooper and Hooper, "The Scripto Strike," 11.

57. Charles A. Black, "Scripto Company May Lose $½ Million Federal Contracts," *Atlanta Inquirer*, January 2, 1965; John Lewis to Bernard L. Boutin, December 9, 1964, Law firm files, 1963–1964, Scripto Strike Records.

58. Hooper and Hooper, "The Scripto Strike," 23, 26.

59. Scripto—Annual Report, 1967–1968, folder 2, box 31, Carmichael Papers.

60. Board Meeting Minutes, June 21, 1966, Scripto—Executive Committee, Minutes, 1965 Nov-Dec-1966, folder 8, box 33, Carmichael Papers.

61. Salter, "Scripto Quits Downtown for Doraville 'Economy.'"

62. Maria Saporta, "Presto! It's Scripto Tokai," *Atlanta Journal-Constitution*, November 2, 1984; Kraul, "Japanese Firm's U.S. Unit Plans Plant in Mexico."

63. "The Final Touch: A Parking Lot," *Atlanta Journal-Constitution*, November 26, 1995.

64. Andy DeRoche, "Andrew Young and Africa: From the Civil Rights Movement to the Atlanta Olympics," in *Globalization and the American South*, ed. James C. Cobb and William Stueck (Athens: University of Georgia Press, 2005), 185–208.

65. Lassiter, "Big Government and Family Values," 88–91.

66. "Lockheed's Workers OK Pact," *Atlanta Journal-Constitution*, December 30, 1977.

15

Beyond Boosterism

Fort Smith and the Creation of a Conservative Economic Culture

ADAM CARSON

At 10:00 a.m. on an unseasonably warm and sunny February 1, 1962, an estimated forty thousand people watched a parade in Fort Smith, Arkansas. It lasted two hours and cost twenty thousand dollars, making it the largest and most expensive parade in the city's history. Leading the parade was a wagon that embodied the parade's theme: "From Ox Carts to Jets." Arkansas's two senators, John McClellan and J. William Fulbright, Governor Orval Faubus, Congressmen Jim Trimble and Dale Alford, Oklahoma senators Robert Kerr and A. S. Monroney, two major generals from Fort Chaffee, and numerous state and local dignitaries followed in a fourteen-car procession. Behind marched military units and school bands from around the region. Interspersed were civic groups, floats, classic cars, horseback riding clubs, chuck wagons, a restored calliope, and "a horse that performs tricks." A trio of jets flying overhead signaled the end of a parade that included over 250 organizations from western Arkansas and eastern Oklahoma. Yet politicians and beauty queens were not the focus of the parade. Alongside Senator McClellan and Governor Faubus rode Les Porter and Robert Ingersoll, president of Borg-Warner and chairman of the board, respectively. Members of upper management sat side by side with elected officials to be feted by the public for Borg-Warner's decision to build an eighteen-million-dollar refrigerator factory for their Norge division in Fort Smith.[1]

More than mere spectacle, events such as this shaped the community's conscience by lionizing business, manufacturing, and entrepreneurship.

Local elites constantly presented Fort Smith residents with economically conservative messages from the late 1950s to the early 1970s. This was not simply an expression of economic ideology. Combined with public celebrations, media coverage, and a steady increase in industrialization, this messaging became an organizing principle for society. It, in effect, became a culture that defined prevailing attitudes about the role of government and who should lead society, and created a narrative that credited increasing local prosperity to the public's hard work and dedication to conservative economic policies. Even though the number of factory workers and union members in Fort Smith increased dramatically over this period, the lack of a competing counternarrative left residents with little choice but to turn to the business community for guidance. Blue-collar workers' acceptance of an economically conservative culture supplements well-known arguments that explain why a strong southern labor movement analogous to its northern counterpart never formed. Recognizing how the business community can monopolize the development and dissemination of culture provides another method to examine the labor movement in the American South.

Though historians have long recognized that southern industrialization occurred at the nexus of race, politics, and business, they have disagreed as to why antilabor policies became the region's defining feature. In *The Selling of the South*, James Cobb argued that the South's reliance on cheap labor as its primary resource after Reconstruction defined patterns of economic development. Industries, like textiles, where competition was greatest and profits smallest were attracted to southern communities whose antiunion regulations, low taxes, and willingness to issue bonds to finance relocation created a low-cost business environment that trapped cities in a race to the bottom. Boosters advertised that their cities' labor forces were hostile or, at least, apathetic to unions, which Cobb viewed as merely a tactic to lure industry.[2] Numan V. Bartley, on the other hand, held that southern workers' inability or unwillingness to form unions as strong or active as their northern counterparts stemmed, in part, from probusiness organizations' continued postwar control of political institutions and voter disfranchisement.[3] Jefferson Cowie, however, argues that continued antilabor practices cannot be wholly explained by historical continuities. In *Capital Moves*, he argues that conservative antilabor policies succeeded due to corporations' ability to relocate in response to workers' attempts at exerting control over the workspace. Despite working-class communities acting "as fundamental sources of power and resistance," for various reasons, including geographical limitations and competition between communities for jobs, no unified movement capable of forcing corporations to adhere to labor agreements was created.[4]

None of these books, however, examine how southerners worked together to attract industry, even if that meant limiting workers' abilities to organize. Recognizing the agency of southerners to accept or reject a culture that promised prosperity through the adoption of economically conservative policies is central to changing historians' understanding of the power relationship between labor and business. An analysis of Fort Smith shows less division between workers and management than there was in other communities in the previously mentioned histories. This does not mean that leaders were free from criticism, that workers wholeheartedly supported their actions, or that labor unions did not vigorously advocate for worker interests. Local elites used their power to hinder the labor movement, amass power for themselves, and limit local democracy. At the same time, they used their control of the media to create a façade of cultural uniformity that hid evidence of discontentment from public view. Yet elites did not impose this culture from above as alternative sources existed. Several smaller local or national media outlets that were more disposed to progressive movements could have provided a different narrative. But the tangible improvements that arrived with manufacturing jobs convinced many voters to support probusiness politicians even after the poll tax was repealed in 1964.

To understand this process, one must recognize the extent to which industrial development improved the material lives of factory workers. Fort Smith's average income surpassed that of Little Rock by 1960 due in part to industrialization. Family income rose to $5,136, while other urban Arkansas communities averaged only $3,184. Sixty percent of homes were owned by the occupier—10 percent more than in Little Rock. Most residents obtained hallmarks of the American Dream by 1970: cars, television sets, radios, and washing machines.[5] This resulted in electoral support for Republican candidates, including those who openly supported right-to-work laws and refused to repeal section 14(b) of the Taft-Hartley Act.[6] This begs an answer to the question of why a majority of residents credited businessmen, instead of unions, with increasing local prosperity even though unions successfully won improved wages and benefits in many of the newly arriving factories.

Fort Smith unions increased the intensity of their organization campaigns, labor actions, and political outreach following the arrival of industry in the late 1950s. The United Furniture Workers of America struck numerous times between 1959 and 1963 against three employers who routinely violated agreements arbitrated by the National Labor Relations Board.[7] Food Handlers Local 425 of the Amalgamated Meat Cutters organized OK Foods, a chicken-rendering plant, in October 1959. Six months later, they began a successful twelve-week strike and boycott for a full slate of worker rights.[8] Fresh off their success, the Food Handlers organized Arkansas Piggly Wiggly and Safeway grocery stores between 1961 and 1962. In 1967, 175 workers from five stores struck for better wages and overtime pay; they won those plus paid vacations.[9] A major strike at Norge two years after its opening was significant for both the number of workers involved and its symbolism, since the plant was the jewel of the business community's efforts to attract industry. Workers chose the Allied Industrial Workers to represent them in 1962 despite opposition from management.[10] Contract negotiations began eight weeks before the old contract was set to expire in 1964, but management refused to budge over demands for improved working conditions and wage increases. AIW workers struck for eighteen days before winning some, but not all, of their demands.[11] Their relationship with workers and the community severely damaged, Norge sold the factory to Whirlpool in 1966. No major labor disputes occurred between Whirlpool and the AIW for the rest of the decade. Labor activity was not limited to strikes, however.

Fort Smith native George Ellison, head of the state AFL-CIO Committee on Political Education (COPE), was a key figure in Arkansas's labor movement. He led several campaigns for a state minimum wage, to abolish the poll tax, and to pass prolabor legislation, and pressured politicians to eliminate right-to-work laws and repeal section 14(b) of the Taft-Hartley Act. Critically, the AFL-CIO defeated legislation in 1959 that would have outlawed picketing and public unions. They also created a labor education school to teach local leaders about unions' legal rights. Ellison's next plan was to increase worker participation in elections by repealing the poll tax. After several failed attempts, COPE created a seventeen-point "program for progress" designed to be a multipronged attack on antilabor politicians and businesses within the state.[12] Despite several high-profile victories, there were signs of weakness within the labor movement.

Principally, unions found it difficult to organize workers even though the number of manufactories in Arkansas increased dramatically throughout the 1960s. The AFL-CIO expressed concern over a lack of cohesion. George Ellison said that the main obstacle to repealing the poll tax was that "light attendance at meetings has been a factor in our failure to inform the average union member."[13] Such communication difficulties may have been a factor in Arkansas having one of the lowest strike rates in the nation, where strikes averaged fewer participants and shorter durations.[14] Barton Westerlund, associate director of the University of Arkansas's Industrial Research and Extension Center, found that the arrival of higher-wage industries did not lead to increased unionization.[15] Only one new union arrived in Fort Smith between 1961 and 1964, bringing the total to thirty-seven, which is a small number for a city that accounted for 20 percent of the state's industrial growth during this period. By comparison, the number of unions in Little Rock and Pine Bluff increased from sixty-seven to seventy-two and thirty-seven to forty-six, respectively.[16] This disparity may have stemmed from Fort Smith's late industrialization, as the other two cities experienced heightened manufacturing growth during World War II. The 1961 state AFL-CIO convention had to address several organizational problems that led to jurisdictional conflicts and rival unions "raiding" each other for members.[17] Also discussed was whether the AFL-CIO should allow the Teamsters Union to reapply for membership.

Though their split did not cause the Arkansas labor movement to falter, this lack of unity would hinder both organizations' ability to take advantage of the state's evolving political landscape and possibly develop a counternarrative to that of the Fort Smith business community. Teamsters Local 373 joined with four neighboring organizations to form an Arkansas-Oklahoma Joint Council to increase cooperation among them and better connect the groups to the larger Southern Conference. Parallel to the efforts of AFL-CIO-affiliated unions, the Teamsters began a campaign to organize Fort Smith workers. Such competition would not necessarily have had a deleterious effect on the broader movement, but the Teamsters' relationship with Winthrop Rockefeller, the former director of the Arkansas Industrial Development Commission (AIDC), hindered any movement toward conciliation with the AFL-CIO.[18] Yet it was logical for the Teamsters to support a moderate Republican since the state Democratic Party had been largely unwilling to back labor.

Despite Orval Faubus's initial populist streak, he and most other Arkansas Democrats began to distance themselves from labor issues by the late

1950s. Facing a shrinking population and economic stagnation, Governor Faubus called for the creation of the ADIC to help bring industry to the state in 1954. Fortuitously, Winthrop Rockefeller, scion of John D. Rockefeller's fortune, had moved to Arkansas to escape a scandalous divorce. Faubus tapped him to be the first director of the ADIC based on his business connections. Relations, at first cordial, grew cool due to Rockefeller's racial moderation, celebrity, and growing political aspirations. Stung by the Little Rock desegregation crisis's impact on industrial redevelopment, Faubus worked to pass legislation favorable to business.[19] He became the state's number-one booster. At a banquet put on by the ADIC and the Fort Smith Chamber of Commerce to welcome the arrival of the Ohio Rubber company in 1960, Faubus boasted that in Arkansas "cooperation between management and labor is still the order of the day."[20]

Indeed, his and other Democrats' ties to industry were so strong that the AFL-CIO admonished them for their refusal to support prounion legislation. In 1962 COPE refused to endorse Faubus, saying that he had lost their support due to "his broken promises and actions against [worker] welfare." Only Rep. Jim Trimble, of the Third Congressional District (which encompassed Fort Smith), retained their unwavering support. For years, state Democrats refused to pass a minimum wage law or reform worker's compensation. The state's poll tax was eliminated only by a referendum on a constitutional amendment in 1964. Readers of the Arkansas AFL-CIO statewide publication, the *Union Labor Bulletin*, were probably not surprised when, during the 1966 election, the paper declared that readers should judge candidates individually and not by party.[21] Exploiting this breach, a reemergent Republican Party began courting labor.

William Spicer of Fort Smith became chairman of the Arkansas Republican Party in 1962 and initiated Republicans' attempts at splitting the labor vote.[22] Advertisements placed in the *Union Labor Bulletin* argued that Democrats had failed to keeps faith with labor, by refusing to establish a state minimum wage or improve workers' compensation and unemployment laws.[23] Ads touted Winthrop Rockefeller's role in attracting industry as head of the ADIC, his statements supporting the right of workers to organize, and his pledge to pass the aforementioned laws.[24] Though his career as governor was mixed, Rockefeller, true to his word, passed Arkansas's first minimum wage law in his first term. When confronted with a choice between antilabor Democrats and antilabor Republicans, Fort

Smith workers chose candidates who seemed most likely to bring more jobs to western Arkansas.

Worker adoption of an economically conservative culture is best evinced through Fort Smith's political realignment. This was not wholly the result of racism, as residents from all wards increasingly supported racially moderate Republican candidates. Perhaps heeding the *Union Labor Bulletin's* anti-Faubus resolution, many Fort Smith blue-collar voters supported the dark-horse Republican candidate, Henry M. Britt, over Orval Faubus in 1962. While Fort Smith voted overwhelmingly for Goldwater in 1964, working-class neighborhoods again voted against Orval Faubus in favor of Winthrop Rockefeller.[25] In 1966, voters helped elect businessman John Paul Hammerschmidt over long-serving incumbent Jim Trimble. Hammerschmidt took a racially moderate position, while Trimble ran partly on his having signed the Southern Manifesto and opposition to the 1964 Civil Rights Act.[26] Voters also supported Rockefeller for governor over Jim Johnson, an arch segregationist.[27] Finally, despite heavy voting for George Wallace and Hubert Humphrey in racially mixed precincts, Richard Nixon gained a plurality in Fort Smith in 1968. Rather than simply pull votes from the middle class, Nixon won many blue-collar neighborhoods and ran competitively throughout the city.[28] In these races, many Fort Smith workers aligned with middle-class residents to support economically conservative, racially moderate Republicans. However, support for segregationist candidates remained strong in and around racially mixed precincts.[29] But support for conservative candidates only increased once business leaders began to fulfill their promise to increase prosperity.

That promise was made only after a series of economic setbacks left Fort Smith vulnerable. After the outbreak of World War II, city leaders sought federal funds for local industry, but received only $543,000 to increase the production of zinc oxide, a chemical used in explosives. However, the federal government decided to build a new training facility, Camp Chaffee, in the area, which increased employment and helped businesses. The local chamber of commerce conducted an economic study in 1945 and concluded that because the city was not a "war plant boom town" it must continue to rely on the federal government for support.[30] The closing of Camp Chaffee in 1946 jeopardized this strategy; only the start of the Cold War caused the base to reopen in 1948, but thousands of young men and women had already left in search jobs. Unlike larger bases, Camp Chaffee was a destabilizing economic force in Fort Smith. Though its status was upgraded to fort in 1956, it was closed again in 1959. Fort Chaffee had been the city's economic lifeblood for fifteen years; its permanent closing forced eighteen thousand military personnel and their families to relocate.[31] The city could no longer rely on the federal government and had to seek alternative means for economic survival.

Only one major factory had opened in Fort Smith prior to the closure of Fort Chaffee and it arrived due to Arkansas's early adoption of a right-to-work law in 1944. Dixie Cup chose Fort Smith in 1947 because unskilled, low-wage labor could be found in abundance, and it soon became the city's largest employer. Otherwise, Fort Smith did not capitalize on the state's antiunion legislation. While the chamber of commerce previously sought to attract industry, none of its efforts were very focused or successful.[32] Between 1944 and 1959 local businesses relied upon federal dollars spent on goods and services for the fort and wages spent by military personnel in town.[33] After the fort's closing, the chamber of commerce began to aggressively court northern industry. Though chamber members were initially not as successful as they had hoped, smaller manufacturers began to trickle in.

The vigorous efforts of Fort Smith's political and business leadership show their desperation and determination. Prominent local businessmen, dubbed "minutemen," organized into groups that traveled north with letters of introduction from Governor Faubus and members of the AIDC upon hearing that a business may have been interested in relocating. There they placed advertisements in newspapers and cold-called businesses to pitch Fort Smith as an ideal location with a loyal and hardworking populace.[34] These "minutemen" were not fundamentally different from groups sent by other southern cities to bring back industrial jobs. But most cities failed to meet industrialists' main requirement: an overabundance of labor educated enough to perform low- to mid-level tasks.[35] Fort Smith met this criterion. Historians have often focused on boosters' appeals, but not upon their efforts to ensure that their communities conformed to industrialists' needs.[36]

Most efforts to mold Fort Smith into a desirable location came from the city's chamber of commerce members who used their status as job creators to leverage themselves into positions of political power in the late 1960s. They developed programs to educate the public on the importance of worker loyalty and corporate expansion to spread their conservative philosophy. During the annual "Fort Smith Industrial Week," presentations about business and the free enterprise system were set up in highly trafficked commercial sites. "Vigorous" young men were encouraged to enter the political arena through a "political education course."[37] Begun in 1950, "Business Education Day" was designed to inform public school teachers about the free enterprise system to influence the students of Fort Smith and the surrounding area. Teachers gathered on a summer morning in the municipal auditorium for an introductory speech by a member of the chamber of commerce on economics, freedom, or a related topic. They were split into groups to visit participating local factories, where they were given a tour and the opportunity to speak with a plant manager about the corporation's goals, needs, and outlook. The teachers were then given another lecture about how the growth of manufacturing would "sustain the economic life of our community." Afterward, they were taken back downtown and tasked with discussing their experiences. A final presentation was given on the necessity for all citizens to understand the free enterprise system's political and economic importance.[38] Though the impact of this program upon teachers and students may not be quantifiable, it is instructive that the chamber of commerce believed it successful enough to continue organizing the event for thirty years.

Another method by which the chamber of commerce sought to guide the community was through its newsletter. For twenty years the newsletter was not simply a publication discussing business matters but an organ written to create a community of businessmen with an agreed-upon set of principles. Big government, high taxes, expansive social welfare programs, and any public policies that infringed on the freedom of businesses were, per the newsletter, inimical to American society. One article declared FDR's New Deal to be "a something for nothing program" where the government took taxes from hardworking people to give to the undeserving poor.[39] Political cartoons lambasted Washington for fiscal irresponsibility and the emerging counterculture for its deviancy. As the newsletter's circulation expanded, it shamed those members by name who let their subscriptions lapse or who had spoken out against the chamber's actions. The chamber's control over the media extended beyond their newsletter, however.

Don W. Reynolds used his status as owner of the *Southwest American* to provide favorable news coverage for the chamber of commerce even before he was elected vice president in 1954.[40] Over the next two decades, the paper promoted events related to industrialization, like the parade for Borg-Warner, to show businesses' vital role in the community. In 1958 when the decision to close Fort Chaffee had been finalized, the newspaper published the chamber's extensive forty-point plan to advance economic development, which stated, "Anything that helps business here helps Fort Smith." The paper assured readers that the chamber would "assist the city on self-government in civic problems" and "co-ordinate chamber activities with city government," thus strengthening the ties between the two.[41] Chamber members' pictures were often printed on the front page alongside columns detailing their personal and professional activities, especially after successfully attracting industry. Critically, the success of the "minutemen," the growing alignment between business and government, and increased efforts to mold the public's consciousness all occurred as a scandal erupted in the municipal government.

Business elites used this opportunity to alter the city's form of government to make it amenable to their economic interests and establish a power base for themselves. In 1960, a grand jury found that the local government was rife with mismanagement, incompetence, and fraud. The most egregious example of this was when the city gardener was paid for ninety-six hours of work in one week.[42] Soon after, the chamber of commerce spoke in favor of replacing the city's mayoral form of government with a city manager system to more closely resemble corporate governance. In that arrangement, the public would vote for a seven-member board of directors who would then hire a city manager to oversee day-to-day operations. Discussions about changing the form of government first occurred in May 1960, when a newly formed Good Government Committee invited Dean Dualey, Little Rock city manager, to speak about the advantages and legal steps necessary to change the form of governance.[43] At the end of the session, 150 of the roughly 300 attendees signed a petition calling for change.[44] Despite early interest, no major progress occurred for the next five years.

In 1965 the Good Government Committee began a serious initiative to change the city's government. State Rep. B. G. Hendrix submitted a bill to allow Fort Smith to hold an election. One day later, the committee met with Mayor James Yarbrough to announce its plans to gather signatures for a special election in 1966.[45] In the year and a half between Hendrix's first bill submission and its approval by the legislature, the committee switched to advocate for a city administrator in which the mayor retained some executive power and selected the administrator, with final approval coming from the board of directors. The newspaper covered the legal minutia in a five-part series one week before the vote.[46] It also gave column space for advocates to argue in favor of the plan.

By doing so, the newspaper surreptitiously extolled the virtues of a conservative political system principally concerned with economic growth and reduced spending. Paul Schlaf, president of the Good Government Committee, pronounced the form of government "more democratic" and better at controlling deficits. Mrs. E. E. Elkins, state president of the League of Women Voters, went further, arguing that Fort Smith's civic groups, clubs, and churches had created more progress than municipal government ever had.[47] These were just two of many individuals covered by the newspaper who argued that the city's budget was out of control, that a system based on corporate governance would be more efficient, and that the city needed to create an environment conducive to further economic development. While the newspaper never directly supported the proposal, no opponents of the change appeared in its articles. However, an exchange of advertisements points to the existence of dissent.

Joshua Cohn, a Fort Smith native and descendent of the city's first Jewish settlers, lived in Oklahoma City but still owned several large commercial properties in Fort Smith. He placed an advertisement that claimed no other city had a city administrator and asked, "Is this not enough to make you want to VOTE NO?" Below, in large bold letters, it read, "Eternal Vigilance is the Price of Liberty."[48] Ten days later, an advertisement posted by chamber of commerce treasurer Bill Pitts listed those for and against the vote. "FOR" garnered the support the chamber of commerce, the League of Women Voters, the Classroom Teachers Association, and numerous other clubs and civic organizations. "AGAINST" registered, "Joshua Cohn (Resident of Oklahoma City), Frank A. Denster (Ex-Fellow Employee of Mayor Yarbrough), and Mayor James Yarbrough."[49] While those organizations supporting the plan read like a list of midcentury respectability, according to Mr. Pitts the opposition could be summed up as follows: a Jew, a lackey, and the mayor. Cohn fired back the next day in an advertisement that extolled citizens not to give up their right to self-government, reminding readers that they could not directly hire or fire the administrator. It finished with, "As you know from experience, anyone who does not agree with the local chamber of commerce is strictly all wrong. The fact that I was born in Fort Smith is immaterial to them."[50] Cohn's efforts were in vain.

On March 28, 1967, voters turned out in numbers similar to those of a midterm election to vote 7,541 to 3,020 in favor of changing their government. All but one of the thirty-five precincts voted in favor of the measure with only a handful being competitive. Precincts in neighborhoods closest to factories where workers may have benefited the most from the efforts of the chamber of commerce had the greatest voter turnout and highest percentages voting "Yea." Not surprisingly, those precincts with the smallest voter turnout and lowest margins of victory tended to be from neighborhoods with higher percentages of African Americans and located away from most of the industrial development.[51] Mayor Yarbrough declared that his final act would be to oversee the creation of a new ward system to ensure its fair and equitable distribution of voters.[52]

Changing the municipal form of government was the culmination of a nine-year push by local elites to spread a conservative economic and political culture. Convincing a sizable portion of the working population to support this culture required trust, which was earned by the tangible material benefits Fort Smith accrued through industrial development. That trust resulted in residents of all classes voting for racially moderate, economically conservative Republicans. Labor narratives often focus on conflict between labor and management. Yet examining how a common conservative culture came to be broadly accepted in Fort Smith can help historians understand why many workers voted for candidates who promoted policies at odds with their interests. Recognizing the agency of southern workers to make this decision provides new insight into the development of the mid-twentieth-century southern labor movement. This is not to say that harmony existed between management and labor or that all workers accepted this culture. Rather, it is to argue that the absence of a strong progressive counternarrative, a unified labor movement, and prolabor political support forced Fort Smith workers to look beyond the New Deal coalition to create economic prosperity. As Winthrop Rockefeller reminded the AFL-CIO, "before you can organize, you have to have something you can organize."[53]

Notes

1. "City Will Welcome Norge With Biggest Parade Ever," "Massive Parade To Say Welcome To Norge," *Fort Smith (AR) Southwest American*, January 31, 1962; "Norge Hold Open House Next Two Days," *Southwest American*, February 2, 1962.

2. James C. Cobb, *The Selling of the South: The Southern Crusade for Industrial Development, 1936–1990*, 2nd ed. (Urbana: University of Illinois Press, 1993), 4, 88, 93, 151, 160–65, 278–81.

3. Numan V. Bartley, *The New South, 1945–1980* (Baton Rouge: Louisiana State University Press, 1995), 138–46, 457–58, 469–70.

4. Jefferson Cowie, *Capital Moves: RCA's Seventy-Year Quest for Cheap Labor* (New York: New Press, 1999), 7–8, 184–90.

5. Francis Fletcher Shaver, "An Economic Base Study of Fort Smith" (master's thesis, University of Arkansas, 1964), 6; *U.S. Census of Population and Housing 1950*, part 4, *Arkansas* (Washington, DC.: Government Printing Office, 1952), 4:46 (table 32), 4:47 (table 32a); *U.S. Census of Population and Housing: 1960*, vol. 1, part 5: *Arkansas* (Washington, DC: Government Printing Office, 1961), 5:15–18, 5:20–21, 5:27–28; *U.S. Census of Population and Housing: 1970, Arkansas* (Washington, DC: Government Printing Office, 1971), 5:169 (table 41), 5:170 (table 42), 5:252 (table 89).

6. "Here Is How the Candidates Answered the Questions Our Readers Asked!" *Southwest American*, November 7, 1966.

7. "Furniture 270 Continues Strike At Rush Mfg. Co.," *Little Rock Union Labor Bulletin*, October 23, 1959; "Furniture Workers Solid in Strike at Ft. Smith Chair Co.," *Union Labor Bulletin*, June 23, 1961; "Furniture 270 in Strike against Ballman-Cummings," *Union Labor Bulletin*, October 27, 1961; "Furniture 270 on Strike at Ballman Cumming," *Union Labor Bulletin*, October 8, 1963.

8. "Morale High among Strikers at OK Processor," *Union Labor Bulletin*, June 17, 1960; "Food Handlers Settle 12-Week Strike at OK Processors, Inc.," *Union Labor Bulletin*, July 1, 1960; "Agreement with OK Processors Reached," *Southwest Labor*, June 1964.

9. "Local 425 Strikes Piggly Wiggly at Fort Smith, Van Buren," *Union Labor Bulletin*, May 5, 1967; "Piggly Wiggly Strike Is Settled by Food Handlers," *Union Labor Bulletin*, June 2, 1967.

10. "Borg-Warner Hearing to Be Held Mar. 21," *Union Labor Bulletin*, March 16, 1962; "Norge Plant Employees Give Big Vote to AIW," "Victory at Norge," *Union Labor Bulletin*, May 11, 1962.

11. "Norge Vote Scheduled," *Southwest American*, May 21, 1964; "Norge Strike Settled," *Southwest American*, May 24, 1964.

12. "Union Members Go to University to Learn about Rights," *Union Labor Bulletin*, June 12, 1959; "Minimum Wage Act Expected on State Ballot in November," *Southwest American*, March 30, 1960; "Should Unions Be in Politics? Sure, Says State COPE Director," *Union Labor Bulletin*, May 8, 1959; "Executive Committee Adopts Massive Plan for Arkansas Progress," *Union Labor Bulletin*, January 16, 1962.

13. "Arkansas COPE Goes Forward; Council at Newport Is Organized," *Union Labor*

Bulletin, April 17, 1959; "Communications Is Big Need in COPE Program, Says Ellison," *Union Labor Bulletin*, April 24, 1959.

14. "Arkansas Strike Rate Is below U.S. Average," *Union Labor Bulletin*, November 27, 1959.

15. "High Wage Plants Don't Bring More Union Activity," *Union Labor Bulletin*, August 17, 1962.

16. "413 Labor Unions in Arkansas Registered with Labor Department," *Union Labor Bulletin*, February 17, 1961; "Arkansas Has 427 Labor Locals, 64% Are in 9 Cities," *Union Labor Bulletin*, November 6, 1964.

17. "AFL-CIO Conventions Solved Its Most Important Problems," *Union Labor Bulletin*, December 22, 1961.

18. "Teamsters Form Two-State Joint Council," *Union Labor Bulletin*, July 29, 1960; "Teamsters 373 Asks Election in Swift and Co.," *Union Labor Bulletin*, December 6, 1963; "Arkansas-Oklahoma Teamsters Re-elect Odell Smith," March 8, 1968.

19. Roy Reed, *Faubus: The Life and Times of an American Prodigal* (Fayetteville: University of Arkansas Press, 1997), 139–40, 214, 259–60; Jeannie Whayne, "Dramatic Departures," in *Arkansas: A Narrative History* (Fayetteville: University of Arkansas Press, 2002), 373–75, 381–84; "Nearly 11,000 New Jobs Are Created in Arkansas," *Southwest American*, January 1, 1960.

20. "After Arrival, Governor Told He Would Welcome New Plant," *Southwest American*, February 24, 1960.

21. "The Anti-Faubus Resolution," *Union Labor Bulletin*, July 20, 1962; "Rep. Jim Trimble Merits Support of State's Workers," *Union Labor Bulletin*, October 23, 1964; "This Is the Stand Your Governor Has Taken on the Repeal of Section 14(b) of the Taft-Hartley Act," *Union Labor Bulletin*, February 11, 1966; "Vote for the Man, Not the Party," *Union Labor Bulletin*, November 4, 1966.

22. "Republicans in Major Offensive against Arkansas Democrats," *Union Labor Bulletin*, October 26, 1962; "Rockefeller Emerges in Firm Control of State Republicans," *Southwest American*, May 22, 1964.

23. "State AFL-CIO Call for Better Protection of State's Jobless," *Union Labor Bulletin*, January 18, 1963.

24. "What Has a Strong Republican Party Got to Do with Organizing a Union?" *Union Labor Bulletin*, May 21, 1965; "What's Wrong with Trained People?," *Union Labor Bulletin*, November 19, 1965; "More Jobs—Better Pay," *Union Labor Bulletin*, September 23, 1966.

25. Earl Black and Merle Black, *The Rise of Southern Republicans* (Cambridge: Harvard University Press, 2002), 24–25, 61–62; "A Proof of Government Based Solidly on Merit," *Southwest American*, March 25, 1956.

26. "Old Friends Oppose Each Other in Election," *Fort Smith Times Record*, October 28, 1964; Floyd Car Jr., "Jim Trimble Sees Bright Future for Area," *Northwest Arkansas Times* (Fayetteville), November 2, 1964; "Here Is How the Candidates Answered the Questions Our Readers Asked!"

27. John L. Ward, *The Arkansas Rockefeller* (Baton Rouge: Louisiana State University Press, 1978), 4, 8; Campaign Material, Winthrop Rockefeller Papers, series 3, box 22,

files 1a and 1b, University of Arkansas Little Rock Archives, Arkansas Studies Institute, Little Rock.

28. 1968 General Election Returns, microfilm, Arkansas History Commission, Little Rock, reel MG00023.

29. Film 1404 E—Secretary of State Election Results, University of Arkansas Library microfilm collection, Fayetteville; Bill Hathorn, "Pratt Cates Remmel: The Thrust toward Republicanism in Arkansas, 1951–1955," *Arkansas Historical Quarterly* 43 (1984): 306.

30. Charles Bolton, "WWII and the Economic Development of Arkansas," *Arkansas Historical Quarterly* 61 (2002): 132–35; J. Fred Patton, *The History of Fort Smith* (Fort Smith, AR: First National Bank, 1992), 125.

31. William Butler, *Fort Smith: Past and Present: A Historical Summary* (Fort Smith, AR: First National Bank, 1972), 127; Betty Zander and J. Fred Patton, "Vignettes & Vision," *Southwest Times Record Centennial Celebration*, April 25, 1976.

32. *Fort Smith Chamber of Commerce Newsletter* 1, no. 6 (November 1953).

33. Shaver, "An Economic Base Study of Fort Smith," 55.

34. Cobb, *The Selling of the South*, 79–89.

35. Cobb, *The Selling of the South*, 151–52.

36. Bartley, *The New South 1945–1980*, 138–46, 457; Cobb, *The Selling of the South*, 79–89.

37. *Fort Smith Chamber of Commerce Newsletter* 5, no. 8 (January 1958); *Fort Smith Chamber of Commerce Newsletter* 5, no. 10 (March 1958).

38. *Fort Smith Chamber of Commerce Newsletter* 1, no. 1 (1953).

39. *Fort Smith Chamber of Commerce Newsletter* 1, no. 2 (1953); *Fort Smith Chamber of Commerce Newsletter* 1, no. 3 (1953).

40. *Fort Smith Chamber of Commerce Newsletter* 1, no. 6 (November 1953).

41. "Plan Outlined To Improve, Promote City," *Southwest American*, September 18, 1956.

42. "Jury Terms City Findings 'Disturbing,'" *Southwest American*, March 9, 1960; "Text of Grand Jury Report," *Southwest American*, April 8, 1960.

43. "LR City Manager Will Speak Here," *Southwest American*, May 8, 1960.

44. "202 City Manager Petitions Circulated," *Southwest American*, May 11, 1960.

45. "Hendrix Hopes to Get Five-Man Commission Bill in Special Session," *Southwest American*, October 29, 1965; "Vote Requested on Abolishing Commission Government," *Southwest American*, October 30, 1965.

46. "Procedure for Director, Mayor, Election Told," *Southwest American*, March 14, 1967; "Qualified Voters over 30 Eligible for City Post under New Law," *Southwest American*, March 15, 1967; "City Would Limit Mayor's Duties," *Southwest American*, March 16, 1967; "Law Says Directors Paid Only for Meetings Attended," *Southwest American*, March 17, 1967; "City Administrator Law Would Require Competitive Bids," *Southwest American*, March 18, 1967.

47. "Group Urges Government Shift," *Southwest American*, March 22, 1967.

48. "Vote NO on Administrator Form of Government," *Southwest American*, March 17, 1967; Caroline Grey LeMaster, *A Corner of the Tapestry: A History of the Jewish Experience in Arkansas, 1820s–1990* (Fayetteville: University of Arkansas Press, 1994), 456.

49. "On Whose Side Will You Be Counted?" *Southwest American*, March 27, 1967.

50. "From Every Mountainside Let Freedom Ring," *Southwest American*, March 28, 1967.

51. "Administrator Government Approved," *Southwest American*, March 29, 1967; Shaver, "An Economic Base Study of Fort Smith," 1–10.

52. "Aligning Panel Named," *Southwest American*, March 30, 1967.

53. "Address to AFL-CIO COPE Convention," Winthrop Rockefeller Papers, series 3, box 36, file 5, Special Collections, University of Arkansas Libraries, Fayetteville.

16

From "the Chosen" to the Precariat

Southern Workers in Foreign-Owned Factories since the 1980s

DAVID M. ANDERSON AND ANDREW C. MCKEVITT

On February 3, 1981, state and local politicians joined with Japanese business executives in Smyrna, Tennessee, to break ground on Nissan Motors' new automobile assembly plant, ushering in the "New Automotive South" phase in the region's industrial development. In Nissan's wake, Japan's other major automakers, Toyota and Honda, established assembly plants in the region, and they were soon joined by their German and South Korean counterparts, along with numerous foreign-owned parts suppliers. By 2012 foreign auto manufacturers and parts suppliers employed some 323,000 U.S. workers across the country, most of them in the South.[1] While southern boosters offered increasingly lucrative incentives packages to lure foreign automakers to the region, the South's primary attraction was its self-professed identity as the anti-Detroit, one embraced by the foreign automakers both in their method of making cars and style of managing workers. Workers, in turn, adopted the anti-Detroit perspective for themselves, convinced of foreign manufacturers' potential to improve their lives and modernize the region without the baggage of the postwar industrial relations system.

Nissan's Smyrna factory, which began production in September 1983, not only marked the shift away from Detroit as the geographical center of the American automobile industry, but it also signaled the industry's drift away from the "Fordist" mass-production regime and toward the Japanese "lean-production" model, which promised maximum flexibility and efficiency through a variety of techniques like the "team concept" and "just-in-time" supply-chain management.[2] As part of this shift, both Nissan and its southern employees rejected the collective bargaining relationship with the United Automobile Workers (UAW) that had governed labor relations in the Detroit-based automobile industry since the New Deal. During the post–World War II economic boom, automobile industry workers had enjoyed rising wages, increasing fringe benefits, and enhanced job protections like strict seniority and shop-floor grievance procedures.[3] When the automobile sector slumped in the mid-1970s, critics cited the Big Three's management errors but reserved special opprobrium for the UAW, which they blamed for rising labor costs and its supposed inflexibility on job assignments and work rules, yet another shortcoming of the ossified Detroit system.[4] In contrast, the southern way of making cars in the future would be "flexible," meaning unions would be unwelcome.[5]

From a historical perspective, the arrival of the foreign-owned automobile factories (and other foreign-owned manufacturing enterprises that followed) represented the continuation of an industrial recruitment campaign that had its roots in the early twentieth century when southern boosters began attracting "runaway shops" from the North. By the 1920s, northern manufacturers, including the major automakers, had established "branch plants" in southern cities to take advantage of the growing regional markets by cutting down on transportation costs.[6] While southern boosters sought to lure northern industries with promises of a union-free environment, almost all of the region's automobile branch plants were unionized, thanks to companywide contracts with the UAW.[7] In addition, workers in many southern industrial establishments, including the region's major steel mills, belonged to unions, along with many workers in the region's extractive industry and transportation sectors. In terms of union density rates across industries, the South may have paled when compared to the northern manufacturing belt, but this disparity reflected the South's agrarian economy and its prominent textile industry, where unions made few inroads. When it came to other so-called basic industries, though, union density rates in the South closely matched those in the North.[8] When southern politicians and boosters in the 1980s promised foreign-owned manufacturers like Nissan a union-free industrial environment, they were hoping to remake the region's industrial sector into a bastion of the open shop that stood in stark contrast to the heavily unionized northern industrial belt with Detroit at its hub.

Nissan's arrival in the South marked the culmination of several decades of foreign industrial recruitment by the region's political leaders, who began looking overseas as early as the 1950s, and they intensified their efforts when confronted by the stagnant economy of the 1970s.[9] As industrial production slowed, southern boosters sought an injection of foreign capital to kick-start local economic growth. Japanese companies, riding the "economic miracle" of the previous two decades and fearful of increasing calls for protectionism in the United States, were happy to oblige. Electronics firms, responding to criticisms of unfair trade practices during the Nixon administration, arrived first, when Sony built a factory near San Diego in 1972. Five years later, Sony constructed a $75 million plant to manufacture Betamax video cassettes in Dothan, Alabama. Reports cited the appeal of rural southeastern Alabama's cheap land and labor and its historical hostility to unions. In contrast to the promises future foreign industrial transplants to the South would make, Sony made no claims to uplift a destitute region; rather, its managers claimed Dothan's workers "know more about putting in a day's work" than those in the industrial heartland.[10]

The turning point in the establishment of foreign-owned manufacturing plants in the South occurred in the mid-1970s when Japanese automobile companies began capturing a larger share of the American domestic market. In 1979, Honda constructed a motorcycle assembly plant in Marysville, Ohio, and it would undertake automobile production there three years later. Nissan, Japan's second largest automaker, followed soon thereafter with its Smyrna, Tennessee, plant.[11]

In deciding to locate its plant in the South, Nissan established a pattern that other foreign-owned automakers would follow. First, Nissan benefited from an intense bidding war among a host of localities that upped the recruitment ante far beyond any previous set of incentives, acquiring land, tax abatements, infrastructure improvements, and funds for worker training. Second, Nissan's new "greenfield" plant would be located in a sparsely populated "exurban" area, situated between the growing metropolis of Nashville and the college town of Murfreesboro.[12] Toyota followed this pattern several years later with its massive plant in Georgetown, Kentucky, sandwiched between a regional metropolis, Cincinnati, and Lexington, home of the University of Kentucky.[13] When Mercedes-Benz arrived in the South in 1993, it chose Vance, Alabama, which lies between the city of Birmingham to the east and the college town of Tuscaloosa to the west.[14] These scattered plants came to define the "Southern Auto Corridor," with access to two major interstate highways, I-55 and I-75, and serviced by ample railroad connections.[15] The other significant area of development was South Carolina's Greenville-Spartanburg region, which had pioneered the recruitment of foreign-owned factories in the 1960s (and which also sits between a metropolis, Charlotte, and a college town, Clemson).[16]

As much as location defined these foreign-owned automobile plants, management's production philosophies and personnel policies also delineated the anti-Detroit nature of work at the transplants. The initial Japanese or German transplants were not especially hostile to unions. In fact, all auto plants in these countries were unionized (although in Japan by so-called enterprise unions, organized by company, rather than by industry). For their part, UAW leaders initially welcomed the foreign transplants and the jobs they brought. The UAW worked to establish unionized plants with those Japanese and American firms that formed joint partnerships, such as Toyota and GM's New United Motor Manufacturing, Inc. (NUMMI) venture in Fremont, California.[17] Similarly, the Volkswagen plant in Westmoreland County, Pennsylvania, was unionized, though the plant closed after a decade.[18] And at first, Honda management in Marysville appeared amenable to working with the UAW. But the union encountered unexpected resistance from the local workforce, a situation it would also face at other southern transplants, beginning with its disastrous campaign at Nissan's Smyrna plant.[19]

The UAW also met stiff opposition from Nissan's original management team, led by former Ford executive Marvin Runyon, who established the labor relations policy that the other transplants would follow. Runyon's policy consisted of three basic assumptions: First, efficient production could be realized only through management-labor cooperation and "mutual trust." As Runyon saw it, the UAW had adopted an "adversarial" position toward management, and accepted conflict as a natural condition of the employer-employee relationship. Second, the modern factory must constantly innovate to eliminate inefficiencies. The retrograde UAW, however, preferred to protect its members' jobs through rigid work rules that stifled creativity and resisted change. Third, modern factory workers were now expected to resemble well-trained engineers ("technicians" was Nissan's preferred term) rather than the manual workers who possessed a narrow skill set and whom the UAW preferred to represent. Nissan's multi-skilled technicians could anticipate a level of collegiality and respect from their superiors, while on the production line they were encouraged to demonstrate individual initiative, develop all-around expertise, and seek to move up the ranks. In return, management guaranteed their job security, offered the promise of lifetime employment, and provided them with the same fringe benefits company executives received.[20]

To ensure a sympathetic workforce, Nissan managers handpicked individual workers through a "carefully structured program of recruitment, application processing, interviewing, training, and phasing-in of new employees."[21] Arriving in the United States amid the double-digit unemployment rates of the early 1980s "Reagan Recession" meant Nissan enjoyed access to a vast surplus labor pool. The company received applications from more than 100,000 jobseekers, the most promising of whom underwent a three-step interview process. Nissan then selected 128 assembly-line workers, whom it sent to its Japanese plant for training sessions and who were expected to "pass on their new knowledge to their fellow workers."[22] As a result of this intensive culling process, Nissan workers by and large "had more education, and usually more technical skills, especially in electronics." Fewer than 5 percent had previously worked in an automobile plant, where, naturally, they would have been UAW members.[23] For their work at Nissan they earned less than UAW members in Big Three plants making $14.00 an hour, but their average pay of $11.80 an hour amounted to "forty percent above the average for manufacturing jobs in the Nashville area" and their benefits (which included discounted leases on all Nissan vehicles) "were considered among the best in the region."[24] Consequently, UAW organizers could not argue that Nissan's workers were undercompensated.

One of those UAW organizers, Jim Turner, who led the union's Smyrna campaign, complained that while one-third of the workers in most industrial factories held prounion sympathies and provided the foundation for a successful union campaign, at Smyrna he "had to start from almost zero"—not because of management's opposition, but because, as he put it, "Nissan workers act like 'the chosen.'"[25] Nissan workers did not self-identify as typical blue-collar workers but instead possessed a unique sense of status—something akin to a middle-class consciousness. Turner was confident, however, that their attitude would change after toiling under Nissan's lean-production system. "We're just waiting," he said, "for those who have never worked in an auto plant to find out what an assembly line is and what it does to you."[26] Only then, Turner believed, would Nissan's "chosen" awaken to their true proletarian status.

With Nissan workers already receiving higher wages and better benefits than those received by any other factory workers in central Tennessee, UAW organizers in Smyrna emphasized that only a union contract could protect them from the physical and mental toll of assembly-line work, accusing Nissan of line speeds that led to injuries (especially carpal tunnel syndrome), excessive fatigue, and mental burnout. The UAW seemed on the verge of a breakthrough in 1987 when an investigative article published in the left-wing *Progressive* magazine made local headlines when it quoted several workers who claimed that Nissan achieved its efficiencies through excessive exploitation and not some mysterious Japanese production system.[27] Indeed, as Mike Parker has shown, the "impressively high productivity and quality numbers and remarkably low unit costs" achieved by Nissan and other Japanese transplants came through the intensification of assembly line work, or what he termed "management-by-stress," which required the unquestioning assent that Nissan was able to extract from its workers. "Superior Japanese productivity," Parker noted, "arose not so much from lower wages or extensive robotics, but from what seemed the willing consent of the workforce, apparent in the more flexible work rules and the greater intensity of labor and utilization of total worktime characteristic of these factories."[28]

The UAW campaign was weakened by internal bureaucratic problems and management's stiff resistance, but given the oppressive nature of work at Nissan, organizers expected to gain a foothold at the plant when it called for a National Labor Relations Board (NLRB) representation election in July 1989.[29] In that election, however, a solid majority of Nissan workers handed the UAW a "humiliating" defeat that drew national attention for its dire implications for both the future of Big Labor and the UAW's ability to organize other southern transplants. In the final analysis, most Nissan workers were not swayed by the UAW's health and safety campaign and instead viewed such issues through the lens of their professional ethic as "the chosen." To them, concern over one's personal safety was a matter of individual responsibility. One antiunion worker dismissed the plant's prounion minority as a group of lazy, unprofessional workers who sought to make a living at other workers' expense: "We . . . have some people who don't want to work, who think they can hide because this is a large company." Equally important, the UAW was stymied when it tried to drum up support through a patriotic appeal, stoking anti-Japanese sentiments by handing out pamphlets adorned with American flags that proclaimed the pressure for more productivity came from "outsiders 6,000 miles away." For Nissan's "chosen" majority the UAW was the outsider, a relic of the discredited Detroit system of automobile production. "As it turned out," one journalist quipped, "most workers here said that they were more concerned about taking orders from Detroit than from Japan."[30] Over the following years, the UAW launched several equally disappointing campaigns, including aborted efforts in 1997 and 2000 and another ill-fated NLRB election in 2001 in which workers again rejected the union by a 2–1 margin. In each case, UAW officials blamed workers' antiunionism on Nissan management's "campaign of fear and intimidation" rather than questioning the lack of appeal Detroit-style industrial unionism held for most of Nissan's "chosen" assembly-line workers.[31]

In May 2001, as the U.S. economy descended into an eight-month recession, the *Washington Post* published a glowing feature on the "New Automobile South." The article lauded the region's expanding automobile sector for transforming the formerly benighted rural South into a thriving center of cutting-edge industrial production. The chief beneficiaries of the transformation were working-class southerners, who had previously confronted two choices: move north and endure the deadening alienation of factory work (immortalized in the country-and-western song "Detroit City") or remain home in a "dead-end job," most frequently in a dirty textile plant, with no hope of achieving the American Dream of homeownership. But inside the new automobile factories, the article asserted, conditions were of such high quality that local pundits declared there were "no more blue-collar workers," just teams of "associates" and "technicians" who supervised their own work in well-lit, high-tech assembly plants. More dramatically, workers now earned enough money to buy homes and even purchase the expensive vehicles they built. Local residents celebrated their good fortune because, in their eyes, globalization—in the form of foreign-owned automobile factories—had ultimately modernized the rural South.[32]

Just as important, the foreign-owned automobile factories' success in the South, based on the Japanese model of lean production and nonunion labor relations, served as a stinging rebuke to the Detroit-based Fordist model of industrial production and its collective-bargaining regime. For decades, the Detroit system had served as the standard model for economic development and working-class progress until it unraveled in the 1970s, confronted by global competition in the form of Asian and

European imports. The South had bested the North by rewriting the rules of the game. Rather than resisting the forces of globalization and retreating behind the walls of protectionism, southern boosters aggressively pursued foreign-owned factories, a continuation of the long-time southern industrial strategy of recruiting manufacturers from outside the region to rural areas populated by residents unfamiliar with factory work.

In 2008, in the wake of the "Great Recession," pundits again sang the praises of the South's automotive sector, which continued to attract new transplants while the CEOs of GM and Chrysler were facing bankruptcy and pleading for a $50 billion "bailout" from the U.S. Congress. "The southern auto industry mocks Detroit," noted Fred Barnes in the conservative *Weekly Standard*. "The transplants make money and aren't asking for help from Washington." Barnes credited the transplants' success to their "progressive anti-unionism," which "consists of one factor: They pay well." Southern automobile workers "make far more than the prevailing wage in the rural areas where most plants are located but also considerably more than every state's average wage. With overtime, they can earn $70,000 or more a year at some plants." Looking toward the future, Barnes speculated that the transplants had nothing to fear from the UAW, because the union had "little to offer" workers in the form of higher pay, job security, or a "voice on the assembly line." The UAW, he concluded, was "left with a handful of weak arguments about on-the-job accidents, overworked employees, and sweatshop conditions."[33] Yet even as Barnes was dismissing the possibility of unionization in the South's automobile industry, southerners who had assumed that a production-line job in a foreign transplant signaled their ascension into the middle class soon realized the hollowness of that assumption. Signs that workers at southern foreign-owned automobile plants were questioning their status as "the chosen" appeared at VW's plant in Chattanooga, Tennessee, and at Nissan's plant in Canton, Mississippi.

VW's Chattanooga plant, which opened in May 2011, marked the company's attempt to increase its share of the U.S. domestic market (a mere 2 percent) by manufacturing its inexpensive Passat model in the United States. To ensure profitability, VW operated its Chattanooga plant with the lowest labor costs of any American automobile factory by driving its workers at a furious pace.[34] To make matters worse, workers were subjected to "a culture of bullying and machismo" fostered by male floor-level supervisors.[35] The combination of lower pay, a punishing work pace, and general disrespect drove workers toward class solidarity, a condition on which the UAW sought to capitalize.

By early 2014, the UAW claimed the support of a substantial majority of the Chattanooga plant's workforce and called for an NLRB election, which it expected to win handily. VW had signed a "neutrality agreement" in which it pledged not to interfere in the election. At that point, antiunion forces across the state emerged to sway the election's outcome. One of Tennessee's U.S. senators, for example, claimed that VW's future expansion plans in Chattanooga were contingent on workers voting against the union. In the final tally, the UAW lost by a margin of 26 votes (712–686), in the closest election ever in a foreign-owned automobile plant.[36] Twenty-two months later, however, the first crack appeared in the foreign transplant's antiunion defense, when 71 percent of the VW plant's 164 skilled maintenance workers voted to affiliate with the union after learning that UAW members in Big Three plants had received a substantial pay raise.[37] While this group of workers represented a small fraction of the plant's workforce, the result indicated that the attraction of working in a foreign-owned factory was beginning to fade.

A second instance in which southern workers in foreign-owned factories questioned their "chosen" status occurred at Nissan's massive $1.3 billion plant in Canton, Mississippi, located thirty miles north of Jackson. The Canton Nissan plant, which began production in May 2003, marked a new phase of southern industrial development that saw the transplants pushing deeper into the rural South. The heavily automated Canton plant, noted one journalist, was "by far the most sophisticated factory of any kind in a state whose economy is still dominated by king cotton and chicken farms." In contrast to the company's original strategy of "chosen" workers at Smyrna, who possessed relatively high levels of education and work experience, "at Canton, Nissan has had to rely on an untested and largely inexperienced workforce—and to grapple with some of the vexing legacies of Mississippi's past, from racial tension to poverty to a dismal educational system."[38] Most significantly, African Americans made up 80 percent of Nissan's Canton's workforce, a much larger proportion than that of any other previous foreign-owned plant, and many of these workers were connected to Jackson's community of civil rights activists.[39]

While the workers at Canton welcomed the opportunities that the Nissan plant offered, many soon soured on the experience. Despite being subjected to preemployment screening designed to weed out prounion applicants, a core group of workers at Canton rejected the middle-class "chosen" identity and began to pursue their class interests. As one prounion worker put it, "we're grateful that Nissan came to Mississippi, but as I grow older, I see there are safety and ergonomic issues that need to be addressed. . . . We want to make sure our voices are heard." Another worker remarked that the only way to "make a difference" when it came to "[my] safety, my health care, my salary" was when she had "10,000 people behind her at the [bargaining] table." In league with Jackson civic activists, they launched an aggressive campaign on behalf of the UAW, reminiscent of the "civil rights unionism" of an earlier era.[40] Among their grievances, the pro-UAW workers at Nissan Canton cited a new and more ominous development: management's use of "temporary" workers, which the UAW estimated at 40 percent of the plant's total workforce by early 2013. One prounion worker, bemoaning the use of temporary workers, claimed that management "gives them easier jobs so they won't leave" while forcing full-time workers to accept less-desirable positions, such as laboring on the night shift. Yet the prounion Nissan workers, in pursuing their class interests, empathized with the temporary workers: "They're standing next to us doing the same job, receiving less pay and less benefits. That's not fair."[41]

Since the early 2000s, the South's foreign-owned plants have relied on an increasing number of temporary employees, procured from third-party contract services. Although management has promised to upgrade these workers to the status of official company employees, the workers most often found themselves stuck in place. Dubbed "permatemps," these contingent workers regularly confront deteriorating working conditions and substandard wages and benefits.[42] In contrast to southern boosters' claims that foreign firms would hasten working-class uplift, these firms' reliance on permatemps has created a level of economic instability and employment insecurity among southern workers that represents a sharp break from the promises made to "the chosen." As such, the permatemps resemble members of what British economist Guy Standing identifies as the emerging "precariat" class, those disconnected European workers produced by neoliberal globalization "who feel their lives and identities are made up of disjointed bits, in which they cannot construct a desirable narrative or build a career."[43] Unlike their European counterparts, who are constantly moving from one job to another, permatemps in the southern automobile sector have steady jobs but, lacking union protections, still share the same sense of helplessness and victimization.[44]

The permatemp precariat steadily filled the ranks of foreign-owned factories in the months following the 2008 financial crash. Nissan once again led the way, with permatemps making up "easily a majority" of its Smyrna plant's labor force by 2014.[45] Nissan contracted with third-party employers like Yates Services in Smyrna and Kelly Services in Canton to hire thousands of workers to fill positions indistinguishable from those of Nissan's own employees. But a job with Yates, which contracted only with Nissan, failed to match permanent direct employment with the company, whose workers would earn roughly twice as much pay and have access to a range of benefits, from leased vehicles to long-term disability insurance, denied to the permatemps. These contingent workers reported work conditions reminiscent of auto plants in the 1920s before industry-wide unionization. "No one's really worried about the fact that you're so exhausted from working seven days a week, you're dependent on some drug to stay awake, or dependent on some drug to go to sleep, or for pain," said thirty-seven-year-old Chris Young, a permatemp at Nissan.[46]

The industrial precariat now occupies the bottom tier of the American South's new three-tiered workforce. At the top tier are workers like Nissan's original hires from the 1980s, who resisted unionization because of the appealing benefits the company offered and who consequently saw themselves as part of a "chosen" cohort. They constituted the essential component of southern boosters' anti-Detroit project: a new middle class of trained "technicians" in white lab coats who contrasted with the rough-and-tumble (and more ethnically and racially diverse) masses who had powered the Big Three's factories until the automobile industry's crisis in the 1970s. Occupying the second tier is the new southern proletariat, those workers in foreign-owned plants committed to traditional industrial unionism or civil rights unionism. While acknowledging the relative benefits the transplants brought to the South, they seek class solidarity and the long-term protections that unions afford. Mired in the bottom third tier is the permatemp precariat, who lack either the "chosen" cohort's middle-class consciousness or the prounion workers' class consciousness that could possibly forge solidarities in opposition to management. Facing bleak prospects, today's southern industrial precariat lack a narrative of hope and change that would justify their exploitation and the public funds that states and municipalities routinely expend to recruit the factories in which they work.

Beginning in the early 2000s, southern workers found themselves laboring more often in Chinese-owned factories. Fleeing rising domestic labor costs, Chinese companies were drawn to the South's cheap and pliant labor force and the monetary incentives doled out by local politicians. In return for hefty public investments, these Chinese companies, like their predecessors, were expected to improve the lives of the region's most downtrodden inhabitants.

This trend was illustrated most acutely in May 2014 when Alabama governor Robert Bentley ventured to the small community of Sunny South to preside over the grand opening ceremony of a $100 million state-of-the-art factory built by GD Copper, a subsidiary of the Chinese-owned Golden Dragon Precise Copper Tube Group, billed as the "world's largest supplier of precision copper products."[47] To attract GD Copper, Governor Bentley, in concert with local civic groups, had labored for three years to win a competitive bidding war against several competitors. GD Copper, for its part, received a generous recruitment package that included a host of financial incentives, infrastructure improvements, and tax breaks valued at $160 million.[48] In return for the state's substantial investment, GD Copper promised to transform remote Wilcox County from "the most impoverished corner of Alabama" to a thriving manufacturing center.[49] Its workers would earn an annual salary of $40,000 in a county whose median household income was below $30,000 and where one out of every five workers was unemployed.

Like the leadership of foreign transplants, GD Copper's management expected a docile labor force that was apathetic or outright hostile to unions. Yet a mere six months after the factory opened, workers rebelled against GD Copper's management practices, which included lower-than-expected pay, Chinese engineers who could not communicate in English, and a dangerous workplace where "minor injuries . . . piled up." In short order, GD Copper workers successfully petitioned for an NLRB election and in November 2014 chose to affiliate with the United Steelworkers by a one-vote margin.[50] Governor Bentley complained that the union's victory would only make it harder for him to lure other foreign-owned factories: "It does hurt in the recruitment of companies to come to Alabama and it does hurt me in creating jobs when a plant is non-unionized and suddenly it becomes a unionized plant."[51]

The case of GD Copper demonstrates how Chinese companies have arrived in the South speaking the same modernization language of the foreign-owned firms that preceded them and praising the various elements—the hardworking local labor force, cooperative state governments, and access to U.S. markets—that drew them to the region. Their actual treatment of workers, however, betrayed an interest in taking advantage of a high unemployment rate and feeble career prospects for the South's most impoverished and ill-educated rural residents, who were willing to accept punishing low-wage jobs in return for steady factory employment. The GD Copper workers' turn to unionization may represent a glimmer of hope for the future or, more likely, a desperate aberration. In Alabama's other foreign-owned factories, the hiring of permatemps proceeds unabated and workers routinely toil in dangerous, even deadly, conditions without rallying to the union cause.[52]

With the establishment of foreign-owned manufacturers in the South, southern elites promised to provide factory workers with a ladder to the middle class, even in a nonunion environment. But the rise of permatemp workers and the arrival of Chinese factories make such a scenario seem increasingly distant. "For global manufacturers," labor journalist Harold Meyerson has presciently remarked, "the United States—more precisely, the American South—has become the low-wage alternative to China."[53] The steady expansion of the region's industrial precariat reveals the grim truth that, at this point, there exists no utopian endgame, no teleological terminus to southern boosters' global development fantasies of regional uplift.

Notes

1. National Association of Manufacturers, "Top 20 Facts about Manufacturing," accessed December 15, 2016, http://www.nam.org/Newsroom/Top-20-Facts-About-Manufacturing/.

2. Mike Parker, "Industrial Relations Myth and Shop-Floor Reality: The 'Team Concept' in the Auto Industry," in *Industrial Democracy in America: The Ambiguous Promise*, ed. Nelson Lichtenstein and Howell John Harris (New York: Cambridge University Press, 1993), 249–74; James M. Rubenstein, *Making and Selling Cars: Innovation and Change in the U.S. Automotive Industry* (Baltimore: Johns Hopkins University Press, 2001).

3. For the history of the UAW, see Nelson Lichtenstein, *Walter Reuther: The Most Dangerous Man in Detroit* (New York: Basic Books, 1995).

4. Parker, "Industrial Relations Myth."

5. Harold Meyerson, "How the American South Drives the Low-Wage Economy," *American Prospect*, July 6, 2015.

6. David L. Carlton, "Smokestack-Chasing and Its Discontents: Southern Development Strategy in the Twentieth Century," in *The American South in the Twentieth Century*, ed. Craig S. Pascoe, Karen Trahan Leathem, and Andy Ambrose (Athens: University of Georgia Press, 2005), 106–26; James C. Cobb, *The Selling of the South: The Southern Crusade for Industrial Development, 1936–1990*, 2nd ed. (Urbana: University of Illinois Press, 1993).

7. F. Ray Marshall, *Labor in the South* (Cambridge, MA: Harvard University Press, 1967), 191–92. For southern elites' historical opposition to unions, see Chad Pearson, *Reform or Repression: Organizing America's Anti-Union Movement* (Philadelphia: University of Pennsylvania Press, 2015), ch. 6.

8. Bryant Simon, "Rethinking Why There Are So Few Unions in the South," *Georgia Historical Quarterly* 81 (Summer 1997): 465–84.

9. James C. Cobb, *Industrialization and Southern Society, 1877–1984* (Lexington: University of Kentucky Press, 1984), 58.

10. Quoted in Robert G. Kaiser, "Sony in Alabama: A Competitor Takes Root in American Soil," *Washington Post*, December 2, 1979.

11. David Gelsanliter, *Jump Start: Japan Comes to the Heartland* (New York: Farrar, Straus and Giroux, 1990), 66.

12. Michele Hoyman, *Power Steering: Global Automakers and the Transformation of Rural Communities* (Lawrence: University of Kansas Press, 1997), 25.

13. P. P. Karan, ed., *Japan in the Bluegrass* (Lexington: University Press of Kentucky, 2001).

14. William Booth, "Letter from Alabama," *Washington Post*, October 24, 1993.

15. "The Southern Auto Corridor: The Past, Present, and Future of the Center of America's Automotive Universe," Randle Report website, accessed December 15, 2016, http://archive.sb-d.com/LinkClick.aspx?fileticket=rYwZguzR8gg%3d&tabid=36.

16. Marko Maunula, "Another Southern Paradox: The Arrival of Foreign Corporations—Change and Continuity in Spartanburg, South Carolina," in *Globalization and the American South*, ed. James C. Cobb and William Stueck (Athens: University of Georgia Press, 2005), 164–84.

17. Parker, "Industrial Relations Myth," 259.

18. John Holusha, "Volkswagen to Shut U.S. Plant," *New York Times*, November 21, 1987.

19. Andrew C. McKevitt, *Consuming Japan: Popular Culture and the Globalizing of 1980s America* (Chapel Hill: University of North Carolina Press, 2017), ch. 3.

20. William Serrin, "Nissan Brings Foreign Ways to Tennessee," *New York Times*, April 20, 1981; Ralph Orr, "UAW May Ask Japan Union for Help," *Detroit Free Press*, September 26, 1981; "Nissan Warns UAW to Stay Away from New U.S. Plant," *St. Louis Post-Dispatch*, December 27, 1981; Marta Warnick, "A Year Later, Nissan Rolling in Tennessee," *Lawrence (KS) Journal-World*, June 24, 1984; Gene Lyons, "Nissan Makes a Stand in Dixie," *New York Times Sunday Magazine*, September 16, 1984, 80–87.

21. John Egerton, *Nissan in Tennessee* (Smyrna, TN: Nissan Motor Manufacturing Corp. U.S.A., 1983), 60.

22. Egerton, *Nissan in Tennessee*, 60.

23. Gelsanliter, *Jump Start*, 66.

24. Harry Reibstein, "Score Another One for Japan Inc.," *Newsweek*, August 7, 1989, 44.

25. Quoted in Gelsanliter, *Jump Start*, 66.

26. Quoted in Lyons, "Nissan Makes a Stand in Dixie," 85–86.

27. John Junkerman, "Nissan, Tennessee," *Progressive*, June 1987, 16–20. See also David Moberg, "Is There a Union in Nissan's Future?" *In These Times*, April 6–12, 1988, 12–13, 22.

28. Parker, "Industrial Relations Myth," 250, 254.

29. Timothy J. Minchin, "Showdown at Smyrna: The 1989 Campaign to Organize Nissan in Smyrna, Tennessee, and the Rise of the Transplant Sector," *Labor History*, 1–27, http://dx.doi.org/10.1080/0023656X.2017.1262080.

30. Warren Brown, "Behind the UAW's Defeat in Tennessee," *Washington Post*, July 30, 1989.

31. Terril Yue Jones, "UAW Loses Bid to Enter Nissan Plant," *Los Angeles Times*, October 4, 2001; Jeffrey Ball, "UAW Loses Second Bid to Represent Workers at Nissan Factory in Tennessee," *Wall Street Journal*, October 4, 2001.

32. Sue Anne Pressley, "The South's New-Car Smell," *Washington Post*, May 11, 2001.

33. Fred Barnes, "The Other American Auto Industry," *Weekly Standard*, December 22, 2008. For other positive assessments of the South's automobile industry, see Andy Sywak, "The South Rises Again! (In Automobile Manufacturing, That Is)," *Newgeography.com*, July 23, 2008; Patrik Jonsson, "America's 'Other' Auto Industry," *Christian Science Monitor*, December 5, 2008; Daniel Gross, "Big Three Meet the 'Little Eight': How Foreign Car Factories Have Transformed the American South," *Slate*, December 13, 2008; Peter J. Boyer, "The Road Ahead," *New Yorker*, April 20, 2009, 44–57.

34. Mike Ramsey, "VW Chops Labor Costs in U.S.," *Wall Street Journal*, May 23, 2011.

35. Mike Elk, "The Battle for Chattanooga: Southern Masculinity and the Anti-Union Campaign at Volkswagen," Working in These Times website, March 13, 2014.

36. For conflicting analyses of the February 2014 NLRB election at VW, see Lydia DePillis, "Auto Union Loses Historic Election at Volkswagen Plant in Tennessee," *Washington Post*, February 14, 2014; Mike Elk, "After Historic UAW Defeat at Tennessee Volkswagen Plant, Theories Abound," Working in These Times website, February 15, 2014; Rich Yaselson, "After Chattanooga," *Jacobin*, February 17, 2014; Harold Meyerson, "When Culture Eclipses Class," *American Prospect*, February 17, 2014; Elk, "Battle for Chattanooga"; DePillis, "The Strange Case of the Anti-Union Union at Volkswagen's Plant in Tennessee," *Washington Post*, November 19, 2014.

37. Rich Yaselson, "A Victory in Chattanooga," *Jacobin*, December 8, 2015.

38. J. Pascal Zachary, "Dream Factory," *CNN Money*, June 1, 2005.

39. Zachary Oren Smith, "Praying for Help at Nissan," *Jackson Free Press*, June 10, 2015.

40. Robert R. Korstad, *Civil Rights Unionism: Tobacco Workers and the Struggle for Democracy in the Mid-Twentieth-Century South* (Chapel Hill: University of North Carolina Press, 2003).

41. Steven Greenhouse, "At a Nissan Plant in Mississippi, a Battle to Shape the U.A.W.'s Future," *New York Times*, October 6, 2013.

42. For the rise of the permatemps, see Sarah Jaffe, "Forever Temp?" *In These Times*, January 6, 2014; Lydia DePillis, "This Is What a Job in the U.S.'s New Manufacturing Industry Looks Like," *Washington Post*, March 9, 2014; Blake Farmer, "Nissan Is Growing Like Crazy in Tennessee, and Most New Hires Are Long-Term Temps," *Nashville Public Radio*, February 4, 2015.

43. Guy Standing, "Who Will Be a Voice for the Emerging Precariat?" *Guardian* (U.K), June 1, 2001.

44. "We're All Precarious Now: An Interview with Charlie Post," *Jacobin*, April 20, 2015.

45. DePillis, "This Is What a Job in the U.S.'s New Manufacturing Industry Looks Like."

46. DePillis, "This Is What a Job in the U.S.'s New Manufacturing Industry Looks Like."

47. "Alabama Officials Welcome Golden Dragon's First U.S. Factory," *Made in Alabama*, May 28, 2014; Stan Diel, "'Rare as Hens' Teeth': Unlikely Partnership Bringing Hope for Alabama Jobs to Nation's Poorest Place," AL.com, February 14, 2014; Andy Nguyen, "Golden Dragon Opens Factory in Wilcox County, Alabama," *Asia Matters for America*, July 8, 2014.

48. Cliff Sims, "Alabama Plant Unionizes in Spite of Bentley's Warnings That It Could Kill Jobs," *Yellowhammer News*, November 18, 2014.

49. Chico Harlan, "A Grim Bargain," *Washington Post*, December 1, 2015.

50. Harlan, "A Grim Bargain."

51. Sims, "Alabama Plant Unionizes"; Gail Allyn Short, "Poster Company for Job Creation Goes Union," *Business Alabama*, January 2015; Kelli Dugan, "Labor Board Certifies USW Representation for Wilcox County's GD Copper USA," AL.com, June 2, 2015.

52. Gary Silverman, "A Death in Alabama Exposes the American Factory Dream," *Financial Times*, February 2, 2017.

53. Meyerson, "How the American South Drives the Low-Wage Economy."

5

Concluding Thoughts

17

The Historiographies of the Labor and Civil Rights Movements

At the Intersection of Parallel Lines

ALAN DRAPER

The labor and civil rights movements were two of the most important and successful twentieth-century American social movements. They each derived their power from their ability to present political issues as moral concerns. Other parallels are well known, such as how blacks borrowed the sit-in tactic from the labor movement, how both civil rights and union organizers were red-baited, and how the South posed the greatest obstacle to both of them. Moreover, they followed similar strategic paths. Just as unions moved from fighting for recognition from employers to battling over wages and working conditions, so did the civil rights movement shift from fighting for "recognition" in the form of black civil and political rights to struggling for economic equality.

With the two movements moving along parallel lines, it is little wonder that the trajectories of their historiographies also resemble each other. For example, prior to the 1960s and 1970s, labor history was defined as trade union history. Practitioners trained in the "Wisconsin School" of John R. Commons described the institutional rise and fall of trade unions and of collective bargaining. But the political ferment of the 1960s and the emergence of the New Left gave birth to a new generation of labor historians who were intent on redefining the field.[1] Impressed by the example of E. P. Thompson's *The Making of the English Working Class*, these historians were determined to put the worker back into labor history—to include the rich texture of working-class life that the institutional histories of the Wisconsin School ignored.[2]

The new labor historians proceeded to produce an insurgent "history from the bottom up" that was "embedded in a mosaic of local studies" outside the Wisconsin school's institutional line of vision.[3] The new labor historians analyzed the ways in which workers negotiated relations on the shop floor in Watervliet, Massachusetts;[4] managed the household economy in the mills of Manchester, New Hampshire;[5] and carved out their own patterns of leisure in Worcester, Massachusetts.[6]

According to the editors of *Who Built America?*, the effect of this history was to "shift the focus from 'presidents, politics, wars, and the life and values of the nation's elite—the familiar framework their profession had consistently favored'—to depict the lives and struggles of ordinary people who the dominant narrative often left out."[7] The new labor history portrayed ordinary people actively shaping their own lives, thereby imparting agency to those who frequently were regarded only as victims. In addition, it revealed a multiplicity of demands, organizations, and arenas of conflict—ranging from the park bench to the work bench—that could not easily be accommodated within the fold of the old labor history.

But the new labor historians were not without their critics. Elizabeth Fox-Genovese and Eugene D. Genovese criticized them for romanticizing their working-class subjects, exaggerating their autonomy, and neglecting how much workers' public and private lives were shaped by relations of power that, mistakenly, were left in the background.[8] Others accused them of sentimentalism, "for overstating the coherence and success of worker resistance to capitalism."[9] Working-class resistance was celebrated at the expense of examining why it so often failed. Finally, there was the nagging question of what all their local studies amounted to collectively. It was unclear whether their research simply revealed blemishes on the face of the traditional job-conscious portrait of the American worker or represented an alternative to it.[10]

The changes that once transformed the field of labor history are now evident also in the field of civil rights. Like their counterparts in labor history, second-generation civil rights historians want to uncover and derive a usable past, and they regard their work as contributing to contemporary struggles on behalf of their subjects. Just as labor historians drew political inspiration from New Left opposition to the Vietnam War, civil rights historians were provoked by the use of the movement to justify complacency toward persistent racial inequalities. They resented how an uplifting narrative of the civil rights struggle has permitted Americans smugly to delude themselves that the scars of race have diminished.[11] They complained that the success of the struggle for political equality has sapped the nation's will to confront enduring racial disadvantages and is used to justify benign neglect in response to them.

Civil rights historians also began to subvert the top-down, institutional focus of their field in ways that were analogous to those employed by their counterparts in labor history. They tried to divert the spotlight from prominent national organizations, such as the NAACP or the SCLC, and from famous leaders, such as Roy Wilkins or Dr. Martin Luther King Jr., and shine it on equally deserving but lesser-known local activists. In contrast to the prevailing literature, which was composed "mainly of studies of the national civil rights leaders and their organizations," these historians explored local struggles against racism and rescued their brave activists from oblivion.[12] They lamented that most scholarship on the movement gave credit to familiar civil rights leaders at the expense of local activists who, according to David J. Garrow, were "the actual human catalysts of the movement, the people who really gave direction to the movement's organizing work, the individuals whose records reflect the greatest substantive accomplishments and had the greatest personal impact upon the course of the southern movement."[13] These historians wanted to make sure that unheralded, exposed, courageous "local people" received the credit they deserved for challenging white power structures in small isolated towns throughout the South. Their detailed histories portrayed how civil rights had to be won town-by-town and how local people in remote southern communities achieved this extraordinary feat.

But the advantages of the bottom-up perspective go beyond merely restoring credit to those who have been overlooked. It also "laid a foundation for reshaping movement history" and "a rethinking of *what* and *who* we think is important."[14] According to Emilye Crosby, local studies "called into question many of the top-down generalizations introduced and reinforced by studies of national leaders, major events, and pivotal legal and political milestones." Studying "the movement's local, indigenous base," she declares, "fundamentally alters our picture of the movement and its significance."[15] J. Todd Moye suggests that as a result of local bottom-up contributions "scholars now understand the civil rights movement to have been more female, more grass-roots, less philosophically non-violent, and less pulpit-directed than they understood it to be thirty years ago."[16] And Jeanne Theoharis asserts that a history focused on the "specific—on a locality, an organizer or a campaign"—has begun to "map the black freedom struggle in new and important ways," including "*who* led and undertook these movements, *what* the movement was actually about, *where* it took place and *when* it happened."[17]

Second-generation civil rights historians also challenge the standard periodization of the movement as one that went from Montgomery to Memphis, or, its even more truncated and legalistic portrayal as beginning with *Brown* and ending with passage of the Voting Rights Act. In contrast, they see the 1960s civil rights movement as part of a continuous line of struggle, a Long Civil Rights Movement, that began back in the 1930s and continued into the 1980s. Moye asserts that "today, a King-centric book that purported to tell the whole story of the civil rights movement but only spanned the years between the Montgomery bus boycott and King's assassination would be laughed out of the academy."[18] The timeline is extended because civil rights were only a phase of a broader struggle that included demands for economic equality, black self-determination, and support for Third World struggles against Western colonialism and imperialism. Theoharis writes that "the black freedom struggle was a movement to end American apartheid, to achieve economic justice, and to foster the liberation of oppressed people throughout the world."[19] Thus it would be more accurate to talk about a more capacious Black Freedom Struggle to capture a more ideological, global, and radical set of demands that went beyond mere civil and voting rights.

Finally, civil rights historians not only extend the movement backward and forward in time and deepen it in terms of the ideological critique of American society it offered, but they extend it geographically beyond the borders of the South as well. Struggles against de jure segregation and the racial caste system in the South, they argue, have obscured black freedom struggles against de facto segregation and institutionalized racism in the North. Moreover the difference between de jure segregation in the South and de facto segregation in the North has been overdrawn. It does not adequately take into account how much de facto segregation was the result of intention and collusion by federal agencies and state and local governments. Finally, to concentrate so much on the South—as standard accounts do—gives the North a moral free pass that it does not deserve, and threatens to overlook both the more radical types of demands that were made there and the organizations and activists who made them. Jacqueline Dowd Hall summarizes these historians' perspective: "By confining the civil rights struggle to the South, to bowdlerized heroes, to a single halcyon decade, and to limited, noneconomic objectives, the master narrative simultaneously elevates and diminishes the movement."[20]

In the same way that the new labor history came to dominate its field, so do second-wave civil rights histories now "have a hint of a new orthodoxy."[21] They began to receive more critical scrutiny as their approach became more popular. These criticisms bear an eerie resemblance to those leveled against the new labor history. Second-wave civil rights historians have been accused of simply replacing a top-down determinism with their own local determinism.[22] They romanticize what local activists could accomplish on their own. Larger relations of power, especially federal action in the form of court decisions, executive orders, and legislation, are belittled, as if acknowledging their significance and influence would somehow take away credit from the brave deeds of local activists and organizers.[23] This is ironic because the Student Nonviolent Coordinating Committee (SNCC) activists with whom second-generation civil rights historians identify believed that federal intervention was necessary to shift an unfavorable local balance of power. They had no illusions about the limits of local resistance and militancy, desperately tried to obtain federal protection for their voting registration efforts, and were deeply distressed when it was not forthcoming. A Council of Federated Organizations (COFO) memorandum states, "There can be no real breakthrough for the Negro, no significant program with the present power structure, unless there is massive intervention on the part of the federal government."[24] Wesley C. Hogan provides a definitive end to the debate between the relative contributions of local activism and federal protection to SNCC voter registration efforts, declaring that "if the federal government did not protect the right to vote in Mississippi, [blacks] would not become full citizens: they would be dead."[25]

Critics are also skeptical of efforts to shift the movement's timeline in order to accommodate broader, more radical goals, as captured in the semantic change from "civil rights movement" to "Black Freedom Struggle" that these historians propose.[26] Critics charge that the change in nomenclature only introduces conceptual confusion over what exactly is included or excluded by the new term. Imagining one continuous movement from the 1930s through the 1970s flattens and diminishes differences among struggles against racism. There is a loss of perspective, as though the racial struggles of the 1960s were equivalent in magnitude to those of other periods. Amalgamating diverse conflicts also fails to capture changes in strategy and demands. Even Charles M. Payne concedes that there "really was something special about the period from the mid-fifties to the mid-sixties" in terms of the salience of racial issues and the new ways people thought about them.[27]

If the point of changing the timeline is to account for a broader, more radical set of demands, then it's not clear why the Black Freedom Struggle begins in the 1930s and not the 1920s to include Garveyism, or the anti-lynching campaigns in the decade before that, or all the way back to the first act of resistance by slaves as the start of the Black Freedom Struggle.

The dangers of collapsing categories are especially evident when civil rights historians blur the distinction between racism in the North and the South; between the indignities of being thrust into the lower class in the North and of being held in contempt as the lower caste in the South. If these species of racism were merely two sides of the same coin, then the decision of almost six million blacks between 1916 and 1970 who escaped the South to start new lives outside of it becomes inexplicable.[28] Nor does the alleged equivalence of northern and southern racism square with what southern blacks reported after venturing north to visit. According to T.R.M. Howard, who founded the Regional Council of Negro Leadership, the leading civil rights group of the 1950s in Mississippi, "blacks who thought they were happy on the plantations of Mississippi" enviously describe blacks in the North "eating better, living in a better house, wearing better clothing, having more spending money, children going to schools and above all having freedom of mind."[29] Their perception that northern standards of living were better was no illusion. In 1964, median family income for blacks in the North was more than twice that of their southern counterparts.[30]

Part of the reason blacks fared so much better in the North was that its class structure was more susceptible to economic, moral, and political pressure than the southern caste system, which was more overt, severe, and inflexible. Gavin Wright notes that "black occupational attainment in northern states—limited as it was—markedly exceeded that of black southerners" in the 1950s because, for example, northern blacks could vote. Political mobilization led to fair employment laws and public-sector jobs for northern blacks that their southern counterparts lacked the political influence to obtain.[31]

But as significant as the gap in living standards and contrast in labor markets were, they paled in comparison to the sense of freedom blacks enjoyed once they left the South. Whatever prejudice and discrimination blacks suffered in the North, the region still offered a sense of security and possibility that the racial caste system foreclosed in the South, where defiance of their region's racial etiquette could be a death sentence.[32]

Labor and civil rights literatures have followed similar trajectories. Old orthodoxies in each field have been replaced by new ones. Second-generation labor and civil rights historians were both propelled by political upheavals to try to derive a usable past. They each took a more local approach, uncovering obscure actors articulating new kinds of demands. But the two literatures diverge when it came to methodology. Second-generation civil rights historians utilize oral histories much more than do their counterparts engaged in labor history.[33] Part of the reason for this, of course, is because historians of the civil rights movement still have access to the people who participated in it. Labor historians of the nineteenth and early twentieth century are not so lucky in being able to interview their subjects. But another reason has to do with each movement's approach toward organizational development. The civil rights movement, especially SNCC, was skeptical of bureaucracy and loosely structured. Field staff freelanced and resisted centralized control, which was not terribly insistent to begin with. The movement was all and the organization nothing. The opposite was the case with the labor movement, where the goal of the movement was to create viable organizations. This led to greater organizational coherence and bureaucracy that yielded more documentation for future labor historians to consult.[34]

Oral history has its virtues. Civil rights histories that rely on oral history have an anthropological quality to them of thick description. Oral history gives civil rights accounts a narrative richness and depth. In comparison, labor histories that take a bottom-up approach appear schematic.

But oral history also has its shortcomings. Memory is selective. People recall events through a prism shaped by their predispositions and prejudices. When second-generation civil rights historians rely upon oral histories and written reminiscences of movement activists they end up reflecting myths and assumptions that circulated among them. As Charles

W. Eagles perceptively noted, second-generation civil rights historians tell the story "essentially from the perspective of the movement," whose recollections they rely upon.[35]

Clayborne Carson claims that it is the tragic fate of all social movements to fail "in the minds of their participants." "Social movements," he argues, "generate aspirations that cannot be fulfilled" and mere reforms are not accepted as evidence of success.[36] New labor historians lament that unionization may have been achieved but at the cost of stifling working-class spontaneity and foreclosing more radical alternatives. Similarly, second-generation civil rights historians complain that political equality may have been obtained but more significant forms of racial inequality persisted.

But in both instances, labor and civil rights historians are guilty of perceiving the results of these movements from the perspective of the activists who harbored such disappointments as opposed to their followers and supporters who appreciated the gains that took place. Nowhere was the gap between social movement activists and their supporters more evident than in Mississippi following the failure of the Mississippi Freedom Democratic Party delegates to be seated at the 1964 Democratic Party convention. Delegates returned from the convention dispirited. For some, their disappointment led them to lose faith in mainstream politics, the Democratic Party, the efficacy of the ballot, and the value of integration. In contrast, however, their base was anxious to participate in mainstream politics from which they had been excluded, to support the Democratic Party that had passed the Civil Rights Act of 1964 and would later secure their right to vote in 1965 with passage of the Voting Rights Act, to cast a ballot for the first time in their lives and achieve a measure of respect, political power, and first-class citizenship through it, and to integrate public facilities that were previously closed to them.

Labor and civil rights activists were radicalized by their experiences, which led them to adopt different standards to judge the success of their movements than those they sought to mobilize. This was especially true of SNCC organizers, who were often disappointed with results because their goals became more ambitious over time. But, as David L. Chappell argues, "measured by historical standards of realism, their achievement was extraordinary."[37] A. Philip Randolph described the challenge facing the movement following passage of the 1964 Civil Rights Act as "a crisis of victory."[38] The civil rights movement lifted the threat of official and unofficial violence that blighted the lives of black people in the South. Black lives mattered more than they did previously as African Americans began to serve on juries and as police officers in the South.

Following passage of the Voting Rights Act in 1965, new black voters elected black officials who changed the agenda "by raising issues salient to their constituents that whites had either ignored or not considered important."[39] According to Bullock and Rozell, "roads in Black neighborhoods got paved, sidewalks got laid, water and sewer lines were extended, new parks were created, and old ones spruced up." Furthermore, black votes now "translated into public jobs above the janitorial staff. African Americans got hired by the police force and as firefighters and attained administrative posts in courthouses and city halls."[40] Political equality meant more economic opportunities open to blacks, better schools, and fairer property tax assessments. It also ended the indignities of Jim Crow laws that denied blacks access to public facilities. The *Negro Motorist Green Book* that black families consulted to learn of establishments that catered to them when they traveled south has been out of print since 1966. Historians taking a bottom-up perspective need to look another level down—not to activists but to the base they sought to organize—to assess the success of the social movements they describe.[41]

Labor and civil rights historians come to their subjects with a sense of political urgency. They want to extract a usable past from it. They would succeed more in doing so if they were less attracted to tragedy in which the only victories ever obtained are the pyrrhic kind in which very real gains are dismissed because significant inequalities remain. The labor and civil rights movements are portrayed as incomplete revolutions. Unions emerged but class divisions remained. Blacks achieved political equality but racial social inequalities endured. To approach the legacy of these movements in this manner is not analytically helpful. All social movements are incomplete and unfinished, especially in the eyes of their proponents.

Rather we should measure the success of the labor and civil rights movements not against the impossible standards that radicalized activists applied but against the more sober benchmarks that workers and blacks used to assess their lives. We need to see these movements through the lived experience, the practical lens of ordinary people that bottom-up historians are supposed to offer. These historians are more likely to succeed in producing a usable past from which others can draw inspiring lessons when they do so.

Notes

1. The editors of *Who Built America?* explicitly acknowledge that the new labor history derived its political inspiration from the New Left. They concede, "The social and political upheavals of the 1960s and 1970s prompted a number of historians—including all of the authors of this book—to expand their inquiries into America's past." See American Social History Project, *Who Built America? Working People and the Nation's Economy, Politics, Culture, and Society*, vol. 1 (New York: Pantheon, 1989), xi. For more on the affinities between the new labor history and the New Left see Robert Zieger, "Workers and Scholars: Recent Trends in American Labor Historiography," *Labor History* 13, no. 2 (1972): 245–66. In a recent memorial to the work of David Montgomery, Nelson Lichtenstein acknowledges that the "turn to the working class" was "inaugurated by activist students, a generation of young social historians, and widespread strike activity and internal union insurgencies on both sides of the Atlantic." See Nelson Lichtenstein, "David Montgomery and the Idea of 'Workers' Control,'" *Labor: Studies in Working-Class History of the Americas* 10, no. 1 (2013): 65.

2. David Brody confesses that labor historians of his generation "wanted not only to write better history, but to change the focus of study so that labor history would become a history of workers," and David Montgomery described the new labor history as one that drew "our attention away from union and party conventions to the communities where workers lived and fought." See David Brody, "The Old Labor History and the New: In Search of an American Working Class," *Labor History* 20, no. 1 (1979): 111–26 (quote on 113); and David Montgomery, "To Study the People: The American Working Class," *Labor History* 23, no. 4 (1982): 501.

3. David Montgomery, *Beyond Equality: Labor and the Radical Republicans, 1862–1872* (Urbana: University of Illinois Press, 1967), x.

4. Dan Clawson, *Bureaucracy and the Labor Process: The Transformation of U.S. Industry, 1860–1920* (New York: Monthly Review Press, 1980).

5. Tamara K. Haraven and Randolph Langenbach, *Amoskeag: Life and Work in an American Factory City* (Hanover, NH: University Press of New England, 1978).

6. Roy Rozenswieg, *Eight Hours for What We Will: Workers and Leisure in an Industrial City, 1870–1920* (New York: Cambridge University Press, 1985).

7. American Social History Project, *Who Built America*, xi.

8. Elizabeth Fox-Genovese and Eugene D. Genovese, *Fruits of Merchant Capital: Slavery and Bourgeois Property in the Rise and Expansion of Capitalism* (New York: Oxford University Press, 1983).

9. Lawrence T. McDonnell, "'You Are Too Sentimental': Problems and Suggestions for a New Labor History," *Journal of Social History* 17, no. 4 (1984): 630.

10. Brody, "The Old Labor History and the New." For further criticisms of the new labor history see Robert Ozanne, "Trends in American Labor History," *Labor History* 21 (1980): 513–21, which defends the old labor history; and Nell Irvin Painter, "The New Labor History and the Historical Moment," *International Journal of Politics, Culture, and Society* 2, no. 3 (1989): 367–70, which accuses it of whitewashing their subjects' racism.

11. Jeanne Theoharis, "Black Freedom Studies: Re-imagining and Redefining the Fundamentals," *History Compass* 4, no. 2. (2008): 349.

12. Clayborne Carson, "Civil Rights Reform and the Black Freedom Struggle," in *The Civil Rights Movement in America*, ed. Charles W. Eagles (Jackson: University Press of Mississippi, 1986), 22.

13. David J. Garrow quoted in Charles M. Payne, *I've Got the Light of Freedom: The Organizing Tradition and the Mississippi Freedom Struggle*, 2nd. ed. (Berkeley: University of California Press, 2007), 3.

14. Emilye Crosby, "Introduction: The Politics of Writing and Teaching Movement History," in *Civil Rights History from the Ground Up: Local Struggles, A National Movement*, ed. Emilye Crosby (Athens: University of Georgia Press, 2011), 6 (emphasis in original).

15. Crosby, "Introduction," 5–6.

16. J. Todd Moye, "Focusing Our Eyes on the Prize: How Community Studies Are Reframing and Rewriting the History of the Civil Rights Movement," in *Civil Rights History from the Ground Up*, 166.

17. Theoharis, "Black Freedom Studies," 349 (emphasis in original).

18. Moye, "Focusing Our Eyes on the Prize," 162.

19. Theoharis, "Black Freedom Studies," 358. Ironically, criticism of the standard civil rights timeline is one shared by NAACP executive secretary Roy Wilkins, whom these historians assail as an example of the staid national civil rights leadership from which civil rights history needs to be rescued. Wilkins wrote, "Nothing delights me more than to meet someone who does not believe that the civil rights movement began with the Montgomery bus boycott . . . or began with the Greensboro N.C. sit-ins in February 1, 1960." Of course, Wilkins was as politically interested in adjusting the civil rights clock back in time as these historians. To start the clock earlier would return it to when the NAACP dominated the civil rights field and could take all the credit for itself, instead of now having to share it with, or be eclipsed by, such new, pesky competitors as CORE, SNCC, or SCLC. See Roy Wilkins to Benjamin McAdoo, November 18, 1965, in part 21, reel 14, NAACP Papers, Library of Congress, Washington, DC.

20. Jacqueline Dowd Hall, "The Long Civil Rights Movement and the Political Uses of the Past," *Journal of American History* 91 (March 2005): 1234.

21. Payne, *I've Got the Light of Freedom*, xiv.

22. Steven F. Lawson, *Civil Rights Crossroads: Nation, Community, and the Black Freedom Struggle* (Lexington: University of Kentucky Press, 2003), 21.

23. Steven F. Lawson, *Debating the Civil Rights Movement 1945–1968* (Lanham, MD: Rowman & Littlefield, 1998).

24. David C. Colby, "The Voting Rights Act and Black Registration in Mississippi," *Publius* 16, no. 4 (1986): 131.

25. Wesley C. Hogan, *Many Minds, One Heart: SNCC's Dream for a New America* (Chapel Hill: University of North Carolina Press, 2007), 58.

26. Eric Arnesen, "Reconsidering the Long Civil Rights Movement," *History's Compass*, April 2009, 31–34.

27. Payne, *I've Got the Light of Freedom*, xx.

28. Sundiata Keita Cha-Jua and Clarence Lang, "The 'Long Movement' as Vampire: Temporal and Spatial Fallacies in Recent Black Freedom Studies," *Journal of African American History* 92, no. 2 (2007): 265–88.

29. David T. Beito and Linda Royster Beito, *Black Maverick: T.R.M. Howard's Fight for Civil Rights and Economic Power* (Urbana: University of Illinois Press, 2009), 70.

30. Cha-Jua and Lang, "The 'Long Movement' as Vampire," 282.

31. Gavin Wright, *Sharing the Prize: The Economics of the Civil Rights Revolution in the American South* (Cambridge: Harvard University Press, 2013), 6.

32. Isabel Wilkerson, *The Warmth of Other Suns: The Epic Story of America's Great Migration* (New York: Random House, 2010).

33. An exemplary exception to this is Peter Friedlander's *The Emergence of a UAW Local, 1936–1939: A Study on Class and Culture* (Pittsburgh: University of Pittsburgh Press, 1975).

34. The NAACP was an exception among civil rights organizations in its bureaucratization and, consequently, left a richer documentary base for scholars to consult.

35. Charles W. Eagles, "Toward New Histories of the Civil Rights Era," *Journal of Southern History* 66 (November 2000): 816.

36. Clayborne Carson, "Civil Rights Reform and the Black Freedom Struggle," in *The Civil Rights Movement in America*, ed. Charles W. Eagles (Jackson: University of Mississippi Press, 1986), 19. For a similar point from a more theoretical perspective see Sidney Tarrow, *Power in Movement: Social Movements, Collective Action, and Politics* (New York: Cambridge University Press, 1994), 170–87.

37. David L. Chappell, *A Stone of Hope: Prophetic Religion and the Death of Jim Crow* (Chapel Hill: University of North Carolina Press, 2005), 8.

38. A. Philip Randolph, "Crisis of Victory," in "Opening Remarks at Conference of Negro Leaders, National Council of Churches, New York, N.Y. January 30–31, 1965," reel 43, frame 1094, SNCC Papers, Microfilm Collection, Library and Archives of the Martin Luther King Jr. Center for Nonviolent Social Change, Atlanta, GA.

39. Charles S. Bullock III and Mark J. Rozell, "African Americans and Contemporary Southern Politics," *The Forum* 14, no. 1 (2016): 71.

40. Bullock and Rozell, "African Americans and Contemporary Southern Politics," 72.

41. See Wright, *Sharing the Prize*, on the substantial material benefits that southern blacks—not simply the middle class—derived from the civil rights movement.

18

So Goes the Nation

Southern Antecedents and the Future of Work

BETHANY MORETON

In the first two decades of the new millennium, fears of a jobless future have become commonplace. "Will a robot take your job?" asks the legitimate mainstream media. A steady stream of scholarly books answers in the affirmative, while the business press assumes the outcome and cuts straight to advice on "how to keep your job when robots take over."[1] (Not that their solutions were particularly comforting: the *Financial Times* recommends preparing for the future by developing a taste for dog food.) The consulting firm McKinsey made waves in 2015 when its analysis showed that almost half of all activities people are currently paid to perform could be automated by applying already existing technologies. Highlighting the data point of particular interest to its own customer base, McKinsey was at pains to point out that not just "low-skill, low-wage" types were in the crosshairs. Rather, they see robots taking on many tasks of "financial managers, physicians, and senior executives, including CEOs."[2] A crisis, indeed.

Technology-driven unemployment and work degradation are hardly new; they could be seen clearly from atop any mechanical cotton-picker in the Delta of the 1950s, or on the floor of the Lordstown Vega plant in 1970. But they are a newly urgent concern for the information economy's class of "symbolic analysts," the white-collar managers and professionals who engineered other people out of work and must now confront the power of algorithm to unmake their own economic niche.[3] Despite the optimistic projections that machines will free humanity from mind-numbing toil, the reality has been much more complex: from the plantation complex to the assembly line, the specific ways that technology has been owned and organized have more often enriched the few and immiserated many more. The exception to this rule was the mid-twentieth-century high noon of liberalism, when increased productivity was translated, by the democratic tools of taxation and labor protection, into increased wages and social investment for at least some of the American workforce. That relationship was decoupled in the early 1970s: increases in productivity—the goal of technology—produced flat wage rates; and since 2000, productivity increases have also failed to produce more total jobs at any wage rate. In the absence of democratic control over technological decision-making, there is no reason to assume that the new divisions of labor will look any different: Google, worth more than the GDP of Austria, employs only sixty thousand people, about the population of Terre Haute, Indiana. Of the ten fastest-growing job categories, eight require less than a bachelor's degree.[4] The United States has a larger share of low-wage jobs than any other rich country, and of those nearly half pay too little to meet basic needs. Individual bootstrapping hasn't saved the over 40 percent of college graduates who are working in low-wage jobs, and the rate of small-business ownership among those under thirty is at the lowest in a generation. The official unemployment rate hides as well the scandal of the largest imprisoned population in world history, a form of labor force regulation that goes by the name of law and order: in a sense, the answer to automation has been hyperincarceration.[5]

In this landscape, the South again steps into its stealth role as America's harbinger. The former heartland of slavery, historians demonstrate again and again, has not in fact lagged behind the American project as some eternal feudal afterthought, peculiarly resistant to remediation except at the point of a federal bayonet. Rather, the region in many cases leapfrogs over industrial liberalism to connect a plantation political economy to a digital age. Rather than catching up to the Keynesian midcentury and the factory-centered dreams of industrial democracy, the South blew right by it and today models a political economy of exploitation buttressed by hyperincarceration and disfranchisement. As House Minority Leader Trent Lott put it so bracingly during the Reagan Revolution, the postindustrial era's triumphant ideals of economy and governance "are the things that [Confederate president] Jefferson Davis and his people believed in."[6]

As Lott's forthright endorsement of the GOP platform suggests, both proponents and detractors recognize that race-based chattel slavery is the DNA of dominance. "Slavery created the modern world, and the modern world's divisions (both abstract and concrete) are the product of slavery," writes historian Greg Grandin. "Slavery is both the thing that can't be transcended but also what can never be remembered" as the basis of transatlantic white wealth and independence—despite its eloquent scholarly formulation by W.E.B. DuBois, C.L.R. James, and Eric Williams in the first half of the twentieth century.[7] The plantation system set the terms of the great transformation—the industrial-scale monocropping that stripped millions of years of sedimented topsoil into a few decades of bonanza staple cultivation; the technologies of the slave ship, the coffle, and the steam ship that transported a million enslaved people to land newly wrested from its Native owners; the innovative fragmentation of the labor process into an increasingly efficient mode of extraction; the intricate architecture of finance, insurance, and real estate that tied Manchester to New Orleans and Providence to Bridgetown; even the cognitive innovations spurred by thought systems like plantation accounting, theological justifications of bondage, and medical experimentation on enslaved bodies.[8]

This economic engine of modernization also set the limits of democratic government for the antebellum nation as a whole. The enslavers' fundamental imperative was to stave off any political instrument that could empower the majority—even just the majority of free white men—to destroy the slave system. This overriding requirement to protect their "property" met increasing challenges via popular sovereignty, as yeomen, clerks, and mechanics in the early republic pushed the states to make good on the promise of manhood suffrage. To maintain their economic dominance through bondage, southern elites employed new legal and statutory tools to insulate the economy from democracy and keep at bay taxation—and the civilization it *buys* under public control—lest it be turned against the single most valuable species of property in antebellum America: enslaved Americans of African descent.[9] Their deepening concern to hold democracy at bay and protect minority rights against the "tyranny of the majority" turned on a tragically ironic definition of minority—namely the enslaving class, inevitably a minority by the sheer logistics of plantation cultivation. Slavery, declared its ablest defender, was "the best guarantee to equality among the whites," the very basis for republican government.[10]

Small wonder, then, that the literal fact of emancipation—"nothing but freedom," the bare cessation of bondage without due process—was not in itself enough to rewrite the fundamental contours of political economy once the bayonets were withdrawn and the rebels restored to their liberties. Unwilling to build out a public sphere on any front, from schools to prisons, the postbellum southern states adopted a libertarian approach to tax avoidance by violent labor extraction in lieu of state-building and shared public investment.[11] Freedpeople were quickly sucked back into rightlessness by the criminalization of poverty, and leased directly to the emerging "free" enterprises now as convicts. A gulag of brutal labor camps subsidized private industries like lumber, railroad construction, and coal mining; chain gangs built the public roads that moved their products to markets. African American women were additionally conscripted to private white homes to serve out their prison terms under an excruciating regime of intimate dominance.[12]

After the Bourbon elites defeated first the reformist Reconstruction governments and then popular insurgencies in the 1890s, legislative restrictions and, eventually, new constitutions in southern states doubled down on efforts to protect private wealth-generation from even the future possibility of democratic governance by limiting the franchise. "That is what we are here for today," proclaimed a delegate to the Mississippi state constitutional convention in 1890, "to secure the supremacy of the white race." Voter participation—white as well as black—plummeted in the face of poll taxes, literacy tests, and residency requirements left to the discretion of local officials. Thus the same states that officially embraced violent labor coercion also perfected the model of neoliberal political economy that demanded national subsidy of private enterprise but rejected oversight as intolerable meddling and public investment as a waste of money: in Houston at the turn of the twentieth century, for example, businessmen successfully courted a record $1.25 million in federal dollars to dredge a harbor for their trade while raw sewage was dumped in the city's bayous.[13] With "Big Government" successfully prevented from aiding any human freedom beyond that of trucking and bartering, white children in some counties attended school ten weeks a year, black children barely more than a month. Alabama employers could legally work a twelve-year-old for sixty hours a week. Landowners forced cash crops onto every available acre while their tenant workforce suffered pellagra-induced dementia from malnutrition on a diet of fatback and cornbread. Across vast swathes of the rural South, electricity, indoor plumbing, and health care were completely absent; but with the tools of democratic decision-making locked out of the majority's reach, wealth could be redistributed only upward, from the fields and mines to the faux Taras lining the Jefferson Davis Drives of southern towns and cities.

Even during the brief midcentury window of national experimentation with enforceable labor protections and social investment, the southern model defined and enforced the limits for the whole. The price of the southern Democratic congressional delegation's participation in the New Deal was the right to administer it at the state level and seal off from its benefits the agricultural and domestic workers, two job categories dominated by African Americans. Through the Depression, the war, and its immediate aftermath, southern Democrats—power brokers of an antidemocratic, authoritarian one-party system enforced by terrorist violence—used their effective veto power over national agendas to blunt progress on two fronts above all: labor legislation and civil rights.[14] As a Florida congressman pointed out in the debate over the Fair Labor Standards Act, "when we turn over to a federal bureau or board the power to fix wages, it will prescribe the same wage for the Negro that it prescribes for the white man." Such an arrangement, he explained patiently, "just will not work in the South. You cannot put the Negro and the white man on the same basis and get away with it."[15] Rather than accept a national labor market that could not distinguish legally between white and black, the South's representatives preferred to deny to all Americans the social citizenship won in every other industrial democracy at midcentury.

The South's history lays bare the ways that antidemocratic governance has been used in this country to protect unfree labor arrangements and to blunt collective decision-making about the conditions of wealth production and distribution. That history helps sharpen our analysis of the current concern over the future of work. The organization of work is a historically specific social arrangement, not a timeless feature of the physical universe. Jobs are only one way of coordinating work and sustenance, and a very recent one at that. They represent not an ideal match between the work that must get done and the goods and services we require, but rather a compromise between competing interests with deep roots.

The contours of the job as we imagine it were defined and limited by the long shadow of slavery. On the one hand, the paradigmatic job emerged from the national trauma of the Great Depression with such crucial accoutrements as unemployment insurance, pensions, wage and hour protections, and legally enforceable health and safety standards, as well as cultural prestige as the arsenal of democracy and the wellspring of national prosperity. On the other hand, the process of enhancing the job demanded that other forms of work suffer deliberate exclusion to meet the centuries-old requirements of the South's properties elites. To protect the pool of cheap Jim Crow labor, the New Deal labor standards enjoyed by whites on the Detroit assembly line did not extend to Filipino fruit-packers in Fresno or African American domestic workers in Atlanta. Likewise, the New Deal's imperative to shore up the status of the male breadwinner ensured that the "women's work" of reproducing the workforce—the intimate labor of feeding, healing, cleaning, rearing and tending—would remain trapped in a twilight zone between moral obligation and biological impulse. Alone among industrial democracies, the United States distributed benefits largely through employment rather than citizenship; the work of contributing to national life qualified only if it took place within contractual, even corporate, formal employment. Many postwar labor markets were thus free in name only, structured by white-supremacist terrorism, the threat of deportation, and entirely legal forms of segmentation, harassment, and discrimination.

If the arguments for the dignity and value of people in service labor held steady over many decades, the resistance to improving their lot remained remarkably consistent as well. Echoing the fears of New Deal–era white southern lawmakers, in 1967 Senator Russell Long of Louisiana criticized work-training provisions in welfare law since they might tend to make welfare recipients hold out for a job like "the top secretary in your office" rather than taking a cleaning job: "You know somebody has to do just the ordinary everyday work. Now if they don't do it, we have to do it."[16] Similarly, the congressional delegates of southern states killed Richard Nixon's proposed Family Assistance Plan—essentially a guaranteed minimum income—because, as one put it, "there's not going to be anybody left to roll those wheelbarrows and press those shirts."[17] While service employees succeeded in achieving some legal protections in the 1960s and 1970s—notably the right of public-sector employees to bargain collectively, the extension of federal labor law to service employees of nonprofit hospitals in 1970, and the inclusion of domestic workers in the

Fair Labor Standards Act in 1974—the South in particular has blunted their impact by the widespread employment of undocumented immigrants in service industries since 1980.

The irony, of course, is that everybody lost in this bargain. DuBois's point about the antebellum order, that "slave labor in conjunction and competition with free labor tended to reduce all labor toward slavery," remains relevant as long as American political economy and labor organization continue on terms constrained by the legacy of enslavement.[18] By elevating only certain forms of work to the status of "real jobs" and limiting even their scope to terms acceptable to midcentury southern senators, we also incentivized job destruction: Why not break every job into its component parts and sell off the work to the lowest bidder who will make the fewest demands on the social fabric? Why not replace employees with robots, or the employment bargain with the "sharing" economy?

Fifty years ago, scientists and activists joined forces to urge a coordinated national response to "joblessness, inadequate incomes, and frustrated lives." Inspired by the March on Washington for Jobs and Freedom—the mass mobilization designed to break the white-supremacist stranglehold over both those priorities—advocates like Bayard Rustin and Gunnar Myrdal teamed up with chemists and mathematicians steeped in cybernetics to ask, "Are there other proper claims on goods and services besides a job?"[19] The question is as pertinent now as when it was formulated, and the South is where it will have to be answered.

Notes

1. See, for example, Eric Sherman and Rebecca Zissou, "Will a Robot Take Your Job?" *New York Times Upfront*, October 10, 2016, http://upfront.scholastic.com/issues/10_10_16/will-a-robot-take-your-job/; Scott Santens, "A Robot Will Take Your Job," *Boston Globe*, February 25, 2016, https://www.bostonglobe.com/ideas/2016/02/24/robots-will-take-your-job/5lXtKomQ7uQBEzTJOXT7YO/story.html; Erik Brynjolfsson and Andrew McAfee, *Race against the Machine: How the Digital Revolution Is Accelerating Innovation, Driving Productivity, and Irreversibly Transforming Employment and the Economy* (Lexington, MA: Digital Frontier Press, 2012); Erik Brynjolfsson and Andrew McAfee, *The Second Machine Age: Work, Progress, and Prosperity in a Time of Brilliant Technologies* (New York: W.W. Norton, 2016); Martin Ford, *Rise of the Robots: Technology and the Threat of a Jobless Future* (New York: Basic Books, 2015); Klaus Schwab, *The Fourth Industrial Revolution* (Geneva: World Economic Forum, 2016); Simon Cooper, "How to Cope When Robots Take Your Job," *FT Magazine*, October 6, 2016, https://www.ft.com/content/ed208574-8b4d-11e6-8cb7-e7ada1d123b1; Tiger Tyagarajan, "How

to Keep Your Job When Robots Take Over," *Fortune*, August 17, 2016, http://fortune.com/2016/08/17/ai-u-s-workforce/.

2. Michael Chui, James Manyika, and Mehdi Miremadi, "Four Fundamentals of Workplace Automation," *McKinsey Quarterly*, November 2015, http://www.mckinsey.com/business-functions/digital-mckinsey/our-insights/four-fundamentals-of-workplace-automation.

3. For an influential early assertion of the benefits of the information economy, see Daniel Bell, *The Coming of Post-Industrial Society: A Venture in Social Forecasting* (New York: Basic Books, 1973); "symbolic analysts" is the term employed by former secretary of labor Robert Reich, in his *The Work of Nations: Preparing Ourselves for 21st-Century Capitalism* (New York: Knopf, 1993).

4. Tiffany Koebel, "The 10 Fastest Growing Jobs," U.S. Department of Labor Blog, March 15, 2015, https://blog.dol.gov/2015/03/15/the-10-fastest-growing-jobs/.

5. Bruce Western and Katherine Beckett, "How Unregulated Is the U.S. Labor Market? The Penal System as a Labor Market Institution," *American Journal of Sociology* 104, no. 4 (1999): 1030–60.

6. Lott, *Southern Partisan* (1984), quoted in Nancy MacLean, "Southern Dominance in Borrowed Language: The Regional Origins of American Neoliberalism," in *New Landscapes of Inequality: Neoliberalism and the Erosion of Democracy in America*, ed. Jane Collins, Micaela Di Leonardo, and Brett Williams (Sante Fe, NM: School for Advanced Research Press, 2008), 23. More broadly see MacLean, *Democracy in Chains: The Deep History of the Radical Right's Stealth Plan for America* (New York: Viking, forthcoming 2017).

7. W.E.B. DuBois, *Black Reconstruction* (New York: Harcourt Brace, 1935); C.L.R. James, *The Black Jacobins: Toussaint L'Ouverture and the San Domingo Revolution* (New York: Dial Press, 1938); Eric Williams, *Capitalism and Slavery* (Chapel Hill: University of North Carolina Press, 1944).

8. Greg Grandin, "Capitalism and Slavery," *Nation*, May 1, 2015, https://www.thenation.com/article/capitalism-and-slavery/. Important recent books that build on the prewar analyses of DuBois, James, and Williams about the relationship between slavery and capitalism include Edward Baptist, *The Half Has Never Been Told: Slavery and the Making of American Capitalism* (New York: Basic Books, 2014); Sven Beckert, *Empire of Cotton: A Global History* (New York: Vintage Books, 2015); Sven Beckert and Seth Rockman, *Slavery's Capitalism: A New History of American Economic Development* (Philadelphia: University of Pennsylvania Press, 2016); Greg Grandin, *The Empire of Necessity: Slavery, Freedom, and Deception in the New World* (New York: Metropolitan Books, 2014); Walter Johnson, *River of Dark Dreams: Slavery and Empire in the Cotton Kingdom* (Cambridge: Harvard University Press, 2013); Matthew Karp, *This Vast Southern Empire: Slaveholders at the Helm of American Foreign Policy* (Cambridge: Harvard University Press, 2016); Kris Manjapra, "Plantation Century: The Global Spread of Industrial Agriculture, 1830–1930," paper presented at the Twenty-First Annual Cultural Studies Conference, Indiana University, Bloomington, IN, October 21, 2016; Jennifer L. Morgan, *Laboring Women: Reproduction and Gender in New World Slavery* (Philadelphia: University

of Pennsylvania Press, 2004); Stephanie Smallwood, *Saltwater Slavery: A Middle Passage from Africa to American Diaspora* (Cambridge: Harvard University Press, 2007).

9. Robin Einhorn, *American Taxation, American Slavery* (Chicago: University of Chicago Press, 2006); Gavin Wright, *Slavery and American Economic Development* (Baton Rouge: Louisiana State University Press, 2006).

10. John C. Calhoun's remark was delivered to John Quincy Adams in a private conversation in 1820; Adam's account of the conversation is quoted in Lacy Ford Jr., "Inventing the Concurrent Majority: Madison, Calhoun, and the Problem of Majoritarianism in American Political Thought," *Journal of Southern History* 60, no. 1 (1994): 41.

11. MacLean, *Democracy in Chains.*

12. Sarah Haley, *No Mercy Here: Gender, Punishment, and the Making of Jim Crow Modernity* (Chapel Hill: University of North Carolina Press, 2016); Talitha LeFlouria, *Chained in Silence: Black Women and Convict Labor in the New South* (Chapel Hill: University of North Carolina Press, 2015); Alex Lichtenstein, *Twice the Work of Free Labor: The Political Economy of Convict Labor in the New South* (New York: Verso, 1996).

13. Joe R. Feagin, *Free Enterprise City: Houston in Political and Economic Perspective* (New Brunswick, NJ: Rutgers University Press, 1988), 119.

14. Ira Katznelson, Kim Geiger, and Daniel Kryder, "Limiting Liberalism: The Southern Veto in Congress, 1933–1950," *Political Science Quarterly* 108, no. 2 (Summer, 1993): 283–306. More broadly, see Jill S. Quadagno, *The Color of Welfare: How Racism Undermined the War on Poverty* (New York: Oxford University Press, 1994).

15. James Mark Wilcox quoted in Ira Katznelson, *Fear Itself: The New Deal and the Origins of Our Time* (New York: W.W. Norton, 2013), 267.

16. Long quoted in Dorothy E. Roberts, "Spiritual and Menial Housework," in *Feminist Legal Theory: An Anti-Essentialist Reader*, ed. Nancy E. Dowd and Michelle S. Jacobs (New York: New York University Press, 2013), 116.

17. Rep. Phil Landrum (D-GA) quoted in Quadagno, *Color of Welfare*, 130.

18. DuBois, *Black Reconstruction*, 19.

19. Ad Hoc Committee on the Triple Revolution, *The Triple Revolution* (Santa Barbara: Ad Hoc Committee on the Triple Revolution, 1964).

19

Why Labor History Still Matters

MATTHEW HILD AND KERI LEIGH MERRITT

There is little wonder why labor history should be more relevant today; one look at statistics of poverty, especially concerning the working poor, reveals a tale of two Americas. While a slight majority of the country lives above the poverty line, far too many Americans—and an even higher percentage of southerners—still struggle to make ends meet in an often unforgiving world. Indeed, recent statistics reveal that about 40 percent of Americans between twenty-five and sixty will live in poverty for at least one year, while half of all children will live in a household that uses food stamps. With a poverty rate approximately twice that of the European average, one journalist wrote, the "American social safety net is extremely weak and filled with gaping holes." Out of all the industrialized countries in the world, the United States now spends "among the fewest resources" to help pull people out of poverty.[1]

The main reason for poverty, of course, is not necessarily the lack of jobs, but the lack of a living wage and a social safety net. A living wage—the minimum pay needed for the basics of living—has become a rallying cry for workers all over America recently, as calls for an increase in the minimum wage have gained steam. While full employment is certainly important, people need jobs that are year-round (as opposed to seasonal work), that pay a living wage, and that provide benefits like health care and retirement funds. Without these things, even people working more than full time can expect to spend years living below the poverty line. Even a better education system cannot help to effect change as much as a living wage and benefits could. As technological innovation and the loss of American jobs overseas further threaten the plight of southern laborers, nothing short of drastic changes to the system will truly help to alleviate poverty and suffering among the region's most impoverished.

The late twentieth and early twenty-first centuries posed new challenges for working-class southerners even as old problems persisted. Some of the new problems resulted from the globalization of the American economy. For most of the twentieth century, textile manufacturing was a major source of jobs in the South (as well as elsewhere in the United States). In 1973, more than 2.4 million Americans worked in the textile and apparel industries. By 1996 that figure had dropped to 1.5 million, and by 2012 it had plummeted to 383,600.[2] Between 1997 and 2006, Georgia lost more than 100,000 manufacturing jobs, about 60 percent of them in the textile and apparel industries. Globalization, or what James C. Cobb characterized as "the lure of even cheaper labor elsewhere on the planet," played a significant role in the decline of the southern textile industry.[3] The replacement of American labor with cheaper foreign labor in the textile industry reached its fruition after the United States ratified the North American Free Trade Agreement (NAFTA) in 1993 and increased further after China joined the World Trade Organization (WTO) in 2001.[4]

By the middle of the second decade of the twenty-first century, major newspapers were touting the "return" of the American textile industry, especially in the South, but with a significant caveat. *USA Today* made note of the "highly automated" nature of new plants, while the *New York Times*, examining a reopened mill in Gaffney, South Carolina, reported that "machines have replaced humans at almost every point in the production process." In 2013, 140 workers were producing an amount of yarn (2.5 million pounds per week) that in 1980 would have required more than 2,000 workers. *USA Today* pointed out one benefit for southern textile manufacturers that had not changed in the twenty-first century: a "nonunion workforce."[5] In fact, unionization rates descended sharply in the South during this era of industrial decline. In Georgia, for example, 14 percent of industrial workers belonged to a union in 1964, but by 2016 that rate stood at a meager 4 percent, fourth-lowest in the nation.[6]

Many of the manufacturing jobs that were lost in the South during this time have been replaced by service-sector jobs, which generally pay much less. When Pillowtex Mills shut down its plant in Kannapolis, North Carolina, in July 2003, putting some 4,800 men and women out of work, many of its displaced employees went to work for Walmart (ironically, since the retail giant's emphasis upon low prices fueled the rising sales of imported textile products), in most cases for significantly less pay and benefits.[7] Many service workers outside of retail have found themselves being classified by their employers as "independent contractors," which means that they are not covered by the Fair Labor Standards Act's minimum wage and overtime provisions. Furthermore, companies that hire independent contractors usually do not cover workers' compensation, payroll taxes, or unemployment insurance. In Georgia in 2016, truck drivers, construction workers, and film industry workers filed lawsuits charging their employers with wage theft via misclassification as independent contractors.[8] Perhaps not surprisingly, then, service workers led a surge of unionization between April 2014 and April 2016 in which labor won thirty-five of forty-seven unionization elections, even as the state's rate of union membership remained flat.[9]

Much like globalization, technological progress will likewise continue to influence labor in the South, and indeed in all of America. As technology continues to displace workers—especially unskilled-sector workers—we, as a nation, are going to have to figure out what to do with a growing pool of unemployed people. For instance, when driverless trucking becomes a reality, 3.5 million truckers will be out of work. How do we plan to reemploy all of these people? Because this seems like such a momentous task, many scholars and theorists are proposing rethinking work and labor altogether. In a new book entitled *Raising the Floor*, Andy Stern has proposed that a universal basic income (UBI) is the best way to deal with the crisis in the labor market that is sure to come with further technological innovation. A type of social security, the UBI would grant citizens an "unconditional wage" from the government.[10]

Ideas like the UBI will certainly gain more traction as globalization and technological change make the current labor market even more unrecognizable in the future. As Derek Thompson wrote in the *Atlantic*, "the share of U.S. economic output that's paid out in wages . . . now stands at its lowest level since the government started keeping track in the mid-20th century." Americans are indeed in an era where technological progress means keeping a large number of people out of the workforce. Taken together, one out of every six "prime-age" men is unemployed, or has dropped out of the workforce completely. We are truly entering an age of crisis where if we do not make concrete, rational changes at the governmental level, extreme inequality will rise, unemployment will continue to increase, and the story of two Americas will never ring more true.[11]

Furthermore, ways to fleece American laborers still abound, with wage theft becoming one of the most widespread violations of workers' rights.

This illegal but ubiquitous practice includes making laborers work off the clock, not paying them overtime, and even the simple violation of minimum wage laws. Like so many other labor problems, wage theft affects women and minority workers most severely. Of course, wage theft is extremely hard to prosecute because there is currently no effective way to enforce labor laws, and thus the practice is prevalent and growing. For example, one study of low-wage workers in Chicago, Los Angeles, and New York showed that two-thirds of laborers experienced wage theft at least once a week, averaging about $2,600 per worker during the course of a year. If these three cities are representative of the rest of the country's thirty million low-wage workers, wage theft effectively steals over $50 billion a year from hardworking men and women.[12]

One other area connected to both labor and the continuing poverty of the South is the criminal justice system. With the end of slavery, the justice system became more powerful and important than ever; its strain of viciousness became the main tool of social and labor control in the South. Indeed, directly coinciding with the "freedom" of African Americans, the number of people arrested in Deep South rose significantly as the substance and enforcement of the laws changed. In contrast to the antebellum period, the vast majority of those arrested in the post–Civil War period were black. To keep up with the rapid pace of arrests, cities and towns that did not have police forces before the war quickly established professional, uniformed forces during Reconstruction. The undeniable proportion of race-based arrests caused concern, even during the initial years of freedom.[13]

Emancipation, therefore, did provide the theoretical framework of black freedom, and laid the groundwork for a path toward citizenship. But the Thirteenth Amendment also provided the former slaveholders with a "slavery" loophole: slavery and involuntary servitude were completely legal in conjunction with criminal convictions, paving the way for convict laborers who are still fighting for their rights today. Since former masters could no longer lord over enslaved African Americans, they created a path whereby the freed people could be returned to legally sanctioned bondage, first in the convict lease system, then to the chain gang, and finally to labor in both public and private prisons. By drastically increasing the severity of criminal punishments, broadening the statutes of behavioral crimes, and effectively preventing jury service by blacks, southern whites could force the convicted to work long hours in ungodly conditions. The grave excesses of this system, of course, are still acutely felt by people of color today, with one in three young African American men either incarcerated or on parole or probation.[14]

In 1994, amidst a rancorous political debate about crime, President Bill Clinton secured congressional approval of a crime prevention program that Congresswoman Cynthia McKinney, an African American Democrat from Georgia, characterized as "an ounce of prevention, a pound of punishment and a ton of politics."[15] The program's provisions included tougher mandatory sentences and a "three strikes" rule that required a life sentence for anyone convicted of a violent felony who had two or more prior convictions, including drug offenses. Twenty-one years later Clinton looked back upon the legislation with regret, conceding that "we had a lot of people who were essentially locked up who were minor actors for way too long."[16] Indeed, federal and state "tough-on-crime policies" ultimately produced what the historian Heather Ann Thompson, in an article published in 2012, called a "severe carceral crisis in the U.S." that "ultimately ensnared more than 7.1 million Americans in the nation's criminal justice system and led to the actual imprisonment of a staggering 2.3 million of them for record lengths of time."[17] African Americans and other communities of color still bear disproportionate shares of both the rising incarceration rates and tougher sentences.[18]

At the same time the use of prison labor, which had finally been banned during or shortly after the New Deal era, not only returned in southern states but also spread to other states and the federal level. Alabama went so far as to revive the chain gang in 1995, and soon Maricopa County, Arizona (which includes Phoenix) adopted the practice as well.[19] By 2000, the list of American corporations that had made use of prison labor included AT&T, IBM, Boeing, Revlon, Starbucks, Target, and McDonald's. Just as globalization resulted in American workers losing jobs to cheaper labor overseas, the use of prison labor cost working-class Americans jobs as well. As the twenty-first century began, one Georgia county laid off fifty workers from its recycling program and replaced them with a labor force of female prisoners.[20] One recent study found that "state prisoner wages range from as low as $0.13 [per hour] for those unfortunate enough to work in one of Nevada's prison camps, to a meager $0.32 even if they work for private industries in states such as South Carolina because certain jobs do 'not fall under Federal Minimum Wage requirements.'" Thus convict labor, a scourge of the South for seven or eight decades after the Civil War, has become a blight upon the entire nation, reducing the availability of jobs as well as wages for working-class Americans—all while exploiting prisoners in workplaces that are often unsafe for the prisoners as well as the prison guards.[21]

Taken together, therefore, globalization, technological innovation, harsh labor laws, and the carceral system have brought the country, and particularly the South, to a time of grave concern for the future. And despite the efforts of recent social justice movements, from Moral Mondays to efforts to unionize to Black Lives Matter, little of substance has changed for working-class southerners. The last time the country faced a crisis of this proportion—during the Great Depression—multiple ideas were discussed and implemented to help ease the suffering of the un- and underemployed. Some economists championed the theory of universal employment, and the U.S. government went to work putting in place safety nets for society's most vulnerable. Yet today, outside of academics, few people are talking about the dire need for change regarding labor—not only how often people work, but when, where, and how. The resolution of these problems will determine whether the American working classes will have the opportunity to achieve the "American dream" in the twenty-first century or whether further millions will slip into the poverty and uncertainty that preceded Roosevelt's New Deal.

This book, then, seeks to contribute to the discussion over labor by bringing past struggles of working-class people to light. By learning from their trials and tribulations, we are hopefully able to come up with realistic, workable solutions to modern problems. As the working classes in the South—and, indeed, in America writ large—continue to descend into poverty, these discussions are now more imperative than ever.

Notes

1. Mark R. Rank, "Poverty in America Is Mainstream," *New York Times*, November 2, 2013.
2. Timothy Minchin, *Empty Mills: The Fight against Imports and the Decline of the U.S. Textile Industry* (Lanham, MD: Rowman & Littlefield, 2012), 1.
3. James C. Cobb, *Georgia Odyssey: A Short History of the State*, 2nd. ed. (Athens: University of Georgia Press, 2008), 123.
4. Timothy Minchin, "'It Knocked This City to Its Knees': The Closure of Pillowtex Mills in Kannapolis, North Carolina and the Decline of the U.S. Textile Industry," *Labor History* 50 (August 2009): 288–89.

5. Marsha Mercer, "Textile Industry Comes Back to Life, Especially in South," *USA Today*, February 5, 2014; Stephanie Clifford, "Textile Plants Humming, but Not with Workers," *New York Times*, September 20, 2013.

6. Cobb, *Georgia Odyssey*, 123; Dan Chapman, "Unions Win Many Battles, Even in Georgia," *Atlanta Journal-Constitution*, May 1, 2016.

7. Cobb, *Georgia Odyssey*, 123; Minchin, "'It Knocked This City to Its Knees,'" 287, 295–96.

8. Dan Chapman, "Ga. Bakery at Center of Jobs Dispute: Lawsuits Allege Flowers Prevents Truck Drivers from Earning OT Pay," *Atlanta Journal-Constitution*, August 21, 2016; U.S. Department of Labor, Wage and Hour Division, "Fact Sheet #13: Am I an Employee? Employment Relationship under the Fair Labor Standards Act (FLSA)," https://www.dol.gov/whd/regs/compliance/whdfs13.pdf.

9. Chapman, "Unions Win Many Battles."

10. Sean Illing, "Why We Need to Plan for a Future without Jobs," *Vox*, October 17, 2016.

11. Derek Thompson, "A World without Work," *Atlantic*, July/August 2015.

12. See UCLA Labor Center, "What Is Wage Theft?" http://www.labor.ucla.edu/wage-theft/; Brady Meixell and Ross Eisenbray, "An Epidemic of Wage Theft Is Costing Workers Hundreds of Millions of Dollars a Year," Economic Policy Institute, September 11, 2004.

13. Edward L. Ayers, *Vengeance and Justice: Crime and Punishment in the Nineteenth-Century American South* (New York: Oxford University Press, 1984), 168.

14. See Michelle Alexander, *The New Jim Crow: Mass Incarceration in the Age of Colorblindness* (New York: New Press, 2010). Also see "Incarceration and Race," Human Rights Watch website, https://www.hrw.org/reports/2000/usa/Rcedrg00-01.htm.

15. Gil Troy, *The Age of Clinton: America in the 1990s* (New York: Thomas Dunne Books, 2015), 121–22.

16. Troy, *The Age of Clinton*, 122; "Bill Clinton Regrets 'Three Strikes' Bill," *BBC News*, July 16, 2015, http://www.bbc.com/news/world-us-canada-33545971.

17. Heather Ann Thompson, "The Prison Industrial Complex: A Growth Industry in a Shrinking Economy," *New Labor Forum* 21, no. 3 (2012): 39.

18. Cynthia Young, "Punishing Labor: Why Labor Should Oppose the Prison Industrial Complex," *New Labor Forum* 12, no. 7 (2000): 44.

19. Young, "Punishing Labor," 43; Mitchel P. Roth, *Prisons and Prison Systems: A Global Encyclopedia* (Westport, CT: Greenwood, 2006), 49; Tessa M. Gorman, "Back on the Chain Gang: Why the Eighth Amendment and the History of Slavery Proscribe the Resurgence of Chain Gangs," *California Law Review* 85 (March 1997): 441–43, 452–58; Quynh Tran, "Earning Their Stripes: Convicted Teens Toil on New Chain Gang," *Arizona Republic* (Phoenix), March 11, 2004.

20. Young, "Punishing Labor," 46.

21. Thompson, "The Prison Industrial Complex," 41–43.

Contributors

David M. Anderson is the William Y. Thompson Endowed Professor and associate professor in the Department of History at Louisiana Tech University in Ruston, Louisiana.

Deborah Beckel is an independent scholar living in Bedford County, Virginia.

Thomas Brown is associate professor of criminal justice and sociology and program coordinator of the Social Science Division Major at Virginia Wesleyan College in Norfolk, Virginia.

Dana M. Caldemeyer is assistant professor of history at South Georgia State College in Douglas, Georgia.

Adam Carson is a doctoral candidate in the Department of History at the University of Arkansas in Fayetteville, Arkansas.

Theresa A. Case is associate professor in the History, Humanities, and Languages Department at the University of Houston-Downtown in Houston, Texas.

Erin L. Conlin is assistant professor of history at the Indiana University of Pennsylvania in Indiana, Pennsylvania.

Brett J. Derbes is a doctoral candidate in the Department of History at Auburn University. He works for the Texas State Historical Association (TSHA) in Austin, Texas, as managing editor of the *Handbook of Texas*.

Maria Angela Diaz is assistant professor of history at Utah State University.

Alan Draper holds the Michael W. Ranger '80 and Virginia R. Ranger P'17 Professorship in Government at St. Lawrence University in Canton, New York.

Matthew Hild is lecturer in the School of History and Sociology at the Georgia Institute of Technology and instructor in the Department of History at the University of West Georgia. He is the author of three books, including *Arkansas's Gilded Age: The Rise, Decline, and Legacy of Populism and Working-Class Protest.*

Joseph E. Hower is visiting assistant professor of history at Southwestern University in Georgetown, Texas.

T.R.C. Hutton is senior lecturer of history and American studies at the University of Tennessee in Knoxville, Tennessee.

Stuart MacKay is a member of the Department of History at Carleton University in Ottawa, Ontario, Canada.

Andrew C. McKevitt is assistant professor in the Department of History at Louisiana Tech University in Ruston, Louisiana.

Keri Leigh Merritt is as an independent scholar in Atlanta, Georgia.

Bethany Moreton is professor of history at Dartmouth College in Hanover, New Hampshire.

Kristin O'Brassill-Kulfan is lecturer and coordinator of public history at Rutgers University in New Brunswick, New Jersey.

Michael Sistrom is professor and chair, Department of History, and director of Quality Enhancement Plan at Greensboro College in Greensboro, North Carolina.

Joseph M. Thompson is a doctoral candidate in the Corcoran Department of History at the University of Virginia in Charlottesville, Virginia.

Linda A. Tvrdy is a civil justice fellow at Blue Ridge Labs at Robin Hood, a social impact tech incubator in New York, New York.

Index